BARGAINING WITH JAPAN

BARGAINING WITH JAPAN

WHAT AMERICAN PRESSURE
CAN AND CANNOT DO

Leonard J. Schoppa

COLUMBIA UNIVERSITY PRESS
NEW YORK

Columbia University Press
Publishers Since 1893
New York   Chichester, West Sussex
Copyright © 1997 Columbia University Press
Library of Congress Cataloging-in-Publication Data

Schoppa, Leonard J. (Leonard James), 1962–
    Bargaining with Japan : what American pressure can and cannot do /
    Leonard J. Schoppa.
        p.   cm.
    Includes bibliographical references and index.
    ISBN 0–231–10590–8 (cl : alk. paper). —ISBN 0–231–10591–6 (pa)
    1. United States—Commerce—Japan.   2. Japan—Commerce—United
    States.   3. United States—Commercial policy.   4. Foreign trade
    regulation—United States.   I. Title.
    HF1456.5.J3S36   1997
    337.73052—dc20   96–34624
                                                                CIP

Casebound editions of Columbia University Press books are printed on permanent and
durable acid-free paper.
Printed in the United States of America
c 10 9 8 7 6 5 4 3 2 1
p 10 9 8 7 6 5 4 3 2 1

For Gabrielle

CONTENTS

TABLES AND FIGURES

ACKNOWLEDGMENTS

I'd like to reverse the usual order and start by thanking the person who, more than any other individual or organization, made this book possible: my wife, Gabrielle. At a time when our young daughters, Melina and Isabelle, needed constant care and affection, she took on the disproportionate share of the duties and thereby made it possible for me to write this book. Her support and encouragement spurred me on to completion while her occasional jabs at my overuse of academic jargon provided a needed corrective which, I hope, will make the book more readable for those of you not enamored of academic prose.

My debt to her in no way lessens, however, my debt to the many individuals who helped improve the book. Haruhiro Fukui may not know it, but it was his paper at the annual meeting of the Association for Asian Studies in 1990, with its effort to apply Robert Putnam's two-level game approach to U.S.-Japan bargaining, that first inspired the book. John Campbell has provided advice and encouragement throughout the process, starting with comments on the first draft of the paper which outlined my argument and continuing right through his service as a referee for the Press. I also cannot thank enough my colleague Herman Schwartz who has been there as a sounding board, reader, and critic throughout the writing of the book. Other colleagues here at the University of Virginia, especially Gary Allinson, John Duffield, Kenneth Elzinga, David Waldner, and Brantly Womack, have also offered advice and support. Also helpful was Yoshihiko Nakamoto who provided research assistance.

In addition, I am especially indebted to John Odell, editor of *International Organization*, for the suggestions he made in the course of reviewing the article which provided the theoretical framework for the book project. Robert Putnam, Kenneth Oye, and anonymous referees for *IO* and the Press also offered advice which improved the analysis. Among the many Japan scholars who read chapters and provided advice, I want to offer special thanks to Skipp Orr, Mark Ramseyer, Mike Smitka, Mark Tilton, Frank Upham, David Weinstein, and Brian Woodall.

In the course of writing the book, I was privileged to have the opportunity to present my work before many fora, and in each case I learned a great deal from comments and questions. For making these exchanges possible, I want to thank Hiroshi Ishida and Bob Uriu at Columbia University, Stephen Haggard at the University of California at San Diego, David Finegold at the Rand Institute, Arthur Stockwin at Oxford University's Nissan Institute, Patricia Maclachlan of the Ph.D. Kenkyūkai in Tokyo, Mary Lea Cox of the Abe Fellows Colloquium in Tokyo, Hosono Sukehiro of the Keiō University Public Choice Seminar, Junko Katō at Tokyo University, the staff of the Library of Congress Japan Documentation Center for their 1995 Symposium, and Meg McKean at Duke University.

I also am deeply indebted to many individuals who assisted me in my fieldwork, foremost among them Ōshima Haruyuki and Ōhahashi Ichizō and the other NHK reporters who generously shared what they had learned by covering the Structural Impediments Initiative and helped me make my initial contacts with Japanese officials involved in the talks. I am also indebted to Kusano Atsushi for his help in arranging an affiliation with Keiō University during academic year 1993–94. Kubo Fumiaki, Tamura Jirō, and the staff at Keiō were all very supportive. I would also like to thank all of the Japanese and Americans who submitted to interviews, but especially Glen Fukushima, Hasegawa Tokunosuke, Noguchi Yukio, Iyori Hiroshi, Unno Tsuneo, and Linn Williams. Others, whom I would otherwise thank by name, chose to remain anonymous.

Finally, I would like to thank the institutions that made it possible for me to write this book. The project was initially conceptualized at Harvard University's Reischauer Institute, which provided me with a postdoctoral year in which to think and catch my breath before starting work as a full time professor. The University of Virginia, where I have worked in that capacity, has provided generous support as well, helping to fund summer research in Tokyo and Washington, D.C., and giving me the time to write through a Sesquicentennial Fellowship in the fall of 1994. The Weedon Fund, based in Charlottesville, and the Association for Asian Studies Northeast Asian Council also provided support for the initial research trip to Japan. The biggest share of the work was done, however, during a year in Japan funded by an Abe Fellowship, administered by the Social Science Research Council and the American Council of Learned Societies and funded by the Japan Foundation Center for Global Partnership.

Charlottesville
May 1996

NOTES ON CONVENTIONS

In this book Japanese personal names generally are given in the Japanese order with the surname first. The exception is when a Japanese scholar has written an article or book in English and chose to list his name in the Western order. Diacritics are used for all Japanese words with long o's or u's except, again, for Japanese scholars writing in English and for city names such as Tokyo and Kyoto that are widely known. Japanese words are not italicized except at their first usage where the term is defined. When sums expressed in yen are converted into dollars, the then-current exchange rate is used.

ACRONYMS

ACTPN: Advisory Committee on Trade Policy and Negotiations (U.S.)
AML: Anti-Monopoly Law
CAABs: Commercial Activities Adjustment Boards
CEA: Council of Economic Advisors (U.S.)
DSL: Department Store Law
EPA: Economic Planning Agency (Japan)
FDI: Foreign Direct Investment
FILP: Fiscal Investment and Loan Plan
GATT: General Agreement on Tariffs and Trade
IAEA: International Atomic Energy Association
JFTC: Japanese Fair Trade Commission
LDP: Liberal Democratic Party
LSL: Large Store Law
MAFF: Ministry of Agriculture, Forestry, and Fisheries (Japan)
MCI: Ministry of Commerce and Industry (Japan)
MHA: Ministry of Home Affairs (Japan)
MITI: Ministry of International Trade and Industry (Japan)
MOC: Ministry of Construction (Japan)
MOF: Ministry of Finance (Japan)
MOFA: Ministry of Foreign Affairs (Japan)
MOJ: Ministry of Justice (Japan)
MOSS: Market Oriented Sector Specific
MOT: Ministry of Transportation (Japan)

NAFTA: North American Free Trade Agreement
NATO: North Atlantic Treaty Organization
NEC: National Economic Council (U.S.)
NLA: National Land Agency (Japan)
NSC: National Security Council (U.S.)
OECD: Organization for Economic Cooperation and Development
SII: Structural Impediments Initiative
USTR: United States Trade Representative
VER: Voluntary Export Restraint
VIE: Voluntary Import Expansion
WTO: World Trade Organization

Bargaining With Japan

1 INTRODUCTION

The more things change the more they stay the same. In the time since the Bush Administration named Japan an "unfair trader" under the Super 301 trade legislation of 1988 and launched a series of sectoral and structural trade talks, the Soviet Union has disintegrated, Japan's long-ruling Liberal Democratic Party (LDP) has been ousted from power, Bush has been replaced by Clinton, and the two nations' economies have moved in opposite directions—with formerly booming Japan suffering from the aftereffects of the burst "bubble" while the United States enjoys a sustained recovery. Economic relations between the two nations, however, seem to have been impervious to all of this change: America threatens, Japan reacts, and the fundamental problems remain unaddressed even as ties between the countries become more and more strained.

The arrival of two new administrations on each side of the Pacific in 1993 was marked by the start of a new round of trade talks, this time known formally as the U.S.-Japan Framework for a New Economic Partnership. The topics covered in these Framework Talks, though, were hardly new. Auto parts and autos, government procurement of telecommunications, medical equipment, supercomputers and satellites, *keiretsu* business groups, and macroeconomic policy have all been the subject of numerous prior rounds of negotiations. Cellular phones and construction market access, subjects of concurrent discussions, have also been staples of the diet of trade rows which has kept several generations of American and Japanese trade negotiators well fed. Lest there be a lull in this never-ending series of trade battles, the Clinton Administration most recently raised the stakes again by threatening Japan with prohibitive sanctions on $5.9 billion worth of luxury car imports in an effort to force the nation to accept American demands for a "results-oriented" deal in the auto and auto parts sector.

The never-ending quality of economic friction between the United States and Japan is enough to make one wonder whether the U.S., like Sisyphus, is destined to spend eternity pushing for one trade agreement after another only to see each one roll back down the mountain. Is there nothing we have learned from all of these years of negotiating that would suggest a better way of dealing with the "Japan Problem"? Is the only solution to call in bigger guns, making bolder threats in an effort to force open the Japanese market? Or might it be possible to make use of weapons that, while less powerful, are more accurate in their ability to hit the intended target—smart bombs, if you will?

It is the aim of this book to search for answers to these questions by looking back at the recent history of U.S.-Japan trade negotiations, focusing in detail on the talks that were at the center of the Bush Administration's effort to deal with the "Japan Problem," the Structural Impediments Initiative (SII), and in less detail on the more recent Clinton Framework Talks. Both sets of talks involved the application of strong American pressure on Japan in an effort to bring about policy change in a range of areas, but the talks produced widely varying results in terms of the Japanese government's willingness to go along with U.S. demands. The Large Store Law, targeted for reform under the SII talks, has been significantly liberalized, allowing firms like Toys 'R' Us to move into Japan and set up retail chains. The Japanese government has consistently refused, however, to take any steps that would force keiretsu business groups to loosen the ties that bind them together, even though such barriers were targeted in both the SII and Framework talks. By examining the pattern of results in these two sets of talks, this book seeks to identify *strategies* for the use of foreign pressure that are more likely to bring about Japanese concessions and the *conditions* under which these strategies are most likely to work.

This book is certainly not the first book about U.S.-Japan trade relations. Economists have written dozens of books and articles addressing questions such as these: How open is Japan? Do the Japanese keiretsu business groups act as a brake on imports? Does the Japanese distribution system slow the inflow of foreign goods? And are there international price differences which suggest that market forces do not work to reduce trade imbalances in Japan the way they do in other nations? These are certainly important questions whose answers should guide American trade policy vis-à-vis Japan.[1] If Japan is actually an open market, as some economists maintain, then we don't need a special Japan trade policy. If there are barriers, we need to know which ones are most important. These questions do not address, however, a very important follow-up question, which also ought to guide American Japan policy. If it's true that there are trade barriers in Japan, what is the best way to get the Japanese government to go along with our interest in seeing that market become more accessible?

This question of trade strategy has also been addressed in a variety of works, but much of this literature similarly fails to adequately explain how the U.S. government is supposed to convince the Japanese to go along with the strategy advocated. "Revisionist" works in particular have been guilty of an unfounded faith in the ability of American pressure to force the Japanese government to go along with the "results-oriented" trade policy they advocate. Revisionists review the recent record of U.S. trade policy and argue that any effort to open up the Japanese market by focusing on specific trade barriers is destined to end in frustration. Rather than trying to negotiate the removal of barriers one layer at a time, they argue, America ought to insist that Japan commit to specific, quantifiable results. While the revisionist argument has been attractive enough to garner a great deal of support in Washington, few of these studies even attempt to explain how the U.S. is supposed to get the Japanese to agree to quantifiable "results."[2]

One of the few revisionist works that does attempt to answer this question is the 1989 report of the U.S. President's Advisory Committee on Trade Policy and Negotiations (ACTPN). According to its authors, all the U.S. has to do to get the Japanese to agree to a "results-oriented" approach is to threaten retaliation: "Japanese government officials have a keen sense of where their national interest lies, and when faced with credible threats of retaliation that adversely affect that interest, they usually choose to accommodate requests from the United States."[3] When the Clinton Administration attempted to put the revisionist approach to work during the Framework Talks, however, Japanese officials steadfastly refused to agree to anything resembling market share targets—making it clear that the Japanese do not always bend in the face of pressure.[4]

As the fate of the Clinton Framework Talks suggests, what has been missing from revisionist works is a realistic understanding of the role played by foreign pressure in the Japanese political system. While threats of retaliation are part of what makes American pressure effective, equally important is the way that pressure reverberates within Japanese domestic politics. When reverberation is relatively positive, it may take only mild pressure to yield a given concession, but when reverberation is negative (as in the case of the demand for "quantitative indicators" during the Framework Talks), the threat of retaliation required to bring about a concession may be so great as to threaten the entire bilateral relationship.[5]

What is required is a better understanding of how foreign pressure operates within the Japanese political system. That foreign pressure, known in Japan as *gaiatsu*, plays an important role in the Japanese policy-making system is widely recognized. It has been credited with giving voice to Japanese consumers, serving as a "surrogate opposition party," and providing LDP prime ministers with support in their struggles to pursue policy change.[6] Policy decisions in areas ranging from foreign aid to macroeconomic policy to the manner in which the Japanese participated in the Gulf Crisis have been explained by gaiatsu.[7] The pattern has been so routinized, some argue, that the Japanese have become addicted to gaiatsu, relying on it to swing the balance in favor of controversial policy changes to the point that many Japanese have come to believe that major change is impossible in Japan in its absence.[8]

That foreign pressure is credited with such influence, however, does not mean it is viewed as a uniformly positive force. Many authors, noting that Japanese associate gaiatsu with the forced opening of Japan by the gunships of Commodore Perry in 1853, emphasize that foreign pressure produces a certain backlash effect even as it yields measured concessions from government officials. The publication of books like Ishihara Shintarō's *The Japan That Can Say 'No'* is cited as evidence of the long-term damage a strategy reliant on heavy-handed foreign pressure can do to U.S.-Japan relations.[9]

Despite this consensus that foreign pressure plays an important but varied role in Japanese politics, surprisingly few studies have attempted to offer generalizations about *when* foreign pressure is likely to yield the most response with the least backlash.[10] Neither have these studies specified *how* foreign pressure produces policy outcomes which were previously blocked due to domestic political constraints. Most studies which have commented on gaiatsu limit their observations to the specifics of their cases and, when crediting policy outcomes to foreign pressure, tend to treat it as just one more interest competing with domestic interests to influence policy outcomes. Much in the way pluralist theory treats the government as a "black box" for processing pressures from domestic interests, many studies of U.S.-Japan economic relations have treated gaiatsu as just another input into the calculations of the Japanese government. It is the aim of this book to look inside the black box in an effort to improve our understanding of when and how foreign pressure influences the policy process.

In seeking to look inside the black box, this study begins by taking a step back from U.S.-Japan relations. Drawing on the broader literature of negotiation theory, it builds in particular on the work of Harvard political scientist Robert Putnam whose "two-level game" metaphor for analyzing the dynamics of bargaining between governments has drawn attention to the importance of recognizing how the outcomes of international negotiations reflect not just the separate force of foreign and domestic demands *but their synergisms as well*.[11] Putnam argues that international bargaining can be likened to a game where the chief negotiator from each country faces two game tables: one at the international level and one at the domestic. Any deal he negotiates must "win" at both tables, since it must be acceptable to both his international counterpart(s) and his domestic constituents. What makes the game complicated—more complicated than can be accommodated in traditional realist models of international relations—is that all parties in this game have at their disposal strategies for influencing the plays of other participants: synergistic strategies. gaiatsu, I propose in this book, is nothing more than an umbrella term for a variety of such strategies.

Many readers may be wondering at this point whether one needs all of this fancy terminology and political science theory to get at the questions addressed by this book: when and how foreign pressure influences Japanese policy outcomes. I propose that my decision to draw on Putnam's two-level game approach is justified on two counts. First, it offers an alternative to the black box as a way of understanding how foreign pressure and domestic politics combine to produce bargaining outcomes in U.S.-Japan relations. Rather than implicitly treating foreign and domestic pressure as the same type of input (as in the black box model), the two-level game approach recognizes that the two types of pressure are fundamentally different. Government leaders respond to domestic pressure because domestic interests put and keep them in power. Leaders respond to foreign pressure, however, only to the degree foreign demands fall within the range of deals which are domestically viable (Putnam terms this the "win-set"). Foreign pressure may shift the outcome from, say, the mid-point of the win-set to the end closer to the foreign demands, and it may at times actually expand the win-set to include outcomes that were not domestically viable prior to international negotiations; but in all cases foreign pressure is constrained by domestic politics. Because the two-level game approach captures the way in which intergovernmental bargaining is "nested" within the primary game of domestic politics,[12] it generates useful insights into how gaiatsu influences Japanese policy.

Second, the explicit focus on political science theory in this book is justified by the fact that much of the other work on U.S.-Japan relations, while not explicitly theoretical, is nevertheless based on certain assumptions about international relations. The ACTPN report cited above is a case in point. In the passage quoted earlier the authors note that "Japanese government officials have a keen sense of where their national interest lies" and suggest that these officials respond to threats of sanctions by rationally calculating whether Japan should give in to foreign demands—suggesting that Japan behaves as a "unitary rational actor." This assumption is literally drawn directly from the tradition of realism which has dominated theorizing and thinking about international relations in America since World War II. While such assumptions may have helped policymakers in devising strategy for the Cold War contest with the Soviet Union, it is debatable whether they are helpful in guiding policymakers today as they struggle to devise a strategy for dealing with U.S.-Japan economic negotiations. If these assumptions are invalid and the implicit model guiding American Japan policy produces distorted policy prescriptions (as this book argues), then it is useful to question not just the policy but its underlying theory as well.[13]

The Argument of the Book

This book argues that gaiatsu does indeed have the power to influence Japanese policy outcomes and that its influence is greatest when the Japanese domestic political arena offers opportunities for employing synergistic strategies that take advantage of divisions of opinion and interest on the Japanese side. Such strategies, described in more detail in Chapter 2, include "synergistic linkage," "reverberation," "participation expansion," and "alternative specification." Opportunities for employing these strategies are greatest when foreign demands can be presented as legitimate, when demands can arguably be characterized as "in Japan's national interest," when latent support for foreign demands can be found outside the bureaucratic and interest-group circles that ordinarily dominate the policy process, and when recognized Japanese policy problems are in search of solutions. This analysis suggests that an American Japan policy seeking to impose policies that fail to meet these criteria will require an extremely high threat level (and may fail completely to produce results) while a policy more sensitive to these considerations should be able to win more Japanese concessions with less backlash.

The book also finds, however, that American officials need to be aware that, even as they seek to employ strategies that take advantage of opportunities within the Japanese domestic arena, Japanese-side actors will be trying to take advantage of opportunities to "use gaiatsu" for their own purposes. They will try to get U.S. officials to make demands that support their own interests and will use every opportunity during the course of negotiations and during the process of policy implementation to turn foreign pressure in their favor. Like the Americans, Japanese negotiators will also be trying to take advantage of divisions on the U.S. side. The case of SII in particular makes it clear that the effort to take advantage of sympathetic Japanese interests must be carefully balanced with the need to limit and focus demands in such a way as to ensure that gaiatsu is not wasted on policies that serve only Japanese interests and do little or nothing for the U.S..

Although this book focuses its analysis rather narrowly on U.S.-Japan trade negotiations, it nevertheless aims to contribute as well to broader theorizing about the nature of international bargaining and international relations. First, it confirms the utility of the Putnam two-level game approach as a source of insights into how international negotiations work in the real world, validating in particular Putnam's emphasis on synergistic strategies. Second, it builds on Putnam's approach by pointing to two synergistic strategies not identified by Putnam or his collaborators, strategies I term "participation expansion" and "alternative specification." Third, it remedies the lack of effort to identify the conditions under which synergistic strategies are likely to be successfully employed (in previous Putnam-inspired work) by using the two-level game approach to identify likely conditions and examining whether this specification of conditions can help us understand the pattern of results across a range of

U.S.-Japan cases. Finally, it seeks to correct the almost exclusive focus on synergistic strategies available to *government leaders* in the work of Putnam and his collaborators by emphasizing that *domestic-level actors* also can and do pursue "reverse" strategies aimed at manipulating and using political pressure generated by international negotiations.

The Cases: SII and the Framework Talks

This book derives conclusions about when and how gaiatsu influences Japanese policymaking and makes the case for the utility of Putnam's model, modified as outlined above, by focusing on two sets of U.S.-Japan negotiations: the SII and Framework talks. Why choose these two sets of negotiations? As with any study that attempts to draw conclusions from a limited number of case studies, my choice was dictated by the need to find cases that provided an interesting combination of similarities and differences: different enough in outcome so that you have variation to explain but similar enough so that you are not left with too many possible explanations.[14]

The SII Talks fit this "most similar" case design quite well. Under the banner of SII, the United States exerted a great deal of pressure on Japan to implement reforms in a range of areas the U.S. government identified as structural barriers to the expansion of U.S. exports to Japan: macroeconomic policies affecting Japan's savings-investment balance, Japan's distribution system, the nation's land policy, exclusionary business practices, and the uncompetitive relations between firms in keiretsu groups.[15] All of these areas were given essentially equal billing in this Bush Administration initiative linked to the aggressive Super 301 provision of the 1988 Trade Act.[16] Nevertheless, results were decidedly mixed. The U.S. achieved much of what it wanted in the first three areas listed above but came away with very little on the last two.

The SII cases thus provide us with a set of cases where there was great variation in the outcome (the degree to which the U.S. succeeded in imposing its demands on the Japanese) even though many circumstances surrounding the negotiations were "constant." The talks all involved U.S. pressure on Japan and were conducted at the same time under the same implicit Super 301 threat—allowing us to rule out many "system-level" explanations for the pattern of results. Also because all issues were dealt with simultaneously, we can rule out explanations based on shifts in the overall domestic political environment (such as changes in domestic institutions or in governing coalitions). The sɪɪ cases therefore allow us to focus on a more limited set of factors—the domestic politics of specific issue areas and synergisms between the negotiations and politics in the domestic arena—in order to explain the variation in outcomes.

Perhaps one can appreciate the value of this case study design better if one puts oneself in the position of a U.S. trade negotiator. Faced at a particular point in time with a decision about how to deal with the "Japan Problem," a negotiator has virtually no control over many of the factors that will determine whether or not U.S. pressure can be successfully applied. She cannot alter the balance of power between the U.S. and Japan or, more broadly, the system-level context of the talks. She also cannot alter Japanese political institutions or bring a new governing coalition to power. The only things she has some control over are the selection of issues to be negotiated and strategies to be applied. She ought to be very interested, therefore, in any information she can get about what kinds of American demands employing what kinds of strategies are most likely to yield Japanese concessions given a fixed systemic and overall domestic political environment. The analysis of the sɪɪ cases provided in this book is designed to provide exactly this kind of information.

If the sɪɪ cases can tell us so much, why muddle things up by adding the Framework Talks to the set of cases? Clearly it is less easy to draw tight conclusions based on a comparison of the sɪɪ and Framework Talks. Too much is different: the Japanese domestic political environment has changed (the institutions and the governing coalition); the international environment has changed (the end of the Cold War and the establishment of the World Trade Organization); and the U.S.-Japan relationship has been altered by time (it is likely, for example, that both sides "learned" something from the sɪɪ experience and have altered their behavior). The factors on which the sɪɪ comparison focused—issue politics and synergisms—are just two among many factors that vary between sɪɪ and the Framework.

Precisely because other factors come into play, however, the comparison is interesting. While issue politics and synergisms are important, they are not the only factors affecting the way gaiatsu works. If the other circumstances listed above also affect the degree to which American demands can be imposed on Japan, we ought to search for clues as to their significance—even if it is impossible to draw definitive conclusions. The Framework Talks are considered in this book therefore in order to get some idea as to whether the issue politics and synergisms are important even when other circumstances change. Only by asking this question will we know whether the lessons learned from sɪɪ can be fruitfully applied by future U.S. negotiators puzzling over the question of how to deal with Japan.

An Overview of the Talks

The sɪɪ and Framework Talks are interesting, not just because of their utility as case studies for examining the role of gaiatsu in U.S.-Japan relations, but also because the two sets of talks have been at the center of America's Japan policy under the past two U.S. administrations. Although the Bush Administration entered into several sets of negotiations with the Japanese in the first six months after it came into office, it soon became clear that the sɪɪ talks were the ones held dearest by Bush officials. Unlike the renegotiation of the fsx deal and the sectoral talks conducted under Super 301 (both largely forced on a reluctant administration by an assertive Congress), the sɪɪ talks were what the administration used to regain the initiative and set forth its own philosophy aimed at countering the growing popularity of the "managed trade" movement on Capitol Hill. As one Bush Administration official put it, "The administration was faced with the question of how best to guarantee opportunities for American firms to enter the Japanese market without having to resort to 'managed trade.' The sɪɪ talks were our answer to that question."[17]

It was no coincidence, therefore, that the Bush Administration proposal of the sɪɪ talks on May 29, 1989, came at the same press conference where Carla Hills, the U.S. Trade Representative, made her much anticipated announcement naming Japan an "unfair trader" under the Super 301 provision of the 1988 Trade Act. While the Administration had been left by Congress with little choice other than to name Japan under the act, it limited the number of sectors targeted in the announcement to just three relatively small ones with specific barriers largely under the control of the Japanese government. It chose not to identify under Super 301 more informal barriers such as those in the distribution system and the network of keiretsu business groups and instead announced that these issues would be dealt with in the sɪɪ talks, officially outside the Trade Act's system of deadlines and threats. This compromise allowed the administration to say that it had made use of the trade policy tool forced on it by Congress while at the same time presenting its own solution to the "Japan Problem." Rather than dealing with informal barriers like distribution by using Super 301 to impose "results" on Japan (as managed traders had hoped), the Bush Administration insisted that it could use sii to negotiate away these barriers.

As the Administration's plans for sii emerged in more detail over the next few months, it soon became clear that Bush officials were proposing reforms in Japanese business, law, and society that would touch virtually every citizen and every firm. Cross-shareholding and a lack of shareholder scrutiny of Japanese firms allowed keiretsu business groups to favor related firms in their procurement decisions at the expense of newcomer firms such as those from America, so the U.S. would ask Japan to open up these groups. A distribution system populated predominantly by small stores, protected from competition by the Large Store Law (LSL), and characterized by exclusive dealership arrangements made it difficult for new American products to reach Japanese consumers, so the U.S. would ask Japan to eliminate the LSL and make it more difficult for firms to maintain closed distribution networks. Lax antitrust enforcement allowed Japanese firms to collude in order to keep out foreign competition, so the U.S. would ask Japan to raise penalties under the Anti-Monopoly Law (AML) and beef up enforcement efforts.

The other two topics covered under sii were inspired by the faith of Bush Administration economists in one of the laws of macroeconomics: that a nation's surplus of savings (S) over investment (I) will necessarily equal its current account surplus. The delay in current account adjustment on the part of the Japanese after the 1985 Plaza Accord could, according to these economists, be explained in part by the persistent "S-I" surplus in Japan and the corresponding "S-I" deficit in the U.S. The Japanese S-I surplus was thus treated as another structural impediment, and the U.S. called on Japan to increase public investment in sewers, housing, parks, and roads in an effort to offset its high savings rate. Relatedly, the administration called for broad changes in land policy aimed at bringing down skyrocketing land prices which, the Americans argued, kept up savings rates and depressed both personal consumption and public investment.

The breadth of the Americans' reform proposals (the media at one point counted a total of 240 separate demands) made it clear that the sii talks represented a new approach for dealing with U.S.-Japan trade friction. Many of the policy areas touched by the American offensive were ones previously considered purely domestic matters. The approach was also novel because U.S. officials deliberately chose to endorse reform proposals they felt would enjoy broad backing from the Japanese public and at least part of the government. Still, any expectation that such demands would win easy acceptance by the Japanese negotiating team was quickly dashed as the negotiating began: the Ministry of Finance (MOF) made it clear it would resist to the end the U.S. effort to force it to increase spending on public investment; small stores and their backers in the Diet opposed U.S. proposals for liberalizing the LSL; big business opposed calls for a tougher AML and any policy that might open up keiretsu; and urban farm landowners opposed U.S. proposals for increasing taxes on their land (aimed at increasing the supply of land for development and bringing land prices down). In fact, the list of interests adversely affected by U.S. proposals looked like a "who's who" of the rich and powerful in Japanese politics.

The stakes were high and the politicking intense, therefore, as the deadlines for the midterm and final SII reports approached in the spring of 1990. In the end, the Americans could point to substantial Japanese movement toward their demands in three areas: the MOF gave in and agreed to spend 430 trillion yen on public investment over the next ten years, an amount government economists estimated would boost the proportion of GNP spent in that category from 7.2% to 8.4% by 2000[18]; the Ministry of International Trade and Industry (MITI) agreed to rewrite the LSL to limit the degree to which established stores could delay a new large store opening to just one year—where it had previously taken as long as 10 years; and the government of Japan agreed to revise its land tax system in order to increase incentives for landowners to sell or develop their land, pledging to dismantle tax loopholes that urban farm landowners had successfully defended for over 20 years.

In the two remaining areas, however, the Japanese promises were either vague or lacking. The government agreed to raise the levels of penalties imposed under the Anti-Monopoly Law and to use the law more aggressively, but Japan's Fair Trade Commission has thus far failed to use the full force of the law against the construction industry and has declined to take action against industries like flat glass, paper, and auto parts where, Americans argue, collusive practices make it difficult for U.S. firms to gain market access. On the keiretsu issue, the Japanese government refused to impose any limits on cross-shareholding and has thus far made only marginal changes in rules that prevent shareholders from subjecting Japanese firm managers to the degree of scrutiny common in the U.S.

The above brief account of the aims and results of the SII talks cannot do justice to the complexity of the issues. Within each issue area there were multiple points of contention, and the degree to which the Japanese conceded often varied across these specific demands. Such complexities will be discussed in detail in the issue-specific chapters later in the book. What the summary emphasizes, however, is the variation in outcomes between the five main issue areas. Why did the Japanese concede more on the Large Store Law than on the Anti-Monopoly Law? Why did the MOF agree to sacrifice a great deal of its autonomy in fiscal policy by committing to a specific sum of spending on public investment while it refused to consider limits on cross-shareholding? It is this variation in outcomes that inspired this book's focus on when and how foreign pressure influences policy in Japan.

While it subsequently became clear that the SII talks had produced more significant changes in some areas than in others, the Bush Administration greeted the 1990 SII Agreement with positive reviews, one official calling it an "historic" agreement.[19] Already, though, there were signs that the entire SII approach was being questioned by the Administration's critics. News reports about the SII agreement featured skeptical comments from the American business community, and advocates of a more "results-oriented" trade policy accused the Administration of using SII primarily as a tactic for avoiding Super 301 and buying time for the GATT Uruguay Round.[20] How, they asked, were extra large stores, more spending on sewers, and lower land prices supposed to help American firms sell more goods in Japan? If anything, the changes forced on Japan in these areas were likely only to strengthen Japan by making it more efficient. The truly significant barriers in areas like keiretsu and exclusionary business practices had been left intact. For these critics, SII was a symbol of the futility of trying to open the Japanese market by negotiating the removal of barriers. What was needed was a truly new approach.

Critics of SII who had long been calling for a more results-oriented trade policy saw Clinton's election in November 1992 as their chance to press the new administration to give their strategy a try. Such an approach had been tried just once before, in the Semiconductor Trade Agreement of 1986 (renewed in 1991), when the Japanese government pledged to help foreign chip-makers expand their share of the Japanese market from 10 percent to a goal of 20 percent.[21] Coincidentally, the Japanese government announcement that foreign firms had finally reached this goal came in February 1993, just as the Clinton Administration was beginning to formulate its trade policy toward Japan, giving added force to the arguments of those who called for the use of a similar strategy in other sectors.

Subsequent statements by U.S. officials leading up to the agreement on "the Framework" in July 1993 made it clear that the administration was intent on following this advice. Future trade agreements, the U.S. insisted, must include "numerical targets" and "multiple benchmarks" for measuring results.[22] Even as the U.S. and Japan were negotiating the text of the joint statement setting up the Framework, however, it became clear that the Americans had few allies this time in their fight to convince the Japanese to agree to this core demand. The Prime Minister pledged that Japan would never again agree to a market share commitment as it had in the Semiconductor deal, Japanese officials from every concerned agency blasted the approach, and even the media (generally sympathetic to the American cause during sii) uniformly came out against the Clinton approach.

While the disagreement on this fundamental issue was patched over in the joint statement setting up the Framework, it reemerged as a continuing source of disagreement as the two sides tried to hammer out agreements in each of the Framework "baskets." The Americans worked to find a formula for quantitative indicators the Japanese could accept, telling anyone who would listen that they were not insisting on specific market share targets as in the Semiconductor Agreement, but the Japanese side refused to accept any form of indicators that even hinted at future growth in imports. Unable to agree on a formula for bridging this gap, the two sides decided to suspend their negotiations in February 1994 after Clinton and Hosokawa came out of their summit meetings unable to find common ground on this issue.

After the failed summit, it took more than three months for the two sides to start talking again and another three before they finally reached a partial agreement covering all priority issues except for autos.[23] Even then, the Japanese refused to agree to specific numbers which would quantify future increases in foreign market access. Although the Clinton Administration attempted to present their last-minute commitment to "progress" in access (according to several measures) as a major concession, the agreements were in fact little different from earlier ones more quietly negotiated by Bush which had also contained quantitative *measures* without specific *target numbers*.[24] The Japanese refused even to agree to that much on autos and auto parts, alone responsible for two-thirds of the bilateral deficit. After failing to reach a deal on this set of issues in the fall of 1994, talks dragged on for another nine months, culminating in another last-minute settlement on June 28, 1995, this time just hours before Clinton had promised to impose $5.9 billion in sanctions on Japanese luxury cars. While the administration claimed victory again, the agreement fell far short of the standards set by Clinton and his trade negotiators. Specific numbers contained in a "Fact Sheet" issued by the Americans were disavowed by the Japanese government in the joint statement issued when the agreement was reached, and even the "voluntary" plans issued by Japanese auto makers were vague on the points of greatest interest to the U.S.: access to their dealer networks and sales of original equipment parts. All in all, the Framework talks produced little to justify the tremendous expenditure of time, energy, and political capital that had been poured into the talks over two long years. The Framework Talks, defining the Clinton Administration's Japan policy just as the SII Talks defined Bush's, thus provide us with another case to contrast with the SII cases outlined above. Why did strong U.S. pressure, including the threat of specific trade sanctions, fail to convince the Japanese to go along with the Clinton demand for meaningful "quantitative indicators" when similar pressure produced Japanese concessions on the Large Store Law, public investment, and land policy under SII? This question too will be answered in the coming chapters.

The Plan for the Book

As noted earlier, this book begins by taking a step back from U.S.-Japan relations in order to draw on the broader literature on international bargaining. Chapter 2 therefore starts with a survey of this literature, stressing the limited utility of traditional realist models in cases of economic negotiations such as those examined in this book and focusing in particular on Putnam's two-level game approach as an alternative to such models. Even Putnam's approach is found to be vague, however, on the crucial issue of how domestic politics operates to limit and make possible the effective use of bargaining strategies by government negotiators. An effort is therefore made to specify in more detail the nature of "domestic politics" and to examine systematically how a variety of bargaining strategies are constrained by their need to "work well" with internal politics. In this way, the modified Putnam approach is used to suggest a range of *strategies* for the positive application of foreign pressure as well as the *conditions* most conducive to the use of such strategies.

The next six chapters are then devoted to examining how the insights gained through the above exercise help us understand the emergence of sii (chapter 3), the course of negotiations (chapter 4), and the results in each of the five main issue areas (chapters 5–8). Unlike many studies of negotiations which take for granted the existence of those talks, the discussion of the emergence of sii in chapter 3 starts by asking how the Americans came to embrace this unusual approach to dealing with bilateral trade tensions. Even at this stage, it is argued, two-level logic influenced the administration's choice of approach, format, and agenda.

While the focus is primarily on American politics in chapter 3, the analysis in chapter 4 takes us deep into the realm of Japanese politics in its quest to explain the course of the sii negotiations. The peculiar structure of Japanese politics under the extended rule of the LDP, it is argued, made Japan particularly vulnerable to a range of two-level strategies. When conditions favored the use of these strategies, the Japanese negotiators ended up agreeing to American demands. When conditions were unfavorable, the Japanese stood their ground. Examining all of the sii issues at once, this chapter identifies patterns in the bargaining outcomes and illustrates them with examples from all of the issue areas.

The next four chapters then focus in depth on each of the five issues covered in sii, surveying policymaking in the area before, during, and after the talks in order to identify exactly how policy was altered by gaiatsu in each case. It is necessary to look at the history of policymaking in each area not just to provide background but also to develop a credible argument about what *would have happened* if the U.S. had not intervened through sii. Only by comparing what actually happened to this counterfactual can we ascertain and begin to understand the impact of foreign pressure. These chapters also go into some detail on what has happened in each area since the sii deal was made in 1990, not just at the level of government policy but at the "ground level" where policy is implemented. The "results" of any set of negotiations are not just what is agreed on paper or even what is achieved in the form of legal changes but ultimately must be evaluated at the level of policy implementation.

The treatment of the Clinton Framework in chapter 9 offers an abbreviated version of the analysis of sii. The emergence of the Framework format, the negotiations, and the results are again explained with reference to the modified Putnam approach. More attention is given, however, to factors other than issue politics and synergisms which were the focus of the explanation for the pattern of sɪɪ results. The world, Japanese politics, and American politics have all changed since sɪɪ, and the possibility that these changes (rather than the factors highlighted in the analysis of sɪɪ) explain the failure of the Administration's effort to convince the Japanese to accept meaningful quantitative indicators is explored. While these factors are important and must be taken into account in any future strategy for dealing with Japan, it is argued, the results of the Clinton Framework can nevertheless be seen primarily as a reflection of the same kinds of processes that produced the results of sɪɪ.

Throughout the body of the book, I have made an effort to examine the dynamics of gaiatsu with a social scientific detachment. I'm interested in when and how gaiatsu can be used by the United States to impose policy demands on the Japanese, but for those purposes I don't need to consider whether or not any specific demand made during sɪɪ or the Framework was "good" or "worthwhile." The question of whether U.S. pressure helped alter the course of Japanese land policy, for example, is therefore considered apart from the question of whether the U.S. should have been intervening or whether this intervention has produced any "positive" result for the U.S. such as a decline in the trade deficit. The final chapter pulls together the lessons drawn from my analysis of the two recent trade talks about when and how gaiatsu shapes Japanese policy outcomes, but it then relaxes this social scientific detachment to evaluate the two initiatives from a normative perspective. Given certain overall aims of American Japan policy, which aspects of each approach can be said to have worked better? This analysis forms the basis for a few final policy recommendations.

2 GAIATSU IN A TWO-LEVEL GAME

The overview of the Structural Impediments Initiative and the Clinton Framework Talks in the previous chapter made it clear that the United States does not always succeed in imposing its demands on Japan. Sometimes gaiatsu works, and sometimes it doesn't. The same point could have been made by looking at other cases involving Japan: the failure of American pressure to convince the Japanese to send support personnel to the Gulf while similar pressure succeeded in getting them to contribute $13 billion toward the war effort; the failure of the International Whaling Commission to stop the Japanese from whaling while similar international environmental pressure convinced them to abandon their imports of endangered turtle shells and ivory. Like the SII and Framework cases introduced in the last chapter, these paired cases make it clear that similar gaiatsu does not always produce similar Japanese concessions.

Somewhere in stories such as these there is a pattern—a pattern that will tell us when foreign pressure is most likely to be effective. What is the best way to identify this pattern? One way would be to jump right into a few case studies, going through all of the details of all of the cases in an effort to find parallels. The danger with this approach, though, is that one is likely to get quickly lost in the particulars, not knowing what sort of data to look for and therefore unable to see the proverbial forest for the trees. Other studies which have examined gaiatsu have tended to plunge right into case studies in this way, so that many are left without generalizable conclusions. Even the best of the previous studies of American pressure on Japan, the volume edited by Destler and Sato in 1982, suffers from this problem. The book goes through the details of a range of cases from the 1970s first and then leaves it to the editors, in their concluding chapter, to draw out the parallels. While their insights are pragmatic and illustrated with examples from the case studies, the ex post nature of their observations leaves them unable to base their arguments on a unified portrayal of how gaiatsu works within the Japanese policy process.[1]

The alternative to the case-first approach is to address a set of cases with questions generated by a particular analytical framework. Such an approach has the advantage of clarifying which details about a given case are likely to be important, making it easier for me to do my research and providing you with a roadmap to use when the narrative account of the cases gets particularly dense. It has the potential disadvantage of leading us both off in an entirely wrong direction, causing us to neglect data which we ought to have taken into account. Care has to be taken, therefore, in order to balance the need for a model with parsimony with the need for a model that does not neglect important explanatory factors. It is my aim here to construct such a framework, drawing on the literature in a range of political science subdisciplines.

What We're Trying to Explain

There are several questions we *could* ask about U.S.-Japan negotiations. We could seek to identify, for example, the conditions that increase the likelihood that the two parties will come to a cooperative agreement. Such a question would have the advantage of making our job of characterizing the results of U.S.-Japan negotiations easy. Either the parties came to an agreement or they didn't. Choosing to focus on such a question would also allow us to employ some of the most popular game-theoretic models as a starting point for our analysis.[2] In the real world (especially in negotiations between interdependent allies like the U.S. and Japan), however, the question of whether or not there will be an agreement is rarely a concern. The U.S. and Japan almost always reach some kind of agreement. The relationship is too important to be put at risk through a failure to reach a deal in any single set of talks. The more interesting questions concern the *terms* of the agreement.[3]

This study is interested in the terms of bargains reached between the U.S. and Japan, and specifically in when and how foreign pressure can be "effective" in improving these terms. While this question is clearly of greater real world interest in this case than the one above, it is unfortunately more difficult to specify. One approach, sometimes used in theoretical studies of bargaining, would be to attempt to quantify the total gains or losses from the bargain as well as the way these are divided. "Better terms" would be obtained by the party that secured a greater share of the gains or had to absorb a smaller share of the losses. While such an approach again has the advantage of being relatively neat and clean, its use with respect to the cases under consideration in this book seems impractical. How can one compare the benefits each side received, for example, in the SII deal to liberalize the Large Store Law? Liberalization was designed to allow in more imports from America (the U.S. gain), but it has also made the Japanese distribution system more efficient (the Japanese gain). Who got the better deal?

Rather than attempting to quantify the economic gains and losses incurred by the U.S. and Japan as a result of their SII and Framework negotiations, this study chooses to measure the terms of the bargain against the standards set by the parties themselves. American pressure is judged to be "effective" when the final deal on an issue is close to *what the Americans had originally demanded.* It is judged to be "ineffective" when the deal leaves Japanese policy little changed from *what would have happened without foreign pressure.* Care is therefore taken in the case studies that follow to identify as clearly as possible the original American demands, to plot out what would have happened based on an examination of what was happening in each issue area before foreign intervention, and to locate the final deal in relation to this scale.[4]

This book, to reiterate, seeks to identify the following: the factors that determine when foreign pressure is likely to be effective in improving the terms of bargains reached between the U.S. and Japan, where "effectiveness" reflects the degree to which the Japanese move from where policy would have been in the absence of negotiations toward the original American demands. What can the range of approaches to international negotiations which are currently employed in the social sciences contribute to our effort to identify these factors?

The Realist Contribution

The dominant paradigm in the field of international relations remains the realist perspective, so it is natural that we start our effort to build a framework by examining what this approach has to offer. As formalized by Waltz, realism argues that international relations reflect the efforts of all states to maximize their security—with the pursuit of power being one of the most important means toward that end.[5] In international negotiations, therefore, we can expect that a given state's negotiating positions will be motivated by its interest in improving or protecting its security and power. Its ability to prevail will depend on the power resources it can bring to bear on the outcome.[6]

Given the centrality of "power" in this approach, how one understands this concept is critical. Most realists emphasize military power, viewing economic power as important primarily in that it is convertible into military power.[7] Other analysts in this tradition have argued, however, that economic power in the form of "asymmetrical interdependence" can also be translated into bargaining power in international negotiations.[8] For example, in bargaining between nations with asymmetrical trade relations (where one nation exports only a small portion of its GNP to the second while the second relies on the first as a market for a large proportion of its GNP), the less dependent state ought to be able to use its leverage to extract concessions from the more dependent.

A further complicating issue is the fungibility of various kinds of power. Some analysts, recognizing that it is difficult to reduce military and economic power to a single denominator, have emphasized that power resources which can be effectively applied in certain relationships (say, between military rivals) may be different from those which can be applied in others (say, between allies in economic disputes). Even within the category of "economic disputes," these analysts note, the power resources which matter in a dispute involving oil may differ from those which matter when the issue concerns shipping.[9]

This brief survey of the realist approach points us to several factors that might be important in explaining when foreign pressure is more or less likely to prove effective in improving the terms of bargains. First, it points to the importance of relative power resources, suggesting that *foreign pressure is most likely to be effective when the power resources of the nation exerting the pressure are greatest relative to those of the target nation.* A second related hypothesis is suggested by the assumption that power resources are not perfectly fungible: *that foreign pressure is more likely to have the intended effect when the targeted issue area can be influenced with the specific kind of relative power resources at a given nation's disposal.*

Both of these hypotheses are intuitively appealing and likely have some validity. When applied to the U.S.-Japan relationship, they tell us why Japan, in general, pays close attention to U.S. demands and concedes to many of them. Japan listens because it has long depended on the American market and security guarantee more than the U.S. has depended on Japan. When one observes how unevenly Japan has responded to U.S. pressure, however, it quickly becomes clear that these hypotheses offer an inadequate explanation. The puzzle that motivated this study was the uneven pattern of Japan's response to America's SII demands. As noted in chapter 1, these talks involved the application of similar pressure within the same bilateral relationship at the same time—and yet resulted in very different degrees of responsiveness. The issues also uniformly fell into a rather narrow category of economic issues subject to bilateral trade sanctions, making it difficult to account for the variation by pointing to differences in the applicability of U.S. power resources. For the cases which constitute the bulk of this book, therefore, power was a constant and therefore cannot tell us much about why foreign pressure was more effective in some cases than in others.

It is still possible, of course, that *changes over time* in the U.S.-Japan power balance might tell us something about why gaiatsu works better at time X than at time Y. In particular, this realist explanation may help explain why the Japanese conceded more in the SII talks than in the Clinton Framework talks held four years later. While this hypothesis will be evaluated relative to other competing explanations in chapter 9, the coexistence of similar power balances with widely varying degrees of Japanese responsiveness in the SII cases raises enough questions to propel us on to see how other approaches might be able to help us refine the basic realist hypothesis.

That relative power balances are such an unreliable predictor of foreign pressure effectiveness should not be that surprising. Critics of traditional realism have been arguing for some years that the growth in economic interdependence over the postwar period has made the exercise of power much more difficult.[10] Some have even likened the economic ties among nations to a "cobweb" which binds states in so many ways that they can no longer make use of their power.[11] The U.S. government has encountered this cobweb each time it has sought to subject a specific list of Japanese products to trade sanctions, for example when it wanted to punish Toshiba in 1987 after the firm was found to have sold sensitive technology to the Soviets. So many American users of Toshiba products protested that sanctions on "their" product would force them to shut down factories and lay off workers that the list ultimately agreed upon was quite short.[12] John Odell has found similar international ties getting in the way of American attempts to pressure an even less powerful Brazil.[13]

What these examples and the literature on interdependence suggest is that, despite America's overall power advantage relative to a nation like Japan, it is rarely easy for the U.S. to exercise this power in pursuit of a specific aim. When it tries to strike out at Japan, it often finds American interests caught in between, seeking to prevent it from acting. What makes foreign pressure effective, therefore, *may not be raw power as much as it is the ability of a nation to take advantage of the web of interests that bind, not just itself, but its partners as well.* Before considering this alternative hypothesis—which will take us deep into the realm of domestic politics and therefore away from realism—we need to consider a final set of realist hypotheses based on the concept of "national interest."

As noted above, realists argue that nations always pursue their interest in maximizing their relative power position. It is possible, then, that the pattern of results in cases of U.S.-Japan trade talks reflect this drive. The results would reflect the *American* national interest if the U.S., recognizing that it couldn't force concessions on all trade issues, used its power to assure that it would at least win its battles in the areas that promised the greatest benefit for its relative power.[14] In multiissue negotiations like sii and the Framework Talks, then, the U.S. could communicate these priorities to the Japanese in order to make sure the Japanese side knew where to concede first. It is also possible that the pattern of results in these and similar cases of U.S.-Japan trade talks reflect *Japan's* national interest. Having judged that it has to concede to some U.S. demands some of the time in order to avoid a rupture in its vital economic relationship, Japan may concede only to those demands where it sacrifices the least.

The problem with these "national interest" explanations is that together they can explain *any* pattern of outcomes. If Japan concedes on issues that are U.S. priorities, a realist can invoke the first explanation. If Japan concedes on issues according to its own list of priorities, a realist can invoke the second view. As will become clear once we get into actual cases of U.S.-Japan negotiations, neither hypothesis consistently explains the pattern of outcomes. The U.S. certainly was not able to consistently win the most concessions on *its* top priorities, but neither was Japan able to consistently avoid yielding on issues at the top of *its* list.

Ultimately, how "national interest" gets defined is left to domestic pol-

itics. Realists too grant that it is here that varying domestic interpretations of national interest are sorted out but are content to "black box" this
part of the story in the expectation that the imperatives of the international struggle for power and survival will guide nations to respond to
their environment "as if" they were unitary rational actors. What the
above survey of realist propositions has shown, however, is that focusing
too much on power can be dangerously misleading. "Misleading" because,
as we have seen, the results of U.S.-Japan trade talks do not seem to correspond at all with the underlying power structure. "Dangerous" because
American trade policies based on the assumption that Japan will react to
foreign pressure "as if" it is a unitary rational actor may simply lead to
fruitless confrontation.

What then is the "realist contribution" to the framework employed in
this book? It lies in its insistence that power does matter. While the analysis above rejects the idea that "raw power" is the key to explaining the
effectiveness of gaiatsu, it is willing to admit that asymmetric interdependence creates points of leverage which *can* be used by more powerful
states to impose demands on less powerful states. How power is translated into results in any specific case, however, depends greatly on
whether government negotiators are able to take advantage of these
points of leverage while avoiding the web of interests that constrain their
own options in that case.[15] In other words, it depends on negotiating
strategies and on how domestic politics constrain and produce opportunities for negotiators to pursue these strategies. Which brings us next to
the school of thought which has the most to tell us about negotiating
strategies: the "negotiation-analytic" approach.

The Negotiation-Analytic Contribution

For analysts working in the negotiation-analytic tradition, epitomized by
Thomas Schelling's *The Strategy of Conflict*, "power" shapes the terms of
negotiated agreements only to the extent it is mated to an effective strategy. Such tactics include the use of credible *threats* that make it clear to
one's negotiating partner that a failure to reach agreement will result in
damage to the partner's interests, action to *improve one's own options* in the
event of no agreement, *linking* agreement on one issue to a deal in
another area where one has leverage over the partner, offering *side payments* to foreign governments for their use in buying the acquiescence of
constituents opposed to compromise, *adding parties* sympathetic to one's

position to the negotiations, *misleading the partner* about one's ability to concede on an issue, deliberately *tying one's hands* so that one cannot concede on an issue, *persuading the partner* that its interest lies in accepting a position closer to one's own, and *making take-it-or-leave-it offers* which limit the choices available to one's partner.[16]

Some of these strategies are related to "power" as discussed above. It is difficult to make a credible threat without the power resources to carry it out. It is also difficult to devise a linkage strategy unless one has leverage over the partner in at least one issue area. Analysts working in this tradition point out, however, that even these more power-dependent tactics do not neatly translate power resources into bargaining influence. Threats sometimes provoke "strong negative reactions, which may overwhelm the original issues at stake."[17] Some of the other tactics enumerated above have even less relationship to the kinds of "power" realists refer to when using the term.[18] If these analysts are right in their insistence that there is much more to negotiations than power (and we will be examining their claims more carefully below), then this approach may point us toward the explanation for why there is wide variation in the effectiveness of gaiatsu even when the U.S.-Japan power balance is constant. The broad hypothesis we must consider is therefore as follows: that the effectiveness of American pressure on Japan depends on the degree to which strategies such as those enumerated above can be pursued in a given case.

The key insight of the negotiation-analytic approach lies in its recognition that all factors affecting the outcome of negotiations do so by influencing the "perceived zone of possible agreement." Each party involved in a set of negotiations goes into the talks with some idea (often ill-defined even to itself) about the range of terms it considers to be better than the alternative of no agreement. When the positions of all parties on all issues are combined, they thus create a "zone of possible agreement" that encompasses all of the possible deals which *all* parties would consider better than the alternative of letting the talks fail (see figure 2.1). The tactics enumerated above all work to improve the terms of the deal for one party either by favorably changing the boundaries of zone of agreement (see figure 2.2) or by influencing *perceptions* about the zone of agreement so that the final terms end up in the corner of the zone which maximizes value for just one party (in figure 2.1, this would be Point A for Party One).[19]

This approach does a good job of demonstrating analytically how various tactics work in one of these two ways. It shows, for example, that threats work to improve terms by giving one's negotiating partner extra incentive to avoid "no agreement." More eager to forestall this result, the partner will expand outward its zone of possible agreement to include concessions it previously would not have considered, again as in figure 2.2.[20] It also is able to capture the major limitation of this tactic: if threats provoke a backlash, they may actually reduce the range of concessions a negotiating partner is willing to offer, thus shrinking the zone of agreement in a way that makes the terms of any likely agreement less attractive to the party which issued the threats. Persuasion works in a similar way, by convincing the partner that it lies in its interest to expand its zone of agreement outward. Issue linkage can also shift zones of agreement, often dramatically, as each side adds the value of resolving a new issue to the previous zone of agreement.[21]

In contrast, strategies like misleading the partner work not by shifting zones but by convincing the partner that one's own zone is smaller than it is, increasing the chance that the final terms of the deal will fall in that corner of the zone which maximizes one's own value. Making take-it-or-leave-it offers can be used to focus attention on a single point within the zone which, if the offer lies above the no-agreement line for one's partner, may be accepted by the partner.

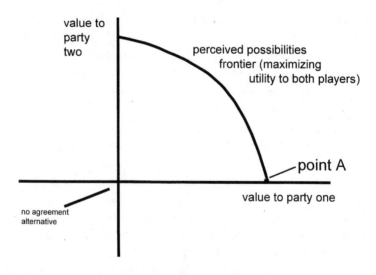

FIGURE 2.1   The Bargaining Set

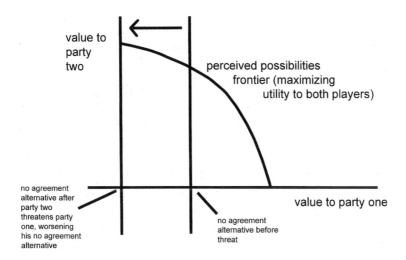

FIGURE 2.2   Impact of Threat on the Bargaining Set

Source: both figures based on bargaining model depicted in Lax and Sebenius, The Manager as Negotiator (New York: The Free Press, 1986), p.248.

What is attractive about the negotiation-analytic approach is that it shows us analytically how all of these strategies *can* work to improve terms. Scholars like Sebenius, Lax, and Raiffa, who formalized the basic model as presented above, also offer careful discussion of case studies to illustrate how these tactics—many only marginally related to realist kinds of power—*can* work.[22] A major limitation of this basic model, however, is that many of the factors that determine *when* these strategies are most likely to work are external to the framework. Take the example of threats. Whether threats work to expand zones of agreement depends on whether they spark a backlash, but in the model this question is a function of a party's "preferences" (or "value function") which are treated as an externally determined input into the model. Likewise, the effectiveness of persuasion depends on whether the target's preferences are amenable to suasive influence. Similar factors external to the basic model condition many of the other tactics enumerated above.

The Domestic Politics Contribution

Because many of these factors are a function of domestic politics, a growing number of scholars have sought to expand the scope of negotiation analysis to incorporate politics at this level. I draw in particular on Putnam's work here because his approach focuses explicitly on international negotiations, but he is certainly not the first to treat negotiations as a two-level game.[23] As explained briefly in the introductory chapter, Putnam argues that international negotiations are like a "two-level game" where each chief negotiator's moves must "win" at both the international table (Level I) and at the domestic table (Level II). The final terms each negotiator agrees to must be acceptable to his international counterparts, but they also must fall within his domestic "win-set," the set of all possible deals that a chief negotiator can have ratified by his domestic constituents. In terms of the basic negotiation-analytic model illustrated above, this means that the parameters of the zone of agreement are determined by each side's domestic win-set.

To a large extent, the domestic win-sets are a given for international negotiators—set by domestic factors beyond their control. Much of what goes on in international talks, therefore, involves the attempts of chief negotiators to make the best of the hands they are dealt, to use their own constrained win-sets to get a good deal (as when Carter used his difficulty in getting 67 votes in the Senate to extract attractive terms from the Panamanian government) or to extract the best terms possible from a counterpart whose win-set is loose enough to accommodate a range of terms.

Like other analysts in the negotiation-analytic tradition, however, Putnam sees international negotiations as giving negotiators some room to shift the parameters of these win-sets to improve the terms of their deals. A chief negotiator can use variations of the strategies listed above, such as threats, linkage, and persuasion, to expand the size of her counterpart's win-set or she can shrink her own win-set by tying her own hands. The difference, the reason Putnam's approach represents an important advance on the basic negotiation-analytic model, lies in the way in which his approach brings domestic politics explicitly into the framework, making it clear how the effectiveness of strategies designed to shift the parameters of "win-sets" depend on the way in which those tactics *interact with* domestic politics.[24] The strategies of international negotiators do not directly produce changes in the size of "win-sets." They affect their size only to the extent that they work their way through domestic politics. The strategies must be *synergistic* (they must work well with domestic politics) if they are to have the kind of effects the negotiation-analytic model demonstrates they *can* have.

As this brief survey of the approach makes clear, Putnam places a great deal of importance on domestic politics. It is domestic politics which sets the basic contours of "win-sets" and it is domestic politics which determines the degree to which the strategies of international negotiators are successful in shifting their boundaries. If Putnam is right, the only way to understand the results of international negotiations, including those involving the U.S. and Japan, is to delve quite deeply into the internal politics of the countries involved. But how deeply? What aspects of domestic politics are most important? If we are to make use of this approach, we need a "theory of domestic politics" to guide our analysis.

It is very tempting, in constructing this theory, to make simplifying assumptions about the domestic game in order to limit the range of variables we need to consider. One scholar working with Putnam's model, for example, has chosen to treat the domestic game as one where the only thing that matters is the ratification vote in the legislature. This allows him to focus narrowly on how the strategies of international negotiators influence the legislature's "median voter" and facilitates the use of formal modeling to test Putnam's hypotheses.[25] The problem with such simplifying assumptions is that they grossly under-represent the complexity of domestic politics. It is precisely because of its complexities, which make it an uneven transmission belt for international pressures, that domestic politics matters. How a nation responds to foreign pressure depends not just on legislative votes but on patterns of interest group mobilization, bureaucratic infighting, public opinion, and even on the process through which specific policy proposals are chosen for top-level consideration. The contours of "win-sets" and how a negotiator's strategies work depend on all of these variables.

The "theory of domestic politics" employed in this book is therefore a modified version of the more complex one used by Putnam himself. Putnam argues that "win-sets" are a function of domestic political institutions and the "power, preferences, and possible coalitions" among domestic constituents.[26] He lists the relevant domestic actors as legislators, bureaucratic agencies, interest groups, social classes, and public opinion. Institutions set basic rules about who is allowed to participate in the "ratification" of international agreements and how much power each actor will have. In the case of societal actors, however, whether a specific group participates and how much power it has also depends on whether it mobilizes for political action and on whether it is part of the ruling coalition. The preferences of the various actors, in Putnam's approach, are based on their perceptions about the costs of "no agreement" in a given set of international negotiations, perceptions which in turn reflect their material interests and their organizational goals.

In this book, I accept the main features of Putnam's theory of domestic politics. I accept the view, implicit in his listing of "bureaucratic agencies" as political actors, that government units can be independent players in the domestic political game, pursuing their own organizational goals.[27] Like Putnam, I also accept and draw on collective action theory to account for variable levels of power and participation by societal actors in domestic politics. According to this argument, the power of societal interests depends on whether individuals choose to organize themselves into groups of a size which is big enough in terms of money or votes to gain preferential access to the policy process. Such choices are in turn a function of history (whether groups have already organized in response to past circumstances) and the nature of an issue (whether the policies at issue involve concentrated or diffuse costs or benefits).[28]

The theory of domestic politics employed here differs from Putnam's in only two respects. First, institutions are seen to do more than just allocate power. Institutions, as Peter Hall has argued, also influence the behavior of actors "by altering their relationship to other actors."[29] Electoral rules, for example, influence the behavior of politicians by creating incentives for them to appeal for votes in certain ways. Rules setting jurisdictional boundaries between government agencies similarly influence the behavior of bureaucrats by creating incentives for them to defend or fight for turf along certain lines. This study will therefore look closely at how institutional structures in both the U.S. and Japan have served to influence the behavior of various actors within their domestic polities.

Second, the theory of domestic politics employed here emphasizes that policy outcomes reflect not just political power but also *ideas*. As John Kingdon has argued, the process through which politicians, bureaucrats, and interest groups sort out their preferences is just one of three streams that must come together before a major policy change can be adopted. Equally important to explaining policy outcomes are the processes through which governments come to recognize that a problem exists and identify specific policy proposals.[30] In these processes, the media and groups of experts in specific areas of policy ("policy communities") play very important roles.[31] The analysis in this book will therefore also consider the possibility that international pressure can affect policy outcomes by influencing these other streams.

We are now ready, finally, to return to the central question with which we started this chapter: when and how is foreign pressure likely to improve the terms of international bargains? The negotiation-analytic approach told us *how*. If international negotiators want to improve the terms of their deals, they have to influence the "perceived zone of possible agreement" by using one of a number of strategies, including persuasion, threats, linkage, adding parties, making take-it-or-leave-it offers, and tying hands. Based on this analysis, I proposed a more specific hypothesis for application to the cases to be examined in this book: that the effectiveness of American pressure on Japan depends on the degree to which strategies such as those enumerated above can be pursued in a given case. The problem with this hypothesis was that it didn't tell us *when* these strategies were likely to be useful. Like the negotiation-analytic approach as a whole, it only told us how.

Putnam's metaphor of the two-level game combined with the theory of domestic politics outlined above has the potential to tell us *when*. Putnam's approach argues that strategies such as those listed above are effective only when they *work through* domestic politics, and our theory of domestic politics tells us what kinds of domestic factors influence how this transmission belt operates. The only remaining task is to connect the various negotiation strategies to our various domestic political factors, a favorable combination of which yields *synergistic* strategies.

Ironically, Putnam himself spends only a little time, in his article laying out the two-level game approach, on the conditions that favor the use of synergistic strategies. Strategies like "reverberation," he argues, are more likely to produce positive results when the nations involved are allies, the issues are economic, and relations between countries are interdependent.[32] These specifications tell us nothing, however, about what kinds of issues within the broad category of economic issues within a given relationship are likely to be more responsive to synergistic strategies. The collaborative project Putnam's article inspired is more ambitious in that it advances numerous hypotheses related to his framework, but many of these are unrelated to synergistic strategies.[33]

In the section that follows, I seek to finish the job that Putnam started, systematically connecting the various negotiation strategies identified by the negotiation-analytic approach to our theory of domestic politics in order to generate hypotheses about when these strategies are likely to prove effective. The section builds on the work of Putnam and his collaborators whenever possible, but pushes it further in several respects. Two of the six synergistic strategies discussed below (participation expansion and alternative specification) are not anticipated in previous work using the two-level approach. In addition, I have generated a number of new hypotheses about when these two strategies and others are more likely to prove effective. The analysis in this section will be used throughout the remainder of this book to guide our investigation of why gaiatsu works in some cases and not in others.

REVERBERATION

According to the negotiation-analytic approach, one of the main ways in which a negotiator can improve the terms he can get out of his counterpart is to expand the size of his partner's zone of agreement through persuasion, threats, linkage, or adding parties. Putnam himself gets us started on this list with his discussion of a strategy he calls "reverberation," which is essentially a synergistic version of persuasion. Sometimes, Putnam argues, a chief negotiator may find "silent allies at his opponent's domestic table" who support his position. If these silent allies constitute a minority within the domestic arena of the target nation at the beginning of negotiations, international pressure may in time succeed in bolstering this movement to the point that it becomes a majority.[34] The phenomenon described is somewhat different from regular old persuasion, however, because (in accordance with the logic of the two-level model) it has to *work through* domestic politics. A chief negotiator must convince more than just his negotiating partner. He also has to convince his counterpart's *constituents*.

But when is such a strategy more likely to prove effective? One of the most important conditions, suggested by Putnam's reference to a "silent" minority, is that *there must already be a sizable coalition of influential domestic actors in favor of the foreign demand*. This condition follows from the way domestic actors form their preferences. As specified above, domestic actors derive their preferences on a given issue in international negotiations from their perceptions of how that issue relates to their *own* interests and goals. They do not care what others (including foreigners) feel about an issue. The only way anyone can change an actor's preferences with rhetoric is to change its *perceptions* of how an issue relates to its goals. What this means is that negotiators are unlikely to be able to change an actor's mind if its material interests or organizational goals are affected in an obvious way. For reverberation to be successful in creating a majority in support of a foreign demand, a sizable minority of those influential actors with an obvious stake in the outcome of a policy debate must already be in support of the foreign position. Reverberation can then go to work on the undecideds, the actors whose interests are not affected in obvious ways and whose perceptions about an issue might be swayed by the arguments of foreigners.

The more difficult question concerns the conditions under which undecideds are prone to be swayed by foreign negotiators. Indeed, as Putnam notes, foreign efforts to convince the people of another country that they should pursue a certain course of action may in some cases cause "negative reverberation," making people more reluctant to back the policy favored by the foreign government.[35] Why is reverberation more positive between certain countries, on certain issues? Putnam himself, as noted above, suggests that it depends on whether the nations involved are interdependent allies and the issues economic. He suggests that domestic actors in allied nations are likely to be more receptive to the suasive arguments of foreign negotiators because cognitive theory tells us that messages from friends are more likely to be taken to heart than those from enemies. Those in interdependent relationships (especially the more dependent of the pair) are more likely to be swayed on matters of economic policy because they are in the habit of listening to what "big brother" has to say on such issues.

While these observations get us part of the way to an answer, they cannot explain why French interests, for example, so often rebel at even the hint of American intervention in their internal affairs even as the Japanese have for so long politely taken note of everything American officials have to say about their country. Neither can they tell us why American arguments on agricultural trade issues are more likely to spark an emotional backlash than U.S. pronouncements on electronics trade issues. What I propose is a modification of Putnam's hypothesis, still true to cognitive theory, which conditions whether reverberation will be positive on *the degree to which domestic actors in a target nation view the intervention of a particular foreign government in a particular issue area as "legitimate."* The legitimacy of meddling by a certain foreign government may be partly a function of whether that country is an ally, but it is also likely to reflect the history of the relationship and may even depend on the institutions of the target country (which may change over time). Foreign intervention in economic matters may be viewed as generally more legitimate, but even within this category, there are likely to be some issues, such as those linked to national symbols or sensitive social problems, where foreign meddling is seen as totally unwelcome. This hypothesis thus predicts that part of the explanation for why gaiatsu works in some cases but not in others may lie in cross-issue and cross-time variation in the degree to which American intervention is seen as legitimate.

Synergistic Threats

While the idea that threats have to "work well" with domestic politics may sound oxymoronic, the logic of Putnam's two-level game metaphor suggests this requirement applies to threats as much as it does to any other strategy. Unlike reverberation which, as we saw, works by changing the *perceptions* of various actors about the cost of no-agreement, threats work by raising their actual costs, by giving exporters of a specific product a real incentive to mobilize by threatening to cut off their export markets, for example, or by giving users of imported oil a reason to mobilize by threatening an oil embargo. Still, according to Putnam's logic, these strategies do not automatically bring about an advantageous expansion of a counterpart's win-set. They do so only to the extent they *work through* domestic politics. As Harrison Wagner noted in his study of economic coercion, "any suggestion that the U.S. government can pressure the Soviet government by making it more difficult for it to buy wheat must take into account . . . the political influence of American wheat farmers and the political weakness of Soviet consumers."[36] Such observations and Putnam's logic make it clear that the effectiveness of threats is conditioned by how they interact with domestic-level factors.

First, the counterpart's decision to give in to a threat has to be ratified by his domestic constituents, meaning that the political support for a concession from domestic political forces whose interests are directly affected by the threat must outweigh the opposition to the concession. As Wagner's comment about the "political weakness of Soviet consumers" suggests, this ability of threatened interests to bring about policy change cannot be taken for granted. Concessions may be ratified at the domestic level with relative ease if the domestic political actors whose interests are most affected by the threat are also the ones with the power to grant the concessions, but they may not be ratified as easily if the threat is directed at interests who are least likely to change their views or at those who are unable to bring about the policy change that is sought.[37] An excellent example of a synergistic threat, cited in the collaborative volume, was the American decision to single out cognac, brandy, white wine, whiskey, gin, cheese, and olives for retaliation in its campaign to remove European Commission barriers to American feedgrain imports in 1986. By no coincidence, the producers of these products happened to be well-organized and influential in the nations which were best positioned to influence the EC's decision—which subsequently went in favor of the U.S.[38]

This example, emphasizing that American pressure works when it is "targeted" at *organized* groups, points to how our theory of domestic politics can help us to refine further our predictions about when threats will work.[39] The model of domestic politics outlined above suggests that *threats will be more effective when the groups affected are organized and/or inside the ruling coalition, when the state actors affected have institutionally derived power, and when the costs imposed through threats are concentrated.* To the extent American pressure on Japan relies on threats, this means it will be effective only when the promised sanctions are targeted at the kinds of groups specified and when the sanctions promise to impose concentrated costs.[40]

The second factor conditioning the effectiveness of threats, suggested by Wagner's comment about the "political influence of American wheat farmers," is the requirement that a threat must "work well" with the domestic politics of the nation which is *issuing* the threat. One of the most interesting arguments made in the collaborative volume which extended Putnam's work is its proposition that threats are effective only when they can be ratified by the state making them. If the country targeted by the threats sees that domestic political problems are likely to prevent the threatening state from carrying out its sanctions, the threats will lack credibility and are unlikely to produce any expansion of the target's win-set. Assuming that the target bases its reading of domestic politics on an implicit theory similar to the one I outline, this means that threats will be credible and effective only when *those groups in the state that makes the threat who will bear the costs of carrying out the sanctions are less influential than those who will benefit from any concessions that might be extracted with the threat,* where "influential" is defined in terms of whether affected groups are organized, inside the ruling coalition, and/or institutionally privileged, as in the previous paragraph.[41] For the U.S.-Japan cases examined in this book, this hypothesis suggests that gaiatsu may vary in its effectiveness depending on whether or not Japanese negotiators perceive American politics as allowing the government to carry out sanctions in support of a particular U.S. demand.

One final factor also conditions the effectiveness of threats. Just as there is likely to be less positive reverberation when foreign intervention is considered illegitimate, threats too are likely to vary in their effectiveness *depending on the degree to which they are perceived as "legitimate."* Studies of economic coercion have long noted that even severe threats from powerful nations often fail to produce concessions, especially when the threat is coming from a power seen as "external" and when the challenge is to a policy identified with "the nation."[42] When threats are seen as totally illegitimate, they are likely to cause a backlash effect which leads the target nation to actually shrink its win-set and refuse to yield. When the threat is seen as coming from a relatively friendly source on an issue seen as "fair game," the threat is more likely to produce the expected expansion of the win-set. The logic here is very similar to that developed above for reverberation, so I will not repeat it in detail. For the U.S.-Japan cases, this hypothesis suggests that gaiatsu may work better on issues seen by key actors as "fair game" for sanctions and when the U.S. is broadly perceived as employing threats only as a last resort and in the interests of "the relationship" rather than in its narrow self-interest.

Synergistic Linkage

Linkage, the third strategy on our list, is on almost everyone's list of effective negotiating strategies. Unfortunately, the kinds of tactics different authors have in mind when they discuss linkage vary, and Putnam adds to the confusion by illustrating his own discussion of the topic with two fundamentally different examples. As we will see, however, the two-level game metaphor makes it clear that all varieties of linkage must "work well" with domestic politics. Win-sets cannot be enlarged, even with the "power politics" version of linkage, unless the strategy resonates in certain ways with the domestic politics of all parties involved in negotiations.

Most commonly, linkage refers to cases where a nation seeks to take advantage of its power advantage in one area by linking it to an issue area in which it has fewer power resources. The Arab OPEC nations, for example, sought in the early 1970s to bring their power in international oil markets to bear on the Arab-Israeli conflict by linking their oil policy to the position taken by oil-importing nations on the Middle East conflict. More recently, the Clinton Administration sought to influence Chinese human rights policy by linking it to American trade policy toward the nation. I will be referring to this type of linkage as the "power politics" variety because, in exactly the way *threats* work, it involves the attempt by one nation to aggressively bring about an expansion in the counterpart's "win-set" by worsening its no-agreement option.

Because this type of linkage is so similar to threats, the domestic factors limiting its effectiveness are essentially the same as those discussed above. *The linkage must be targeted at the right domestic groups in the "linkee" country, it must be ratifiable within the "linker" country, and it must be seen as legitimate.* Thus Clinton's linkage strategy for China, for example, was doomed by the fact that the China trade lobby was much more organized and plugged into the system than American human rights interest groups. China recognized that the linkage was not likely to be ratified and so did not find it necessary to make significant concessions. The legitimacy of linkage argument also applies to the China case. The Chinese government consistently argued that human rights and trade were two separate issues and that America was unfair to try to link them.

Some negotiation analysts have insisted, however, that not all linkage has to be one-sided and aggressive. In some cases of "mutually advantageous issue linkage," a decision to link the settlement of two previously separate issues can benefit *both* nations, providing the parties involved in negotiations with a currency with which to resolve distributional problems associated with deals where a cooperative bargain on one issue alone is difficult to achieve because it inevitably leaves one side with an unfair advantage.[43] Tollison and Willett point to the example of how such linkage can facilitate agreements to concentrate production of military equipment for an alliance in a single country. While agreements of this type (which provide scale economies for the alliance as a whole) are notoriously difficult to reach because the benefits of any single deal are by definition skewed toward the party that gets all of the production work, Tollison and Willett point out that such deals can nevertheless be facilitated by linking them to deals on other issues where distributional asymmetries are skewed in the opposite direction.[44]

While the cooperative "mutually advantageous" type of linkage on first glance seems quite different from the one-sided "power politics" type discussed first, the domestic-level factors that condition the effectiveness of the two types are surprisingly similar. Because the agreement to link issues in this case is supposed to be mutual, it is difficult to speak of a "linker" and "linkee." Nevertheless, "mutually advantageous" linkage involves a tradeoff across issues in each nation, which is likely to complicate the task of getting the linkage to work well with domestic politics. By definition, with this type of linkage, both sides agree to accept less than what they could have bargained for on one issue for more than what they could have bargained for on another. Since the bureaucracies, interest groups, and other actors involved in the two issues are likely to differ, it is likely that the actors asked to settle for "less than they could have bargained for" are going to object even as those who get "more than they could have bargained for" press for the deal. *Whether the deal comes off and the strategy works, according to our theory of domestic politics, depends on which of these two groups of actors are more "influential," again defined as above.*[45] The only advantage "mutually advantageous" linkage has over the "power politics" variety, in terms of their domestic viability, lies in the likelihood that there will be less of a backlash effect with "mutually advantageous" linkage since both sides will be getting something out of the agreement.

Interestingly, one of the two examples Putnam cites under his discussion of "synergistic linkage" is a clear case of the mutually advantageous type. At the 1978 Bonn Summit, the U.S. on the one hand and West Germany and Japan on the other agreed to a tradeoff where the U.S. received more than it could have bargained for on macroeconomics (when Japan and Germany agreed to reflate) while the latter received more than they could have bargained for on energy policy (when the U.S. agreed to decontrol oil prices).[46] What is odd is that Putnam's other example of linkage does not involve an international tradeoff. A brief look at this case can help clarify how this third type of linkage—which I call "target-nation linkage"—differs from the "mutually advantageous" type of linkage discussed above.

Putnam's other case is a stylized example of a case of trade negotiations where two issues are linked, which he calls "beef and oranges."[47] Not coincidentally, the U.S. reached a deal with Japan on beef and oranges in 1988, but Putnam's example is not based on the actual politics of that deal. He points out that in many such cases, a negotiator has trouble getting concessions out of the other side when issues are dealt with separately. The interest groups and bureaucracies that care most about the issue are often the ones that are most adamant that no concession should be made, and if they dominate the policymaking process for that issue, they can block all concessions. When issues are linked, however, the logjam can be broken and the negotiator can often get *some* concessions on both issues. Note that the story here is different from the "mutually advantageous" type in an important way: the nation employing the strategy is not giving up anything! Where it previously was not getting concessions from the target nation on any issue, it ends up getting some concessions on both. No matter how this happens, it is clear the domestic politics of such a strategy are going to be different from those discussed above.

Putnam is vague about the domestic politics that lie behind this type of strategy.[48] The theory of domestic politics outlined above, however, tells us how "target-nation linkage" can work. According to this theory, the groups that mobilize for political action are those with the most at stake. When the orange issue, a demand for trade liberalization, is dealt with by itself, the only groups who mobilize are likely to be those representing protected orange farmers. Consumers, potential beneficiaries of liberalization, are unlikely to mobilize because the costs they face are so widely dispersed. At the same time, the "orange bureaucracy" is likely to be active in seeking to fend off a challenge to its organizational mission: to maintain the domestic orange industry. No other bureaucracy will be involved since the narrowly focused negotiations affect only the organizational mission of the "orange bureaucracy." With the actors most opposed to concessions being the only ones involved, no concessions will be offered. The story will be the same for beef, with beef producers and the "beef bureaucracy" mobilizing to block any concessions.

"Target-nation linkage" can change this situation and provide the nation employing the strategy with *mobilized* support. If the nation employing the strategy can make it clear that it will trade off concessions on oranges for concessions on beef, orange interests suddenly have a stake in making sure that beef interests give up "their share." Likewise, beef interests have a stake in making sure orange interests make some sacrifices. Each bureaucracy too will have an organizational interest in making sure that it is not the only part of the government asked to make concessions. With this mobilized support, the nation employing the strategy has an opportunity to win some concessions on both issues.[49]

What are the domestic political factors that condition the effectiveness of this type of linkage strategy? One constraint, which limited the ratifiability of the other two kinds of linkage, is noticeable in this case for its absence. Because the "linker" country is not giving up anything it could have extracted without linkage, the domestic politics on that side are not likely to get in the way of employing this strategy. On the side of the "linkee," however, domestic political factors *are* likely to determine how effective this strategy will be in expanding win-sets. Given that the tactic draws its impact from sectoral and bureaucratic rivalry, I would posit, first, that *this strategy will have the most impact when policymaking is highly segmented.*[50] Sectoral and bureaucratic rivalry are likely to be most intense (and hence provide greater support) when the issues that are linked are handled by rival ministries (or rival sections of functionally segmented ministries) and when the pressure groups have few common interests. This hypothesis suggests that we should look closely at the degree to which policymaking is segmented (especially in Japan) in order to understand when and how gaiatsu brings about policy concessions.

Participation Expansion

We are now ready to turn to the final strategy identified in the negotiation-analytic literature as a way negotiators can expand their counterpart's win-set: adding parties. This tactic is analyzed in particular by Sebenius who, in his work, draws primarily on examples of how negotiators have been able alter zones of possible agreement by manipulating the number of participating *governments.* This tactic, he argues, can be used by negotiators to create zones of possible agreement where no mutually agreeable terms existed before and can alter the parameters to the advantage of one of the parties.[51] There is no reason to suppose, however, that the parties available for adding to negotiations are limited to other governments. If we recognize, as we already began to do in our discussion of "target nation linkage" above, that the set of actors who participate in the domestic ratification process is not a constant, then it follows that "participation expansion" at the domestic level may provide a similar mechanism through which negotiators can improve the terms of their deals.[52]

The proposition that the set of actors participating in the domestic policy process is *not* a constant is in fact widely accepted in studies of policymaking processes but has strangely been neglected in other works that have attempted to develop Putnam's two-level model. Many of these studies take Putnam's use of the term "ratification" too literally and so implicitly or explicitly treat the domestic game as one where the goal is to secure a majority vote in the legislature where, of course, the number of participants is fixed.[53] Even Putnam, who explicitly recognizes that levels of participation vary across issue areas and can change because of the politicizing impact of international negotiations, discounts the likelihood that politicization is ever likely to be a useful strategy for a negotiator looking to improve the terms of his deal.[54] The strategy discussed below is thus "new" in the sense that previous work employing the two-level approach has not given it significant attention.

The importance of participation levels in determining policy outcomes, though, suggests we should not be so quick to dismiss this factor. No less an observer of American policymaking than E. E. Schattschneider placed critical importance on the number of participants involved in making a decision, arguing that "the number of people involved in any conflict determines what happens; every change in the number of participants, every increase or reduction in the number of participants affects the result."[55] If an international negotiator can use a deliberate strategy of participation expansion to increase the number of participants in his counterpart's domestic arena, and the ranks of the previously uninvolved domestic actors include many who support his demands, then this change in the domestic political game ought to produce an expansion in the size of his counterpart's win-set that allows him to extract a better deal.

The key condition determining whether this strategy is likely to be of any use is the question of whether the ranks of the uninvolved actors include latent supporters of the foreign demand. Unlike Putnam, who assumes that politicization is almost always likely to shrink win-sets and is therefore unlikely to be of any use as a synergistic strategy, I treat this question as open to empirical analysis. It is possible, particularly in cases where foreign pressure seeks to change policies that have been kept in place through the entrenched power of privileged domestic actors, that politicization may bring into the game other elite actors with less of a stake in maintaining the status quo or that it may even motivate the public (who may have previously been unaware of an issue) to become aroused and bring the weight of public opinion to bear on the outcome. In such a case, where participation expansion works *synergistically*, it may serve as a useful tool for international negotiators.

The analysis above suggests that, in our study of U.S.-Japan negotiations, we should examine what effect an American decision to target an issue area had on participation levels in that area: who was involved in policymaking before gaiatsu, and who became involved after? If we find participation levels increasing, if the ranks of the previously uninvolved actors included supporters of the American position, and if the participation by these groups helped shift policy in a new direction, .we can draw the conclusion that "participation expansion" can under certain conditions serve as a strategy through which negotiators can improve the terms of their deals.

Alternative Specification

According to the negotiation-analytic literature, expanding the other guy's win-set through the kinds of tactics discussed above is just one way a negotiator can improve the terms of her deal. She can also focus attention on a specific distributionally-advantageous point within the zone of possible agreement. We now turn to the two-level implications of this second class of strategies, the best known example of which is the tactic of making take-it-or-leave-it offers. As Sebenius writes, "if party A can make a single advantageous part of the Pareto frontier salient to party B and obscure the rest of the zone of possible agreement, A may have a better outcome." In making this point, he cites Schattschneider's famous line: "the definition of the alternatives is the supreme instrument of power."[56] But the "definition of the alternatives" is rarely going to be left to foreign negotiators alone, as Schattschneider himself would have pointed out. The logic of Putnam's two-level metaphor suggests that this tactic too has to "work well" with domestic politics. Because the two-level implications of this strategy have not been explored in previous work employing Putnam's approach, I have coined my own term for the synergistic version: "alternative specification."

According to the classic formulation of the take-it-or-leave-it strategy, a negotiator was supposed to "define the alternatives" for his counterpart by giving him only two choices: take this deal or no deal.[57] Negotiation analysts have long noted, however, that such aggressive tactics frequently cause the negotiating climate to deteriorate, leaving the parties with "Pareto-inferior agreements, deadlocks, and conflict spirals."[58] While this bad blood may be explainable partly in terms of the psychology of negotiators, Putnam's metaphor suggests that the backlash seen in such cases probably also reflects the reaction of the counterpart's domestic constituents: they object to having foreigners tell them what ideas they should consider. *The degree to which strategies of this type are effective, therefore, would seem to depend on factors similar to those which condition the effectiveness of persuasion and threats.* Is the country telling them what proposals to consider an ally? And is the issue on which the proposals are being made one where foreign intervention is legitimate?

Putnam's metaphor also suggests, however, that a negotiator's efforts to specify the alternatives his counterpart should consider are likely to be more effective when they resonate positively in his counterpart's domestic arena—the relevant part of the domestic arena in this case being the part where policy alternatives are already being studied and weighed. According to the theory of domestic politics outlined above, this process is in many cases dominated by "policy communities" of experts who are constantly debating and researching, sifting through a wide array of potential approaches for dealing with a problem in an effort to identify a few particularly promising approaches. To the extent this is an accurate description of how policy proposals are generated in a given issue area, then it follows that *foreign negotiators are likely to encounter much less resistance to their efforts to "define the alternatives" if the proposals they make: 1) are already being considered within the policy community; or 2) address a problem that is recognized as such by the policy community.*[59] In a policymaking process where whether a policy proposal makes it onto the short list of policy proposals can be as important as the political squabbles among politicians and bureaucrats, a foreign negotiator may under these conditions gain a significant advantage in bilateral talks by making sure that a policy proposal he favors gets advantageous consideration in the policy debate.

This analysis suggests that, in our study of the sii and Clinton Framework talks, we should look carefully at the "policy communities" that were already involved in devising proposals on the issues targeted by the Americans. If the proposals made by the Americans were among those being considered in these communities, if these proposals received more attention than they would have as a result of gaiatsu, and if this extra attention contributed to the enactment of new policies, we can conclude that this strategy too can, under certain conditions, serve as a way in which negotiators can improve the terms of their deals.

Tying Hands

The final way negotiators can improve the terms of their deals, according to negotiation analysts, is to shrink the size of *their own* win-sets. Because a leader who is weak domestically, who cannot win support for any concessions, can paradoxically end up being "stronger" in international negotiations because of his ability to insist that his partner make all of the compromises required to get to an agreement, negotiators have an incentive to tie their own hands.[60] As with all of the strategies examined above, however, this tactic too is limited in important ways by domestic politics (in this case largely on the side of the negotiator employing the strategy). Only when a negotiator's attempt to tie his hands "works well" with the politics of his own domestic arena is he likely to be successful.

Before looking at the domestic constraints that limit the utility of this strategy, though, we should look at one important reason why the idea of shrinking their own win-sets is inherently less attractive to negotiators. As Putnam points out, a negotiator's motives vis-à-vis his own win-set are mixed. While a negotiator always wants his counterpart's win-set to be as large as possible, he wants his own to be both small enough to get a good deal *and* large enough to accommodate an agreement.[61] As a result, even when negotiators *might be able to* improve the terms of their deals by tying their own hands, they often refrain to avoid the risk that they might eliminate their maneuvering room.[62] For this reason, in U.S.-Japan negotiations, we should expect to see American negotiators using this tactic less often than the other tactics discussed above.

Nevertheless, it is possible that the variation in the effectiveness of gaiatsu reflects the degree to which domestic conditions in the U.S. supported the use of this tactic in specific cases. We therefore need to consider which domestic factors are likely to have been relevant. Interestingly, the conditions limiting the use of a strategy of tying hands parallel those limiting a negotiator's ability to use reverberation—except that the audience who needs persuading this time is her own rather than her counterpart's. Again, since a leader cannot change the objective cost-benefit calculations of domestic actors, she can do little more than affect their perceptions of how a set of negotiating positions relate to their interests. *She thus needs a sizable coalition of those influential actors with an obvious stake in the outcome of the negotiations to be already supportive of a more hawkish posture*, so that she can then go to work trying to influence the perceptions of the undecideds. *Institutions* too condition the effectiveness of this strategy, so that a dictator, for example, has a harder time tying his hands than a leader who has to have his agreement ratified by his legislature. In U.S.-Japan negotiations, it is possible that the fact that Clinton's party controlled Congress during most of the Framework Talks (making him more like a dictator?) made it more difficult for him, than for Bush, to take advantage of this strategy by playing "good cop, bad cop" with Congress.

Now that we have identified and thought a little about the above six synergistic strategies, we have a more specific understanding of how the kinds of negotiating tactics identified in negotiation-analytic studies are conditioned by domestic politics. Instead of the vague sense that many of the factors which determine whether these tactics will be successful lie outside the model, we now have a somewhat better idea of how each strategy depends on how it interacts with domestic politics—which are now inside our model. This set of hypotheses, emphasizing how strategies employed by international negotiators are only effective when they "work well" with domestic politics, will serve as the basis for this book's evaluation of why American pressure on Japan has not produced uniform results.

Domestic Politics Reversed

Before we turn to that task, however, we need to consider one implication of the Putnam two-level game approach that has been neglected in much of the work that has sought to develop it. Putnam's approach, unlike the basic negotiation-analytic framework that inspired it, does not restrict the use of "strategy" to actors at the international level. Because Putnam's two games are played simultaneously, without one game taking priority over the other, there is no reason to expect that strategic options should be available only to statesmen. Even as international negotiators seek to manipulate domestic politics to achieve international objectives, sophisticated domestic actors should also be able to use international negotiations to further their domestic objectives.

Strangely, this side of the framework has received only minimal attention. Putnam himself fails to discuss domestic strategies even as he devotes a large section of his article to the two-level strategies available to international negotiators. Moravcsik, in his introductory essay to the collaborative volume, notes that "the two-level games model also implies that domestic groups have opportunities to develop similar strategies and counter-strategies," but goes on to admit that the essays in the volume focus primarily on the strategic options available to statesmen.[63]

The one exception to this general neglect of domestic strategies is Jeffrey Knopf's study of the U.S.-NATO-Soviet negotiations on intermediate nuclear force (INF) reductions in the 1980s, but even he does not capture the full range and potential of these strategies. Briefly, Knopf argues that the U.S. decision to embrace the "zero option" in 1981, a decision that reversed the American government's previous insistence that NATO needed to concentrate on getting intermediate weapons deployed even as it began negotiating with the Soviets, cannot be understood without looking at how West German antinuclear groups pursued a "cross-level" strategy that gave Reagan little choice but to begin the talks this way. He refers to the strategy as "cross-level" because, in the inter-alliance bargaining, domestic groups on one side of the talks (Germany) appealed directly to the international negotiator on the other side (the U.S.) in order to pursue their domestic objective of blocking deployment of INF weapons in Germany. Based on this example, Knopf argues that those employing two-level analysis should not concentrate on the strategic options available to statesmen to the point that they fail to see how statesmen are constrained in their choices by "cross-level" strategies pursued by domestic actors.[64]

While I agree with Knopf's conclusion, I do not think his choice of a case study actually supports the point he is making. In the U.S.-German negotiations, Knopf claims that the German antinuclear forces reached "cross-level" to get what they wanted. In fact, however, the influence of these groups was not based on the sympathy of American officials for their position. The U.S. wanted to get INF forces deployed. Rather, these groups had influence in the negotiations because of their power within Chancellor Schmidt's Social Democratic Party. They limited the range of U.S.-German deals Schmidt could accept. What Knopf describes, therefore, is not a "cross-level" tactic but the more conventional ability of domestic groups to limit the size of their *own state's* win-set and to use this influence to secure terms which are more attractive to them.[65]

A better example of strategic behavior by domestic actors would tell the story of how a domestic group, failing to achieve its policy goals on its own, appealed to sympathetic actors or a sympathetic government in *another state* in order to change the nature of the domestic game and secure its objectives. If it is true that international negotiators can influence the domestic policymaking process by increasing the number of participants, creating opportunities for cross-issue tradeoffs, and specifying policy alternatives (as suggested above), then it seems obvious that losers in domestic policy battles which see an opportunity to gain influence by "internationalizing" an issue ought to be interested in doing so. Do they? Under what conditions are they most likely to play the "international card"? Given the lack of theorizing about domestic-initiated two-level strategies at this point, we will have to leave it to the case studies to provide first-cut answers to these questions.

One more question about these domestic-initiated strategies brings us back to where we started this discussion: if it is true that domestic actors also have two-level strategic options, what are the implications for states-men seeking to use their own such strategies to improve the terms of their bargains? Ironically, despite his failure to base his conclusions on a case study of a true "cross-level" strategy, Knopf gets it right when he argues that such strategies work to limit the options of statesmen. International negotiators cannot create allies in their counterpart's domestic arena out of thin air. They are limited at least to some degree by what is already there. And when domestic groups reach out to them and solicit their help in "internationalizing" an issue, negotiators are vulnera-ble to being manipulated, for these groups are likely to have objectives that differ in subtle but important ways from their own goals. In fact, because cases where statesmen seek to "work with" domestic politics by definition involve interaction with domestic forces seeking to pursue their own goals, there are likely to be many cases where *both* international negotiators and domestic groups are seeking to take advantage of strate-gic opportunities to use each other at the same time. Who has the advan-tage in such cases? While international negotiators have the advantage of sitting at both game tables, domestic actors have the advantage of being in the position where they control exactly how much and in what way the win-set for their side will be widened. This question too can be answered only by empirical analysis.

Conclusion

In our search for an analytical framework upon which to base our case studies of s11 and the Clinton Framework, we have come a long way from "power." The negotiation-analytic approach showed us that strategies hav-ing relatively little to do with power can influence the terms of interna-tional negotiations, and the Putnam two-level game model showed us that the success of these strategies depends critically on how they res-onate with domestic politics. Even strategies like threats that draw explicitly on power resources, we found, operate more effectively when they "work well" with domestic politics. Other synergistic strategies like reverberation, participation expansion, alternative specification, and tar-get-nation linkage rely for their impact almost entirely on how they inter-act with domestic politics. The effectiveness of gaiatsu, this analysis sug-gests, depends not just on the force behind a particular application of pressure but also on the contours of the domestic political topography which it encounters. What is more, the section on domestically initiated strategies reminds us that this topography is not fixed, but shifting, with a mind of its own.

In the chapters that follow, we will be using the framework developed here as a "roadmap" to guide our analysis of how the topography of American and Japanese domestic politics influenced the pattern of results in the SII and Clinton Framework talks. As we will see, the kinds of factors highlighted in this chapter did prove to be decisive in determining whether or not gaiatsu would work. When it did work, as in the SII talks on public investment and the distribution system, it was effective because domestic conditions in Japan and the U.S. favored the use of several synergistic strategies. When it didn't work, as in the SII talks on keiretsu and the Clinton Framework demand for numerical targets, it failed because domestic conditions would not support any strategy capable of influencing the parameters of their zones of possible agreement. Without any further delay, it is time now to turn to the actual cases where America has sought to pressure Japan.

3

AMERICAN POLITICS AND THE BIRTH OF SII

The Structural Impediments Initiative: It was an unusual name for an unusual approach to trade relations—so unusual in fact that the *Washington Times* became confused and kept referring to the talks as the *Strategic* Impediments Initiative, recalling the Cold War arms control talks with the old Soviet Union.[1] Negotiations in those days certainly were simpler. While Democrats and Republicans sometimes disagreed as to whether SALT or START was a better approach, all could agree that a deal which put tough limits on Soviet arms was a "good" deal in terms of the "national interest." The debate was merely about how much the U.S. should give up in terms of limits on its own deployment plans in order to extract such concessions from the Soviets.

When it comes to trade relations in general and relations with Japan in particular, however, there has been no American consensus on the "national interest." Some Americans insist that persistent U.S.-Japan trade imbalances are the problem, arguing that the U.S. must force Japan—if necessary with the threat of sanctions—to reduce its surpluses. Others call for an approach rooted in the multilateralism of GATT, insisting that the greater threat to U.S. interests is not trade imbalances but rather the damage that would be inflicted on the world trade order by American unilateralism. Finally, a third group has for many years called on successive U.S. administrations to prioritize security ties in relations with Japan, insisting that economic interests pale in comparison with the strategic objectives at stake in the region. If there is disagreement about the nature of the problem, there is even more disagreement about the appropriate means. In addition to those favoring approaches centered on "results" and on GATT, others have advocated: (1) tough bilateral sector-specific trade negotiations; (2) pressure concentrated on addressing the macroeconomic causes of the trade imbalance; and (3) a dialogue on the structural causes of this imbalance. The Structural Impediments Initiative can be seen as a product of *all* of these perspectives, but its unusual approach and format is more than the vector sum of these divergent views. The SII talks were born of this multiplicity of interpretations of U.S. interests, *processed through* domestic politics and refined to reflect what I call "two-level logic."

This chapter tells the story of the birth of the SII talks, but it also aims to describe how nations define their negotiating objectives when the international system fails to define for them a clear-cut national interest. Many previous studies of international negotiations, such as those of SALT and START, have examined cases where each nation's objectives were neatly specified for them by their place in the world order.[2] In Putnam's terms, a nation's preferences in such cases are "homogeneous" in that all or almost all parties agree that the "best" deal lies at one end of a continuum. In such cases, it may indeed be possible to "black box" domestic politics and still derive interesting and practical insights about how negotiations work. In many other negotiations, however, the preferences of various constituencies within a domestic arena pull negotiators in two or more directions. In such cases, when a negotiator faces "heterogeneous" preferences, black boxing domestic politics is clearly problematic.[3]

It is problematic because biases in the way domestic politics mediates international incentives are most likely to be decisive when those signals are mixed. Thus, for example, analysts of U.S. foreign economic policy have argued that American ideas and institutions have had their greatest impact on U.S. trade policy in the early 20th century and since 1970, when the changing position of America in the world has given rise to new pressures competing with the old. At such times, these analysts argue, established ideas and institutions have helped perpetuate previous trade policy orientations even after the nation's objective situation has given rise to incentives and pressures to shift course.[4] This chapter's examination of trade policy under the Bush Administration confirms that institutions and ideas do play an important role in setting constraints on how international incentives are converted into a trade policy. It finds, however, that it is also important to take into account another variable which tends to get ignored in deterministic accounts of how domestic political *systems* produce trade policy: the strategic behavior of political actors.

Strategy comes into play because in trade policy, unlike other areas of policy which have less of an international dimension, political actors are making moves that have implications at two different game tables. As argued in the previous chapter, this interactive nature of "two-level games" forces us to look at both levels simultaneously rather than at just the domestic-to-international or international-to-domestic lines of causality. "Two-level logic" may lead a chief negotiator to make moves at the domestic level designed to secure a better deal at the international level. Likewise, it may lead him to make moves at the international level designed to serve his interests at the domestic level. To further complicate matters, in cases of "domestic politics reversed," other domestic actors may intervene in the international game in an effort to further *their* domestic interests.

The Bush Administration's decision to go with the sii format and agenda, I argue here, can be understood only when one has taken into account such "two level logic." Interests, institutions, and ideas set important constraints on how the Bush team set their negotiating objectives, but exactly how the team chose to proceed within these constraints was dictated by strategic considerations: Bush's desire to use the sii talks to mend his fraying Republican free trade coalition; his negotiating team's desire to minimize conflict among themselves while taking advantage of conflict among actors on the Japanese side; and the efforts of Japanese actors to use gaiatsu to secure their sectional policy objectives. The sii talks thus serve as an illustration of how, even at the stage where governments frame their negotiating objectives, strategic two-level considerations influence policy decisions.

The Changing World Order and U.S. Trade Interests in the 1980s

In the early postwar years, American trade policy was driven by mutually reinforcing strategic and economic incentives which led the nation to become the champion of free trade. The Cold War with the Soviet Union led it to open up its own market to its allies in Europe, Japan, and elsewhere in an effort to bind them in a global free-trading alliance. Its strong competitive positions in almost all sectors gave it an incentive to seek out new markets through negotiated trade liberalization. Its economic size, accounting at its peak for more than half of global production, gave it the clout to set the international trade policy agenda while at the same time giving it the willingness to tolerate some free riding. And rapid economic growth and current account surpluses kept down the number of domestic interests seeking protection. The combination of all of these incentives propelled the U.S. to a leadership role in a series of tariff-reduction talks which, by 1979, had reduced the average rate of tariffs in the U.S. to three percent.

By the 1980s, however, the international environment was not sending such clear signals. Nothing symbolized the changing world order better than a pair of trade balance statistics: in 1987, the U.S. ran a record deficit of $160 billion while the Japanese ran a record surplus of $96 billion. For several years in the mid-1980s, the two nations' bilateral imbalances averaged close to $50 billion a year (See figure 3.1).

Beneath such numbers lay a more concrete reality: American firms lost billions of dollars in sales at home and abroad to foreign competitors; factories were forced to shut down; and thousands of jobs were lost. While U.S. manufacturers lost sales to firms from a wide range of nations, the challenge from abroad was symbolized by the Japanese. Japanese auto makers increased their share of the U.S. auto market from

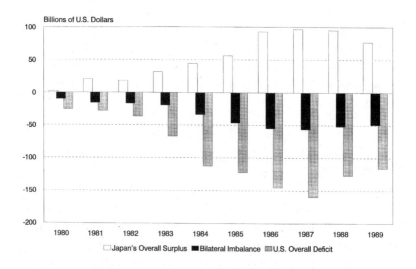

FIGURE 3.1   U.S.-Japan Balance of Trade, 1980-1989

Sources: Bank of Japan for Japan's surpluses; U.S. Department of Commerce for U.S. deficits and bilateral balances.

3.7 percent in 1970 to 21.2 percent in 1980 while increasing their annual exports to the U.S. from 380,000 units to 2 million units over the same period.[5] In successive waves, Japanese exporters increased their sales in other sectors from $2 billion to $4 billion in steel between 1975 and 1981; from $2 billion to $12 billion in office machines between 1981 and 1990; from $5 billion to $10 billion in semiconductors and telecommunications equipment between 1981 and 1987; and from $3 billion to $9 billion in auto parts between 1985 and 1988.[6]

Given the magnitude of the foreign (and especially Japanese) import surge, it should come as no surprise that there was soon a long line of protection-seeking interests clamoring for help from the federal government. Among the most important of the converts from free trade to protectionism was organized labor—whose membership was concentrated in exactly those sectors hardest hit by the increase in imports from Japan. Some unions, in sectors like textiles, had been calling for protection since the 1950s, but by the 1980s they were joined by the steel, auto, and other major unions to the point that organized labor became "a major national, cross-industry organization—a coalition, more accurately—which took an across-the-board trade-restrictive stance."[7] Also significant, however, was the growth in the number of firms and industry associations who began to call for protection and/or a more aggressive trade policy. Not just firms in rust belt industries but even high-technology firms like Corning Glass, Motorola, and Hewlett-Packard began to voice support for a tough line— and if necessary protective retaliation—in trade talks with Japan.[8]

What was happening was the first step in a process which E.E. Schattschneider had described many years earlier as the natural workings of pluralist politics. Groups hard hit by import competition have more of an incentive to organize and demand protection than do the consumers who benefit from the lower prices trade competition brings. Hence the protection-seeking pressure groups tend to out-muscle advocates of free trade in the political marketplace.[9] With the surge of Japanese and other imports in the 1980s, this political market effect was simply accentuated.

It would be a mistake, however, to focus only on the effects of imports on pressure group activity in our examination of the incentives created by the changing world order of the 1980s. Also important were fundamental shifts in the global balance of power which created incentives for American government officials to think in new ways about the "national interest." As noted above, when the U.S. was an undisputed economic hegemon and was challenged only by the Soviet Union, the "national interest" had been quite clear: free trade with the allies and contain the Soviets.[10] By the late 1980s, however, U.S. economic hegemony was no longer undisputed and (under Gorbachev) the Soviets were looking less menacing. Given this new situation, a growing chorus of academics, analysts, and government officials began to call for an American foreign policy which would take into account this new reality.

Once again, those who called for a new foreign policy focused their attention on Japan. That nation, which in 1960 had a GNP which was only 8.6 percent the size of America's, had by 1989 caught up to the point that its GNP was fully 55 percent that of the U.S.. If both nations maintained their growth rates, some calculated, Japan's economy would actually be *larger* than that of the U.S. by early in the next century.[11] The nation was amassing huge annual balance of payments surpluses, as noted above, and was using them to buy up American property, companies, and Treasury bonds. Through its aggressive exporting, it had virtually destroyed the American consumer electronics industry, and in the 1980s it was threatening to do the same thing to the steel, auto, semiconductor, and machine tool sectors. Even America's ability to defend itself, some argued, was threatened by the Japanese economic challenge.[12]

Of particular concern were Japan's trade practices which were variously labeled "adversarial," "unequal" and "unfair."[13] For most of the economists who did the econometric studies to back up these charges, the problem was *not* Japanese trade surpluses. These, they recognized, resulted as much from U.S. macroeconomic policy as from anything Japan was doing.[14] The problem was the *pattern* of Japanese trade. What made Japanese trade "adversarial" was the fact that the nation tended to import relatively low levels of manufactured goods even as it was exporting such goods in massive quantities. The raw numbers were striking: in 1987, Japan's manufactured goods imports as a share of its GDP stood at only 2.4 percent compared to numbers like 7.3 percent for the U.S.; 14.4 percent for West Germany; and 20 percent for Sweden. Moreover, Japan's manufactured import level in that year was virtually unchanged from levels 15 years earlier whereas virtually every other developed nation had seen a marked rise in this index. Even taking into account standard explanations for why Japan might have such low levels of manufactured exports (its resource poverty; its distance from other developed economies), econometric analyses in general have found that Japan is still an outlier, importing—according to one of the most influential studies—

some 40 percent less manufactured goods than it would if it behaved like other industrial economies.[15]

Other commonly-cited measures of Japan's "adversarial" posture have been that nation's unusually low level of intra-industry trade, the imbalance in its inward and outward foreign direct investment (FDI) flows, and price differentials for the same items sold inside and outside Japan. According to one study of intra-industry trade, Japanese levels in the 1980s were under half those in the U.S., Germany and France; and like Japan's manufactured import ratios, this study found, Japan's intra-industry trade levels had remained static for many years despite a global trend toward increasing trade within industries.[16]

Studies of FDI levels in Japan similarly describe the nation as an outlier. According to Ministry of Finance figures, Japanese in 1989 had outstanding investments worth 16.9 times as much as foreigners had in Japan in that year. In contrast, comparable government figures were 1.17 times for the U.S.; 1.7 times for the U.K.; and 2.2 times for Germany.[17] What these numbers mean, according to a leading critic of Japan's investment restrictions, is that American multinationals have been unable to use investment to expand their market share in Japan in the way they have been able to do everywhere else and in the way the Japanese have been able to do in the U.S.[18]

For anyone who has spent time in Japan recently, the most obvious indicator suggesting that something odd is going on in its trading patterns is the *nai-gai* price differential: the difference in prices for an item purchased inside Japan compared to the price for the same item purchased abroad. When the Japanese Economic Planning Agency (EPA) conducted a study of such price differences in 1988, it found that color film costs 47 percent more in Tokyo than in New York, color TVs cost 100 percent more, and bread costs 27 percent more. Strangely, the EPA found, price differences were greater for some manufactured goods with little or no formal trade barriers than they were for some heavily-protected farm products (See table 3.1). For some economists, these price differences for manufactured goods are the clearest evidence that the Japanese economy has within it significant structural barriers to the importation of such goods. Particularly incriminating, one analyst argues, is the fact that many Japanese-manufactured products can be purchased more cheaply in the U.S. and the fact that many U.S.-manufactured goods are subject to higher mark-ups than competing Japanese goods.[19]

TABLE 3.1
International Price Differentials

Item	Tokyo	New York	Hamburg	London	Paris
bread	100	79	95	64	76
beef	100	40	52	71	54
pork	100	66	87	65	71
chicken	100	59	41	54	80
eggs	100	71	136	130	133
sausage	100	94	90	93	62
cabbage	100	47	35	90	70
onions	100	72	110	160	110
bananas	100	46	87	131	144
sugar	100	61	61	58	60
cooking oil	100	82	87	103	59
business suit (winter)	100	78	50	70	115
dress shirt	100	93	56	76	284
men's briefs	100	134	193	148	237
skirt (winter)	100	138	159	110	179
color television	100	50	97	91	87
men's leather shoes	100	114	90	91	99
laundry detergent	100	82	89	80	107
color film	100	68	96	108	110
gasoline	100	38	69	83	81
telephone call (local)	100	130	170	200	160
hair cut	100	66	86	55	111
permanent	100	133	116	147	135
dry cleaning (suit)	100	110	144	94	162

Source: Economic Planning Agency, *Bukka Repooto* '88 (Price Report '88), p. 32.

For advocates of a new American foreign policy toward Japan, a group that came to be known as the "revisionists," all of the above statistics were evidence that trade with Japan was rigged so that the Japanese enjoyed an unfair advantage that would allow them, over time, to destroy the American industrial base. For them, the evidence proved that Japanese manufacturers, by restricting manufactured imports (particularly in the industries where they excel—hence the low intra-industry trade), were able to earn excess profits at home that they could use to subsidize exports (hence the price differences). American manufacturers, in contrast, were kept out of the Japanese market by hidden barriers which resulted in higher markups on their products and barriers to investment that kept them from using a base within Japan to expand their markets.

The "Japan Problem" was diagnosed by these revisionists to mean that Japan had organized itself so thoroughly for the purpose of catching up economically with the West that it was unable to stop, even though it was stuck in a course that was bringing it increasingly into conflict with its principal allies.[20] As James Fallows put it,

> There is a basic conflict between Japanese and American interests—notwithstanding that the two countries need each others as friends—and it would be better to face it directly than to pretend that it doesn't exist. That conflict arises from Japan's inability or unwillingness to restrain the one-sided and destructive expansion of its economic power. The expansion is one-sided because Japanese business does to other countries what Japan will not permit to be done to itself. It is destructive because it will lead to exactly the international ostracism that Japan most fears . . .[21]

Fallows's words clearly invoke a realist rationale for the new U.S. foreign policy he advocates. Japan's interests are in conflict with America's, Japan is expanding its power at American expense, and the U.S. needs to check this expansion. Not coincidentally, his editors chose to make the parallel with the Cold War rationale for dealing with the Soviet threat blatant by titling his article "Containing Japan."

Interestingly, it is not just amateur realists like Fallows who have identified the Japanese challenge as a reason for the U.S. to adjust its foreign policy. Stephen Krasner, a neorealist by profession, surveys the evidence about Japanese economic behavior and agrees that if the Japanese continue to operate as they have been, the U.S. should move toward a tougher policy of "specific reciprocity," providing only as much access to Japanese firms as the Japanese provide for American firms.[22] His conclusion follows from the core realist assumption: that nations in an anarchic world care more about relative gains than about absolute gains.[23] Given that the Japanese seem to be gaining more than Americans are from a trading relationship tilted in their favor, the U.S. ought to be concerned about its long-term loss of relative power and therefore has a strong incentive to do something to restructure this relationship. While this incentive may have been muted during the years of U.S. hegemony and Cold War rivalry with the Soviet Union (because of America's greater willingness to tolerate free-riding and its prioritization of the East-West military rivalry), it should have come to exercise increasing influence on American foreign policy as the gap between U.S. and Japanese economic power narrowed and as the Soviet threat diminished.[24]

Up to this point, I have emphasized exclusively the *changing* signals from the international system which began to confront the U.S. in the

1980s: the rise in imports and the growing saliency of the Japanese economic challenge. It would be misleading, however, to end the story there, for as I argued at the start of this chapter, it is the *mixed* nature of the incentives confronting the U.S. in this case that makes it interesting. While the above trends pushed the U.S. government toward a more assertive Japan policy, other forces continued to signal moderation.

First, it is important to recognize that even in the political marketplace where protectionist interests tend to dominate (as noted above), there were organized and influential forces calling for moderation even in the 1980s. Such forces existed because U.S. exports to and investment in Japan, though low compared to the corresponding numbers of Japanese exports to and investment in the U.S., represented a substantial economic stake in good bilateral relations. Japan in 1989 was America's second largest export market overall, purchasing $44.5 billion of U.S. merchandise, and it was at or near the top of list of American customers in each of the following areas: food, feed and beverages ($8.5 billion); computers and computer parts ($3.1 billion); logs, lumber, plywood and veneers ($2.4 billion); aircraft and parts ($1.8 billion); aluminum ($1.5 billion); industrial chemicals ($1.3 billion); artwork and antiques ($1.3 billion); semiconductors ($1.2 billion); paper base products ($1.0 billion); telecommunications ($1.0 billion); tobacco products ($874 million); and pharmaceuticals ($870 million).[25]

While firms and industry groups in each of these sectors had incentives to push for an aggressive American trade policy aimed at expanding these markets, they also had an interest in avoiding an economic rupture. Even if they felt Japan would hesitate to retaliate openly against the U.S., they knew that the powerful Japanese bureaucracy had ways of throwing roadblocks in their way if it identified them as ringleaders in a campaign to threaten Japan with trade sanctions. Many firms, furthermore, had sweetheart deals, often blessed by the Japanese bureaucracy, which gave them niche markets that, while small, generated generous profits. These firms knew that such generosity could be quickly withdrawn if the bureaucracy or their private sector partners wished to punish them.[26]

The American insurance firms AIG and AFLAC are examples of firms that enjoyed privileged positions in Japanese niche markets—at least until recently. The Japanese insurance market, regulated by the Ministry of Finance, has been strictly segmented, with Japanese firms forced to operate in either the life insurance or non-life insurance sector, but not both. U.S. firms like AIG and AFLAC, while excluded from these areas, were allowed to offer "third area" insurance such as personal accident, cancer, nursing care, and hospitalization coverage which was not clearly "life" or "non-life." Because the MOF let these U.S. firms provide such products while at the same time making it difficult for the firms' Japanese competitors to get into this market, they were virtually guaranteed healthy profits. By giving these firms their niche, however, MOF also guaranteed that they would be defenders of a segmented system that, on the whole, worked to exclude foreign firms from core areas of the insurance business in Japan. In fact, during the Framework talks on deregulation in this area, the firms prevailed upon Clinton to make a *slow down* in deregulation their central demand.[27]

It is not just export interests, however, that have a stake in good U.S.-Japanese economic relations. While the investments of U.S. multinationals in Japan are relatively small, they did by 1991 have some $8.5 billion invested in the country.[28] When combined with the interests of these and other U.S. firms in maintaining their access to imported components, those of U.S. retailers in continuing their access to imported consumer goods, and those of U.S. employees of Japanese "transplants" in keeping their jobs, it is clear that there is within the American political system a significant basis for "anti-protectionist" groups to organize and mobilize in an effort to prevent serious U.S.-Japan economic conflict.[29]

An example of the ability of such groups to influence the process is the story of Toshiba's campaign to limit the breadth of sanctions it would face after its subsidiary was found in 1987 to have sold sensitive military components to the Soviet Union. It promptly directed its 4,000 American employees to contact their Congressmen and convinced U.S. firms who relied on Toshiba components (Apple, Compaq, AT&T, etc.) to do the same. While Congress in the end voted for sanctions, it allowed numerous exemptions and it is now estimated that Toshiba lost only a few million dollars of business (compared to the $3 billion in total U.S. sales which it had at stake).[30]

If the political marketplace has thus tended to be split on the issue of Japan policy, the structural incentives created by the international system have been similarly mixed. In the mid-1980s, in the years leading up to the Bush Administration's decision to go with the SII format, the Cold War was waning, but it was not yet over. The U.S. therefore had a continuing incentive to make sure its economic conflicts with the Japanese would not threaten its vital security alliance with that nation. Throughout the Cold War years, the importance of this security relationship had led U.S. policymakers to view the nation's Japan policy "through a Soviet lens," as Joseph Nye put it. "Economic disputes were isolated from and generally subordinated to security interests."[31]

Even in the emerging post-Cold War environment, however, it was clear that the U.S. would have a continuing strategic interest in nurturing this alliance—if necessary by moderating its trade demands. As many analysts argued, the emerging situation in Asia was quite different from that in Europe—where Gorbachev's policy toward Eastern Europe was in the process of eliminating the primary target of U.S. deterrence strategies. In Asia, the Gorbachev revolution was playing out much more slowly, with the Soviet navy still rated a destabilizing factor. Furthermore, the threats to regional stability from North Korea, from renewed Japanese nationalism, and from potential Chinese mischief were clearly going to remain regardless of what happened to the Soviet Union. All of these factors argued for a continuing American role in the region and specifically for the maintenance of good relations with Japan.[32]

As if this were not enough, structural incentives arguably created additional incentives for the U.S. to cooperate with Japan in an effort to preserve the international trading regime. The two may have had reason to fight over the division of their spoils from this system, but both also had ample reason to make sure the system did not completely collapse. The analysis of David Lake suggests that great powers will have an incentive to cooperate in maintaining an open trading system, despite relative gains concerns, under certain conditions: if all have high rates of labor productivity, if moderate levels of uncertainty lead each to worry somewhat that the system will collapse unless they do their part to maintain it, and if regimes facilitate the process of cooperation by providing rules as to what constitutes cheating and information that makes it easier for each partner to spot such cheating when it happens.[33] It is not much of a stretch to argue that all of these conditions were operative for the U.S. and Japan in the 1980s. Both economies were among the most productive in the world, there was moderate uncertainty about the future of the trading regime, and the GATT regime did fulfill the basic function of providing rules and information. If Lake's logic is correct, both states under these circumstances should have had this additional systemic incentive to moderate their positions in trade disputes.[34]

The Mediation of U.S. Trade Interests by Institutions and Ideas

The above analysis of American trade interests generated by the positions of American societal actors and the U.S. as a nation in the international system confirms the point with which we began this chapter: that the incentives were distinctly mixed. Societal actors in sectors challenged by Japanese imports had a clear incentive to devote energy and political capital to the task of stemming the inflow of those goods, but firms in sectors with a significant stake in the Japanese market, as well as those inside the U.S. who were dependent on Japanese components and investment, had reason to counter that pressure. The Japanese challenge, in particular the evidence that Japan was gaining relatively from a trading relationship tilted in its favor, pointed to a "national interest" in restructuring that relationship through an aggressive trade strategy, but continuing common strategic interests in Asia as well as common interests in preserving the liberal trading regime simultaneously cautioned against such an approach.

How do nations frame their trade policies and negotiating strategies when the incentives confronting them are mixed in this way? One answer provided by the political economy literature is that policy outcomes are critically affected by the way in which they are mediated by domestic ideas and institutions. Incentives may be mixed, but the way they are processed by domestic politics may tilt the outcome in favor of one set of incentives rather than another. First, the political marketplace where *societal* interests are sorted out is not neutral. Institutions left in place by past policy battles and affected by the ideas and social balance of power of that day privilege certain interests over others.[35] Similarly, the ideas of *state* actors bias the way they perceive the "national interest." Even when the structural incentives are mixed, they may see only the interests that fit their worldview.[36]

One way to understand the Bush Administration's decision to go with the sii talks as the centerpiece of its Japan policy would thus be to focus on how institutions and ideas biased the way domestic politics processed the incentives discussed above. As I develop the argument below, it will become clear that institutions and ideas *did* affect the result. One can point to many ways in which the liberal ideology of the executive and the institutional relationship between the executive and Congress conditioned the administration's choice of policy and negotiating demands. What I argue, however, is that institutions and ideas did not dictate "structural talks" as the *only* choice the American political system could have produced in 1989. Much less did it dictate the final sii format and agenda. To account for the specific choices made by Bush and his team, we will have to look (in the final section) at the "two-level" calculations of various players.

For most analysts looking at how American institutions affect the nation's trade policy, the key variable is the institutional relationship between Congress and the executive. Congress, on the one hand, is described as being predisposed toward protectionism—as was most dramatically illustrated in the congressional free-for-all which led to the Smoot-Hawley tariff in 1929.[37] As I. M. Destler describes it, "Congress is a decentralized, undisciplined institution, particularly susceptible to pressure from organized interests. So if it 'does what comes naturally,' if the politics of benefit-seeking and logrolling goes unimpeded, the result will be a high level of trade barriers, to the benefit of certain groups and the detriment of the nation as a whole."[38]

The executive, on the other hand, is generally described as being predisposed toward a liberal trade policy (at least since the 1930s). As a representative of the entire American electorate, the President is better able to resist the claims of narrowly based interest groups when he sees their demands as contradicting the good of the people as a whole. Furthermore, charged with watching out for the "national interest," the President has been more likely than Congress to be influenced by incentives arising from the position of the U.S. in the international system. As argued above, these incentives for most of the postwar period have favored a free trade policy. Both America's hegemonic/competitive position and its military rivalry with the Soviet Union argued for such a trade policy.

In its institutional relationship with the liberal executive, Congress has always had the upper hand *at the constitutional level*. The American Constitution clearly says that Congress has primary responsibility for regulating international commerce. In the years after the Great Depression, however, Congress consented to a series of changes in the institutions that govern trade policy—changes that reduced its ability to dominate the process. Specifically, Congress delegated much of its authority to executive branch officials through a vehicle known as the "bargaining tariff," giving the President the power to reduce tariffs in exchange for reductions by America's trading partners. As the system operated through 1974, Congress did not even have to approve final trade agreements. At the same time, Congress protected itself from pressure politics by: (1) giving a great deal of authority to strong committee chairmen on strong trade committees who could resist pressure to bring product-specific trade bills to a vote; (2) creating new trade remedies such as adjustment assistance which took pressure off the legislature; and (3) writing trade remedy rules so that presidents were given ample discretion not to invoke sanctions.[39]

Still, these steps did not end tensions between Congress and the executive. As pressure from import-affected industries and labor unions grew in the 1970s and '80s, and as reforms in the institutional structure of Congress reduced the power of the committees and committee chairs, Congress gradually began to take back some of the powers it had delegated to the executive. The "bargaining tariff" was superseded by a new "fast track" procedure for dealing with trade negotiations which required Congressional approval of trade deals after the fact (albeit under restrictive rules limiting amendments and delay); trade remedy rules were rewritten to leave the President less discretion; and the office of the U.S. Trade Representative and the Commerce Department, the two agencies seen by Congress as most willing to pursue a tough trade policy, were given greater statutory responsibility.[40]

As this brief history of trade policy institutions reveals, there has been a great deal of back and forth in relations between Congress and the President. While the President has had a great deal of authority to negotiate trade liberalization pacts, he has had to be sensitive to Congressional sentiment lest he drive it to assert its constitutional primacy in trade matters. The coexistence of some trade-restrictive policies with American presidential leadership in promoting global liberalization can thus be explained by this tension in the institutions governing U.S. trade policymaking. As we will see, Bush's decision to emphasize the SII talks in his Japan policy can partly be explained by this institutional tension.

Before examining the institutional origins of SII, however, we need to look at another aspect of domestic politics that mediates between international incentives and policy outcomes: ideas. For some who have examined the impact of ideas on policy, the dynamic is closely related to institutions. Judith Goldstein, for example, argues that the decision of Congress to delegate much of its authority over trade policy to the executive starting in 1934 simply reflected the ascendancy of liberal ideas about trade after the Great Depression delegitimized the old Smoot-Hawley approach.[41] Similarly, the privileged status of the political departments (State and Defense) in the management of trade disputes with U.S. allies in the postwar period can be seen as the institutional result of the Cold War conventional wisdom that economic disputes had to be subordinate to the overriding importance of maintaining the Western alliance.[42]

Slightly different from this institutional approach to the impact of ideas on policy is one that sees them as having more of a direct impact on the way policymakers perceive interests. Ellis Krauss and Simon Reich argue, for example, that an "embedded American ideology of free trade" conditions the way presidents perceive demands for state intervention in the economy. Demands from noncompetitive industries threatened by foreign competition are seen as illegitimate and are thus discounted while demands from competitive industries hurt by unfair competition from abroad are greeted more sympathetically.[43] Likewise, the tendency of American presidents to see U.S. interests abroad strictly in terms of the Cold War rivalry with the Soviets even after the international environment began to present more mixed signals can be seen as a function of habits of thinking born during decades in which the Soviets truly were the only significant rival.

Ideas are important, these analysts argue, because through institutions and habits of thinking they have a prolonged effect on policy—outlasting the circumstances that gave rise to them in the first place. Only when the current conventional wisdom (that a liberal trade policy is best for America and that the world should be seen in terms of the East-West conflict) has been delegitimized by war, depression, or other dramatic sign of failure are institutions and habits of thinking likely to be changed to the point that the system produces new and different policy outcomes. In analyzing how domestic politics mediated the mixed incentives produced by the international system in the 1980s, therefore, these arguments tell us we should pay particular attention to the influence of ideas as well as institutions.

The following survey of major American trade policy decisions leading up to the decision to go with SII in 1989 shows how, in each case, policy was influenced by the mediating effects of competing institutions and ideas. As Presidents Reagan and Bush struggled to deal with protectionist demands from Congress, and as liberal and Cold War ideas that had guided U.S. trade policy were challenged by a new ideology based on "strategic trade theory," U.S. policy vacillated wildly from principled support for free trade (as seen in support for the new Uruguay Round of

GATT), to unabashed protectionism (as seen in Reagan's acceptance of requests for voluntary export restraints on autos, steel, and machine tools), to a novel experiment in managed trade (the semiconductor agreement). As we will see, similar institutional and ideological conflicts helped produce the novel trade policy approach which is the major subject of this book: the SII.

THE FIRST REAGAN ADMINISTRATION

Fresh in office and staffed by a group comprising a large number of ideologues committed to free market economics, the new administration was slow to develop a cohesive trade policy beyond a rhetorical defense of free trade dogma. Rather than formulating its own approach, the administration tended to wait until pressure built up before taking any action. The pattern was set, in fact, just months after Reagan came to office when, under pressure from Congress, the administration was forced to work for voluntary export restraints on Japanese autos. Had the administration not acted when it did, Congress was poised to adopt a unilateral quota bill. Later in his first term, Reagan accepted a similar deal on imports of foreign steel—this time acting when he did because an International Trade Commission (ITC) ruling calling for import relief had given him just 60 days to decide on a response.[44] In the meantime, the administration worked successfully to strip the 1984 Omnibus Trade Act of protectionist provisions added during congressional deliberations, but the trade gap continued to grow.

THE SECOND REAGAN ADMINISTRATION

Tired of always being on the defensive, the Reagan team finally put forward an initiative of its own in January 1985 when it announced that it was proposing a new set of Market-Oriented Sector-Specific (MOSS) talks with the Japanese. Modeled after the Treasury Department's just-completed high-level talks with the Japanese on financial liberalization (the Yen-Dollar Talks), the MOSS talks were to involve subcabinet level officials in an intensive series of negotiations with Japanese counterparts aimed at removing a wide range of barriers to foreign access in a set of four sectors: telecommunications equipment and services, medical equipment and pharmaceuticals, forest products, and electronics. The MOSS approach suited the Reagan team because it focused on sectors where U.S. industries were widely recognized as competitive internationally, because it aimed to remove barriers to exports on a most-favored-nation basis rather than to restrict imports, and because it focused on "rules" (product standards, testing, licensing, and government procurement practices) rather than "results." In all of these ways, it was perfectly consistent with the administration's liberal economic ideology while also serving to satisfy to some degree the continuing political pressure for a tougher trade policy.[45]

Even as the administration was attempting to reclaim the initiative, though, congressional demands for a more aggressive trade policy were reaching new heights. During the 1985 calendar year more than 300 trade bills were introduced as members of Congress, faced with mounting pressure from industry and labor, rushed to introduce harshly worded resolutions and protectionist bills.[46] One resolution, passed 92–0 by the Senate in March 1985, blasted Japan for its unfair trading practices and urged retaliation unless the nation significantly increased its imports from America. The most notorious of the legislative initiatives, though, was the Gephardt Amendment, based on legislation first introduced by Representatives Richard Gephardt and Dan Rostenkowski and Senator Lloyd Bentsen in the summer of 1985. This amendment, which would have required Japan and other nations with which the U.S. had large deficits to reduce those deficits by 10 percent a year under the threat of sanctions, was included in the omnibus trade legislation reported out of the House Ways and Means Committee in 1986 and was passed by the House that year by a lopsided vote of 295 to 115.[47]

Even before the verdict was in on the MOSS Talks, therefore, the Reagan Administration was forced once again to respond to Congressional saber-rattling. If it didn't do something more to reduce the trade deficit, officials realized, Congress might pass something like the Gephardt Amendment over presidential objections even if Reagan vetoed the measure.

The first area where the administration concluded it had to shift course was on exchange rates. For the first four years of the Reagan presidency, even meddling with foreign exchange markets was considered a violation of Reagan's free market ideology, and the administration had done little but watch as the soaring dollar destroyed the competitiveness of one industry after another. When it realized that it risked provoking restrictive trade legislation, however, the administration ended up embracing an exchange rate intervention strategy which entailed massive and coordinated action by the G-5. The Plaza Accord of September 1985, which followed quickly upon the administration's change of position, committed these governments to intervention aimed at devaluing the dollar, and within a year the U.S. currency had lost over a third of its value relative to the Japanese yen.[48]

While the administration saw Plaza as its primary strategy for dealing with the deficit, it realized that Congress would not tolerate an exclusively macroeconomic approach. So even as the Plaza intervention was underway, the president announced a new "action plan" involving more aggressive use of the government's authority to go after unfair trading practices, the targeting of copyright violators, a "war chest" to counter foreign trade subsidies, and a new push for GATT talks.[49] From the point of view of Congress, one of the administration's most important reversals was its decision to self-initiate a series of unfair trade and dumping cases. While both the unfair trade (Section 301) and dumping provisions of U.S. trade law allowed the executive to self-initiate cases, officials in the past had always waited until industry filed a complaint. By taking the initiative in these cases, the administration signaled Congress and its trading partners that it was getting serious.

Among the cases self-initiated in the fall of 1985 was a dumping case against the Japanese semiconductor industry filed by the Department of Commerce. Together with the USTR, which was investigating a U.S. industry complaint under Section 301, these two agencies put intensive pressure on the Japanese to deal with trade practices the U.S. industry saw as predatory. American firms seemed to be stuck with a single-digit share of the Japanese market even as Japanese firms were selling massive quantities of chips in the U.S. market at below the cost of production. After heated negotiations, the two sides finally reached a landmark agreement on July 30, 1986, committing the Japanese government to monitor costs and prices in order to prevent Japanese firms from dumping in the U.S. and in third markets *and* committing the government to "make efforts to assist foreign companies in reaching their goal of a 20 percent market share [in Japan] within five years."[50] Less than a year later, when confronted with evidence that Japanese firms were still dumping chips in third markets and that the market share of foreign firms in Japan remained stagnant, Reagan imposed stiff sanctions to show that the U.S. was intent on making this agreement stick.[51]

What was notable about this agreement, of course, was that it represented the first experiment with what has come to be known as a voluntary import expansion (VIE), a kind of "managed trade" which had been fiercely resisted by elements within the Reagan administration. Even as the USTR and Commerce were aggressively pushing for such a deal, Treasury, the National Security Council, and State voiced arguments like the following: "Dumping benefits the society receiving it"; "We think Japan will endorse SDI [the Strategic Defense Initiative] and we don't want to do anything that would undermine that"; and "If we do this, are we moving toward an industrial policy?"[52] Interestingly, these arguments echo quite clearly the ideological habits of thinking noted above, reflecting the liberal economics and Cold War mindset of the executive. In this case, however, ideological purity suffered a defeat to the realization by the Reagan administration that it had to do something to deal with the Congressional challenge on trade as well as pressures from the growing segment of the business community that favored a new "strategic" trade policy.[53] Over the following years, however, it only redoubled the efforts by executive branch officials in Treasury, State, the NSC, and in the Council of Economic Advisors, to prevent another slippage of this sort as the debate continued.

That debate entered a new phase when, following significant Democratic Party gains in the 1986 midterm elections, Congress began to move concertedly toward adopting new trade legislation. Despite MOSS, Plaza, and the Semiconductor Accords, it soon became clear, Congress was still intent on embarrassing the president on the trade issue. And with deficits still setting records (refer back to figure 3.1), the president was very vulnerable.

Once again, activism on the House side centered on the Gephardt Amendment which, as noted above, proposed to strengthen U.S. trade policy by imposing deficit reduction targets on nations with large bilateral deficits. On the Senate side, however, the focus this time was on a set of revisions to Section 301 of U.S. trade law designed to reduce presidential discretion and provide trade negotiators with a bigger stick—or a "crowbar" as it came to be known. The Super 301 provisions, first added to the Senate bill in July 1987, required the USTR to compile a list of countries maintaining a consistent pattern of trade distortion and negotiate the removal of offending barriers within a set period of time. Throughout the debate, it was clear that members of Congress had Japan in mind when they discussed this "unfair trader" provision. The final version of the legislation actually included a "sense of the Congress" passage that referred specifically to Japan as an example of a nation with a consistent pattern of barriers.[54]

While the Reagan administration opposed both the House and Senate approaches, it became clear that resistance was futile after the Senate approved its Super 301 version of the bill by a vote of 87–7. The Omnibus Trade and Competitiveness Act of 1988, including an undiluted Super 301 provision, was finally enacted on August 23, shortly before Bush won the right to succeed Reagan as the next president. How to respond to this latest Congressional challenge to the executive's leadership thus became the first item of trade policy business for the new administration.

THE BUSH ADMINISTRATION

Although their seats were barely warm, the new Bush team faced tight deadlines imposed by the new Trade Act. By April 30, the USTR was obliged to compile a new version of its annual National Trade Estimate Report on Foreign Trade Barriers which was to serve, this time, as a basis for the subsequent decisions on which countries and which practices to label as "unfair" under Super 301. This latter decision, closely watched by Congress and the world, was in turn due by May 31. All spring, as Bush's cabinet appointees appeared before the Senate for confirmation hearings, Senators like John Danforth and Max Baucus (both of whom had led the fight for the Super 301 provision of the Trade Act) made it clear that Congress would not be satisfied unless the administration "named" Japan.[55] Deputy USTR S. Linn Williams, recalling that 90 percent of his three-hour grilling by the Senate was devoted to his views on Japan, describes the atmosphere on the Hill in those days as, "not Republicans versus Democrats, but rather Congress versus the administration."[56] Like the two Reagan administrations, therefore, the new Bush team was quickly forced into the reactive mode, formulating its trade policy in response to the Congressional challenge.

At least as important as this institutional challenge in influencing the new administration's thinking on trade policy, however, was the *ideological* challenge, which was gaining momentum at this time as well. The "revisionist" views discussed earlier in this chapter had by 1989 become almost conventional wisdom on Capitol Hill and even in business circles. Particularly worrying for free traders in the Bush Administration was the endorsement of a "results-oriented trade policy" by the President's Advisory Commission on Trade Policy and Negotiations—a group composed primary of business executives—in February, just as the administration was trying to decide how to handle Super 301. In sectoral talks with Japan, the report recommended, the U.S. should "insist on appropriate sectoral import levels" reflecting the competitiveness of U.S. firms and should force Japan to comply with agreements to meet these targets by using Section 301 of its trade law.[57] Even the Business Roundtable, the champion of numerous prior battles for trade liberalization, began in the late 1980s to call for a more aggressive policy for dealing with Japan.[58]

At the root of this ideological challenge were two related propositions calling into question the orthodox "ideas" that had guided American trade policy since the Great Depression. The first one, based on the work of economists, questioned the liberal view that protectionist policies of other nations can safely be ignored because they almost always hurt the offender more than they hurt you. In some high-technology sectors, according to this view, the "spillover benefits and excess returns" available to the nation sucessfully dominating the industry are such that nations ignore at their peril the benefits of promotional and protective policies aimed at fostering success in these sectors.[59] If a nation falls behind in the race to develop one generation of technology in such a "strategic" sector, according to the extreme version of this view, it may find it difficult ever to catch up. For those who applied the new "strategic trade theory" to the real world, the industrial policy of the Japanese government was the prime example of how a nation can actively work to claim these first mover advantages for itself while the liberal trade policy of the U.S. was the favorite example of the "sucker's" approach.[60]

The second proposition, articulated most clearly by frustrated civil servants in the economic agencies of the U.S. government, questioned the Cold War habits of thinking which subordinated U.S. economic disputes with its allies (especially Japan) to political and strategic interests in maintaining good relations. Clyde Prestowitz at Commerce, Glen Fukushima at USTR, and Kevin Kearns at State, among others, reacted vociferously against the continuation of this tendency at a time when, they felt, the U.S. had just as much at stake in its economic competition with Japan as it did in its military rivalry with the Soviet Union. All eventually left their positions after finding the Reagan and Bush administrations unwilling to listen to their warnings, but each continued to press for a reorientation of American foreign policy.[61]

Just as the Bush team was formulating its response to the Super 301 deadlines, these two strands of revisionist philosophy came together in a particularly stark way in the debate over the Memorandum of Understanding Reagan had signed with the Japanese in the waning days

of his administration, agreeing to transfer some of America's most sophisticated aircraft technology as part of a deal to codevelop a next-genera-
tion Japanese fighter plane—the FSX. Critics of the deal argued that aero-
space was a classic case of a "strategic sector" where the U.S. should be
jealously protecting its technological lead. Instead, in the interest of continued good relations with Japan, it was turning over technology at what
they considered to be a bargain price. While Bush ultimately prevailed on
the specific issue of the FSX deal, the debate provided an opportunity for
"revisionists" to trumpet the dangers of traditional ways of dealing with
Japanese trade problems just when the administration was engaged in
deciding how to deal with Super 301—an area where similar issues were
at stake.[62]

Within the administration, there was some support for the active use
of Super 301 to open up the Japanese market. Commerce and the USTR,
the government agencies whose missions naturally led them to view the
national interest in terms of economic interests and the agencies closest
to Congress and industry on matters of trade policy, had gradually started
advocating a more aggressive strategy for dealing with Japan during the
Reagan years. The two agencies had proposed a "results-oriented
approach" prior to the decision to go with the MOSS Talks in 1985, and
they had been the leading advocates of the market share expansion provisions of the Semiconductor Accords.[63] Commerce (most recently under
Bush's new department head, Robert Mosbacher) had also taken the lead
in the fight to keep the FSX deal from becoming a technology giveaway.

Yet, even within these agencies there was disagreement about what
kinds of Japanese practices should be named. While willing to go along
with Congress by naming *some* practices, U.S. Trade Representative Carla
Hills was also concerned about how the Super 301 decision would affect
the willingness of America's trading partners to cooperate in bringing the
Uruguay Round of the GATT talks to a successful close by the end of
1990—her top priority. Both she and her new deputy in charge of trade
talks with Japan, Williams, were on record as opponents of "managed
trade." Given the challenge of this "new and very sexy" approach, one of
their priorities was therefore to put forward an alternative means of dealing with the "Japan Problem": one that would deal with the kinds of barriers which concerned industry without resorting to "managed trade" and
one that would allow the administration to take the initiative in trade policy back from Congress.[64]

The rest of the administration, however, was even cooler to the controversial provision of the Trade Act. The CEA under Michael Boskin and the Office of Management and Budget under Richard Darman were hostile to the idea of naming any country under Super 301.[65] If Japan had to be named, Darman argued, it should be cited without the mention of any specific practices. For these economic ideologues, the main worry was that the law was GATT illegal and contrary to American liberal economic principles.

Treasury's position was somewhat more complex. As economists, senior officials like Undersecretary for International Affairs David Mulford and his deputy Charles Dallara were instinctively repelled by the kind of "aggressive unilateralism" inherent in the Super 301 approach. Given the time and energy they had devoted to the U.S.-Japan bilateral deficit problem over the previous four years, however, they felt that the administration needed a new approach. Starting with the Yen-Dollar Talks in 1984, in fact, Treasury had taken an unusually prominent role in the effort to deal with the Japan problem. It had taken a lead in proposing the MOSS talks, committing the time of senior officials to dealing with the negotiations on medical equipment and pharmaceuticals. It had then orchestrated the Plaza Accords. Despite all of these efforts, however, the U.S. deficit with Japan remained at close to record levels.[66]

Dallara recalls the thinking within the agency at that time as being particularly preoccupied with the slow impact of Plaza on the U.S.-Japan bilateral imbalance:

> The Plaza Accords were designed to reduce imbalances through macroeconomic policy coordination and exchange rate adjustments. But exchange rates will only work to bring about this result when goods prices move in response to currency shifts. In the case of Japan, even though the value of the dollar relative to the yen declined by 40 percent, there were innumerable cases in which there was unusual inflexibility, where this change was not reflected at all in prices.[67]

This lack of movement in wholesale and retail prices in Japan, Treasury officials concluded, was evidence that structural barriers were getting in the way of the market mechanism. For their macro approach to work, they realized, they would have to tackle barriers like government regulations, inefficiencies in the distribution system, and exclusive dealing arrangements within keiretsu business groups. The idea of addressing structural barriers in some way (if not through Super 301) was therefore of much greater appeal to officials in Treasury than to their economist-brethren in places like the CEA. Lower-ranking officials at Treasury had advocated a new structural initiative even before the Omnibus Trade Act passed. Once Super 301 and the competition to devise a new strategy to deal with Japan heated up after Bush's election, therefore, it was quite natural for Mulford and Dallara to emerge as the architects of SII.[68]

The final significant faction was made up of the State and Defense Departments along with the NSC. Long accustomed to viewing the U.S.-Japan relationship through Cold War glasses, officials of these agencies in Washington and senior diplomats in Tokyo were quick to warn of the backlash the U.S. could expect if it named Japan under Super 301. One USTR official recalls an argument made by a member of this faction during interagency meetings: if the U.S. pressed Japan too hard, this official worried, "the Socialists and Communists may come to power and throw the U.S. armed forces off the Japanese archipelago."[69] It was just the kind of attitude one would expect from a foreign policy establishment nurtured in the Cold War environment.

The process through which the Bush administration came to a decision on Super 301 allowed all of the divergent views discussed above to be expressed. An interagency team based in the USTR, but with representatives from all of the departments with a stake in the outcome, first devoted its attention to the question of which barriers should be listed in the agency's trade estimate report at the end of April. The USTR then compiled a memorandum listing various (nonexclusive) options the administration could pursue in its trade relations with Japan. Options at this point included: (1) multilateralizing pressure on Japan; (2) export promotion measures; (3) targeting sector-specific barriers with Super 301; (4) using non-trade leverage to open up the Japanese market; and (5) "a structural initiative combining macro-economic and trade policy measures."[70]

The decision on how do deal with Super 301 was then left to a meeting of the cabinet-level Economic Policy Council, with President Bush present, on May 22. The group was divided. Hills of USTR and Mosbacher of Commerce argued that Japan had to be named for specific practices, emphasizing in particular their expectation that Congress would not tolerate anything less. Darman and Boskin were opposed to naming practices. It was at this point that the structural initiative being discussed at the subcabinet level was presented as part of a possible compromise.[71] According to USTR's Williams, members of the subcabinet who had been working on plans for structural talks with Japan had no expectation going into this meeting that the cabinet would endorse sii. Structural talks, it was thought, would be proposed later, so as to avoid the possibility that the Japanese would see sii and Super 301 as the same thing. Cabinet officials at the meeting who were familiar with the work being done by the subcabinet (Hills, Nicholas Brady of Treasury, and James Baker of State) felt, however, that structural talks should be called for at the same time the Super 301 decision was announced "in order to show that we were thinking of alternatives to Super 301." This was the first cabinet meeting where the Bush administration was going to be setting out its trade policy, and they were reluctant to have it pass only on the Super 301 hit list. They wanted to communicate to the world trade policy community "that our trade policy is not Super 301, although Super 301 is a piece of it, that we have a broader policy."[72]

Finally, on May 25, 1989, Carla Hills made her much-awaited announcement on Super 301, revealing what had been agreed three days earlier. Japan would be named, but only for three practices: government procurement practices in satellites and supercomputers and technical barriers in forest products. These practices were the ones most directly under Japanese government control. Japan would *not* be listed for barriers in the distribution sector, for anticompetitive practices, or keiretsu business groups—as many on Capitol Hill had hoped. Instead, Hills announced, the White House was proposing that such problems be discussed in a separate set of talks outside Super 301 which it proposed to call the Structural Impediments Initiative. At the same time, in order to further soften the blow of naming Japan, Hills announced that Brazil and India were also being listed as unfair traders.[73]

The sii talks thus came to be launched at a press conference with 19 television cameras and hundreds of journalists from around the world in attendance,[74] linked to Super 301 (despite the assertions that they would be separate) by the very fact that the talks were proposed at the same time Japan was listed under the provision. By all accounts, the talks would not have been proposed when they were or acquired the high profile they eventually did if they had emerged, more like the moss talks, from the depths of the bureaucracy without the significant involvement of the President and Congress.

That the sii talks *were* launched when they were and in the form they were can be seen—based on the account of the decisionmaking process up to this point—as the product of an institutional battle between Congress and the executive and of the ideological battle between traditional liberal economic and Cold War principles on the one hand and emerging "revisionist" views on the other. The importance of the Congressional challenge cannot be understated. As one Congressman long active on the free trade side of the debate put it, Super 301 was "terrorizing the administration" in 1989:

> I think the first objective was how are we going to deal with Super 301 without getting egg on our face, and SII helped to some extent on that. The second thing was how do we stay out of future 301s? How do we keep Congress off our backs? Well, we start these wonderful negotiations which can go on forever and we'll tell them we're making progress. I think SII was quite successful, but mostly it was successful in giving the administration the running room it needed to proceed with its other priorities—especially the Uruguay Round.[75]

Without Super 301 and the Congressional challenge it represented, it is very likely that the administration would have put much less energy into structural talks. It may not have launched the talks at all.

It would be a mistake, however, to focus only on the battle between Congress and the administration. Arguably the talks were just as much a product of disagreements within the administration, reflecting different perceptions of America's national interest. Commerce and elements within the USTR, focusing on the economic competition between the U.S. and Japan, were coming to see barriers in Japan as being beyond the reach of traditional rule-based market-opening initiatives and were edging closer to an embrace of a "results-oriented" strategy. Without a more aggressive approach, they felt, Japan would continue to reap disproportionate benefits from the trading relationship and would continue to challenge the competitiveness of U.S. firms. Most of the rest of the executive, on the other hand, saw such creeping revisionism as a threat to U.S. leadership of the global trade regime and to its continued good relations with its Western allies. For these officials, SII represented a chance to articulate a constructive alternative to the managed trade approach, to tackle exactly those barriers that bothered the revisionists, but with a rule-based approach.

That ideological considerations were important in shaping administration thinking is again not something one has to divine from decisionmaking outcomes. The principals have said as much. John Taylor, the member of the CEA who represented it in the SII talks, told the *Financial Times* that the administration saw SII as a "a workable alternative to managed trade."[76] The USTR's Linn Williams put it this way: one of the objectives of SII was "to stop managed trade."[77]

Two-Level Logic and the SII Format

The above discussion of the origins of SII makes it clear that America's domestic institutions and ideas had a great deal to do with the administration's decision to embrace this novel approach to trade relations with Japan. Without the institutional challenge from Congress and without the ideological challenge of the managed trade movement, it is likely the Bush administration would have handled the trading relationship much differently. It is another matter, however, to suggest (as most analysts have) that SII was the *only* decision that the American political system could have produced in 1989. Glen Fukushima (then of the USTR) suggests, for example, that the administration was caught between the blades of a pair of scissors: on the one hand a Congress that had to be appeased and on the other hand a Japan that could not be offended. SII was "a cost the administration had to pay" in order to satisfy both parties.[78]

While I agree with the conventional analyses that domestic institutions and ideas did constrain the administration in important ways, I argue here that these factors did not *determine* the administration's negotiating posture. Just as the international environment—with the mixed incentives discussed in the first section of the chapter—were indeterminate, the domestic political environment also left the administration a fair degree of latitude. To fully account for the decision to go with SII and for important details about the way the administration chose to pursue the initiative, the analysis cannot be conducted one level at a time, looking first at international incentives and then at how the domestic system processed them. One must look simultaneously at both levels, at how the two levels interacted.

My argument here, insisting that two-level considerations came into play even before the SII negotiations began, flows naturally from the theoretical framework developed in the previous chapter. If it is true that negotiators have opportunities to widen win-sets in their counterparts' domestic arenas through a range of strategies, it makes sense that they will formulate their demands and attempt to manipulate the format (rules) for the negotiations in order to maximize their ability to pursue these strategies. As David Lax and James Sebenius argue, "like tactics within a fixed game, tactics that change the game itself are intended to create and claim value."[79] Before the negotiations start, in fact, is the time when negotiators have the greatest flexibility to add parties, add and subtract issues, and otherwise alter the rules of the game in order to make possible their synergistic strategies.

In this final section, I want to take a look at three ways in which strategic considerations (attempts to use one level to pursue objectives at the other) influenced administration decisions on the format and agenda for SII: the way Bush's decision to go with SII was influenced by his desire to use the negotiations to shore up his fraying Republican free trade coalition; the ways his negotiating team sought to minimize their own differences while taking advantages of differences on the Japanese side; and the way Japanese domestic actors sought to use the negotiations to pursue objectives within their domestic arena.

First, I propose, we need to take a step back from the point reached at the conclusion of the last section, asking ourselves whether we can really ascribe a liberal economic ideology to "the executive" in accounting for the Bush decision to fight the managed trade movement. According to Krauss and Reich, postwar presidents have been inherently biased toward free trade because: (1) they represent the American state and therefore have to be concerned about the "national interest"; and (2) because America's national interest has been to pursue a free trade policy.[80] By the time Bush became president, however, it was not as clear as it had been in the 1950s that America's national interest *did* lie in a free trade policy. As argued in the first section of this chapter, by the mid-1980s there were clear national interest arguments for a more aggressive trade policy, perhaps for a policy of selective reciprocity. Some parts of the American state (Commerce and USTR) had in fact begun to swing distinctly toward the view that America's interest lay in a "results-oriented" trade policy.

Nevertheless, Bush paid no heed to the advice he was getting from these parts of his administration. Instead, he chose to side with the advice coming from the CEA, State, and Treasury, all of which argued that the national interest lay in staying the course. In the previous section, this decision was described as being the natural result of Cold War and economic "habits of thinking" as well as the privileged institutional status of these departments. It is my contention, however, that the "presidency" was not as constrained by this domestic environment as the analysis thus far has led us to believe. Under Reagan, Commerce and USTR actually had some success pushing the administration toward a "results-oriented" posture (as seen in the Semiconductor Accords). Another president (a Mondale/Dukakis/or Clinton?) probably would not have been as quick to stay the course as was Bush. In fact, in circumstances not too different from those facing Bush, Clinton embraced a "results-oriented" trade policy just four years later.

Rather than attributing Bush's decision to fight managed trade to the executive ideology, I propose, we should recognize that he was guided by his interest in using international negotiations with Japan to pursue his domestic interest in shoring up the coalition that brought him to office. In the late 1980s, this coalition was starting to fray as more and more firms and industry associations were calling for a more aggressive trade policy. As noted above, even the Business Roundtable advocated specific reciprocity in dealings with Japan. Bush had reason to worry: some of the defecting business and opinion leaders (e.g. Hewlett-Packard's John Young; former Reagan administration officials like Clyde Prestowitz and Glen Fukushima) had by 1992 signed on with the Clinton campaign partly out of their conviction that he would offer a tougher trade policy.[81] The Bush team had to do more than appease Congress if it wanted to avoid this potential loss of support, and this is where the SII came in: Bush needed SII to show potential supporters of the managed trade approach that he had a constructive and fruitful alternative approach that could deal with "the Japan problem" as well as or better than could managed trade. By doing so, he hoped to keep traditional Republican supporters inside his coalition.[82]

If Bush's decision to go with SII reflected his interest in using the international talks to pursue domestic goals, his team's decisions on the format and agenda for the talks reflected two-level logic of the opposite kind: the desire to manipulate domestic politics to pursue international objectives. The influence of such logic can be seen, first, in the way in which administration officials consciously conspired to add agencies to their own negotiating team in order to add parties sympathetic to their demands to the Japanese team—expanding participation in the Japanese policymaking process. As noted above, the idea for a new round of structural talks originated in the Treasury Department. Almost immediately, however, Treasury decided that it wanted the USTR involved, with Dallara (of Treasury) approaching Williams (of USTR) in March 1989 to see whether the two agencies might not be able to cooperate in launching a new Japan initiative.[83] Treasury was usually not very keen on sharing control, but in this case it had a clear purpose for reaching out. Having exhausted its attempts to influence Japanese fiscal policy on its own through the G-7 and through one-on-one Treasury pressure on the Ministry of Finance, the department was eager to bring the pressure of the Ministry of International Trade and Industry—a known advocate of the kind of fiscal stimulus sought by Treasury—to bear on the Japanese policy process. It realized that one way to increase MITI involvement would be to engage it, along with MOF, in a two-by-two dialogue.[84]

A similar rationale lay behind subsequent decisions to expand the U.S. SII negotiating team to include the Justice Department and the Council of Economic Advisors. According to Williams, the administration knew going into the talks that the Japanese counterparts to these two U.S. agencies, the Fair Trade Commission (JFTC) and the Economic Planning Agency (EPA), sympathized with many U.S. negotiating demands. They also knew the Japanese would "match a bishop with a bishop." They therefore conspired to add the CEA and Justice in order to add allies on the Japanese side of the table.[85]

While adding parties to the Japanese team in order to magnify internal divisions on that side of the table, the U.S. team had to be careful to minimize their own differences. Divisions on the U.S. side over what to do about "the Japan problem" had, as noted above, grown to be substantial over the previous few years. Therefore the danger existed that the Japanese might be able to play one U.S. agency off against the other just as the U.S. was hoping it would be able to do with Japanese ministries. To minimize this possibility, USTR and Treasury initially aimed to keep the State Department out of SII. According to USTR and Treasury officials, there was seen to be little value in adding the Ministry of Foreign Affairs (MOFA) on the Japanese side—since it was so powerless—whereas there was a real danger (in their eyes) that State could sabotage efforts to maintain a tough united front in the talks. As one participant noted, they were afraid State would be "absolutely obstructionist."[86] State's credibility was particularly low on structural issues since the department's experiment with a "Structural Dialogue" with Japan in 1985–86 was widely perceived as having failed to produce anything of value.[87] Treasury and USTR therefore went out of their way to avoid letting State find out about their initiative even as they began to approach the MOF and MITI, their Japanese counterparts.[88]

By the end of April, however, it had become clear that the initiative was going to be too big to exclude State and MOFA and a decision was made to bring them into the game. By bringing them in after the USTR and

Treasury had convinced MITI and MOF to go along with the basic format, however, the two departments hoped to limit State's opportunity to water it down.[89] Shortly afterward, a decision was also made to bring in Commerce, despite the opposite risk: that Commerce would be critical of the approach for not going far enough. This time, the decision to include the extra agency was based not so much on inevitability as it was on the hope that Commerce criticism of the initiative would be muted if it were given a role to play. But not too big a role. The Treasury and USTR conspired to limit Commerce's role by giving it the largely peripheral task of doing a price survey.

As the talks got under way in the fall of 1989, the team of officials heading the U.S. delegation made another decision that reflected their strategic interest in minimizing divisions on their side: they would emphasize all of their demands equally. By this time, the list of U.S. demands numbered over 200 and ranged from macroeconomic demands to increase Japanese public investment to more micro-level demands calling for the abolition of regulations. Rather than prioritizing this list of demands, however, the group consciously decided to submit an unprioritized list of them to the Japanese.[90] Clearly, the American delegation would have faced turf battles if it had attempted to rank its demands. By avoiding that step, it helped keep the team united.[91]

By staking out middle ground within the administration and by avoiding decisions that might provoke turf battles, Treasury and the USTR were surprisingly successful in maintaining unity among the U.S. negotiators. At the staff level, the core group of a dozen junior officials who devoted full time to SII worked closely together—often co-authoring position papers across departmental lines. A number of them remarked in interviews that the cohesiveness of their interagency group during the SII talks was unlike their experience with any U.S.-Japan negotiations before or since. At more senior ranks, there were real turf battles, most notably over the question of which department should lead the U.S. delegation, but even this issue was resolved in a way that probably served the Americans' strategic interest in maintaining their unity. Bush decided that the delegation would have three co-chairs: Dallara at Treasury, Williams at USTR, and Undersecretary of Economic Affairs Richard McCormack at State.[92]

The final related way in which the U.S. delegation aimed to manipulate Japanese domestic politics to its advantage can be seen in its selection and packaging of agenda items. As originally conceived within Treasury, the structural initiative was designed to deal with barriers to a market-based balance of payments adjustment (which, it was felt, wasn't functioning as it should after Plaza). Given this priority, the issue at the top of Treasury's list was Japan's surplus of savings relative to investment which, through macroeconomic equations, produces an equivalent current account surplus. Declining levels of public investment and land policies in Japan were seen to be part of the macroeconomic problem. Closely following the macro issue was one which particularly interested Dallara: bank-centered keiretsu business groups. The idea was that these privileged networks propped up declining firms and subsidized rising ones so that structural adjustment would not work as it was supposed to.

Over at the USTR, which joined the SII project next, the priority was not structural adjustment but market access, and so the issues at the top of its list were different. Given Williams's background as an anti-trust lawyer, it was not surprising that he focused especially on this issue. There was also common concern in these agencies, as well as at State, about structural barriers in the distribution system. State had in fact organized and sent an interagency mission to Japan in late February to look into barriers in the distribution sector.[93] All of these issues were discussed during the course of interagency meetings in April and May, prior to Hills's May 25 announcement proposing the SII talks. The administration still had little idea, however, about how it wanted to package its agenda, much less about what specific demands it wanted to make in each issue area.[94]

It was in the next stage, when the administration began to identify specific demands and frame talking points, that two-level strategy clearly came into play. During the summer and fall, as the interagency team prepared position papers, a conscious decision was made to appeal to potential supporters of the U.S. demands within Japan. As Williams put it, "we wanted to mine Japanese constituencies."[95] The team scoured Japanese government reports for clues as to how different ministries stood on various issues. The Maekawa Reports of the mid-1980s, the product of a reformist advisory council sponsored by Prime Minister Nakasone which had led to extensive debate but little policy change, were a particularly rich source of ideas for the American team.[96] Increased public investment, liberalization of distribution sector regulations, and land policy reforms were all proposed or discussed during the Maekawa period.

The U.S. team was intent, however, on tapping support for their demands beyond the confines of the bureaucracy. As Williams recalls:

Early on, a strategic decision was made that this thing could not be won if we dealt exclusively with *kasumigaseki* [the Tokyo district where most Japanese ministries have their offices]. Even the politicians becoming involved a little wasn't going to make enough of a difference. The only way we were going to succeed was if we could appeal to the public interest.[97]

The U.S. wanted to go over the politicians' and bureaucrats' heads and appeal directly to consumers and the general public. The list of demands and the way they were packaged was therefore carefully tailored to appeal to the average Japanese citizen. The land issue, which Williams and others recognized was probably only marginally related to U.S.-Japan trade problems, was given special prominence because support for reforms was especially great among a general public upset that spiralling land costs were pricing them out of the market for home-ownership. The U.S. focused its demands under distribution on the Large Store Law hoping their argument about how regulations jacked up consumer prices would make their demands attractive to ordinary Japanese shoppers. In the area of the savings-investment imbalance, the U.S. packaged its demands so that they emphasized the new infrastructure that public spending could bring for average Japanese (sewers, parks, housing)—rather than calling for policies to lower Japanese savings rates, which would have had the same effect but were not as popular.

In the next chapter, we will examine how all of these tactics fed into the Japanese policy process. Before leaving this story of how the Americans framed their sii negotiating demands, however, we need to examine the final way in which two-level logic influenced the process: what was called in the last chapter "domestic politics reversed." Even as the Americans were trying to "mine Japanese constituencies," these constituencies were seeking to manipulate American pressure to achieve their own domestic objectives. The economists the Americans contacted for advice about how to frame their land policy demands (people like Noguchi Yukio and Hasegawa Tokunosuke) helped the U.S. delegation, but each had an ulterior motive—to influence the demands so that they stressed the policies they were advocating in the policy debate. Noguchi was a firm believer in market-based solutions to the land problem, and seems to have used his access to U.S. negotiators in order to skew their demands toward market-based (rather than regulatory) approaches to lowering land prices.[98]

The decision to focus on distribution problems and the Large Store Law in particular may also have been influenced by Japanese political actors. The head of large Japanese retail chains, including Daiei's Nakauchi Isao, are reported to have been in touch regularly with the U.S. Embassy in Tokyo. These chains had a particular interest in how the U.S. framed its demands since the Large Store Law directly affected the profitability of their existing stores and their prospects for expansion. The head of one smaller newcomer chain, Shimizu Nobutsugu, sued the government for what he charged was its illegal administration of the law—even though he knew he could never win—because he hoped to use the publicity to influence the Americans' demands. He then sent all of the documents he prepared for the trial to the U.S. Embassy.[99] He describes the reaction of Japanese officials when he told them what he was doing: "Of course there were people who said it was a disgrace for me to be going to the Americans and using gaiatsu, but the Japanese government's policy was wrong and the government itself wasn't doing anything to correct the situation. There was nothing to do besides using gaiatsu." And Shimizu was not the only one who sought to "use gaiatsu" to achieve their aims. Almost the same words were used by the Economic Planning Agency's Unno Tsuneo when speaking of how he too felt there was nothing he could do other than to "use the Americans" to overcome the Ministry of Finance's resistance to the public investment increase he favored.[100]

It is difficult to measure the degree to which U.S. demands were influenced by all of these Japanese attempts to influence the process. After all, the Americans were deliberately looking for reform proposals that had support in Japan, so they were bound to pick up on the advice of Japanese political actors. The key question is whether American negotiators ended up pushing demands that served the interests of Japanese constituencies more than "American interests." Critics have pointed out, for example, that firms like Shimizu's, more than American retailers, benefited from the changes in the Large Store Law forced on Japan at great cost to the Americans in terms of time and political capital. Ordinary Japanese got the extra sewers and parks. The Ministry of Finance secured a new source of land tax revenue. All of that may be fine if the U.S. gained something too, but for American critics the SII did not produce nearly enough.[101]

Conclusion

Putting aside for now the question of how to evaluate the SII approach, let us return to the question with which we started this chapter: how do nations faced with mixed incentives emanating from the international system frame their negotiating demands? While the argument in the middle section of the paper emphasized that U.S. domestic institutions and ideas placed important constraints on how these incentives were translated into negotiating demands, I argued in the last section that two-level considerations also played a critical role in shaping U.S. negotiating demands. Bush didn't have to embrace a structural initiative in order to appease Congress but did, partly because he and his advisers saw it as a way to convince business and industry interests which were on the verge of defecting from their free trade coalition that the administration had an approach which would address their concerns. American institutions and ideas similarly did not dictate that the administration structure agency participation in the negotiating team in the way it did: to enhance divisions on the Japanese side and minimize them on the U.S. side. Nor did the domestic structure dictate that the team frame their negotiating agenda to appeal to Japanese constituencies—or to respond to their efforts to "use gaiatsu." The administration nevertheless did these things because it was operating in a two-level environment where it and other actors had incentives to behave strategically.

What I have argued here is that we can understand trade policy only by looking at both international and domestic politics at the same time. It may be possible to understand how nations arrive at something like "incomes policy" or "tax policy" by looking at the two levels sequentially: first at how the international system structures incentives and then at how domestic politics mediates those incentives. But when a policy area—such as trade—requires that governments *negotiate*, it becomes impossible to separate the levels. The international system provides incentives and domestic politics still mediates them, but the government must again take into account the international system (and the domestic politics in the countries that make up the international system) as it frames its negotiating demands.

While the argument in the final section of the chapter was based on a detailed analysis of a single trade policy decision, it does not take much effort to find other cases where American trade policy positions have been sensitive to two-level considerations. Take just two examples touched on earlier in this chapter: the 1985 Plaza Accords and the 1981 voluntary export restraint agreement on Japanese autos. While both of these decisions were described as being constrained by domestic institutions—specifically the Congressional challenge—important features of the administration's approaches in each of those cases cannot be accounted for without examining how the negotiated nature of the policy brought two-level considerations into play. When the U.S. chose in 1985 to emphasize exchange rate manipulation as the core of its strategy to deal with the macro sources of the deficit, the decision reflected a sensitivity to the fact that Japanese and German domestic politics were unlikely to be responsive to a strategy that called on them for fiscal stimulus.[102] Likewise, the Reagan Administration's decision to call for a VER arrangement rather than domestic content legislation reflected its realization that such an arrangement would appeal to MITI and, by promising greater per-vehicle profits, to the Japanese auto industry. While it is beyond the scope of this chapter to examine cases in other bilateral relationships and other (non-trade) policy spheres, the analysis suggests that policy decisions in other such cases *where international negotiations come into play* are likely to reflect two-level considerations even at the pre-negotiation stage.

The SII pre-negotiation stage ended on July 14, 1989, when Bush and Prime Minister Uno Sōsuke issued a joint communique prior to the Paris G-7 gathering announcing that the two sides had agreed on a format for their SII talks. The Japanese had accepted the U.S. suggestion that they talk about Japanese structural issues, but they insisted that the talks be "two-way." They wanted to be able to talk about structural sources of the imbalance on the American side: such issues as the U.S. budget deficit and low levels of private savings.[103] After a series of two meetings during the summer, the Americans agreed to this Japanese demand in return for the Japanese agreeing to a set of tight deadlines.[104] The negotiators committed to producing a midterm progress report by early April 1990, in time for it to be factored into the decision on whether or not to re-list Japan under Super 301, and a final report within a year.[105] In September, the SII talks officially began.

4
JAPANESE POLITICS AND
THE SII NEGOTIATIONS

After a year of often tense negotiations and a final session that stretched from the scheduled two days to four, the American and Japanese officials assigned to the sii talks finally agreed on a "Joint Report" which settled their primary differences. It was June 28, 1990, just under a year since Uno and Bush had set the process in motion in Paris. At the final negotiating session, the Japanese agreed to add 15 trillion yen (more than $100 billion) to the 415 trillion yen ten-year public investment package they had brought to the table, but they refused to give in to American demands that they commit to a specific higher level of fines for anti-trust violators.[1] On the other primary issues raised during the course of the year, their responses were also mixed. They had already agreed to far-reaching and very specific changes in the Large Store Law and land tax policies in an interim report released in early April, but on the issue of keiretsu their refusal to even talk about limits on cross-shareholding left the U.S. with little to show for its efforts.

While the previous chapter demonstrated that two-level logic influenced the Americans' choice of format and agenda in the sii talks, the true test of the approach developed in this book lies in its ability to account for this pattern of negotiating *outcomes*. After all, the "effectiveness of foreign pressure" (the dependent variable of primary interest in this book) can be judged only by looking at the results of negotiations. This chapter examines how a year's worth of sii bargaining produced widely varying degrees of responsiveness to American demands and tests whether the approach outlined in chapter 2 can help us explain this pattern.

The bottom line of the argument developed in this chapter, that the effectiveness of foreign pressure depends on how it works with domestic politics in Japan, is not too controversial. A wide range of practitioners and scholars writing about gaiatsu—Robert Orr, Ed Lincoln, Amelia Porges—have noted that its impact depends on the domestic political environment it encounters.[2] None of these works, however, attempt to specify *what specific domestic political conditions* are likely to be conducive to the successful application of foreign pressure. With the insights gained from the abstract analysis of bargaining tactics and domestic politics in chapter 2 and a carefully chosen set of cases, we are poised to do that in this chapter.

We begin with a brief summary of the Americans' SII demands and the results of the negotiations in each issue area. The story of how the course of policymaking in each issue area was altered by SII is explored in much greater detail in the issue-specific chapters to follow, but in order to identify overall patterns, it is necessary to provide a rough sketch of the results up front in this chapter. The analysis next turns back to the approach developed in chapter 2 and applies it to the Japanese political system. A variety of synergistic strategies, it is argued, should be particularly effective (*under certain conditions*) given the structure of Japan's political regime under LDP rule. The final section of the chapter then lays out the core argument of the book, linking the pattern of results in the SII cases to the predictions generated by the two-level game approach.

The SII Demands and Results

The SII talks started slowly, as most U.S.-Japan negotiations do. At the first two negotiating sessions, held September 4–5 in Tokyo and November 6–7 in Washington, the two sides exchanged views on the main issues—with time divided between America's complaints about Japan and Japan's complaints about the U.S.. When the topic was Japan's structural barriers, the Japanese delegates energetically explained and defended *all* of the regulations and practices the Americans had criticized. The comments of American delegates ranged widely over the SII issue areas, but avoided (at these first two sessions) making specific demands.[3]

By the time the two sides met for a third time in late February, however, the Americans had made their demands explicit, compiling them in a thick document which was delivered to the Japanese shortly before the negotiating session.[4] When the press obtained a copy of the list of demands, it promptly published them and trumpeted the fact that the Americans were making over 200 specific proposals.[5] Because this list was published, we have an opportunity to compare exactly what the Americans were demanding with what they got, allowing us to measure the "effectiveness" of U.S. pressure.

Starting in February, the Japanese also began to budge on a few issues, initially on land and the distribution system. Within about a month, after a concerted campaign to bring public opinion, media pressure, and LDP leadership to bear on the Japanese negotiating team, Japan had agreed to even more concessions. The results of the year-long talks—spelled out in an April 1990 interim report and a June final report—were widely heralded as a breakthrough in resolving U.S.-Japanese tensions. Given that the Japanese had shown little ability or willingness to deliver any concessions at the start of the negotiations, that nation's willingness to agree to significant concessions in some areas was a pleasant surprise. For the purposes of this analysis, however, it is particularly important that the Japanese did not yield uniformly across the five targeted areas. Rather, they offered significant concessions in two areas (macroeconomics and the distribution system), compromised somewhat in one (land policy), offered minimal concessions in another (exclusionary business practices), and offered virtually no concessions in the last (keiretsu business groups). What follows is a brief summary of the issues, the primary American demands, and results in each of these areas.

SAVINGS-INVESTMENT BALANCE

Based on the macroeconomic rule that a nation's surplus savings equal its current account surplus, the U.S. called on Japan to take a number of steps to boost public investment to offset the nation's high savings rate. Until the late 1980s, Japan's persistent private sector surplus savings had been largely offset by large government budget deficits. As the government succeeded in stemming its deficit spending, however, the net surplus of savings began to grow—contributing, according to the Americans, to Japan's growing trade surplus.[6] The solution was obvious: the Japanese government needed to start spending again. Pointing out that the nation's social infrastructure in areas like sewers and parks lagged way behind other industrialized nations, the U.S. urged Japan to set high targets for improvements in its five-year public investment plans. The core demand in this issue area, however, was the one where the U.S. called on Japan to increase its rate of public investment from the 1989 ratio of 6.7 percent to 10 percent of GNP over a three- to five-year period. Making obvious their hope that all of the spending would force the Japanese to rely on deficit spending, the U.S. added for good measure the suggestion that Japan fund the increased spending with construction bonds.

Throughout the talks, the Japanese were very resistant to these American demands. In particular, the Ministry of Finance (MOF) resented the American interference with its plan to restore fiscal responsibility after more than a decade of annual budget deficits. It also considered the U.S. attempt to secure concrete spending commitments to be a gross intrusion into the nation's right to devise its own budget to meet its own economic needs. Nevertheless, in April 1990 the Japanese government agreed to draw up plans for achieving specific social infrastructure targets and in late June, after more hard bargaining, agreed to commit a specific sum (430 trillion yen) on public works over the next ten years. The 430 trillion yen (approximately $3 trillion) was still less than the amount the Americans had demanded but marked an increase over the original Japanese offer of 400 trillion yen and amounted to a commitment to a substantial increase in the ratio of GNP spent on public works (from 6.7 percent to about 9 percent).[7] Significantly, the Japanese have by all accounts lived up to this pledge.

THE DISTRIBUTION SYSTEM

The Americans were concerned that excessive regulation by the Japanese government and collusive practices among distributors limited the ability of newcomers (especially foreign firms) to get their products to market at an affordable price. Over the course of the talks, one particular law became the symbol of U.S. frustration with Japan's distribution system: the Large Store Law (LSL). Under the terms of that law, large retailers planning the expansion of an existing store or the establishment of a new store were required to notify the Ministry of International Trade and Industry (MITI) and participate in a formal adjustment process designed to consider the interests of local merchants and consumers. The law functioned in such a way, however, that local small retailers were able to hijack the process and delay the opening of new stores for years (often as long as six years but sometimes as long as ten), thereby forcing many stores to give up their expansion plans. This system, the U.S. argued, prevented the expansion of large stores that were more likely to sell imported goods— thus making it all the more difficult for U.S. producers to break into the Japanese market. When Toys 'R' Us came forward midway through the negotiations with stories of how it had been frustrated in its efforts to set up a chain of giant toy stores, the U.S. focused as well on the way the LSL excluded U.S. retailers from entering the Japanese market. The Americans called for the repeal of the law.

As in the case of the U.S. demand that Japan drastically increase its public works spending, this second demand by the U.S. also met with fierce resistance from elements within MITI, the Ministry of Home Affairs (defending the right of local governments to enforce their own regulations), and the LDP, which was very sensitive to pressure from the politically influential small business lobby. Because of this resistance the Japanese had been unable to deal with the LSL issue on their own despite efforts dating back several years, and not surprisingly, the Japanese side of the SII negotiations strongly resisted the American call for repeal. Nevertheless, faced with the Americans' concerted pressure tactics, the Japanese side suddenly came forward with major concessions. As spelled out in the April interim report and the June final report, the Japanese government agreed to some very specific changes in the LSL. These included implementing changes in the administration of the law that reduced the delay between request for and opening of new stores to 18 months and agreeing to rewrite the law within a year to reduce the delay to 12 months. That these changes (all implemented) were having an effect became clear as MITI announced that it was processing a record number of requests to open new large stores. By 1992, new large stores were opening at twice the rate that had prevailed in the latter half of the 1980s.[8]

LAND POLICY REFORMS

This issue was on the SII agenda because Japan's urban land prices— already among the highest in the world—had skyrocketed in the 1980s and because the Americans saw those high land prices as aggravating the trade imbalance in three ways: first, by discouraging foreign firms from establishing operations in Japan; second, by placing new (landless) foreign firms at a distinct competitive disadvantage relative to established Japanese firms that had bought land when it was much cheaper; and third, by aggravating the macroeconomic savings-investment imbalance. The last argument, reflecting the rationale of the first issue-area discussed above, pointed to the ways in which high land prices forced Japanese consumers to save more (to buy exorbitantly priced homes) and spend less (as high prices depressed spending on home construction and consumer durables)—while also depressing government spending on social infrastructure by pushing up the cost of land-acquisition.[9]

Unlike the cases of public works and the distribution system, however, the U.S. did not have a simple, straightforward demand in the case of land policy. Reflecting the complexity of the problem, the U.S. side called for a range of changes in tax and regulatory policies designed to increase the supply of land and allow its more efficient use—thus bringing down the price. Of particular concern to the Americans were tax policies encouraging urban farmers to keep their land in farming and firms to hold onto idle land for use as collateral, as well as regulatory policies that discouraged multistory and rental construction. Such tax and regulatory policies, the U.S. argued, created an artificial shortage of land, which aggravated the land price problem.

In pressing these demands, the Americans encountered a mixed response. A few actors, including the National Land Agency and the Construction Ministry, supported many of the U.S. proposals. On the other hand, the American demands for land tax increases were strongly opposed by the affected groups (farmers and big business) and by their bureaucratic and LDP patrons. In fact, land policy reforms of the type proposed by the Americans had been brought up in the past and had been emasculated to the point that they had no lasting effects. Nevertheless, this time, limited tax and regulatory changes were adopted in many of the areas targeted by the United States. Especially notable was the virtual elimination of loopholes that had allowed urban farmland to largely escape inheritance and land holding taxes. By the summer of 1992, 70 percent of the farmland in urbanization promotion areas which had previously escaped taxation at the rate of surrounding residential areas was slated for higher taxes and development. Because the tax and regulatory changes did not go quite as far as the Americans had sought, however, I have characterized the response as more limited than in the first two areas discussed above.

EXCLUSIONARY BUSINESS PRACTICES

This category of structural problems was of concern to the Americans because they saw the lax enforcement of antitrust policy by the Japanese government as permitting a range of private-sector collusive practices that had the effect of excluding foreign firms from Japanese markets. The Americans were concerned about: (1) the rigging of construction project bids; (2) a slow patent process and collusive arrangements among firms to delay purchase of technologically advanced foreign products until Japanese firms were able to replicate foreign advances; (3) cartels designed to protect uncompetitive industries by keeping out foreigners, fixing prices, and dividing the Japanese market; and (4) manufacturer-controlled distribution networks that effectively excluded foreign products. The U.S. called for increased funding and staffing of the Japanese government agency in charge of policing anti-competitive behavior (the Japanese Fair Trade Commission, JFTC), changes in the Anti-Monopoly Law (AML) designed to give it more teeth by increasing civil and criminal fines and opening up opportunities for private parties injured by collusive practices to recover their damages, and more vigorous enforcement of the law.

In pursuing these demands, the Americans encountered at least as much opposition as on any other issue. For many Japanese, the entire antitrust system was a foreign creation (adopted during the U.S. Occupation after World War II) not in conformance with the traditional Japanese emphasis on informality in business dealings. MITI and the business community had already fought many battles to limit the powers of the JFTC and the AML, and they were not about to give in easily to the latest foreign demands. Even the JFTC, though sympathetic with the need to increase its staff, funding, and powers, was defensive about its preference for informality in dealing with anticompetitive cases. In addition to this general lack of enthusiasm for more vigorous antitrust enforcement, specific U.S. proposals such as those aimed at ending the rigging of construction project bids and breaking up cartels in long-protected segments of the economy ran up against the potent opposition of powerful interest groups and their LDP supporters.

Faced with this negative response, the U.S. side made much less progress in achieving its objectives in this case than in the previous three. The Japanese agreed to draw up guidelines to clarify which practices were illegal under the AML and to increase staffing and funding of the JFTC. Most of their commitments, however, were phrased in vague terms, and in the year following the adoption of the SII report, it became clear that the Japanese were going to interpret those commitments in the most conservative way possible.[10] Although the government decided to revise the AML, the new maximum levels for fines and criminal penalties were felt by the Americans to be still too low to deter collusive behavior. Despite steps by the JFTC to increase the number of cases pursued and to publicize its decisions, many on the U.S. side remained pessimistic about what had been achieved through the SII process on this issue.[11]

KEIRETSU BUSINESS GROUPS

The U.S. pointed to Japan's famous business groups as one of the most important structural barriers making it difficult for foreign firms to break into the Japanese market. The Americans charged that firms participating in these networks, such as those in the Sumitomo, Mitsubishi, and Mitsui groups as well as the groups of suppliers and distributors dominated by manufacturing giants like Toyota, Nissan, and Matsushita, systematically discriminated against non-group firms (including those located in the U.S.). Such groups, the U.S. side pointed out, were locked in tight relationships based on cross-shareholding, interlocking boards of directors, and stable business deals that sometimes seemed to defy economic logic. In sum, Treasury delegate Dallara charged, "keiretsu ties foster preferential group trade as the cost of outside suppliers, help facilitate exclusionary business practices, and deter foreign direct investment, especially mergers and acquisitions."[12]

To remedy this problem, the United States demanded that the government of Japan limit cross-shareholding, increase shareholders' rights, and force firms to make public more of their business decisions. Such changes, the U.S. hoped, would make it easier for American firms to get involved in the Japanese market through mergers and acquisitions while at the same time forcing Japanese firms to be more responsive to market forces when deciding on suppliers. Once removed from the protective womb of cross-shareholding and limited disclosure requirements, managers would have a more difficult time defending questionable business deals based on group connections.

Like all of the American demands described above, these demands encountered a storm of criticism. The Japanese business community, professional economists, and government bureaucrats all defended keiretsu arrangements, describing them as economically rational and not overly exclusionary.[13] It was the Americans who should change their own system, the Japanese argued. Thus, in the 1990 SII agreement, the Japanese side insisted that the Americans agree to a clause recognizing "certain aspects of economic rationality of keiretsu relationships" and agreed to make only limited changes in the way it regulated cross-shareholding: the Japanese government would increase JFTC monitoring of intra-keiretsu deals, and if it found that cross-shareholding among keiretsu firms led to restraints on competition, it would limit such practices. Not surprisingly, when the JFTC issued its February 1992 report based on a study of six major keiretsu, it found no preference for intragroup trade within such groups.[14] Consequently, the JFTC has proposed no new restrictions on cross-shareholding.

EXPLAINING THE PATTERN

The above summary of the results of the SII talks emphasized the variation in the degree to which Japanese conceded to U.S. demands in the talks on the five issues. The Americans attempted to apply gaiatsu in all of the issue areas, but it worked only some of the time. How to explain this variation is the central puzzle addressed in this book.

As noted in chapter 2, simple realist explanations do not help us much in explaining this pattern of results because America's relative power advantage over the Japanese was a constant for all five issues. Attempts to invoke "national interest" explanations are also unconvincing. The *Americans'* top priorities, given either a strategic-trade or interest-politics understanding of how nations derive their interests, should have been changes in the AML and the opening of the keiretsu business groups. These were the barriers that were most distorting U.S.-Japan trade patterns (depriving the U.S. of access to Japan's manufactured goods markets), and they were also the ones of greatest concern to politically-powerful groups like the National Association of Manufacturers.[15] And yet these were the areas where the U.S. got the least concessions.

The flip side of this argument, that the pattern of results might have reflected *Japan's* national interest in minimizing its costs of adjustment, is equally weak. While it is difficult to disagree with such an argument in the abstract, that rationale begs the question of how those costs might have been calculated. Was it less of an adjustment for the Japanese to agree to give up a great deal of autonomy in their fiscal policy (by committing to a specific sum of public works spending) than for them to agree to raise the upper limit on surcharges imposed under the AML to the level demanded by the Americans? Ultimately, it is domestic politics that determines how these costs will be calculated, and realists have not yet been able to devise systematic propositions about how this is done.

One other alternative explanation deserves attention. This one, which

I encountered on occasion while presenting this research at public forums, argues that the pattern of SII outcomes may be explained less by "politics" than by Japanese policymakers' desire to make concessions only where they would have a relatively easy time implementing the agreed changes.[16] They avoided making concessions on exclusionary business practices and keiretsu, according to this view, because following through on promises in these areas would require them to confront behavior in the *private sector*. They agreed to changes in the Large Store Law and in the area of public investment, on the other hand, because these were policies directly under the control of the government. Unfortunately, this simple explanation cannot get us very far. In fact, many of the policies at issue during SII in the areas of exclusionary business practices and keiretsu were just as much under government control as, for example, large store regulations. The government could have easily set and enforced limits on cross-shareholding if it wanted to. It could have eased the burden of proof in antitrust cases and written guidelines so that previously tolerated exclusionary practices were clearly made illegal under the Anti-Monopoly Law. It also could have set penalty levels under the law even higher. The reason the government did not agree to any of these changes was not because the policies were impossible to adopt or enforce but because they were strongly opposed by Japanese interest groups, politicians, and bureaucrats. This is what made them "hard" to implement. Similarly, changing the LSL was "easier," not because the regulation was based on government law, but because there was support for liberalization among Japanese bureaucrats, politicians, and interest groups. In other words, "easy" and "hard" were very much a function of "politics."

The puzzle of the SII results thus forces us to confront once again the conclusion we came to in chapter 2: one cannot explain the results of international negotiations without looking at *politics* at both the domestic and international levels. The approach developed in that chapter was more complex than the competing realist and intuitive approaches surveyed briefly above, but, I argue here, also more fruitful. To recall, in that chapter we identified a range of foreign pressure tactics with the potential to deliver better terms in international negotiations. We then identified a list of domestic political conditions which, all things being equal, should favor the use of each of these strategies. Reverberation and threats, we concluded, should produce better terms when domestic actors in the target nation view the intervention of a particular nation in a particular issue area as "legitimate." Target nation linkage should tend to have the most impact when policymaking is highly segmented. Participation expansion should only yield distributional gains when the ranks of uninvolved actors in the target polity include latent supporters of the foreign demand. And alternative specification should be more productive when the proposals a nation makes are already being considered within the policy community and/or address a problem recognized by the policy community.[17]

It is the argument of this book that the explanation for the pattern of SII results lies in the presence and absence of domestic political conditions such as these. When conditions were operative, pressure tactics worked and produced concessions, but when they were not operative, the tactics failed and Japan was able to hold out against concessions. In the remainder of this chapter, I propose to develop this argument in two stages. First, I will examine the Japanese political system as a whole and identify ways in which the system (at least as it operated under the LDP) was broadly conducive to the use of synergistic tactics. As in chapter 3, the focus will be on the impact of domestic institutions and ideas—in this case their role in conditioning the effectiveness of pressure tactics. Only by understanding the role gaiatsu played within the Japanese political system, I propose, can we begin to understand why a nation as powerful as Japan was generally responsive to U.S. pressure. Then, in the final section of the chapter, I will return to the SII talks to show how *issue-specific* domestic political factors conditioned the impact of gaiatsu tactics along the predicted lines and thus can account for the pattern of negotiating outcomes.

The Role of Gaiatsu in Japanese Politics

To understand why Japan has been generally responsive to U.S. pressure over the postwar period, one must begin by examining how the *institutions* and *ideas* of the "1955 System" combined to provide the U.S. with unusual opportunities to employ synergistic tactics. The term "1955 System," of course, refers to the system in place during the prolonged rule of the Liberal Democratic Party (LDP). The party, formed in that year, held power continuously from its birth until it split and was defeated in elections during the summer of 1993. Not coincidentally, the 1950s was also the decade when the Cold War was reaching its peak both outside and inside Japan. Both the length of LDP rule and its association with the Cold War, we will see, structured institutions and ideas in ways that made Japan broadly responsive to gaiatsu tactics. Understanding how gaiatsu worked under the LDP regime is critical to understanding the pattern of SII outcomes because, when those talks were going on, the party was still firmly entrenched in power. As we will see when we get to chapter 9, this discussion also sets the stage for a comparison of how gaiatsu worked during the SII talks with how it worked during the Clinton Framework Talks—when LDP-dominant rule and the Cold War were both history.

INSTITUTIONS OF THE LDP REGIME

The Americans had unusual opportunities to employ gaiatsu under the LDP, first, because of the way the party's extended rule combined with the nation's political institutions to create a rigid, segmented, and often immobile policymaking system. This tendency of the system has been emphasized in much of the work characterizing the LDP-dominated policymaking system as one of "patterned pluralism." The policymaking system was described as "pluralist" because a wide variety of interests were represented through their ties to segments of the LDP and the concerned ministry. It was described as "patterned" because, over almost 40 years of LDP rule, the party had come to delegate its policymaking authority to loyal bureaucrats in the ministries and to policy specialists within its own ranks, to members of "policy tribes" known as *zoku*.[18] The party was content, except in exceptional circumstances, to let its zoku Diet members work out policy decisions with interest groups and bureaucrats in the policy area such that policymaking involved a wide variety of actors but was almost always confined to a "subgovernment" defined by the jurisdictional boundaries of a specific ministry.

"Subgovernments," of course, are not unique to Japan. The term was originally coined in studies of policymaking in the U.S.[19] They came to be particularly entrenched in Japan, however, because the organizational cleavages that divide the nation's bureaucracy were replicated within the LDP's Policy Affairs Research Council, the party's policy organ.[20] Each ministry was paired with a specific PARC division (*bukai*) which served as its champion at budget time and was regularly briefed and consulted on all policy issues in its jurisdiction. Interest groups too had no choice but to tie up closely with a specific ministry and zoku, lacking any incentive to maintain their distance as long as the LDP was the only party that won power. This segmentation, where each zoku was in charge of maintaining relations with a different set of interest groups, suited the LDP because it allowed the party to maintain ties with a wide variety of interest groups. It meant, however, that battles between competing interests, such as conflicts between protectionist farmers and export industries advocating trade liberalization, were fought between subgovernments, with the LDP itself torn and often immobilized by its competing commitments.[21]

While the rigid subgovernmental structure of the policy process served as one source of immobilism in the LDP-dominated system, the multimember electoral system for the Lower House of the Diet contributed further to the problem by making politicians extremely sensitive to interest groups demanding particularistic benefits. This system provided for the election of from two to six members from each district with voters casting a single nontransferable vote for a specific candidate. Any party seeking a majority was therefore forced to put up several candidates in each district, which is exactly what the LDP did. It was then left to these LDP candidates to make sure in any way they could that they got enough of the party vote to secure their election.

Because they could not compete with each other based on different voting records (due to strict party discipline), the only way LDP Dietmen could gain electoral security under this system was to build a "personal support network" (koenkai) which would guarantee them an adequate share of the LDP party vote at election time. And the easiest way to build such a network, many Dietmen found, was to specialize in a specific issue area (such as agriculture, construction, or small business) which would provide them with a loyal bloc of voters and/or a reliable source of political funds. All they had to do was to demonstrate their commitment to their favored pressure group by working to secure for their clients "private goods" in the form of subsidies, tax breaks, and/or regulatory protection from competitors allowing them to earn excess rents.[22]

Such clientelism, not uncommon in democracies of all types, might not have been a large problem had it been pursued only by a few politicians in a few sectors. When such strategies were pursued by hundreds of Dietmen in a wide range of issue areas over an extended period of time, however, they created a system that was extraordinarily biased toward private goods. Over time, whole ministries were sucked into this particularistic system so that such ministries as Agriculture, Construction, Posts and Telecommunications, and even those parts of MITI and MOF dealing with favored LDP clients like small retailers and small banks, came to be strongly oriented toward providing particularistic favors for LDP-favored interest groups.

As one would expect, this extreme bias toward private goods created tensions in the system. As Ramseyer and Rosenbluth note, the under-provision of public goods in such a system will at some point drive away more voters than can be bought with pork and special favors. It was there-fore in the interest of the LDP leadership to make sure that clientelism was reigned in short of this point.[23] That LDP leaders did for a long time succeed in providing public goods when they had to (environmental pro-tection and welfare programs in the 1970s; deficit reduction and more open markets in the 1980s) is for those authors evidence that the system had *within it* the ability to correct for its excesses.[24] Margaret McKean, in another recent survey of this problem, is similarly impressed with the ability of the LDP-dominated system to provide public goods when nec-essary. She describes the LDP as a "peak association" with "long time hori-zons" which encouraged it to anticipate demands of the unorganized masses before they reached the point where voters revolted. McKean also points to the power of other peak organizations such as *Keidanren* (the Federation of Economic Organizations) which, because they represent a wide cross-section of society, call for public goods like fiscal responsibil-ity and freer trade.[25]

While these authors' arguments go part of the way toward explaining the government's periodic adoption of public goods policies, they under-state the rigidities created by the segmented policymaking system described above. LDP leaders may have had an interest in reining in excessive spending, but having delegated a great deal of authority to LDP zoku leaders in each sector, they could not lightly intervene against the wishes of those zoku Diet members. Keidanren may have made pro-nouncements calling for rice liberalization, but these statements were not likely to change anything as long as the decisions on rice policy were being made exclusively by actors inside the agriculture subgovernment. Those who suggest that LDP leaders and "peak organizations" could inter-vene easily to restrain particularistic policies ignore the fact that, except at extraordinary times, the Japanese policymaking system under the LDP resembled a "truncated pyramid." Those in charge of the big picture, like the prime minister, were often powerless to act.[26]

The key modifier in the previous sentence, however, is the phrase "except at extraordinary times." When there was a "crisis," when the dis-tortions created by the particularistic bias of the LDP became so great that they threatened to deprive the party of its Diet majority, LDP leaders could and did intervene in subgovernmental affairs.[27] Environmental problems in Japan had become so serious by the early 1970s that citizens were dying of pollution-related illnesses, so LDP leaders worried about losing the next election to progressive forces were finally able to force MITI and industry to accept limits on pollution. It was only after Japanese deficits ballooned from 4.2 percent of the budget in 1970 to 35.4 percent in 1979 that LDP leaders were able to declare a fiscal emergency and clamp on the budget ceilings.[28] In both of these cases, the media played a prominent role in heightening public awareness of the problems, speaking almost with one voice in representing the concerns of ordinary (largely unorganized) citizens, placing the issues firmly on the political agenda, and giving LDP leaders the "excuse" they needed to impose limits on previously untouchable particularistic policies.

Which brings us to the role of gaiatsu in the policymaking system under the LDP regime. Many of the particularistic policies that resulted from the LDP's insistence on favors for its clients were protectionist: closed markets for agricultural goods; regulatory barriers protecting uncompetitive firms; and bidding rules protecting the construction market, for example. In ordinary times, with policymaking on these issues left to the subgovernments, liberalization of these policies was unlikely. The interests concerned, through their LDP zoku, would simply veto any reform proposal. Even if LDP leaders felt that the inefficiencies resulting from protecting uncompetitive sectors were starting to be a drag on the overall economy, that consumers were being burdened, or that protection was likely to increase tensions with Japan's trading partners, it was impossible for LDP leaders to intervene *until America made specific and insistent demands.* They needed gaiatsu as an *excuse* to break the rigidities of the subgovernmental system.[29]

As in the case of the internal "crises" discussed above, the media played an important role in nourishing the crisis atmosphere in cases involving gaiatsu. As former USTR official Glen Fukushima has noted, Japanese journalists sometimes self-consciously sensationalized American trade demands—exaggerating the degree of American concern, overplaying the threats—in order to give the Japanese government the cover to respond to demands. He quotes a number of journalists as having explained their reasoning this way:

> That's true. You're right that our stories are sensationalized. But it's only because our stories emphasize America's pressure that the government is able to more easily overcome domestic resistance, producing concessions for the Americans. If we didn't exaggerate your demands, the Japanese

government wouldn't be able to concede. For that reason, you should be thankful to the Japanese media for its sensationalized stories.[30]

As we will see, the Japanese media played this role to the hilt during the SII negotiations, providing even notoriously weak Prime Minister Kaifu with the excuse to take a lead in resolving the U.S.-Japan impasse by intervening in policy affairs usually left to status quo-oriented bureaucrats and zoku politicians.[31]

What this discussion emphasizes is that gaiatsu had a specific role to play in the Japanese policymaking system under the LDP regime. It provided party leaders with an excuse to intervene in subgovernmental affairs, to change policies backed by privileged interest groups, bureaucrats, and zoku politicians in the sector, to counteract potentially self-destructive particularism within the system, and to offer public goods policies with appeal to consumers and salaried workers—the great "middle mass" of the Japanese public whose support LDP leaders knew they needed to keep their party in power. Not only LDP leaders, but the media, business leaders, and bureaucrats of internationally oriented ministries like MITI, MOFA, and the Economic Planning Agency similarly recognized the importance of gaiatsu as one of the few forces able to counteract the tendency toward particularistic policy in the LDP-dominated system.[32]

That gaiatsu was accorded this role meant that, under the LDP regime, it was especially well suited for several of the synergistic strategies discussed in chapter 2. First, it was in general well-suited to strategies of target-nation linkage and participation expansion. As we have seen, Japanese policymaking in ordinary times tended to be confined to tightly demarcated subgovernments, but gaiatsu was recognized as an excuse to expand participation and link issues. Issues previously handled by a single ministry were bumped up to the cabinet level where they received the attention of the prime minister. Issues left to zoku Dietmen were given scrutiny by the LDP leadership. Television cameras and print reporters swarmed around issues they had previously neglected, in some cases bringing the weight of public opinion to bear on policy outcomes. And in some cases at least, there were bureaucrats, politicians, business leaders, and reporters eager to take advantage of their expanded opportunities to participate in order to push for policy changes that had been blocked in the absence of gaiatsu. As we will see, this kind of dynamic played a critical role in bringing about concession in the SII issue areas where gaiatsu worked.

The LDP-dominated system, for similar reasons, made it easier for the Americans to shift Japanese win-sets with persuasion and threats. Recognizing that the regime had difficulty dealing with policy change, a wide range of political actors treated gaiatsu as a "necessary evil," a force that had a *legitimate* role to play in the policy process. Both American and Japanese observers have gone so far as to liken the attitude toward gaiatsu in Japan to a drug addiction. Political actors seemed to believe that foreign pressure was a *necessary* ingredient in the mix of conditions required for policy change, and so they waited for U.S. pressure to do the dirty work rather than taking political heat by attempting to mobilize domestic pressure for change (*nai-atsu*).[33] While participants on all sides recognized the long-term damage this kind of "addiction" could do to U.S.-Japan relations, it contributed to a widespread acceptance of foreign pressure under the LDP regime as something Japan could not go without. Persuasive arguments were more likely to be heeded and threats were tolerated with less of a backlash, I propose, because actors in Japan recognized that their political system would spin out of control—centrifugal forces outstripping the centripetal ones—without the corrective influence of American pressure.[34]

The "1955 System" and the Idea of the Cold War

In the last chapter, we saw how the Cold War conditioned attitudes toward Japan in Washington and nurtured "habits of thinking" that out-lasted the international environment which produced them. In much the same way, the "1955 System" froze in place Cold War attitudes in Japan, influencing how U.S.-Japan relations were viewed in Tokyo in ways which, like the institutions discussed above, made Japan generally responsive to U.S. pressure. Here again the issue relates to "legitimacy." As the nation that had defeated, occupied, reformed and democratized it, as the nation that defended it against the Red Menace just miles off Japan's coast, as its patron in most of its dealings with the world, the United States was accorded a tremendous degree of deference by the Japanese—especially in the early years of the Cold War.

It was in these early years that Prime Minister Yoshida Shigeru charted a course for Japan's foreign policy from which it has yet to depart: the Yoshida Doctrine. Japan would not attempt to rearm itself but would depend on the U.S. for its defense, all the while concentrating on economic growth to catch up with the Western powers. For choosing this course, however, Japan had to pay a price. It had to listen carefully to its patron, the U.S., and at times, it even had to be a "sycophant."[35] Even as

Japan became stronger, more able to defend itself and powerful enough to stand up to the U.S., it found it hard to break free of "habits of thinking" nurtured over many years of following the Yoshida line. Again, this tendency for the U.S. and Japan to continue acting as senior partner-junior partner was unhealthy for the relationship, but it did give U.S. pressure a legitimacy that made threats and persuasion easier to use.

The above discussion, focusing on how Japan's overall domestic structure under the LDP made it easier for the U.S. to take advantage of synergistic strategies, helps explain why the Japanese conceded at all during the SII talks. While some might assume that America's "brute power" forced Japan to concede, this discussion suggests that a more subtle process was at work. U.S. pressure was generally effective because the nation's pressure tactics played to a domestic structure with institutions and ideas that made it predisposed to respond to gaiatsu. Were its domestic structure to change, this analysis suggests, we cannot assume that the tactics which worked during SII would have the same effect. We will return to examine this relationship between Japan's domestic structure and its overall responsiveness to foreign pressure in chapter 9 when we look at the Clinton Framework talks.

Gaiatsu and the Pattern of SII Results

At this point, however, we are still left with the question of why the Japanese responded on some SII issues more than on others. The discussion of factors affecting Japan's overall responsiveness to gaiatsu provides us with some clues about which strategies might have been most important, but they cannot on their own account for variation across issues. Fortunately, the logic that helped explain why Japan responded in general to foreign pressure can also help us explain why its response varied. The American negotiators responsible for the SII talks attempted to apply strategies relying on participation expansion, alternative specification, threats, reverberation, and linkage *across the board*. But these strategies produced concessions only part of the time. As we will see, the pattern of Japan's response corresponded closely to the presence and absence of domestic political conditions identified earlier as being supportive of these various tactics.

PARTICIPATION EXPANSION

American negotiators knew from previous experience about Japan's segmented policymaking process, and as we saw in chapter 3, they planned the SII format expressly to take advantage of opportunities to influence policy outcomes by bringing previously excluded players into the game. The Treasury Department wanted MITI brought in to help overcome MOF resistance to reflation, and Williams of USTR had a plan to bring Japanese consumers into a process dominated by organized interests with a stake in the status quo.

The American negotiators were correct. Many of the policies targeted in their list of 200 demands were classic examples of the kinds of particularistic politics protected by the small group of actors who dominated the policymaking process in the issue area. For example, decisions regarding the Large Store Law tended to be dominated by the regulatory agency (MITI), retail interest groups, and LDP politicians with close ties to the retail industry. The collusive bidding process for construction projects, tagged as an "exclusionary business practice" by the Americans, was closely guarded by the Ministry of Construction, construction interests, and the members of the LDP construction zoku. Another SII issue, public investment, was different from the above in that it was not protected by a collusive triad, but policy in this area too was dominated by limited elite participation. In fact, a single bureau of the MOF (the Budget Bureau) dominated fiscal policymaking.[36] At the start of the SII process, therefore, there was ample room for participation expansion in most of the SII issue areas.

The Americans achieved a significant participation expansion effect, first, merely by putting specific issues on the SII agenda. Many of these issues were considered "purely domestic" matters before SII, involving only those domestic political elites who were part of the subgovernment. By placing them on the SII agenda, the U.S. guaranteed that they would henceforth be considered "U.S.-Japan issues." This change in issue-definition by itself promised to involve a host of new elite actors. Ministries with a stake in the overall U.S.-Japan relationship (like MITI) could now rightfully demand a say about policies previously dominated by MOF, MOC or MAFF. LDP leaders previously lacking an excuse to intervene in subgovernmental affairs could declare a "crisis" and bring their weight to bear on a policy outcome.

The U.S. negotiators were not content, however, to sit back and wait for this process of participation expansion to build up momentum on its own. Whenever they could, they tried to help the process along. They did this, first, by repeatedly quoting from Japanese government reports critical of established policy in an effort to bolster advocates of reform within the Japanese government. At the first formal SII negotiating session in Tokyo on September 4–5, the Americans repeatedly cited Japanese government documents to support their case, mentioning the Maekawa Report at least six times and other reports as well. Treasury's Dallara, for example, cited a publication by the Japanese Economic Planning Agency (EPA) which documented how the nation's sewerage connections, phone connections, and paved road ratios were all well below OECD averages—backing up his point that Japan needed to invest more in public infrastructure. Later in the same session, State's McCormack pointed out that the Maekawa Commission and a variety of other government reports had called for the liberalization of distribution system regulations.[37] After one meeting later in the year in which his agency's reports had been cited repeatedly by the Americans, EPA delegate Unno Tsuneo jokingly complained to Commerce undersecretary Michael Farren that he didn't know how to respond when the U.S. side kept quoting statistics and using arguments straight out of his agency's publications. Farren replied, "You should come and sit on our side of the table."[38]

While seeking to take advantage of bureaucratic rivalries, the U.S. also devoted extensive effort to a campaign to bring LDP leaders into the policy process.[39] This phase of their strategy picked up momentum especially after the third formal SII negotiating session in February failed to produce the concessions the U.S. delegates had hoped to see. The U.S.agreed to put off this meeting for a month when it became clear that the Japanese side would not be able to agree to any significant concession prior to the Japanese general elections, held February 18. With these elections out of the way and the LDP fresh from an unexpectedly comfortable victory, the Americans had hoped the Japanese would be more receptive to their recently delivered list of 200 demands. Instead, they got little more than another round of excuses: MITI insisted it could not abolish the Large Store Law; MOF fumed at the temerity of the Americans, with their monstrous budget deficits, telling them what to do with their fiscal policy; and the JFTC insisted that it saw no need for Japan to set tighter limits on cross-shareholding or to revise the Anti-Monopoly Law.[40] After the meeting, Williams charged in his comments to the press that Japanese officials had nothing to offer but "a defense of the status quo."[41]

Within hours of that meeting, Bush had placed a call to Prime Minister Kaifu. Could he meet, on short notice, in Palm Springs? What ensued was the most hastily arranged U.S.-Japan summit meeting in history. The two leaders met March 2 and, amidst palm trees and sun, declared afterward that they were intent on resolving the two nations' differences. As Kaifu put it, "I am determined to firmly tackle structural reforms [in] Japan as one of the top priorities of my new cabinet with a view to improving the quality of Japanese life." Bush was equally upbeat: "We got everything out of this meeting that we had hoped for."[42]

Upon his return to Tokyo, Kaifu quickly announced that he was setting up a cabinet-level task force charged with putting together the government's response to the Americans' SII demands. He urged the group to approach their task with a positive attitude, noting that many of the U.S. demands were also in Japan's interest.[43] The initial reaction of many LDP backbenchers, however, was critical. They worried that Kaifu had promised too much in Palm Springs, and they insisted that he avoid concessions on the Large Store Law and Anti-Monopoly Law. As one LDP Diet member put it, "The American demands calling for the abolition of the LSL and strengthening of the AML present us with greater difficulties than the consumption tax [an issue that cost the LDP dearly during the 1989 Upper House elections]. The only issue on which we can respond is the demand for increased spending on public investment."[44]

Kaifu, without a strong base of his own inside the party, was not well-positioned to overcome this opposition. He had been chosen as Prime Minister the previous summer only because he was one of the few LDP members of his generation who had not taken discounted shares from the Recruit corporation, and he had only recently angered some of the most powerful men in the party by refusing to name any members tainted by scandals to his cabinet. His faction of the party, the smallest, had only 25 Lower House seats.

Well aware that Kaifu was unlikely to be able to overcome bureaucratic and back-bench resistance on his own, the Bush team spent the month of March calling on other LDP leaders as well. On March 12, Bush and Baker each spent a full hour with former Prime Minister Takeshita, urging him to carry back to Tokyo the message that substantial concessions would be required before Bush could sell an SII deal to Congress. It seems that Baker pressed Takeshita especially hard on the issue of public investment where, it was hoped, the former Finance Minister could use his connections to convince MOF of the need to accept a deal.[45] Over the next several weeks, the U.S. kept up this pressure as Treasury Secretary Brady met with Finance Minister Hashimoto in Los Angeles and as Commerce Secretary Mosbacher met with a number of LDP influentials in Tokyo.[46]

While the U.S. had sought to take advantage of ministerial rivalries and the intervention of LDP politicians in previous trade negotiations,[47] the final part of the administration's participation expansion strategy was more novel. This time, the Americans wanted to enlist the Japanese consumer as an ally as well—a tactic that became obvious at the first negotiating session in Tokyo.[48] Holding press conferences at the U.S. Embassy at the end of each day of talks, the Americans sought to take their case over the heads of Japan's bureaucrats. "We are not here just to help the U.S.," USTR delegate Williams said. "The Structural Impediments Initiative is . . . also a great benefit to the Japanese people." Emphasizing that many of the proposals the U.S. was raising were drawn from Japanese government documents like the Maekawa Report, he added, "SII is not [an idea] that we came up with; it was made in Japan by Japanese."[49] Interestingly, the media seems to have been aware of exactly what the Americans were trying to do. "The U.S. officials apparently came to Tokyo with a new approach . . . : through the news media, they appealed to consumers to back their proposals to change Japan's market structure."[50]

As the year of talks wore on, it became clear that the media were not merely passive observers of this U.S. strategy. On many issues, they were on America's side, and they were intent on using their influence to abet the U.S. effort to give voice to Japanese consumers. In the month that elapsed between Kaifu's trip to Palm Springs and the interim settlement the first week of April, for example, *Asahi shimbun* ran a total of six editorials supportive of the American position. Kaifu should use the gaiatsu of SII, one editorial suggested, to overcome resistance to change in the bureaucracy and party and pursue his promise to improve the livelihoods of ordinary Japanese.[51] "The Anti-Monopoly Law should be strengthened," another was titled.[52] A third *Asahi* editorial, after reviewing all that was wrong with the Large Store Law, concluded that the government should consider "revising or even abolishing the law."[53] A fourth backed up the Americans on their demands for increased public investment.[54] A fifth called for increased land-holding taxes as a means of reining in the land price spiral—another American demand.[55] And the last, summing up a theme developed in the series, reiterated the paper's view that the Americans' SII demands were generally in the Japan's own interest. LDP politicians were going around saying we have to do this because of gaiatsu, the editorial noted, but this was merely evidence of the LDP's "abdication of responsibility."[56]

The power of the media in Japan should not be underestimated. The *Asahi* and four other dailies based in Tokyo enjoy huge national circulation and often speak as if with one voice.[57] This tendency reflects in part the fact that most reporters are based, not at newspaper offices, but at ministry "press clubs" where they interact extensively with each other, exchanging their latest tips and trading information about how they plan to pitch their stories. Often, they are quite self-conscious about their power. As one NHK reporter told me, he and others at his network realized that the topics being discussed as part of the SII talks were "too important to be left to bureaucrats." They gave the issue extra prominent coverage, making sure that the issues being discussed in SII "were thrashed out in a major way in public." They broadcast all press conferences related to SII in their entirety, led their evening news shows with stories about SII for days at a time, and ran a six-hour miniseries-length documentary on the talks shortly after the interim SII report was released in April.[58]

The print media were just as thorough in their treatment. Between September 1989 and December 1991, Japanese weeklies and monthlies listed in the Japanese Diet Library data bank published 199 stories with "SII" in their titles and certainly many more that touched on the subject in their stories.[59] Over a similar period, the three leading dailies ran 196 news stories and 33 editorials on SII. Of these news stories, 43 percent of them were on the front page, and of the stories that were biased one way or another, 80 percent presented only "pro-SII" views.[60]

That the Americans' efforts to reach out to Japanese consumers and the media's amplification of their message has some effect is suggested by public opinion polls that showed more than 80 percent of the public supported at least some of the American demands and that 86 percent agreed that the government should "respond positively" to American demands.[61] Particular noteworthy are the figures for the share of this latter group which felt concessions should be made "because [the changes demanded] are related to improvements in the quality of life within Japan, because they are problems for Japan itself." Over half felt this way while only 42 percent felt concessions should be made primarily because of the importance of maintaining good U.S.-Japan relations. These last figures in particular suggest that the U.S. message got through to average Japanese citizens.[62]

It is more difficult to establish how Americans were able to bring this public support to bear on negotiation outcomes. U.S. delegates bragged about the support they had within Japan in their negotiating sessions with their Japanese counterparts. They also on occasion dramatized this fact, as when U.S. Ambassador Michael Armacost hosted a dinner for both delegations following the negotiating session in February and made a point of inviting, in addition to the Japanese delegates, a number of prominent Japanese economists and businessmen who had helped the Americans draw up their list of demands.[63] Probably the most important way in which the U.S. was able to bring public support to bear, however, was by providing Prime Minister Kaifu with a reason and power to intervene in favor of U.S. demands.

As noted above, Kaifu lacked support within his party. His only power resource, it was often noted, was the high approval ratings he enjoyed with the general public. Japanese leaders had in the past been motivated to intervene in favor of U.S. interests by their desire to win public approval through their skillful handling of U.S.-Japan relations. By winning the public over to their side on many SII issues, the U.S. gave Kaifu an extra reason to stake his cabinet's prestige on a pledge at Palm Springs to "firmly tackle" the challenge of bringing the SII talks to a successful conclusion. As one newspaper put it, "Washington succeeded in winning Kaifu to the American side by making friends with the consumer, the premier's de facto power base."[64]

The Americans' strategy of participation expansion worked on many SII issues because domestic conditions generally conformed with the hypotheses advanced in chapter 2. There was room for expanding participation because most issues were dealt with by a narrow elite, and in many cases, there was latent support for U.S. positions outside this privileged group. As we will see when we look at the specific case of public investment in chapter 5, there was support for these U.S. demands from other agencies (especially MITI and the EPA). At several negotiating sessions, this conflict among Japanese delegates broke out into the open as MOF protests that they couldn't discuss macroeconomic policy and that they couldn't commit to specific public investment figures were disputed by delegates representing other agencies. The U.S. also enjoyed the support of LDP leaders and backbenchers on this issue. When these advocates of increased infrastructure spending were finally able to wrest control of decision-making from MOF, therefore, the outcome favored the U.S.

The story was similar on the Large Store Law issue, although this time it was the support the U.S. enjoyed among the Japanese public that helped Kaifu overcome the opposition of LDP Dietmen who for many years had prevented liberalization of the law. The *Nikkei* explained the results of the talks on this issue as follows:

> Washington has implemented the perfect diplomatic negotiations in that it won the Japanese public to its cause. A case in point: the LSL. Washington raised the banner of "consumer benefits" and succeeded in isolating Japanese government agencies which all to often represent business interests in conflict with Japanese public opinion.[65]

Kaifu, sensing this public mood, took advantage of the U.S.-Japan crisis to intervene in a usually subgovernmental issue area and bring about a settlement that went against the interests of the party's small retailer supporters. As we will see when we look at this issue in more detail in chapter 6, MITI too was eager to use the opportunity afforded by SII to launch a campaign to liberalize and modernize Japan's notoriously inefficient retail sector.

On other issues, however, the Americans did not have the kind of latent support they enjoyed in these first two issue areas. On land, the problem was that the issue was already so politicized by several years of runaway price increases that there was little room for the U.S. to affect policy outcomes by expanding participation. On keiretsu and the Anti-Monopoly Law, the problem was that there was scant sympathy for the American demands.

This lack of support was particularly noteworthy on the keiretsu issue. If you refer back to the *Asahi* editorials quoted above, you will note that none of them backed up the American position on this issue. And note that the *Asahi*, as the most left-leaning of the major dailies, was the most likely to sympathize with U.S. criticisms of Japanese big business. In fact, in all of my reading of media and government publications on this issue, I found none that backed up the American call for limits on cross-shareholding or increased shareholder rights. Even the Fair Trade Commission, the antitrust watchdog agency, which in the end sympathized somewhat with the U.S. demands on the Anti-Monopoly Law, never expressed support for the U.S. demands on keiretsu. Because of this absence of support, I propose, U.S. pressure tactics which worked in other issue areas did not work at all on keiretsu.

On the issue of antitrust, there was limited support for some U.S. demands. Note the *Asahi* editorial supportive of the call for tougher antitrust enforcement. Other newspapers, however, came out explicitly against these demands, questioning in particular the demand for a more effective private damage remedy system to give firms extra reason to avoid collusive practices. The *Yomiuri*, for example, singled out this demand as an example of one that it felt might cause more problems than it would solve.[66] USTR negotiator Linn Williams admits that public support was weaker on this issue. "On the things that affected the general public directly (public investment, the Large Store Law, land prices), we got a lot of support," he noted, "but on stuff that they sort of had an idea about but it didn't really affect them directly (like antitrust), we did okay with the general public, but nothing like the others."[67] Through their high-profile campaign, the Americans do seem to have sparked greater interest in antitrust issues inside Japan, with possible long-term implications, but they did not enjoy enough support to use participation expansion as a tactic for extracting immediate and significant policy concessions. We will return to this issue in chapter 8.

Overall, participation expansion was certainly the most important tactic employed by the Americans during the SII talks. They devoted extensive thought to the strategy, and were able to use it on some issues to extract significant concessions. Part of the explanation for why the U.S. was unable to extract concessions uniformly across the SII issues lies, however, in the more limited nature of the support they enjoyed on issues like keiretsu and antitrust.

ALTERNATIVE SPECIFICATION

In chapter 2, we drew on John Kingdon's model of the policymaking process—with its emphasis on the importance of the process through which policy proposals are generated—in proposing that international negotiators might be able to improve the terms of their deals by influencing the way this process proceeds in a target country. American pressure, we suggested, might be able to tilt the policy debate in its favor by highlighting specific policy proposals that favored American interests. In considering how domestic politics might condition the effectiveness of this strategy, we hypothesized that it would prove more effective when foreign proposals are already being considered within the policy community and address problems already recognized as a priority by the policy community. The pattern of SII outcomes suggests that this kind of strategy can actually make a difference and confirms the above prediction about the conditions favoring its use.

The strategy of alternative specification had the greatest impact on the land policy issue-area. This was an issue very much on the domestic policy agenda even before the Americans made it an SII issue. Prime Minister Nakasone had set up a cabinet-level advisory council to deal with the issue in 1987, and the problem had become more manifest in the intervening years. Yet, there was little agreement about which policies ought to be adopted to address the problem. For some, the land price explosion was primarily a result of speculation encouraged by a soft monetary policy. The solution was to raise interest rates, raise taxes on short-term profits from speculation, and place stricter regulations on land transactions and land use. For others, the problem was more deeply rooted in tax and regulatory policies that artificially restricted the supply of land.

The Americans who stepped into this fray had little chance, as argued above, of influencing the result by bringing in new participants and thereby altering the balance of power. The results suggest, however, that they were able to influence the result with ideas. The Americans did not, of course, invent solutions to Japan's land price problem. They consulted with experts in the Japanese land policy community. In particular, they favored the advice of reform economists like Noguchi Yukio and Hasegawa Tokunosuke, who argued for far-reaching changes in tax and regulatory policies designed to bring urban farmland and idle corporate land holdings onto the market and to encourage the more efficient use of property. As we will see in the more detailed discussion in chapter 7, the Americans were able to tilt the results of the policy debate in their favor by highlighting the proposals of these reform economists. Prior to SII, the Ministry of Finance was still firm in resisting a tax reform-based solution to the land price problem. By the time the first year of SII talks was over, however, they had set up a special Land Tax Subcommittee of their Tax Commission and named Noguchi and Hasegawa as expert members. In the end, the Americans gave just enough added credence to these economists' ideas to get some of them enacted.[68]

The limits of the above strategy, confirming the hypotheses advanced above, can be seen again in the keiretsu issue area. In this area as well, the Americans had specific policy proposals. They wanted the Japanese government to set limits on cross-shareholding and to revise its regulations to toughen disclosure requirements and increase shareholder rights. These were not ideas circulating in any Japanese policy community, however, and the Americans made no attempt to link them to any recognizable Japanese "problem." Given these less favorable conditions, the strategy that had worked in the land policy area was doomed to fail.

As with the strategy of participation expansion, therefore, this discussion of how the strategy of alternative specification played out in the SII talks helps explain why gaiatsu worked in some cases but not others. The strategy was, in effect, applied across the board, but issue-specific domestic politics determined whether or not it would be effective.

THREATS AND TARGET-NATION LINKAGE

The remaining two tactics discussed in this chapter, in contrast to participation expansion and alternative specification, help explain why the Japanese made at least some concessions on *all* of the SII issues.[69] Even in the keiretsu issue area, the Japanese agreed to change a few policies along the lines called for by the Americans. In antitrust, they agreed to raise statutory limits on surcharges and criminal fines under the Anti-Monopoly Law. Such concessions, even in the absence of the conditions supportive of the more effective strategies of participation expansion and alternative specification, can be seen as resulting from the set of strategies discussed here.

Gaiatsu, in the form of threats and target-nation linkage, produced limited concessions across the board because these tactics depended for their effectiveness not on issue-specific domestic politics in Japan, but on broader domestic conditions which favored their application in U.S.-Japan relations. The effectiveness of threats, I argued in chapter 2, depends in part on whether the intervention of a particular nation in the affairs of another is seen as legitimate. Because the innate immobilism of the LDP-dominated political system led many in Japan to view gaiatsu as a "necessary evil" and because the Cold War had nurtured deferential attitudes toward America on the part of Japanese elites, U.S. threats were treated to some degree as a legitimate intervention, and Japan thus responded by making at least some concessions to U.S. demands in all five of the SII issue areas.

Target nation issue-linkage, readers may recall from chapter 2, works when foreign pressure can take advantage of organized support from within a target polity by making demands for concessions in two or more issue areas and then relying on forces in each segment to pressure other segments in order to avoid having to make more than their share of compromises. Such a strategy, I hypothesized, would be more likely to prove effective in highly segmented policymaking systems. As the discussion of the Japanese policymaking system earlier in this chapter made clear, one can hardly conceive of a system more segmented than Japan's system of patterned pluralism. Because the system as a whole was conducive to the use of this strategy, it too helped produce at least some concessions from the Japanese on all of the sii issues.

The role of each of these tactics can be seen in the course of the first year of sii negotiations. Even as the Americans were trying to portray themselves as the friend of the Japanese consumer, they never abandoned the leverage they could derive from old-fashioned threats. During the first two negotiating sessions in the fall of 1989, the Americans drummed home the message that they needed concrete results by the time of the spring interim report.[70] Senator Max Baucus, back in Washington, made sure it was taken seriously by talking about how he might introduce legislation to require listing under Super 301 if sii didn't work.[71] And when Carla Hills made her debut in Tokyo in October, she stressed that the administration needed a "blueprint" on reform by spring and a "down payment" before the first year of talks were over—so that progress could be evaluated before the administration had to make a decision about whether or not to relist Japan under Super 301.[72] The message to the Japanese was clear: unless the Japanese made enough concessions, the U.S. would relist Japan and begin moving toward economic sanctions.

As if this threat were not enough, American delegates raised the prospect that U.S.-Japan *security* relations might be affected by Japan's response to the sii demands at the negotiating session in February 1990. At this meeting, Williams revealed to his Japanese counterparts that Defense Secretary Richard Cheney, prior to a recent visit to Japan, had dropped by the usTR office to get a report on how the sii talks were proceeding and had stayed for a full hour. It was the first time, Williams claimed, that a Defense Secretary had expressed such interest in the progress of economic negotiations.[73]

The American's strategy of target nation issue-linkage was implicit in the whole multi-agency design of the sii format. U.S. negotiators knew from previous experience that the Japanese ministries were bitter rivals, always eager to force their counterparts to bear the brunt of concessions, and they hoped to draw them into an internecine battle by making far-reaching demands across the sii issue areas and leaving it to MOF, MITI, and MOFA to fight over who should concede the most.[74] By February, these machinations were beginning to have effects. The Japanese had discovered that sii really was going to have to produce bloody concessions in order to satisfy Congress, and each ministry struggled to make sure its own blood was not the only one shed. Japanese reporting on what was going on inside the ministries suggests that the pressure on MOF to concede on public investment at this point was partly the result of MITI's efforts to get MOF to share in the pain of adjusting its policies. The focus on abolishing the Large Store Law was partly the result of MOFA and MOF's attempts to make sure MITI paid a price.[75]

While it is difficult to ascribe any specific concession to either of the two American strategies discussed in this section, the analysis emphasizes how both tended to have broad, cross-issue effects relying on domestic political conditions, which contributed to their effectiveness across-the-board. That the Japanese agreed to make *some* changes even on issues where there was not substantial domestic support, this discussion suggests, can be attributed to American threats and efforts to take advantage of interministerial rivalry.

Conclusions

At the beginning of this chapter, I noted that the proposition that gaiatsu has the power to influence Japanese public policy is widely accepted. The puzzle is why gaiatsu proves more effective in some cases than in others— why it produces an uneven response even when it is applied uniformly. The key to solving this puzzle, I proposed in this chapter, lies in disaggregating gaiatsu into its component parts: gaiatsu as participation expansion; gaiatsu as threats; and so on. Once one appreciates how each of these types of foreign pressure works differently and is conditioned in unique ways by domestic politics, one can begin to understand why Japan came through with significant concessions on some issues but not on others.

In the case of the SII talks, most of the variation in the degree to which the Japanese agreed to concessions across the five SII issue areas can be explained by how issue-specific political conditions supported the use of strategies of gaiatsu as participation expansion and gaiatsu as alternative specification. Whereas the Americans were able to draw on latent support for their demands in the case of their Large Store Law and public investment demands and on support for their land policy proposals within the Japanese policy community, they were unable to take advantage of such conditions in the case of their antitrust and keiretsu demands. The U.S. was able to convince the Japanese to make some (more limited) concessions in these latter two areas, however, because gaiatsu as threats and gaiatsu as target nation issue-linkage depended on domestic political conditions that favored these strategies across-the-board rather than on an issue-specific basis.

Having disaggregated gaiatsu in this way, however, it is time now to put it back together. Where foreign pressure worked during sii, it did so because several of these strategies were operating simultaneously and in mutually supportive ways. Japan agreed to make changes in its Large Store Law because conditions favored the use of threats, linkage, and participation expansion all at the same time. Efforts to expand participation by making the lsl the subject of U.S.-Japan negotiations probably would not have produced concessions without the threat of Super 301 in the background. The contrary example is provided again by the cases of antitrust and keiretsu. Here conditions favored threats and linkage, as with all of the sii issues, but without latent support for U.S. demands, the Japanese concessions were vague and ultimately implemented in ways that do not constitute significant policy change.

To fully appreciate how gaiatsu interacted with the ongoing policy process in the sii issue areas, one must look at the whole: the policy process before sii, the U.S. demands, the way these demands reverberated inside Japan, and the policy changes actually implemented. In the next set of four chapters, I take each sii issue in turn and look at it as a "whole."

5 THE PUBLIC INVESTMENT ISSUE

On what should Japan spend its public investment budget? The government official had before him all of the options: more on public housing, more on roads, more on sewers. . . . The list went on and on. Sewers. That was the answer. Japan should concentrate its funds especially on sewers in an effort to rapidly increase the number of homes connected to underground sewage systems. Who was the official who came to this conclusion? A junior staffer with the *American* Council of Economic Advisors.

Why should an American official care how much Japan spent on sewers? What business was it of the U.S. to tell the Japanese it should spend more on this type of public investment? Observers on both sides of the Pacific sometimes puzzled at the irreverence of it all, but there was an economic rationale behind this American demand. And by the end of the first year of the SII talks, the U.S. had employed enough gaiatsu to convince the Japanese that they should alter their public investment policy, including an increase in their budget for sewers. This chapter looks at how the U.S. demands on public investment played off of the domestic politics of this issue area in ways that made it possible for America to force changes in Japanese policy. We will look, first, at the background to the debate that was going on in 1989 about whether Japan should spend more on public investment; then at the American demands; and then at how these demands, and the American gaiatsu tactics, took advantage of opportunities to influence the policymaking process in Japan and brought about a late retreat by the long-resistant Ministry of Finance at the end of the first year of sii talks. In the final section, we will then review the implementation of the Japanese sii commitments in this issue area.

The Public Investment Debate in Japan Before SII

Despite the seeming absurdity of America's telling Japan how to spend its public investment funds, this topic was in many ways the most "traditional" of the five sii issue areas. The United States has expressed its views about Japan's macroeconomic policy through diplomatic channels on a regular basis ever since the end of the U.S. postwar occupation. Initially, American concern was motivated by the fear that economic weakness in Japan would make it an unreliable ally in the Cold War fight with the Soviets, but at least since the late 1960s, the U.S. has been driven to intervene by the fact that its own economic well-being (American trade deficits, exchange rates, interest rates, inflation rates, and unemployment rates) have been to some degree influenced by fiscal and monetary policies pursued in Tokyo. Since the mid-1970s, furthermore, the process of consultations on macroeconomic policy has been formally organized through regular meetings of finance officials of the G-5 (and later G-7) and through the annual Western Summits.

This ongoing process of consulations had become particularly heated on two previous occasions. In 1977–1978, the United States pressured Japan and Germany into accepting economic growth targets that forced Japan to ratchet up its reliance of deficit-financing bonds. And again in 1986 and 1987, after the appreciation of the yen engineered with the Plaza Accords slowed down the Japanese economy, the U.S. again pressured Japan to adopt supplemental budgets aimed at stimulating growth in domestic demand. In many ways, the Americans' public investment demands during the sii talks were just the latest in this ongoing series of run-ins stemming from from the need to coordinate U.S. and Japanese macro policies.

America has long cared about Japanese macroeconomic policy because of the effects Japanese fiscal and monetary policy can have on U.S. trade balances (and indirectly on American economic growth rates) through a mechanism know as the savings-investment (or S-I) balance. Because of the operation of this mechanism, nations with S-I surpluses necessarily run trade surpluses while nations with S-I deficits necessarily run trade deficits.[1] Americans worried about U.S. trade deficits thus have every reason to pay attention to Japanese macro policies which influence that nation's savings and investment rates.

In the early 1980s, when the Japanese government was running annual public sector budget *deficits* on the order of 4 to 5 percent of GDP (see figure 5.1), its fiscal policy served to offset high private sector savings rates and thus, by reducing the savings surplus, served to restrain the size of the nation's overall (and bilateral) trade surpluses. Over the decade, however, the Japanese government gradually succeeded in reducing the size of its fiscal deficits to the point that it began to run *surpluses* starting in 1987. As figure 5.1 shows, by 1989 when the SII was underway, the Japanese government was running a surplus of 2.5 percent. By that time, rapidly growing private sector investment was consuming a growing proportion of Japanese savings, enough so that the nation would have registered a savings deficit were it not for the government, but because of the nation's fiscal policy, Japan ended up with a savings surplus amounting to 2 percent of GDP (with an equivalent current account surplus).

American government officials intent on tackling the macro sources of the U.S.-Japan bilateral imbalances therefore focused quite naturally on Japanese fiscal policy as the most important source of the problem on the Japanese side. According to one economic simulation, Japanese fiscal policies in 1980–85 increased Japan's surplus by 1.9 GNP percentage points while worsening America's deficit by 0.2 points. It has to be

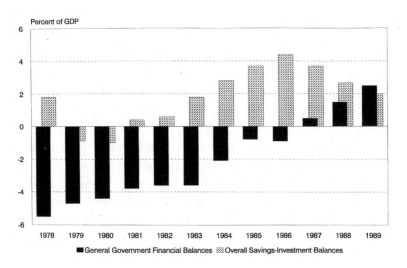

FIGURE 5.1   Government Financial Balances and Overall S-I Balances in Japan, 1978-89

Sources: OECD, Economic Outlook 56 (December 1994) and IMF, International Finance Statistics

emphasized that this simulation (and others) have demonstrated that *American* fiscal policy over this period was an even greater contributor to the imbalance, but the data made it clear that Japanese policy itself was important enough to make a difference.[2]

The question for U.S. officials was how best to attack Japan's fiscal policy. What the U.S. wanted was for Japan to engage in deficit-spending, or at least for it to run smaller surpluses, but coming from a government known world-wide for its inability to deal with its own very real budget deficit problem, a demand to "be a debtor like us" did not promise to have much appeal. Given that the Japanese economy was in the midst of an economic boom, the U.S. also could not appeal for deficit-funded stimulus packages (as it had in 1986–87). The strategy these officials hit upon was therefore to call for sharply higher levels of public investment spending by the Japanese government.

Spending on infrastructure projects like roads, airports, land conservation, and sewers is treated as "investment" in the Japanese budget process and is financed partially with construction bonds—the logic being that such spending provides benefits to society over many years. Therefore, by pressuring the Japanese to increase levels of public investment, U.S. officials could indirectly pressure them to issue more bonds. Instead of having to point to abstract figures for things like "general government financial balances" and making weak arguments for more deficit spending, the U.S. could point to "real" problems like the small size of Japanese homes, the limited park space, and the low level of sewage connections.

There was a great deal of data to support the U.S. argument that Japan lagged in its levels of social infrastructure. Measured against averages for other major advanced industrial nations, Japan had only 50 percent of the sewers, 10 percent of the park space, 32 percent of the expressways, and 63 percent of the housing floor space—even though Japan's per capita GNP was 131% that of these countries (see table 5.1). Other evidence of the need for greater investment in infrastructure was more anecdotal but just as telling: having found that older Japanese men (ages 30–50) were physically stronger and more athletic than teenagers, the Ministry of Education suggested that the explanation lay in the grueling commutes which provided daily exercise for salaried workers. Such workers, the ministry noted, had to weave in and out of rush-hour crowds and had to struggle to maintain their balance while standing on trains frequently carrying more than twice their capacity.[3]

TABLE 5.1

Japanese Social Infrastructure Levels Relative to
Those in Other Advanced Industrialized Nations

Category	Japan	U.S.	France	U.K.	Germany
Sewers (connection rate)	40%	73%	64%	95%	91%
City Parks (m^2/person)	2.5 (Tokyo)	19.2 (N.Y.)	12.2 (Paris)	30.4 (London)	37.4 (Bonn)
Expressways (km/10,000 cars)	0.91	4.55	2.59	1.26	2.85
Housing (m^2 floorspace/person)	25.2	60.9	31.2	35.2	32.0

Source: Ministry of Construction, Nichibei kozo mondai kyogi to kensetsu gyosei (The U.S.-Japan Structural Problem Talks and Construction Administration (Tokyo: Taisei Shuppansha, 1990), p. 52. Data are not all for the same year: most Japanese data is for 1988 and 1989. Data for other countries is for years ranging from 1976 (for park space in London and New York) to 1988.

Neither could these deficiencies be blamed entirely on Japan's status as a poor island nation with a limited land area. The European countries, with similarly limited land, had more spacious housing, much larger parks, and less crowded public rail systems. While the causes of Japan's housing-size deficiency will be discussed in more detail in chapter 7, it is interesting to note that the average newly constructed Japanese dwelling actually *shrank* between the years 1980 and 1989.[4] Over that period, the size of dwellings built with the help of public funds increased significantly—demonstrating that public policy *could* be used to provide Japanese with larger homes—but government simply did not build enough of these homes to make a difference in the overall average.[5]

What was required, the Americans emphasized, was that the Japanese government devote more resources to social infrastructure investment. In the late 1970s, Japan had devoted more than 10 percent of its GNP to "public investment,"[6] but the government's fiscal austerity drive in the decade of the 1980s had steadily reduced this percentage to a low of 7.6 percent of GNP in 1989 (see figure 5.2). This austerity drive had cut, in particular, into central government expenditures on public works (a component of the broader category of "public investment"). From 1981 until 1983, public works spending was frozen, and then from 1984 until 1987, it was held to "negative ceilings" which forced the various min-

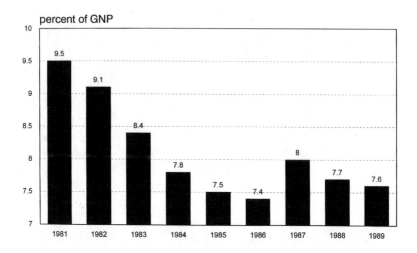

FIGURE 5.2 Japanese Public Investment, 1981-1989

Source: Based on data in Kensetsu keizai kenkyūjō, Nihon keizai to kōkyō tōshi: 23 (The Japanese Economy and Public Investment: 23) (July, 1994), based on EPA, National Income Accounts

istries to absorb actual declines in funding levels. Only in 1987 were the restrictive policies lifted, and then only for that single budget year, as public works spending was used to counteract the effects of the Plaza Accords.[7] Even as the sii was being negotiated, the government was in the process of imposing further cuts in public works spending.[8]

The evidence of social infrastructure deficiencies, combined with the data showing that the government was devoting less and less to fixing the problems, gave American negotiators a basis from which to argue that Japan ought to increase its public investment spending. As we know, however, international negotiations like sii are rarely won with the force of argument. In this case, as with all of the other sii issues, the outcome would be determined by how America's demands and tactics interacted with the domestic politics of the issue area. And, with literally trillions of dollars of public works and Japan's macroeconomic policy at stake, the forces involved in the politics of this issue area were not the kind that could be easily pushed around.

The Americans who entered into the debate over macroeconomic policy and public investment in 1989 were stepping into the middle of a domestic debate that had been going on for a long time. The best place for us to pick up the story is perhaps the mid-1980s. Until this time, there had been a fairly broad consensus among Japanese political elites that the nation's unusually high levels of public works spending and the runaway budget deficits of the late 1970s had to be curtailed. Following the oil shock of 1973–1974, Japanese politicians had been slow to adapt to the slower growth in revenues that came with the end of double-digit economic growth. Instead of restricting spending, they added new health and pension programs and embarked on an infrastructure-building binge, forcing the government to issue "deficit bonds" for the first time in 1976 and pushing up the share of the budget financed by borrowing above 30 percent (see figure 5.3). On top of this, in 1978, the Fukuda Administration committed— under pressure from the United States—to use fiscal policy in an effort to turn Japan's economy into a "locomotive" for world growth, pushing up borrowing levels to a high of 35.4 percent in 1979.[9]

Pressed by business community leaders who feared that Japan was destined to catch the "British disease" unless it reined in its excessive spending habits, the Japanese government decided shortly after the above episode that it had to impose some discipline on its spending habits. An Administrative Reform Council (*Rinchō*) was set up, strict budget ceilings were imposed, and the government committed to a series of targets: it aimed to stop issuing deficit bonds by 1990; and it sought to reduce its total reliance on bonds to 5 percent by 1995. As can be seen simply by glancing at the even, downward-sloping lines in figure 5.3, the government proved to be remarkably successful in carrying out this policy.[10]

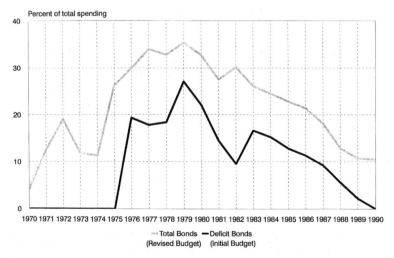

FIGURE 5.3 Japan's Current General Account Deficit, 1970-90

Source:Bank of Japan & Ministry of Finance in JEI Report 17A (7 May 1993) p. 3.

While this graph demonstrates the continuity and consistency of Japanese fiscal policy going into the sii talks, it does not reflect the growing controversy over this policy inside Japan which began to emerge in the mid-1980s. By this time, Japan was well on its way to reducing its annual reliance on borrowing to levels of the early 1970s, leading critics of the continued austerity policy to ask whether it was necessary to persevere in the face of evidence that the policy was beginning to cause more problems than it was solving. The austerity policy had led Japan to rely almost exclusively on export-led growth to get out of the recession early in the decade, and this had caused Japan's trade deficits and foreign complaints to rise in tandem. By 1985, as noted in chapter 3, Japan was facing a firestorm of Congressional criticism in the U.S.

The initial calls for a reevaluation of Japan's fiscal policy were motivated almost exclusively by concerns that a failure to act could push the U.S. to adopt protectionist legislation. Ministry of Finance officials, however, were loathe to let international concerns dictate the nation's fiscal policy. The last time they had let international concerns intrude, in 1978, Japan had ended up with record levels of deficit-financing. Because of that episode, Japan still had record levels of *cumulative* debt, equal to more than 40 percent of GNP in 1985. Japan might have succeeded in bringing down its *annual* debt-financing levels, but it would have to stay on a diet of austerity budgets for many more years before the nation's cumulative debt would come down significantly (see figure 5.4). In short, MOF's experience with the 1978 "locomotive strategy" and its aftermath had left ministry officials resolved to protect the nation's fiscal policy from international pressure.[11]

In the short term, MOF officials succeeded in deflecting pressure on fiscal policy by agreeing to the Americans' strategy of using exchange rate realignments to take pressure off current account imbalances. As Yoichi Funabashi notes in his account of the policy process leading up to the Plaza Accords, MOF strategy at Plaza was to accept currency realignment first, and then interest rate reductions, but under all circumstances to leave the "main castle [fiscal policy] free from attack."[12] As we will see, this was to be MOF's strategy for the rest of the decade.

As it turned out, the Plaza Accords offered MOF only a temporary respite from the pressure on Japanese fiscal policy, and while the pressure came mostly from abroad before the exchange rate realignment, after Plaza it came increasingly from *inside* Japan. Domestic pressure increased because the rise of the yen, especially after it broke through the 160 and 150 yen marks, forced Japan to confront the fact that it could no longer rely on

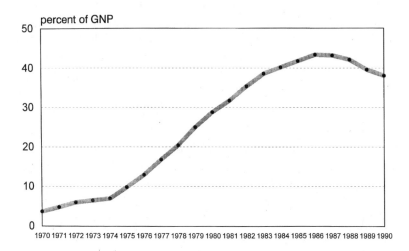

FIGURE 5.4 Japan's Cumulative General Account Deficit, 1970-90

Source: JEI Report, No., 17A, page 4.

exports to fuel economic growth. Japan had to shift to domestic-demand-led growth, and government macro policy had to play a role in that shift.

The first step in the process of reevaluating Japan's macro policy came when Prime Minister Nakasone established the Advisory Group on Economic Structural Adjustment for International Harmony in October 1985, shortly after the Plaza Accords. Maekawa Haruo, the retired central bank chairman who headed the commission, was known as an advocate of shifting Japan from export-led to domestic demand-led growth, and the Commission did engage in a vigorous debate on how fiscal policy ought to fit into the mix of policies needed to move Japan in this direction. The group's final report, however, was a disappointment. It called on the government to commit itself to the goal of "steadily reducing the nation's current account imbalance to one consistent with international harmony," but fell short of suggesting a specific reduction target. It also suggested that the government "put firmly into place domestic demand expansion policies," but was not specific about what kinds of policies should be adopted. In the section which addressed the issue of fiscal policy directly, the commission was even more timid. "In implementing fiscal policy," it said, "it is necessary to maintain the basic policy stance of fiscal reform to end its dependency on deficit-financing bonds. . . ."[13]

The Maekawa Report, it soon became clear, had been watered down by the same "protect the main castle" attitude on the part of MOF officials. Maekawa admitted as much when, at a press conference, he contradicted the statement quoted above by saying that his commission "did not favor the fundamental governmental goal of balancing the national budget by 1990."[14] And yet, this goal did remain sacrosanct as the Ministry of Finance, in an attempt to stick to the long-term plan, delayed the adoption of any real fiscal stimulus until May 1987. While earlier "stimulus packages" were announced, the 1985 packages were literally hollow (containing no public works component) and the 1986 ones were small.[15] Despite rising calls for fiscal stimulus to get Japan out of its high yen (endaka) recession, when the government announced its budget for fiscal year 1987, it contained the smallest expenditure increase in 32 years and an actual cut in public works spending.[16]

With growth stagnant during 1986, however, pressure for fiscal stimulus continued to increase over the two-year period following Plaza—especially after Miyazawa Kiichi became Finance Minister in the summer of 1986. Miyazawa was known as an advocate of expansionary fiscal medicine to stimulate growth. He had in fact been a central figure in the 1978 decision to adopt the locomotive strategy under U.S. pressure. Nevertheless, for almost a year, MOF was able to put off Miyazawa by insisting that monetary policy, rather than fiscal policy, be used to stimulate the economy and fight the strong yen. Thus, due to MOF's continued insistence that the "main castle" of fiscal policy not be influenced by international concerns, interest rates were lowered in successive steps until they reached a postwar record low of 2.5 percent in February 1987.

Although MOF officials were able to postpone the adoption of fiscal stimulus in this way, under the combined pressure of the U.S. and LDP expansionists, they were eventually forced to relent (briefly). Desperate to stem the ever-rising value of the yen, Miyazawa had gone to Washington in January 1987 in hopes of making a deal under the terms of which the U.S. would help stabilize currency values. The deal, as it emerged over a series of meetings with his counterparts in the U.S. and other G-7 powers, featured lower interest rates in Japan and Germany, but it also called on Japan to adopt a "comprehensive economic program" of domestic demand stimulus measures after the passage of the 1987 budget. Using this international pledge, and later ones that specified the size of the fiscal stimulus package, Miyazawa and other LDP expansionists were finally able to prevail upon MOF to allow a one-year departure from their carefully scripted austerity plan. At the end of May, just prior to the Venice G-7 summit, Nakasone announced a six trillion yen stimulus package, which marked the only real fiscal response to the post-Plaza slowdown.[17]

The fiscal policy debate detailed above supports in several ways the argument I make in this chapter about the sii debate on public investment. First, it supports my contention that the public investment policy changes adopted in the wake of sii *would not have happened* without foreign pressure, the counterfactual. The MOF was firmly resolved to carry through with its policy of fiscal reconstruction, this episode shows, and even a recession did not (until after a substantial delay) convince it to alter its course. Even when it did adopt a stimulus package, it did so for only one budget cycle, and it quickly returned to the old policy line once economic growth resumed. A measure of the MOF's commitment to deficit reduction, and its ability to dominate policy in this issue area, was the reassertion of the original deficit reduction goals (eliminating deficit bonds by 1990) in the medium-term economic plan announced by the government in the spring of 1988.[18] Despite the slight detour of 1987, MOF was saying, it was going to steer Japan back onto the roadmap it had drawn up in the early 1980s—and as can be seen in figure 5.3, it did.

The Ministry of Finance was able to dominate the fiscal policy process because during the 1980s it had developed institutions and norms that gave it, and especially its Budget Bureau, the power to exclude almost all others from fiscal policymaking. Its power was derived, most importantly, from its status as the only "responsible" player in the process. Look what had happened, it warned repeatedly, when politicians and foreigners were allowed to intervene in the late 1970s. Only by sticking firmly to a long-term plan with specific deficit-reduction goals and strict rules of balance providing for all ministries to share in budget-cutting pain, they insisted, could Japan avoid a repeat of that earlier debacle. Repeated often enough, in Administrative Reform Council documents and statements by officials, this interpretation of the causes of the 1970s deficits and its lessons created powerful norms that prevented LDP politicians from going against MOF policy—despite their nominal authority to overrule the bureaucrats.[19]

The MOF lock on the policy process was particularly strong in 1989, going into the sii talks on public investment. Unlike the 1986–1987 period, Japan was by this time in the midst of an economic boom. Some officials, in agencies like MITI and the EPA, continued to call for increased public investment, but without a recession to fight they had no chance of influencing policy. LDP backbenchers too continued to favor an increase in the public works budget, but MOF's control of the budget process limited their influence to the issue of *where* public works were going, preventing them from influencing overall spending levels. This was the background for the comment of EPA official Unno Tsuneo, quoted in chapter 3. He and other advocates of increased public investment had no way of overcoming MOF resistance going into the SII talks, he claims, other than to use American pressure.[20]

While supporting my counterfactual assertion that changes in Japanese public investment policy would not have happened without the foreign pressure that came with the SII talks, the 1986–1987 episode also serves as another case study illustrating how gaiatsu works to bring about policy change in Japan. As seen in the brief account of the episode above (and in much more detail in Yoichi Funabashi's book *Managing the Dollar*), foreign pressure played a critical role in bringing about the eventual fiscal policy change. Maekawa, Miyazawa, and others like them were pressing for stimulus all through 1986, but MOF successfully kept them out of the policy process by insisting that it, and only it, knew what was good for the Japanese economy. It was only after Miyazawa was able to insert a commitment for stimulus into an international agreement at the Louvre meeting of the G-7 finance ministers that MOF was forced to relent.

It is telling that LDP leaders then relied heavily on this international promise to push the policy change through. LDP leader Abe Shintarō, for example, advocated stimulus in this way: "The austerity policy to reconstruct government finances is necessary, but Japan has made an international pledge and we must change the present course if needed to meet the world's request."[21] That Japan was in a recession, it seems, was not reason enough for a politician like himself to go to MOF and argue that domestic economic fundamentals required a change in policy. LDP politicians like Abe and Miyazawa needed the excuse of gaiatsu to intervene in the policy process. As we will see when we examine the course of public investment policy during SII, foreign pressure played a very similar role in bringing about change by expanding participation.

Thirdly and lastly, I devoted attention to this earlier fiscal policy debate because decisions made at the time shaped the economic conditions that drove the policy debate in 1989–1990. If Japan had made a fundamental shift to domestic-demand-led growth in 1986, when recession and the high yen were pushing it to do so, if it had done then what Maekawa wanted it to do, SII would not have been necessary. Instead, by its delay, it diverted all of the pressure for stimulus onto monetary policy with (as it turned out) disastrous long-term consequences. As noted above, MOF attempted for two years after Plaza to protect its "main castle" (fiscal policy) by redirecting pressure onto currency realignment and then monetary policy. The Bank of Japan lowered its official discount rate to a then-record low of 2.5 percent in February 1987 and then kept it there for two long years.

While this policy sparked an economic boom that allowed MOF to avoid giving up its cherished deficit-reduction goals, the resulting "bubble economy" grossly distorted the operation of the economy for the remainder of the decade and left behind a seriously damaged economy when it inevitably imploded.[22] When SII started in 1989 the implosion was still in the future, but the government had already been forced to react to speculative excess by increasing interest rates and using administrative guidance to restrain bank lending.[23] By the start of 1990, these policies had begun to bite. What economists in the U.S. Treasury Department sensed when they made public investment an issue in the SII talks was that Japan was going to need some fiscal stimulus to offset the effects of monetary tightening if it was going to maintain the trend toward domestic-demand-led growth and smaller current account surpluses which the bubble had temporarily brought about. It was not long before they were proved right.

The American Demands

As noted above, the Americans decided early on to pitch their demands in this issue area indirectly. Rather than calling specifically for a shift in fiscal policy, they emphasized the need for Japan to invest more in social infrastructure. They pitched it this way partly because the former approach did not seem very promising. They judged, correctly, that an appeal from the U.S. for the Japanese to engage in deficit spending at a time when the nation's economy was booming would have about as much appeal as a down jacket in the heat of summer. Their choice was also dictated, however, by the fact that the Ministry of Finance refused to talk to them about fiscal policy in the SII forum—insisting that this subject should be reserved for the regular meetings of G-7 finance officials.

As the discussion of the 1986–1987 episode makes clear, MOF officials were not keen on talking about Japanese fiscal policy in *any* international forum. Forced to discuss it somewhere, though, they preferred the secret, closed meetings of the G-7 finance officials to any other forum. Being multilateral, these meetings provided MOF with the opportunity to rally support from other governments (usually Germany) whenever the U.S. started talking about stimulating demand. Limited to treasury and central bank officials, these meetings also maximized MOF's ability to dominate the process of establishing Japan's negotiating positions. The SII format, in contrast, promised to be more public, to involve a one on one dialogue with the U.S., and (probably most threatening to MOF) promised to involve the ministry's rivals from within Japan.

MOF's objections to a direct discussion of fiscal policy in SII therefore emerged almost immediately when U.S. Treasury official Charles Dallara approached Utsumi Makoto, Vice-Minister for International Affairs, with the original concept for the talks. Utsumi put it bluntly: the MOF would not participate in the talks unless macroeconomic policy was proscribed from the SII agenda. Needing MOF's go-ahead to proceed with the task of building support for the SII initiative within the Bush administration, Dallara quietly agreed to this condition in what came to be known as the "secret promise."[24]

Thus limited in their ability to attack Japanese fiscal policy directly, U.S. officials concentrated on Japan's public investment policy as they set about framing their demands. At the September negotiating session, Dallara was actually somewhat tentative as he laid out the U.S. position for the first time. He pointed out some of the Japanese infrastructure deficiencies cited above and then called on Japan to adopt a "medium-term investment plan," urging the government to devote higher levels of investment to social infrastructure projects.[25] As the negotiating year progressed, however, U.S. demands in this area became more insistent and much more specific. Dallara, it seems, was pushed along by others in the American delegation who saw SII (and especially the public investment issue area) as an opportunity to press the Japanese on fiscal policy—regardless of the "secret promise." Robert Fauver, formerly of Treasury but reassigned to the State Department as a Deputy Assistant Secretary for East Asian Affairs after his boss (James Baker) moved from Treasury to State, was particularly hawkish on this issue. So was Ambassador Michael Armacost, who at one point skipped an important regional meeting in Australia to attend an SII negotiating session and press Japan on this issue.[26]

Both of these men saw the public investment issue as the only SII agenda item with the potential to make a serious dent in the U.S.-Japan trade imbalance. Antitrust and distribution might open the market somewhat, but these issues couldn't move the savings and investment balance which ultimately dictated current account figures. They therefore pressed Dallara and Council of Economic Advisors delegate John Taylor, the two men charged with leadership on this issue area, to frame the U.S. demands in such a way as to maximize the impact on Japanese fiscal policy.[27] Fauver pressed in particular for the demand to include a call on Japan to issue more bonds. Both pressed for the U.S. to demand a specific and very large increase in public investment—large enough so that MOF would be forced to adjust its fiscal policy in order to fund the increase.

By the time the U.S. presented its list of 200 demands after New Years, therefore, its demands on public investment had emerged as among the boldest and most prominent.[28] As noted in the previous chapter, the U.S. called on Japan to increase its rate of public investment to 10 percent of GNP, its rate during the late 1970s. Publicly, Dallara justified this figure by claiming that it was what the U.S. calculated to be necessary if Japan was to attain the social infrastructure targets spelled out in various plans Japan itself had adopted as early as 1973.[29] He thus maintained the fiction (necessary to avoid a complete violation of his "secret promise") that the U.S. was primarily interested in social infrastructure levels such as sewage connection rates and park space. That Japan had been forced to depend heavily on borrowing in the days when it devoted 10 percent of GNP to public investment, and that it might have to do so again to reach that figure, Dallara would insist, was merely a coincidence.

In fact, however, the American delegation had carefully chosen the 10 percent figure based on economic models which showed that an increase in public investment of that magnitude would force MOF to issue more bonds, postpone its fiscal reconstruction targets, and ultimately stimulate the economy. It was in this context that the U.S. official described in the opening of this chapter concluded that sewers should be a particular focus of U.S. demands. Sewers (unlike road-construction, for example) do not require significant land purchases. Because the multiplier effect of land purchases tends to be lower than that for construction, the U.S. had an interest in emphasizing categories of public investment like sewers that had a low land-purchase component and consequently promised to have a higher stimulus effect on the Japanese economy.[30]

TABLE 5.2

Summary of the Americans' Public Investment Demands

---

1. Establish concrete expenditure targets in medium-term public investment plan.
2. Raise public investment expanditures as a share of GNP to 10 percent within three to five years.
3. Accelerate annual expenditures under the area-specific five year plans.
4. Focus on housing, sewers, transportation, and urban infrastructure in the plans.
5. Reevaluate four comprehensive public investment plans as part of planning for the next ten years.
6. Shift from annual budgeting to multi-year and open-ended (*mukigen*) budgeting for public investment.
7. Modify allocation of public investment by category and region in budget process.
8. Make use of construction bonds.
9. Expand public investment beyond the construction bond issue framework.
10. Reinvest the increase in the social security fund surplus.
11. Increase public investment, especially in urban areas, by allocating the majority of Fiscal Investment and Loan Program (FILP) budget to such areas and by making a variety of laws governing FILP more flexible.
12. Use public lands for public investment projects.
13. Make it easier and cheaper to use subterranean areas for such projects.
14. Promote the markets access of foreign construction firms.
15. Relax regulation of interest rates.

Source: List of 200 American Demands (translated from Japanese by the author)

The details of the American demands in this issue area are summarized in table 5.2. Other than the brief reference to bonds, one will note, the Americans did not make their ultimate interest in fiscal policy obvious. By framing their demands in this way, they avoided criticism from MOF and deflected charges that the U.S. was in no position to make recommendations on fiscal policy. As we will see in the section below, however, the American's decision to frame the issue as a "public investment" issue rather than a fiscal policy issue also helped maximize their ability to affect the Japanese policy process in ways that improved their chances for an attractive deal. In the terminology of this book, it facilitated their exploitation of synergisms in the nexus between international and domestic politics.

Synergistic Strategies and the Deal on Public Investment

Going into the SII talks, the mandarins of the Ministry of Finance sat comfortably in charge of policy in this issue area, surrounded by thick walls protecting their turf from others who might wish to intervene. As we saw in the discussion of the 1986–1987 fiscal policy debate, the MOF had succeeded in establishing a set of norms and budget rules that effectively insulated it from outside interference. The ministry might be willing to negotiate with LDP leaders about how to divide up the budget pie, and it might be willing to respond with some fiscal stimulus in times of serious recession, but it was not about to let politicians, spendthrift bureaucrats, or foreigners alter the overall level of spending it had deemed to be fiscally prudent.

Once it became clear that the level of spending on public investment would be the subject of U.S.-Japan negotiations, however, these walls around the MOF began to crumble. At the very first negotiating session and again throughout the negotiating year, delegates representing the MOF's rivals within the Japanese bureaucracy questioned the ministry's policy line. And later, in the end-game leading up to the April 1990 interim report and the June 1990 final report, LDP politicians became actively involved in brokering a deal. Far from maintaining control of policy, MOF had by the end of the first year of SII talks agreed to a long-term commitment of a specific sum of money to public investment, just months after it had dismissed this American demand as a gross interference in Japan's internal affairs, potentially inflationary, and worse.[31] What follows in this section is the story of how all of these actors became involved in the decisionmaking process and how foreign pressure made it happen.

The first Japanese individual to take advantage of the opportunity SII afforded for participation expansion was the EPA delegate, Unno Tsuneo. Unno, readers may recall, was the official who commented that he and other advocates of increased public investment had no way of gaining access to the decisionmaking process prior to SII other than to "use the Americans." His agency was a known supporter of this type of policy change, and his former boss, Miyazaki Isamu, had pushed hard as a member of the Maekawa Commission and the Economic Council for greater government efforts aimed as stimulating domestic demand. Despite all of their efforts, however, they had been frustrated by MOF's success in deflecting their pressure. Now, as Unno sat alongside MOF delegate Utsumi, waiting to debate the Americans on Japan's public investment policy, he could not help but be thankful for the opportunity the Americans had given him.[32]

In their opening comments at this meeting, however, Utsumi and Dallara—reflecting their "secret promise"—ruled macroeconomic policy to be outside the SII agenda. "Macroeconomic policy coordination,"

Dallara announced, "would be handled within the G-7 framework." Unno's response was immediate. Noting that the issue could not be separated from that of balance of payments adjustment, which motivated the talks, he insisted that the group *should* talk about macro policy. Utsumi's reply, in turn, was equally blunt: "I would like to inform Mr. Unno that the discussion of macroeconomics is beyond the mandate of the SII talks. I would like him to better understand the limits of our jurisdiction."[33] It was an unusually open airing of interministerial conflict for an international meeting, and it opened a wedge within the Japanese position that U.S. delegates proceeded to exploit over the next several months.

MOF, however, persisted in defending its policy. When the U.S. pointed out deficiencies in Japan's social infrastructure at the September meeting, MOF responded by noting that Japan's public investment rate remained more than double the analogous figures for the U.S. and other industrialized nations.[34] Faced with another challenge at the November meeting, MOF pointed out that Japan was devoting more of its public investment budget to quality-of-life categories like sewers, parks, and housing than it had in earlier decades. Furthermore, its infrastructure levels were much improved from where they were in the 1960s.[35] Leading up to the February meeting, even as other ministries began to offer concessions on land policy and the Large Store Law, MOF refused to give an inch.[36]

Instead, facing the Americans' specific demands in this issue area for the first time, MOF officials seemed to become even more vehement in their defense of the status quo. Japan was already spending a great deal on public investment, Utsumi noted, and the question of how to allocate the investment budget was a political matter. Another MOF delegate, Shinozawa, called the U.S. demands "shocking." For MOF to commit to spend a specific share of GNP on public investment would rob the ministry of the ability to respond flexibly to economic conditions. Dallara's response was ingenious. The Ministry, he pointed out, had operated under strict deficit reduction targets and had never complained about the constraints these placed on the government's flexibility. Utsumi, completely frustrated, proceeded to change the subject by pointing out that the group needed to talk about other SII issues.[37]

Despite MOF's refusal to budge, the ministry was increasingly isolated. The U.S. had quoted over and over again from Economic Planning Agency documents, to the point that American delegates could joke with Unno about his coming over to their side of the table. Behind the scenes,

MITI was pressing MOF to make its share of the compromises as the government formulated its response to the Americans' 200 demands. And even as the February negotiating session was going on, the Minister of Construction held a press conference announcing his ministry's support for more spending on public investment.[38]

The Ministry of Finance did not begin to retreat from its position, though, until the politicians became involved. Kaifu's announcement, after meeting with Bush at Palm Springs, that he would set up a cabinet-level task force to draw up the government's response to the Americans' SII demands was a particular blow to the MOF since it meant the issue had truly been raised above the level where it alone could dictate the Japanese negotiating position. As senior bureaucrats from all of the concerned ministries gathered to hammer out a draft of the government's offer, MOF was forced to make its first concession (albeit a vague one): the government would agree to "steadily increase investment in social capital over the medium term."[39]

Kaifu and other LDP executives who were given a report on the bureaucrats' draft, however, felt it would not be enough to satisfy the Americans. In the days between the completion of the draft (March 16) and the departure of the Japanese delegation leaders for an informal meeting with the Americans (March 20), MOF was pressed to consider a more significant concession: committing to speed up the rate of the increase in the eight five-year public investment plans up for renewal that year from an average annual rate of 7 percent to one of 10 percent.[40] This was too much for Utsumi and other MOF officials, however. When Utsumi made his presentation of the government's offer on the investment issue at the informal meeting, he limited the offer to the vague one about "steadily increasing investment."

Once again, Utsumi's hard line provoked a split within the Japanese delegation. At the coffee break, a Ministry of Foreign Affairs official approached Utsumi and asked him how he could continue to resist when Kaifu and Ishihara (the cabinet official in charge of the task force) had already decided that Japan *should* commit to specific numbers. As the Japanese delegate who related this story put it, "Their voices were rising higher and higher and they were making quite a scene." The American delegates in the room may not have understood the heated debate in Japanese, but they certainly could see that the Japanese team was split.[41]

Ultimately, the pressure from the politicians proved to be too strong for MOF to resist. Throughout March, LDP backbenchers clamored for the government to concede on the public investment issue. Stand fast on the Large Store Law, they argued, but not on this one where conceding actually means we'll have more pork to deliver to our constituents.[42] Predictably, the movement was led by the don of the LDP's construction interests, Kanemaru Shin. After meeting with Mosbacher, Kanemaru embarrassed the Japanese delegation by announcing publicly that he had told the Commerce Secretary that he felt Japan should commit to increase the share of GNP it spent on public investment to 8 percent.[43] Coming at a time when MOF officials were telling the Americans they could not sign off on any deal with specific numbers because such a commitment would limit their flexibility and lead to inflation, the Kanemaru comment was a bombshell.

The politicians who made the most difference, however, were former Prime Minister Takeshita and Finance Minister Hashimoto. As noted in chapter 4, the U.S. made a special effort to target these men with personal appeals for them to intervene in bringing about a resolution to the impasse. Both of these LDP leaders, unlike Kanemaru, were respected by MOF for their willingness to stand up to backbencher demands for "irresponsible" tax and budget policies. When, after the March 20 informal meeting, they quietly began to hint that MOF needed to retreat, the ministry could no longer resist.[44] By the time Utsumi returned to Washington on April 2 for the formal negotiating session due to produce an interim report, MOF had accepted the politicians' demands that it agree to spend a specific sum on public investment over a ten year period. The exact figure was left to be specified in the "Joint Report of the SII Working Group" due in June. While MOF continued to drag its feet on this specific number, it was eventually bumped up from MOF's offer of 415 trillion yen over ten years to 430 trillion yen after Finance Minister Hashimoto upped the offer and Kaifu called Bush on the phone to reiterate that the 430 trillion was the best the Japanese could do.[45] A deal had finally been struck.

So what does all of this tell us about the role of gaiatsu in the Japanese policy process? First, as in the case of the 1986–1987 episode, we have circumstantial evidence that foreign pressure made a difference in policy outcomes. Before gaiatsu, MOF was in control of the policy process and was successfully resisting pressure for it to adjust its policy. After gaiatsu, MOF lost its control of the process and was forced to accept a policy it had consistently opposed. Foreign pressure, it seems clear, does make a difference.

What I have tried to do by offering a careful chronology of the SII negotiations and Japanese response on this issue, however, is to flesh out the mechanism through which gaiatsu had an impact in this case. What the telling of the story suggests is that the key to the outcome in this case was the role of foreign pressure in expanding *elite* participation. Despite the presence of support for policy change along the lines advocated by the Americans among the ministry's bureaucratic rivals and LDP back-benchers, the MOF was able to keep these other elite actors from having a say in the decisionmaking process until well into the negotiating year. As American pressure increased, however, LDP leaders were confronted with a "crisis" and were forced to raise the issue up to the cabinet level (forcing MOF to deal with bureaucrats from other ministries) and to get involved themselves in brokering a deal. Once the process was opened up in this way, the path was clear for the many advocates of increased public investment within Japan to bring their weight to bear on the decision, and MOF was forced to give in.

What about the other synergistic strategies? It is possible that gaiatsu facilitated policy change by bringing the widely dispersed preferences of the general public to bear on the policy process (participation expansion at the mass level). Although no public opinion polls asked people whether they favored increased government spending on sewers and parks, cir-cumstantial evidence suggests that the public was supportive of such a policy. The best evidence is the fact that Prime Minister Miyazawa, who became leader after Kaifu stepped down in the fall of 1991, based his leadership campaign on a promise to make Japan a "lifestyle superpower." What Japan needed, Miyazawa argued, was increased public investment in areas like parks, sewers, and housing, aimed at bringing the quality of life of the Japanese up to the level commensurate with Japan's high per capita GNP. Miyazawa would not have stressed this issue if there were not public support for it.

What is interesting is that previous prime ministers had not cam-paigned on this kind of platform. Tanaka, in the 1970s, had called for remodeling the Japanese archipelago, but his vision was directed mostly at providing infrastructure for the countryside, not the average salaryman in Tokyo. That Miyazawa picked up on this issue when he did suggests that the Americans, through SII, may have helped represent and bring to bear on the policy process diffuse public demand for this kind of policy.[46] If so, the decision by the Japanese government to give in on public investment during SII may be partially attributable to the perceptions of LDP politi-cians that this urban demand could no longer be ignored.

Evaluating the Policy Change

Since the debate on this issue was both about public investment and fiscal policy, there are in fact two ways in which the policy change can be evaluated. Has Japan's rate of public investment significantly increased as a result of sii? And has Japan's fiscal policy changed significantly because of the talks? Because the Americans framed their demands in terms of public investment and because the Japanese concession was also quantified in those terms, I propose that we should focus first and most importantly on this measure. According to this measure, I will demonstrate that sii can be shown to have produced a marked change in Japanese public policy. Nevertheless, because the Americans' ultimate motivation was to change Japanese fiscal policy, we cannot ignore the question of whether sii can be credited with producing change in this area. In the second part of this section, I also examine recent fiscal policy and show that there has been change. Given the role of the prolonged Japanese recession in driving recent fiscal policy, though, it is my conclusion that much less of this change can be attributed to sii.

The bottom line by which the American's success in this area has to be evaluated is specified quite clearly in the final sii agreement. Japan agreed to spend 430 trillion yen on aggregate public investment over the decade from FY 1991 to FY 2000, up from an estimated 263 trillion yen in the preceding decade. To reach this level, economists quickly calculated, Japan would have to increase the expenditures on public investment by an average of 6.3 percent each year. Assuming Japan kept its promise and the Japanese economy grew at a nominal rate of 4.75 percent (the rate predicted in the government's economic plan), these economists calculated, Japan's rate of public investment would rise from an estimated 7.2 percent in 1990 to 8.4 percent by the end of the decade (see figure 5.5). Japan was agreeing, in other words, to a policy shift involving 1.2 percent of its GNP, according to its own projections. Considering that Japanese public investment had actually declined as a percentage of GNP over the previous decade, these calculations suggest that Japan's promise to spend 430 trillion yen cannot but be described as a significant change in direction—even if 8.4 percent was somewhat less than the original U.S. demand that Japan commit 10 percent of GNP.[47]

Both the Americans and Japanese knew, however, that the real significance of the 430 trillion yen pledge would depend on actual Japanese growth and inflation rates. And initially, U.S. officials were quite worried

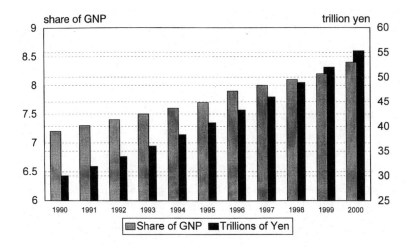

FIGURE 5.5 Projected Impact of Japanese Commitment to Invest
430 Trillion Yen Over A Decade

that a nominal growth rate higher than the one predicted by the government might mean that 430 trillion yen produced a net *decline* in the share
of GNP Japan devoted to public investment.[48] As it turned out, however,
Japan experienced an early and extended recession which kept its nominal growth rate well *below* the government's projections. What that
meant, in a reversal of the logic behind the Americans' fears, was that the
430 trillion yen commitment was bound to push Japan's public investment rate up more quickly and to a higher level than the government had
initially projected.

A look at government expenditures (planned and actual) show that
Japan has more than kept its promise. In the FY 1991 budget, the first put
together after the sII commitment, Japan budgeted a six percent increase
in its general account allocation for public works—approximately the figure it needed to keep Japan on pace to reach the full 430 trillion yen figure over a decade. It did so primarily by creating a new 200 billion yen
line in the budget for "improvements in the quality of life" (*seikatsu kanren
waku*) which was to go primarily for parks, local roads, and sewers.[49] In
its planning for the FY 1992 budget, the government again penciled in
numbers just high enough to keep it on course to meet its public investment target: general account expenditures on public works were to
increase 5.3 percent, the FILP (investment budget) allocation for public
investment was to increase 10.8 percent and local government spending

on public investment was to increase 11.5 percent for a net planned increase in public gross fixed capital formation, again, of six percent.[50]

As with all budgets, however, final government expenditures—by which the government's public investment policy ultimately has to be judged—varied significantly from these numbers (see figure 5.6). This variation has been particularly great for Japan's public investment spending since 1992. Midway through that year, the government adopted a large supplemental budget which boosted public works sharply in an effort to counteract the effects of a serious recession. As one can see, the government increased its actual general account allocation for public works by 34.2 percent in 1992 and a whopping 59.5 percent on top of that in 1993!

While general account expenditures represent only part of aggregate public investment, these boosts had the effect of pushing up Japan's annual public investment totals much more quickly than it had projected. As figure 5.7 shows, Japan increased its aggregate public investment level markedly in 1992–1993, pushing its investment rate up to 9.4 percent of GNP in 1992 and to 10.6 percent the following year. By 1994, the government had increased its expenditures on public investment so steeply that there was no doubt the government would fulfill its 430 trillion yen commitment. In fact, given that it had spent an estimated 184 trillion yen in the first four years of the ten-year plan (1991 to 1994), the govern-

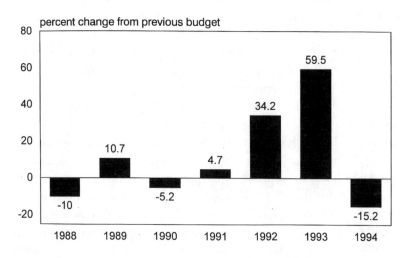

FIGURE 5.6 Japan's General Account Expenditures on Public Works, 1988-1994

Source: Ministry of Finance final revised budget figures.

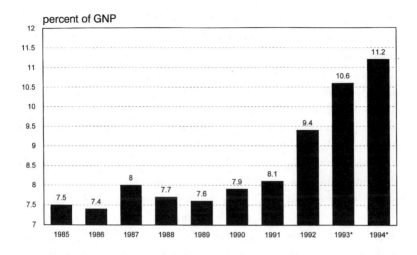

FIGURE 5.7 Japanese Public Investment, 1985-94

Source: Based on data in Kensetsu keizai kenkyūjo, Nihon keizai to kōkyō tōshi: 23 (The Japanese Economy and Public Investment) (July 1994), based on EPA, National Income Accounts.

* 1993 and 1994 numbers are estimates.

ment was in a position where it could meet its 430 trillion yen target even if it spent 23 percent *less* in 1995 and held that level steady for the rest of the decade! Demonstrating that it had no intention to retrench, however, the government in the fall of 1994 announced that it was going to go way beyond its sɪɪ commitment, planning to spend 630 trillion yen between 1995 and 2005.[51]

To summarize, Japan has clearly and completely fulfilled its sɪɪ pledges in the public investment issue area. While the pace with which it fulfilled them was accelerated by the 1991–1995 recession, the fact that the government started making efforts to attain the 430 trillion level even before the recession and that it recently decided to embark on another, bigger ten-year plan is all evidence that the policy change has been real. After the decade of the 1980s in which Japan's public investment ratio dropped, the government has reversed course and sharply increased its ratio in the 1990s—a policy change that can largely be attributed to sɪɪ.

If my evaluation of sɪɪ's impact on Japan's *public investment policy* is unequivocal, my evaluation of its impact on Japan's *fiscal policy* is more cautious. What the Americans were trying to do, readers must remember, is to force the Ministry of Finance to moderate its fiscal reconstruction plan—to reverse, or at least slow, the government's campaign to reduce the share of its budget funded by bonds. By getting MOF to commit to a major increase in public investment, they hoped, the government would be forced to borrow more than it would have without this commitment. Because public works, in particular, tend to be financed with construction bonds in Japan, the U.S. hoped MOF would be led as a matter of course to increase its issuance of construction bonds in lock step with its increase in public works expenditures.

The Ministry of Finance, however, quickly figured out how to avoid changing its *fiscal* policy, even as it agreed to a major increase in public works spending. The key was to end the habit of financing public works with bonds. This was exactly what was recommended by the ministry's Fiscal Systems Council in a report issued on March 1, 1990—just as the Americans were pressing Japan to boost public investment. Public works, it suggested, should increasingly be financed with tax revenues. By making this shift, it noted, Japan would be able to increase spending on social infrastructure even as it continued to work toward the government's goal of reducing the share of the general account budget financed by bonds to 5 percent by 1995.[52]

What MOF was plotting to do, of course, was to maintain its established fiscal policy direction regardless of SII. In fact, a senior MOF bureaucrat confidently predicted shortly after the SII agreement had been reached that Japan would be able to meet its 430 trillion yen commitment even while it continued to reduce its dependence on construction bonds.[53] For exactly one budget cycle, this official's prediction proved on the mark. Even as the government budgeted an extra 200 billion yen for public works in FY 1991, it managed to reduce the share of its budget funded by bonds from 10.5 percent to 8 percent—on track to reduce the ratio to 5 percent by 1995.

And then the recession set in. The impact of the economic slowdown on public investment levels has been described above, but its impact on fiscal policy was just as dramatic. In an effort to fight the recession, MOF abandoned all hope of reaching its 1995 goal. Instead, it ended up presiding over budgets which, in 1992 and 1993, drew 13.3 and 20.9 percent (respectively) of their revenue from bonds. And in the initial budget for 1994, MOF was actually forced to do what its officials had sworn they would never do again. It called for 4.3 percent of the general account budget to be financed with *deficit* bonds.[54]

The impact of this fiscal policy change on Japan's savings-investment balance can be seen in figure 5.8. After contributing an increasing amount

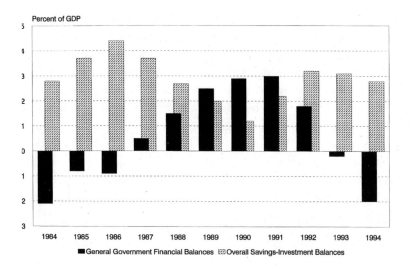

FIGURE 5.8 Government Financial Balances and Overall S-I Balances in Japan, 1984-94

Sources: OECD, Economic Outlook 56 (December 1994) and IMF, International Financial Statistics.

to the savings surplus throughout the 1980s, the general government financial balance declined for the first time in 1992 and moved into negative territory in 1993. While the overall savings surplus actually increased (primarily because a sharp drop in private investment created a growing private sector savings surplus), the effect of the shift in fiscal policy was to make this surplus smaller than it would have been without a change in fiscal policy. Due to the logic of macroeconomics, this meant that fiscal policy also helped produce a smaller trade deficit than would have been the case otherwise.

On first glance, this reversal of Japanese fiscal policy might seem to be evidence that sɪɪ had a real impact in this area. Just as the Americans hoped, an increase in public investment forced the government to issue more bonds—providing real fiscal stimulus for the economy, serving to reduce Japan's S-I surplus from where it would have been otherwise, and thus ultimately narrowing the trade gap from where it would have been *ceteris paribus*. It is my evaluation, however, that sɪɪ can actually be credited with *only a little* of this impact—in contrast with my more generous evaluation of the sɪɪ impact on public investment levels. The key difference is in what the government did in 1991 before the recession really set in. In that budget year, the government *did* significantly increase spending on public investment, but it *did not* engage in any fiscal stimulus. Had the recession not set in, it is very likely that MOF would have persisted with this approach, continuing to boost public investment in line with its SII commitment but funding the increase largely through tax revenues.

That said, it would probably be a mistake to conclude the SII had *no* impact on fiscal policy. What is interesting about the government's response to the 1991–1995 recession is the weight given to public works in the initial stimulus packages. While this has been typical of Japanese stimulus packages in the past as well, it is likely that the attention given to social infrastructure problems during SII and the broad political support mobilized in the course of that debate helped push the government to put together public works packages larger than anything it had crafted in the past. For that reason, I do give SII "a little" credit for fiscal policy shifts following the onset of the recent recession.

Conclusion

Macroeconomic policy has been a recurrent source of tension in U.S.-Japan economic relations, prompting the U.S. to exert significant pressure on Japan in 1977–78, 1986–87, during SII, and again during the Clinton Framework Talks. As the most "typical" of the SII issues, therefore, it is particularly important that we examine how gaiatsu worked in this case. What is interesting about the U.S. approach to this issue during SII, compared to its approach in each of the other episodes, is that the Americans made much more of an effort to appeal to Japanese supporters of the U.S. position. Framing the issue as "public investment" rather than "macroeconomic policy" and pointing to real social infrastructure deficiencies in Japan, the U.S. attempted to broaden participation in a Japanese decisionmaking process that had been dominated by the Ministry of Finance.

As the analysis in the last section showed, this approach proved to be extremely effective at one level even as it proved not so impressive at another. On the one hand, the impact of SII on Japanese public investment levels cannot be denied. Before the talks, the nation's public investment rate had been falling for a decade. Ever since, it has been rising. On the other hand, the Americans' approach did not seem to make as much of an impact on Japan's fiscal policy. Until the recession, MOF was able to fund the increase in public investment with tax revenues, and it abandoned this austerity policy only after the 1991–1995 recession became so severe that the ministry realized fiscal medicine was required. If Japanese growth resumes its previous levels, one can expect that MOF will go back as soon as it can to its old austerity policy.

The mixed record of the American approach to macroeconomics during SII reaffirms the validity of the hypotheses advanced in this book in several ways. First, as emphasized in chapter 4, the success of the U.S. in getting the Japanese to accept their public investment demands points out how effective gaiatsu can be when it works well with domestic politics. In this case, there was a great deal of latent support for higher levels of public investment in Japan, and the U.S. strategy of seeking to expand participation to include these supporters and isolate MOF on this issue proved to be remarkably successful. Because conditions supported the use of a participation expansion strategy on the issue of public investment, gaiatsu worked.

The more limited impact of the strategy on the related issue of fiscal policy, however, also confirms the validity of the approach developed in this book. When one looks closely at what political actors inside Japan liked about the U.S. demand, one realizes that most (especially the LDP politicians) were motivated primarily by a desire to increase expenditures on public works. They were not interested in whether the boost in spending would be funded by tax revenue or bonds. While the U.S. succeeded in taking advantage of latent support on the issue of overall public investment levels, they were unable, in the absence of allies, to overcome MOF's resistance to a relaxation of its austere fiscal policy. With the conditions not operative on this level, gaiatsu failed to produce meaningful policy change.

Today, several years after the SII talks, many more Japanese are connected to sewers, and some of these individuals can thank the U.S. for their cleaner and better-smelling environments. For American citizens, the payoff from the expenditure of U.S. political capital on this issue is much less tangible. The long-term change in Japan's public investment policy may have a limited effect on the nation's savings-investment balance, perhaps contributing to marginally lower trade deficits down the road. In the short term, however, because SII did not force MOF to significantly move its fiscal policy from where it would have been without gaiatsu, the impact on the bilateral imbalance has been small. The SII approach in this issue area may tell us how gaiatsu can work to change Japanese policy, but it is probably not the best example of how to advance U.S. interests.

6
THE DISTRIBUTION ISSUE

Exploring the shopping streets (*shōtengai*) of urban Japan is one of the great pleasures of touring that country. On the typical shopping street in the typical Japanese city one can find a string of specialty shops selling kimono fabric, office supplies, toys, cosmetics, traditional Japanese sweets, French pastry, and on and on. Many of them, interestingly, are "mom and pop" outfits, run by the same family for several generations. The contrast with the retail world of America is glaring. In the United States, most merchants abandoned central city districts years ago. While some have found new homes in suburban strip malls, the retail world of the U.S. has come to be dominated by giant chains: Walmart, the Limited, the Gap, Mrs. Fields, and Toys 'R' Us. In comparison, the Japanese retail world seems like the land where time stood still.

In fact, it is not just Japan's proximity to its feudal past that accounts for its "quaint" retail distribution system. The government, through intrusive regulations, has been involved in slowing (if not stopping) the progress of time in the retail sector since the 1930s when it first adopted the Department Store Law, requiring all large stores to obtain permission from the government before opening new outlets. As recently as the 1980s, local merchants were able to use the successor to this law, the Large Store Law (LSL)[1], to delay the opening of new stores for as long as 15 years. Many localities, furthermore, imposed complete bans on new "large" stores—a category actually comprising stores as small as 500 square meters, about the size of your average American McDonald's.

With such protection and financial assistance through special loan programs, it is little wonder that central city shopping districts and traditional "mom and pop" retail stores continue to survive in large numbers in Japan.

While the Large Store Law was just one of a number of barriers cited by the American sii negotiators in the area of distribution, it emerged as the dominant issue in the area and as the most-publicized of all of the structural impediments covered in the talks. In many ways, it was the archetypal sii issue: the symbol of broader barriers facing U.S. firms as they sought to make their products available to Japanese buyers *and* an example of how the U.S. was on the side of Japanese consumers who were being forced to pay higher prices in order to protect inefficient businesses. The Large Store Law, the U.S. argued, may have served its purpose of protecting shopping districts and the livelihoods of many small merchants, but it imposed heavy costs both on Japanese consumers and on foreign firms.

The Americans' main argument was that the law limited opportunities for foreign firms to get their products to market by slowing the expansion of large stores which for a variety of reasons tend to sell more imported goods.[2] Because these stores have more shelf space, they are more likely to make room for new foreign products. Also, because they are bigger, they have the capability to develop their own direct import operations and can bargain harder with the agents who distribute imports to keep the prices of such goods down. Shifting the balance of power between retailers and distributors was particularly important to the Americans, since they had evidence that Japanese distributors tended to mark up the price of foreign products at a much higher rate than they did domestic goods—operating "like a privately administered set of tariffs."[3] By getting the government to liberalize the Large Store Law, the Americans hoped to bring market forces to bear on the distribution system in ways that would force distributors to make foreign goods available at lower prices.

As described in chapter 4, the U.S. ultimately succeeded in obtaining Japanese government acquiescence to its demands in this issue area. MITI, the regulatory agency in this case, agreed to amend the lsl and limit local government attempts to thwart the intent of liberalization, and the actual number of large store openings shot up sharply when the promised reforms were implemented. This chapter, like the last, begins by reviewing past government policy in this area—emphasizing how

MITI had repeatedly caved under pressure from established retailers eager to protect themselves from new competition. As recently as the summer of 1989, MITI had been forced to back off from an announced policy of liberalization after it encountered resistance from the industry and its supporters within the LDP and local government. Through the SII process, however, U.S. negotiators were able to tap into a vein of support for liberalization within MITI, among the more aggressive large store chains, and within the Japanese public. By expanding participation to include these groups, gaiatsu changed the domestic game in Japan and made possible policy changes that previously had been blocked.

Lest American officials become overconfident based on this experience, however, we will also look in this chapter at what the U.S. was *not* able to extract from the Japanese government: the total abolition of the law. On this point, MITI officials—worried that they would lose control of the distribution sector—were at odds with the U.S. negotiators. Not coincidentally, they succeeded in keeping the liberalization from going that far. As we will see when we look at how the process of liberalization has actually been carried out (in the last section), this compromise has allowed MITI to continue "managing" the retail sector in ways which make it impossible to describe the results of the SII talks in this issue area as an unqualified success.

The Large Store Law Debate in Japan Before SII

The pattern of Japanese government involvement in the retail sector was actually set way back in the 1930s. At that time, as would happen again with enactment of the Large Store Law in 1974, and again with the addition of revised administrative rules in 1979 and 1982, policy outcomes reflected the political power of small merchants. By the time the Americans became interested in this issue in the late 1980s, these merchants had succeeded in slowing the pace of large store openings to a trickle, and they showed every sign of being able to beat back the attempt of MITI, in 1989, to place a limit on their ability to delay store openings. As in the previous chapter, this section on the background to the SII debate on the issue is designed to show *what would have happened* if the Americans had not become involved. The record suggests that the LSL was unlikely to have been liberalized to the degree it was or as quickly as it was without gaiatsu.

THE DEPARTMENT STORE LAW

At the time of the enactment of the Department Store Law in 1937, the government's involvement in this sector of the economy was already driven by demands from politically influential small merchants who, facing competition from department stores and suffering from the effects of the Great Depression, petitioned the government for help. The Ministry of Commerce and Industry (MITI's predecessor) was initially opposed to the idea of a Department Store Law, seeing it as hampering the modernization of the retail sector, but after attempts by the department stores to "regulate themselves" failed, the ministry had no choice but to insert itself into the high-stakes battle between small merchants and their new competitors. Under the law, the MCI required stores larger than 1,500 square meters to obtain permission from the government before expanding existing outlets or opening new ones.[4]

The Department Store Law, in force until it was repealed under pressure from occupation authorities in 1947 and again from 1956 until 1974, succeeded for many years in maintaining a rough balance of interests between small merchants and the large department stores. Small merchants liked it for obvious reasons, and over time department stores came to realize that the law served their interests too by making it difficult for new large stores to open in their territory.

By the late 1960s, however, both department stores and small merchants faced a challenge from a new breed of stores, the superstores, which had found a way around the DSL. Since the DSL required permits for stores larger than 1,500 square meters, each superstore organized itself as a collection of *separate* stores, each smaller than 1,500 square meters but housed in a single large building. With each unit specializing in a different product (food, clothing, pharmaceuticals, etc.), the superstores were able to offer the variety and convenience of the department stores—but at a much lower price. By the early 1970s, these stores had opened branches across Japan and emerged as among the largest of the retail chains.[5]

THE LARGE STORE LAW

MITI officials recognized that the arrival of the superstores was causing turmoil in the retail sector and in 1972 announced that they were willing to revise the DSL to close the loophole which had allowed these stores to expand at will by applying its restrictions to *buildings* with more than

1,500 square meters of retail floor space rather than to "stores" over that size. At the same time, however, the ministry announced that it planned to relax overall limits on large stores, hoping that the freer competition would lead stores to modernize and pursue efficiencies. The DSL's permit system, it proposed, should be replaced by a system of prior notification in which stores were in principle free to expand. In addition, a MITI panel recommended, "assuring the interests of consumers" should be one of the purposes of the new law.[6]

Predictably, MITI's proposals for relaxing the DSL encountered a barrage of criticism from small stores. During the postwar period, small shopkeepers had emerged as a powerful force in Japanese politics. In Kyoto, the nation's ancient capital, they had elected a communist mayor. Elsewhere, they formed the core of many conservative politicians' electoral support groups. No party could ignore them.[7] Thus, when MITI came out with its proposal to relax limits on large store openings, politicians from parties as disparate as the Communists, Socialists, Kōmeitō, and LDP all attacked the proposed legislation. In the end, MITI succeeded in keeping the reference to consumer interests and the notification system in the new law, but it was forced to add a requirement that large stores participate in an "adjustment" (chōsei) process, taking into account the views of a variety of interests.[8]

The emergence of the LSL is a good example of how regulations in Japan reflect the balance of power in the political arena.[9] Portions of the final law testify to the power of small stores while others reflect the preferences of department stores, superstores, and MITI officials. It was very much a compromise.[10] What is particularly interesting about this case, however, is that MITI was able to continue adjusting regulatory policy to the political balance of power for almost two decades after the enactment of the LSL while only once changing the letter of the law. Throughout this period, MITI sought to bring some order to the regulatory regime, but each time it ended up being pulled along by societal forces beyond its control.[11]

In order to understand what happened to the LSL and what was at issue in the SII talks, one needs to look at the law itself. Unlike the Department Store Law, which forced large stores to obtain permits before opening stores, the LSL required only that they notify the authorities and participate in an adjustment process. Developers were required, first, to notify the minister of international trade and industry of their plans to construct a building (Article 3 Notification) and then to notify the minister again with detailed plans spelling out which stores would operate as tenants in the building (Article 5 Notification). At this point, the minister was supposed to refer the matter to the Large Store Council (*Daitenshin*) composed of businessmen, consumers, and representatives of the public interest which was in turn supposed to consult the chamber of commerce in the affected area. Based on advice from these groups, the minister was then to issue a recommendation as to whether or not the merchant should alter the details of his store-opening plans[12] (see figure 6.1).

On paper, the LSL sounded more liberal than the DSL. MITI could not legally prohibit a large store from opening, and time limits imposed under the law promised developers that they would have a verdict from the ministry on the details within seven months. The problem was that these details (floor space, business hours, and number of store holidays) made the difference between profit and loss for developers interested in opening new stores. Under the terms of the law, for example, MITI could force a store near a train station to close at 6 P.M., just as commuters were returning from work.[13] It could also force it to cut the size of its store in half. For nearby small merchants too, these details held the potential to determine whether or not they would survive.

MITI officials thus found themselves in charge of arbitrating bitter dis-

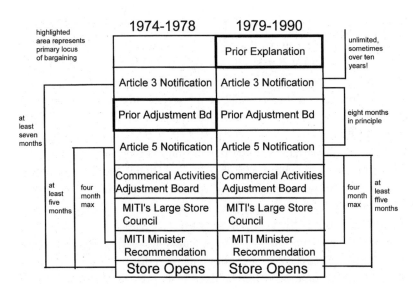

FIGURE 6.1 The Large Store Law Process

putes over the terms of store openings that, while make or break issues for the principles, were a far cry from the "industrial policy" matters they considered to be the ministry's primary mission. Their solution: delegate the task of settling disputes to local chambers of commerce. Consequently, even before the law went into effect, the ministry issued an ordinance directing local chambers to set up Commercial Activities Adjustment Boards (CAABs) with representatives of local merchants, consumers, and academics and to base their recommendations to MITI upon the settlements worked out within these committees. This system promised to significantly reduce the burden on MITI staff, but it also allowed the ministry to keep some control over the process since staff from MITI's regional bureaus were supposed to participate in the CAAB meetings, and since this formal adjustment process was governed by a four-month time limit set in the LSL.[14]

Almost immediately, however, MITI began to lose control of the process. Realizing that they couldn't do anything to stop store openings once the clock started ticking at the beginning of the formal adjustment process, merchants pressured MITI officials into allowing local chambers of commerce to concentrate the real work of "adjustment" within *Prior Adjustment Boards* charged with working out a deal prior to Article 5 notification—a practice that was eventually sanctioned in administrative guidance issued by the ministry. Free of the four-month time limit on the formal adjustment process, merchants were able to drag out negotiations at this stage in order to extract more concessions from large stores.[15] Further, merchants upset that many stores were avoiding the LSL by building stores just under 1,500 square meters went to their local governments and convinced many to adopt regulations restricting the expansion of stores as small as 200 square meters. Finally, small shopkeepers also went to their Diet members and asked them to keep up the pressure on MITI.[16]

For MITI officials, the LSL was turning out to be a real headache. It was causing large stores enough trouble to make them complain about the arbitrary and often extended prior adjustment process, but it had not slowed down the expansion of large stores enough to satisfy small stores and their patrons in the Diet. On top of that, localities were taking matters into their own hands by passing regulations stricter than MITI's. By 1977, MITI officials had come to the conclusion that they had to do something to bring some order to the disorderly process. First, bowing to pressure from the LDP, they proposed legislation that created a new class of medium-sized stores (500 to 1,500 square meters) which were then required to go through a process parallel to that of the large stores. These amendments to the LSL passed in 1978. Then, in 1979, MITI used administrative guidance to add a new set of time limits: large stores would be required to submit their initial (Article 3) notification 13 months before their projected store opening date, but large stores could be assured that the prior adjustment process would take no longer than eight months (see figure 6.1).

With these changes, MITI temporarily brought its official LSL policy into line with the political facts on the ground. By amending the LSL to bring medium-sized stores under its regulatory umbrella, it supplanted uneven local regulations. And by placing a time limit on the uncontrolled prior adjustment process, it recognized that this was where the real bargaining was already taking place. Before MITI officials could even catch their breath, however, small merchants were already creating a new set of political facts on the ground. First, unwilling to work under MITI's time limits, they began to concentrate the adjustment process at an even earlier point in the process: before Article 3 notification.[17] Since there were no time limits governing this "prior explanation" phase, they could drag out the negotiations as long as they wanted. Second, they continued to press local governments for relief. In city after city, they succeeded in getting local assemblies to pass laws freezing retail expansion.[18]

Once again in 1982, therefore, MITI was forced to adjust its policy to better reflect political reality—this time relying entirely on administrative guidance. First, it bowed to the trend toward concentrating the bargaining at the earliest stage by *requiring* parties to come to a settlement before officials would accept Article 3 notification. This move was significant because it confirmed the superior bargaining position of local merchants. If large stores wanted to open without endless delays, they would have to accept virtually all of the local demands.[19] Second, MITI responded to the growing number of local government "freezes" by agreeing to designate certain areas as "areas of store opening restraint" where it would not accept any applications for store openings. By 1989, some 340 cities or wards (or about half of the total) had received this designation.[20]

With this last set of changes in its administration of the LSL, MITI ushered in a period in which the expansion of large stores was finally slowed to trickle. As figure 6.2 shows, the number of new large stores (over 1,500 square meters) fell from 247 in 1981 to less than half that rate by

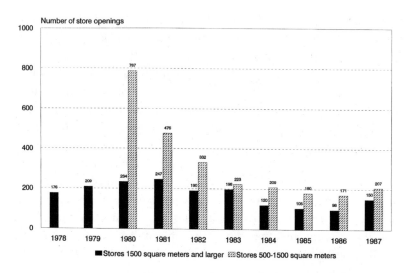

FIGURE 6.2 Large Store Openings, 1978-87

Source: MITI, 90-nendai no ryūtsū bijon (Vision for the Distribution Industry into the 1990s) (Tokyo: MITI, 1989), p.90. Note: MITI did not keep data on medium-sized stores before 1980.

1984 while the number of new medium-sized stores (500–1,500 square meters) fell even more sharply from 787 in 1980 to just 171 in 1986. From a total of more than 1,000 in 1980, the combined number of medium and large store-openings fell to 269 by 1986. While developers were able to open some stores during this period, those that did typically had to endure agonizingly long and expensive delays—averaging over seven years by the end of the decade.[21]

The cumulative effects of the government's policy of restricting large store openings can also be seen by examining time series and international comparative data on the size of retail outlets. Table 6.1 shows that there has been only a very gradual change in the proportions of large versus small stores in Japan. In 1974, the "mom and pop" stores—those with just one or two employees—accounted for fully 62.5 percent of the total, and this figure had fallen just 5 percentage points by 1988. During that time, large stores (those with more than 20 employees), increased their share of the total by just 1.1 percentage points. This slow pace of change left Japan as an outlier (along with France, which has a law similar to the LSL) in terms of the size structure of its retail system. As table 6.2 shows, Germany and the U.S. both have fewer small stores and a significantly greater proportion of large ones.

TABLE 6.1

The Size of Japanese Retail Stores, 1974–1988

Number of Employees	1974	1976	1979	1982	1985	1988
1-2	62.5%	61.9%	61.1%	60.2%	57.7%	54.0%
3-4	23.3	23.7	24.0	24.0	25.1	26.1
5-9	10.2	10.3	10.5	10.9	11.7	13.2
10-19	2.7	2.7	2.8	3.1	3.6	4.3
20-49	1.0	1.1	1.3	1.4	1.6	1.9
50+	0.3	0.3	0.3	0.4	0.4	0.5

Source: MITI, *90-nendai no ryutsu bijon* (A Vision of Distribution for the 1990s), p. 18.

TABLE 6.2

International Comparison of Size of Retail Stores

Number of Employees	Japan (1988)	U.S. (1982)	France (1982)	Germany (1985)
1-2	54.0%	40.0%	66.7%	14.7%
3-9	39.3	40.5	30.1	62.8
10-19	4.3	10.4	1.9	14.7
20-49	1.9	6.5	1.0	5.7
50-99	0.3	1.9	0.2	1.2
100 and over	0.1	0.7	0.2	0.9

Source: Economic Planning Agency data reported in JEI Report 43A (November 10, 1989), p. 3.

THE "VISION" INITIATIVE OF 1989

The record of Japanese policymaking in this issue area up to the late 1980s establishes a clear pattern against which to measure the policy changes adopted in the wake of the sii talks. From 1974 through the end of the decade, MITI's administration of the law had steadily *tightened* restrictions on store openings—in stark contrast to the movement toward liberalization which came after the negotiations with the U.S.. Just prior to the sii talks, however, MITI made one more attempt to bring order to the LSL regulatory regime, an initiative outlined in its "Vision for the Distribution Industry in the 1990s."[22] This report proposed a number of steps which, *if implemented as planned*, would have accomplished much of what the U.S. later convinced Japan to do through sii. As in the case of the previous initiatives, though, this one too immediately ran into stiff resistance—causing MITI to shelve the plan pending the outcome of the SII talks. While MITI's initiative reflected the fact that there *was* support for change within Japan, a close look at the course of this "Vision" initiative suggests that this last MITI attempt to clean up the LSL on its own (minus extensive gaiatsu) was unlikely to have turned out any differently than the initiatives of the 1970s and early 1980s.

Having had little luck in its previous attempts to reform the LSL, MITI officials were not eager to take up this problem again.[23] They were forced to do so, however, after a series of government advisory councils—starting with the Maekawa Commission report of 1986—pointed to the Large Store Law as an example of regulatory excess that was limiting the growth of domestic demand. The Maekawa report had actually been very vague, calling only for the "streamlining of distribution mechanisms" and a "review of the various restrictions pertaining to distribution and sales."[24] A subsequent report from the Administrative Reform Promotion Council in December 1988, though, was more specific, criticizing MITI for letting its administration of the LSL get away from the original purpose of the law.[25]

Confronted with a call for reform from a council set up by the cabinet to lead the deregulation process, MITI officials felt they had to take another shot at "streamlining" the LSL process. To this end, they set two of MITI's own advisory councils to work drawing up concrete proposals. That this process involved two councils was a sign of how MITI was itself divided in its approach to the distribution industry. While one council was organized under the Distribution Industry Division of the Industrial Policy Bureau, long viewed as an advocate of modernization and closer to the large retail chains, the other was organized within the Small and Medium Enterprises Agency, the section of MITI charged with watching out for the interests of small businesses, including the "mom and pop" shops. The division of power and responsibility within MITI on the distribution issue thus perpetuated the tendency on the part of the government to seek a "balance" between economic and political interests.

Significantly, however, this process of "balancing" did not involve representatives of consumer interests or other broad-based interests. The process that led to the "Vision" report, like that which preceded each of the previous MITI attempts to bring order to its administration of the LSL, was instead a classic example of subgovernmental policymaking. MITI officials consulted a range of distribution interest groups and LDP politicians active in the issue area, but the consensus building process was limited to this small circle of elite actors. As a result of the need to please opponents of change within this circle, MITI's eventual "Vision" proposals were already somewhat weaker than reform proposals that had been floated earlier. It did not propose changing the text of the law. It also rejected such proposals as the one from the Economic Planning Agency, which had proposed that CAAB members be designated "quasi-public servants," subjecting them to bribery statutes and thus limiting their ability to exploit their role.[26]

What the "Vision" report did propose was the following: for the first time, MITI would put a time limit on the "prior explanation" phase of the adjustment process, limiting it to eight months; furthermore, MITI would institute an overall time limit of two years for the entire process; authorities would be directed to accept recommendations from one step to the next even if agreement had not been reached; and local authorities would be prevented from adding extra regulations to those set out in the LSL.[27]

As noted above, these proposals would have marked a significant move toward liberalization, *if implemented as planned*. Based on MITI's previous record in administering the law, however, there is clearly a basis for doubting whether MITI could have implemented them faithfully. Given MITI's decision to continue to rely on informal processes like "prior explanation," there was no guarantee small merchants would not find yet another way to circumvent the two year time limit. Critics suggested, furthermore, that the government might start restricting large stores by forcing sharp cuts in planned floor space—something it would still be able to do.[28] MITI officials contributed to such speculation by insisting that the ministry still saw it as its mission to "protect local retailers from any potential injuries to their business."[29]

As it turned out, however, MITI never got far enough with its proposals to establish what would have happened if it had tried to implement them. As soon as the "Vision" report was released in June 1989, it encountered an "icy welcome." The first to voice its opposition was the Ministry of Home Affairs, acting as the defender of local governments' constitutional right to pass their own ordinances regulating local commerce. The MHA had not been part of MITI's consensus-building process, and it promised to oppose to the bitter end the ministry's plan to keep local governments from instituting regulations tougher than MITI's.[30] Given that local governments had played an important role in forcing MITI to ratchet up its enforcement of the LSL in the past, the opposition by the MHA was a serious blow to MITI's "Vision."

Perhaps more serious, however, was the renewed opposition MITI faced from members of the LDP commerce zoku, the group of Dietmen active in small business affairs who had been carefully cultivated by the ministry during the consensus-building process. While these Dietmen had signed off on the MITI proposals prior to their release in June, they rethought their position after the LDP suffered a major blow in the Upper House elections in July. The party lost its majority in the Upper House for the first time since 1955 in these elections, and analysts uniformly pointed to a small business revolt over the controversial new consumption tax as one of the primary reasons for this defeat. With small merchants already upset over the consumption tax, the last thing the LDP commerce zoku wanted to do was to add to their ire by forcing them to accept a reduction in LSL protection. These politicians therefore went to MITI and quietly urged the ministry to put its "Vision" on hold.[31]

MITI had announced, when it released its vision report in June, that it planned to implement the proposals through written administrative guidance (tsūtatsu) in September. That date came and went, however, without MITI action, and the ministry eventually announced that it was putting its plans on hold pending the results of the SII talks. As one MITI official put it, "We could have sent the notice last September, but we thought it won't make sense if nobody followed it."[32]

The Pattern of LSL Policymaking Prior to SII

The above history of retail regulation establishes a clear pattern of Japanese policymaking in this area leading up to the SII talks, both in terms of policy *outcomes* and policy *process*. The consistency in policy *outcomes* is fairly obvious: MITI tried several times to steer policy in a more orderly direction, but in each case ended up either putting off its initiative (1989) or further tightening its restrictions on store-openings (1979 and 1982). The result was a falling rate of large store openings, lengthening delays, and glacial change in the structure of the retail sector.

The consistency in policy *process*, however, is equally noteworthy. Throughout this period, the process was dominated by political actors inside the distribution policy subgovernment: the sections of MITI dealing with distribution, a variety of interest groups representing large and small retailers, and LDP Dietmen with ties to these interests. In 1974, 1979, 1982, and even in 1989, the policy debate excluded consumer interests, involved few LDP leaders, and allowed other ministries a say only when proposals had a direct bearing on their interests. Policy in this sphere is thus an excellent example of "patterned pluralism": the Japanese system's tendency to compartmentalize the policy process and limit involvement to a small but stable group of actors.

Similarly, policymaking in this sphere is a classic example of the tendency toward "particularistic policymaking" in Japan. As described in chapter 4, the structure of the Japanese system (at least through the political reforms of 1994) encouraged politicians to pursue electoral security by targeting particularistic policies at groups of voters who could deliver a loyal personal vote. Small merchants, influential in their communities and tied in with local political bosses, were especially well-positioned to exploit their critical position in this structure. Given that these voters had shown a willingness to switch their votes (when they voted for leftist mayors in some cities and when they punished the LDP in the 1989 Upper House elections), politicians were especially keen on courting their support by offering targeted political goods.

While parties offered a variety of favors to small businesses, the Large Store Law was especially well suited to the politicians' need to provide a policy offering particular favors to this group of voters. Limitations on market entry by new large stores allowed all existing stores to avoid price competition and generate extra profits. It also provided merchants with a "property right" in the status quo which many were able to use during extended negotiations with large stores to extract special concessions: the right to relocate a store inside new retail buildings; sometimes outright bribes. Politicians could often take personal credit for the deals worked out under the shadow of this law by serving as brokers, extracting political contributions and loyal support as a price for their help.[33]

As long as participation in the policymaking process was limited to the subgovernmental elite, the incentives arising from the structure of the Japanese political system guaranteed that interest groups with a stake in maintaining the restrictiveness of the LSL would win out. The politicians most involved, after all, were the LDP backbenchers whose electoral strategy was based on appealing for personal votes from economic groups with vested interests in the status quo.[34] And these politicians naturally did everything they could to force MITI to do their bidding. As one MITI official put it: "MITI doesn't have the power to legislate; that's the power of the LDP." MITI was actually interested in liberalizing the LSL, he claimed, but it had no choice but to tighten restrictions under the law because "we knew that if the LDP put together a law providing for a licensing system for large stores [a more restrictive system than the LSL], all the opposition parties would support them. It would pass in a flash."[35] As long as the policy *process* followed this pattern, the policy *outcome* would continue to be the same: MITI would be forced to continue to recalibrate its administration of the law to reflect the interests of existing stores.

The American Demands

Although the distribution issue area was not one with a long history of American intervention, the SII talks were not the first time the U.S. raised concerns about trade barriers in the sector. The U.S. brought up the LSL issue for the first time in 1985 at one of the regularly scheduled U.S.-Japan Trade Committee meetings, and the law had been listed as a "trade barrier" in the USTR's annual *Trade Estimate* report each year since 1986.[36] Distribution issues in general and the LSL in particular were also one of the primary subjects of the "Structural Dialogue" between the U.S. and Japan in 1986–1987.

Until SII, however, the U.S. had not made specific demands for Japanese action in this issue area. The issue was actually quite low down on the list of topics covered at Trade Committee meetings, where sectoral issues were given priority during the Reagan years, and the Structural Dialogue, designed as an exercise in exchanging information about each side's economic systems, provided no opportunities for the U.S. to press Japan for policy concessions. Instead of making high profile demands, the U.S. during this period took time to study the issue and let the Japanese government know that trade negotiators were interested in it. To this end, the U.S. Embassy in Tokyo did a detailed study of the LSL, and a member of the embassy staff kept in touch with MITI officials in order to follow the course of the Distribution Vision initiative.[37]

Nevertheless, foreign opinion gradually became more and more of a consideration in the Japanese policy debate over the LSL as the 1980s wore on. Advocates of liberalization, for example, began to point to foreign pressure. "The law, if left uncorrected, will turn out to be a target of even louder blame from Western retailers as a non-tariff barrier," the head of one large superstore chain warned in 1988.[38] The fact that the Maekawa Commission, the Administrative Reform Council, and eventually MITI all took up the LSL issue in the mid- to late-1980s was at least partly attributable to their realization that this issue was rising to the top of the U.S.-Japan agenda. By the spring of 1989, those who follow the relationship closely already knew that Japan's distribution system was likely to be the subject of "the next major trade confrontation."[39]

In fact, as the new Bush Administration was setting up shop in Washington in January 1989, U.S. agencies were doing everything they could to make sure the distribution issue was part of their brief. The State Department, which had already invested time in studying the issue, announced it was organizing an interagency mission on the issue which it wanted to send to Tokyo in February. Treasury, upset that State might "do another Structural Dialogue" (all talk and no results), quickly scrambled to bring its staff up to speed on the issue so that it would be represented in the mission.[40] And at the USTR, the issue was on the list of Japanese practices being considered for targeting under Super 301.

Given this widespread interest in the subject, there was never any doubt that the distribution sector was going to have a prominent place on the SII agenda. It was mentioned specifically by Carla Hills when she outlined her proposal for the talks in May, and the Japanese press, in its first coverage of SII, immediately focused on the Large Store Law as the most likely target of the new initiative.

Nevertheless, if anything, the issue became *more* prominent as the negotiating year progressed. While the U.S. did not formulate specific demands on the issue until December, U.S. negotiators led MITI officials to believe—early in the process—that they would be satisfied with a faithful implementation of the MITI "Vision" proposals.[41] The State Department had been given primary responsibility for distribution, and the less aggressive push on this issue early on may have reflected that agency's traditional go-soft attitude toward negotiations with Japan. Deputy Assistant Secretary Robert Fauver and Ambassador Michael Armacost, who took the lead in dealing with MITI on the issue, may also have played down their demands in hopes of cultivating MITI's support for the U.S. position on public investment—the issue both felt was more important in terms of its impact on the U.S.-Japan trade balance.

As the negotiations got underway, however, several forces combined to force the U.S. negotiators to toughen their demands. First, a major U.S. retail chain, Toys 'R' Us, weighed in on the issue with U.S. Trade Representative Carla Hills just before her scheduled visit to Japan. Until this point, the American demands on the Large Store Law had been based on the argument that the law slowed the expansion of large *Japanese* stores which sold more imports—an indirect argument at best. Since no

American chain of large retailers had even tried to get into the Japanese market up to this point, the U.S. could not easily make the more direct argument that the law blocked American retailers. Then in October, Toys 'R' Us executive Charles Lazarus met with Hills to discuss the problems he was having with the LSL. Toys 'R' Us planned to open 100 stores and set up its own direct import operations in Japan, but it was worried that the LSL would screw up its plans. His chain had established similar operations in Germany, Britain, and elsewhere, Lazarus pointed out, but had never encountered anything like the barriers it was facing in Japan.[42]

For Hills, the news that large stores faced long delays was a major revelation, so when she arrived in Tokyo, she cited the Large Store Law specifically as she laid out the Bush Administration's demand that the U.S. wanted a "down payment and blueprint for further action" from Japan by April. With the entry of Toys 'R' Us and the Hills visit, officials in Tokyo and Washington knew that the stakes had been raised on this issue. Congressmen like Max Baucus, following SII closely and threatening to introduce legislation to target structural issues with Super 301, began to concentrate more and more on the Large Store Law as a test of whether Bush and the Japanese were serious. Advocates of liberalization in Japan also pressed the U.S. not to settle for the "Vision" proposals. MITI officials soon realized the U.S. would insist on an actual revision of the law. And by December, the Americans had decided to seek its abolition.

Table 6.3 summarizes the Americans demands in the distribution issue area. As one can see, there is much more to the list than just the Large Store Law. In the final negotiating sessions and in the end-game bargaining, however, the LSL was virtually the only one of these issues to receive the attention of senior officials.[43] In Congressional testimony in March, for example, Linn Williams of the USTR pointed to the plight of Toys 'R' Us:

> [The firm] faces the prospect of considerable expense and delay as a result of the Japanese government's implementation of a law, the Large Retail Store Act, that permits its Japanese competitors to control its destiny in Japan. Japanese companies, by contrast, can buy entire shopping centers in Hawaii and have to obtain little more from the government than a zoning permit.[44]

Congress and U.S. officials thus waited anxiously during the early spring months of 1989 to see how far the Japanese government would be willing to go in liberalizing a regulatory regime deeply rooted in the political structure of the nation.

TABLE 6.3

The Americans' Distribution Demands

1. Improve import processing infrastructure (airports, harbors, customs-clearance facilities).

2. Implement procedural innovations, computerization, and other improvements designed to facilitate more expeditious customs-clearance and import processing.

3. Relax truck transportation regulations.

4. Abolish the Large Store Law by a set date in the future; in the meantime, reduce delay under the law to six months; allow large stores to add floorspace for import sales without any restrictions; prohibit localities from adopting restrictions beyond those at the national level.

5. Reduce regulations and allocate more licenses for liquor sales.

6. Devise guidelines clarifying which practices in the distribution area are considered anti-competitive and illegal under the Anti-Monopoly Act and enforce these rules. Clarify that the following practices, when designed to restrict competition, are illegal: refusal to deal; the rebate system; exclusive contracts with distributors; resale price maintenance.

7. Have the Fair Trade Commission investigate a number of specific sectors where a few large firms dominate the distribution system.

8. Allow foreign firms to participate in processes leading to new policies on standards, licensing, and testing.

9. Abolish Fair Trade Commission supervised fair competition codes which ban the use of premiums to promote new products.

10. Implement various programs designed to promote and facilitate the distribution of imported goods.

Source: Americans' List of 200 Demands.

Synergistic Strategies and the Deal on the Large Store Law

Because it *was* deeply rooted, the task of getting the Japanese to accept a significant liberalization of the Large Store Law was not easy. Initially, even MITI officials sounded off in opposition to the American demands. "We won't accept unilateral U.S. demands to change our marketing system just for the sake of increasing American imports," one official said. "We intend to make the upcoming meetings a place to offer information on Japan's distribution system, not a place of negotiations."[45] The most vocal opposition came, however, from the biggest beneficiaries of the status quo: small retailers. Especially as the expansion plans of Toys 'R' Us were announced, its threat to the livelihoods of thousands of small toy shop owners became the focus of the protest movement. "The Toys 'R' Us plan means that we'll be killed," one toy shop owner complained in the national press.[46]

And this shop owner's worry was more than justified. The average toy store in Japan at the time had floor space of only 60 square meters, too small to hold much inventory and certainly too small to compete with the Toys 'R' Us discounting strategy. Even the largest toy store in Japan, in the Ginza, had only 2,000 square meters, less than half the size of the stores Toys 'R' Us was planning to build in *provincial* cities.[47] When the international toy retailing giant made its debut in Britain, the head of Japan's toy store association pointed out, the number of toy retailers fell from 6,000 to 1,500.[48]

At the local level, fears of a similar fate fueled vigorous activity aimed at defending restrictions on large store openings. In Niigata, a city where Toys 'R' Us planned to open a store even though merchants there had enforced a freeze on all new store openings for several years, store owners got together and announced that they would demand that the chain reduce the size of its planned store from 5,000 to 500 square meters.[49] Responding to protests like this one, several local governments—including Kyoto and Fukuoka—passed unanimous resolutions opposing liberalization of the LSL. "The abolition of the LSL will cause social chaos at the local level," Tokyo's resolution stated.[50]

At the national level, the Japan Federation of Specialty Store Associations (Nihon Senmontenkai Renmei), the umbrella organization representing groups like the toy store association, headed a vocal campaign aimed at forcing the LDP to weigh in on its side. It organized a demonstration outside the LDP headquarters building; it called a rally and invited the entire LDP delegation; and interest group leaders met with usually reliable members of the LDP commerce zoku.[51]

But all of this didn't work. At the final SII negotiating session prior to the April midterm report, the Japanese government brought to the table a proposal to significantly liberalize the LSL, and by the time the session was over the two sides had agreed on a three-phase liberalization plan that promised to open the door much wider to large store expansion. In Phase 1, starting immediately, MITI would issue new administrative guidance limiting the time of the adjustment process to a total of 18 months and allowing stores to add up to 100 square meters for import sales, free of restrictions. It would also relax the closing time and vacation day para-

meters so that stores could stay open until 7 P.M. and open all but 44 days
a year regardless of what local merchants had to say. In Phase 2, implemented the following year, the Diet would pass legislation amending the
LSL so as to reduce the time of adjustment to one year and enhance "the
clarity and transparency of adjustment procedures." In Phase 3, two years
after the passage of the law, the government would review the law and
consider the possibility of abolishing LSL restrictions in specific geo-
graphical areas.[52]

How did this happen? Why did the small stores and other interests
with a stake in the LSL regulatory regime fail to stop the liberalization of
the law this time when they had stopped it so many times in the past? The
short answer, of course, is gaiatsu. The long answer, to be developed in
this section of the chapter, is that the different policy outcome resulted
because gaiatsu helped change the policy process, expanding participation to include new elite actors but also (perhaps more importantly in
this case) expanding it to "include" the general public. It was important
that elements within MITI and some interest groups were on the U.S.
side, but it was also important that the public eventually weighed in on
the U.S. side as well.

PARTICIPATION EXPANSION AT THE ELITE LEVEL

As in the case of the negotiations on public investment, the bargaining on
the Large Store Law was dominated by the lead agency, in this case MITI,
up through the February negotiating session. At that meeting, while the
Americans called for the abolition of the law, the MITI delegation held
fast to its initial position. It was willing to implement the ministry's Vision
proposals, but it was not willing to revise the law, and it was certainly not
willing to abolish it. To do away with the law would mean MITI would lose
all of its influence over the retail sector. It would also have no way of stopping local governments from passing even stricter regulations than
existed under the LSL regime.[53]

In sticking to its Vision proposals, MITI officials were doing what they
had always done with the LSL. They were taking their cues from the political winds. Throughout the first six months of the SII talks, MITI delegates
had been convinced the Americans would settle for the Vision reforms,
and they doubted the LDP would stand for anything more than that. As
recently as February 9, during the general election campaign, Kaifu had
been forced to promise retailers that he would not agree to revise the

LSL. He would merely seek to return to an approach more faithful to the original purpose of the law (i.e. the Vision proposals).[54]

Once the Americans demanded the abolition of the law and put it at the top of their list, however, these officials were forced to scramble to find a new policy equilibrium suited to the changed political environment. This environment was different, first of all, because LDP leaders became involved in an LSL policy debate previously dominated by zoku Dietmen. The leaders' involvement began, as in the other issue areas, with Kaifu's trip to Palm Springs on March 2–3. During his private meeting with Bush, Kaifu reportedly offered a specific set of policy concessions on the LSL. He was willing to consider administrative reforms aimed at reducing the LSL delay to around one year, and he suggested Japan might be willing to revise the letter of the law in 1992.[55] Upon his return to Tokyo, Kaifu was forced to deny that such specifics had been discussed (since his proposals had not been cleared through proper channels), but by setting up a cabinet task force and directing it to come up with a package of concessions that would satisfy his *public* promise to "firmly tackle structural reforms," he nevertheless involved his entire cabinet in the task of resolving the impasse over the LSL and other SII issues.

Over the next several weeks, MITI officials were forced to deal with additional "interventions" by LDP leaders intent on making sure the LSL would not jeopardize U.S.-Japan relations. The first "intervention" came from an unexpected source: Mutō Kabun, the Minister of International Trade and Industry, who proposed at a press conference that the government consider abolishing the LSL in three years if administrative reforms did not prove effective.[56] Mutō's initiative was unexpected because he had long been one of the small stores' most loyal defenders in his capacity as a senior member of the commerce zoku. In subsequent weeks, Mutō went back to defending MITI's preference for administrative reforms along the lines of the Vision proposals,[57] but his call for the government to consider abolishing the law was cited by several MITI officials as a turning point in their deliberations which pushed them to offer more far-reaching concessions.[58]

While it is impossible to establish Mutō's motives for making his controversial comment, one possibility is that he was seeking to establish himself as "above" zoku politics—that he wanted to demonstrate to his colleagues that he could, as a cabinet minister, bow to considerations of the "public good" even when these went against particularistic interests he had long championed. In this regard, it is interesting that other Dietmen, at similar points in their careers, have behaved in similar ways. Ozawa Ichirō, a don of construction interests, helped obtain the consent of these groups to American demands in 1988. And Hata Tsutomu, a senior member of the agriculture zoku, played a brokering role in the resolution of U.S.-Japan disputes on plywood (1985), cigarettes (1986), and beef and citrus (1988).[59] Both of the latter moved up to leadership positions in the party in subsequent years.

What I am suggesting, therefore, is that the dichotomy between LDP "backbenchers" and "leaders" discussed in chapter 4 needs to be seen as a little more nuanced. Senior zoku members often find themselves straddling the line between the two camps: they retain close ties to particularistic interests, but to the extent many of them aspire to "leadership" status, they have an incentive to take a more independent position in favor of the "public good."[60] Note that the main argument advanced in the earlier chapter still stands, however, for it seems that zoku leaders are prompted to behave in this way only when there is a "crisis" such as a threat to the U.S.-Japan relationship. In this case, Mutō could advance his career by demonstrating that he could rise above small store interests while at the same time avoiding the wrath of these groups by blaming it all on gaiatsu (and taking credit for brokering the deal for side-payments to affected groups—see below).

The second major political intervention on this issue came from Kaifu himself who became much more intimately involved in the resolution of the LSL issue than he was in the settlement of any of the other SII issues. In the final days before the Japanese delegation left for Washington to negotiate the terms of the April interim SII report, Kaifu quietly pushed for the total abolition of the LSL, against the preferences of most MITI officials and much of his party, motivated by his belief that the Americans would settle for nothing less and his conviction that the Japanese public was behind this more radical reform.[61] While he was ultimately unable to win party and MITI support for this position, his intervention helped convince all parties to accept more far-reaching changes in the LSL than had been considered up to this point.

But Mutō and Kaifu were not the only LDP politicians involved. According to one MITI official, LDP leaders like Takeshita and Ozawa played equally critical roles: "Because these two put such a premium on maintaining good relations with the U.S. and because they are both such powerful figures in the LDP, we were able to achieve changes which MITI alone could never have accomplished."[62] Ozawa's role was particularly interesting. As secretary general of the LDP, his job was to represent the party's position on issues like the LSL. Having staked his career on making the Kaifu Administration a success, however, he could not ignore Kaifu's push for abolition of the law. In the end, he played the classic broker's role, convincing Kaifu to give up his call for abolition and convincing the party and MITI to accept the final Japanese negotiating position, including a reduction in the LSL delay to one year, the revision of the law in addition to administrative changes (both concessions suggested by Kaifu at Palm Springs), and a promise to consider exempting major metropolitan areas from LSL restrictions in three years.[63]

In addition to these highly publicized concessions, we also need to note here another concession which came more quietly but was probably as important as any of the above. Remember that when MITI originally proposed its Vision reforms, the opposition of the Ministry of Home Affairs was critical in forcing the ministry to postpone implementation of the changes. This time, as MITI went through the process again, it was able to win the MHA's acquiescence to restrictions on the right of local governments to adopt their own regulations governing retail expansion, and so a specific commitment along these lines was part of what the Japanese delegation brought to Washington in early April.[64] The fact that MITI officials were able to win the MHA's cooperation this time when they were not able to do so just a few months earlier can be attributed only to gaiatsu and the role it played in pushing this issue up to the cabinet level. MITI could therefore cite Kaifu's pledge at Palm Springs to convince reluctant MHA officials to go along with the liberalization plan.

The Japanese negotiating position softened significantly between February and April, and the fact that this softening took place at the same time LDP leaders became involved in resolving the impasse suggests that participation expansion at the elite level was an important cause. A MITI official put it this way:

> As long as policy is being discussed only within the sphere of distribution, policy proposals are decided based only on their effects on the distribution industry. But when such an issue becomes a subject of negotiations with the U.S., people begin to focus on the broader implications of policy: the effect on the trade balance and the possibility that the U.S. might

retaliate in other areas with charges of "dumping." As long as we were talking only about the "Distribution Vision," the only people who participated
in the discussions were those from the distribution industry. But when we
talked about these issues in the context of the SII, many others joined in
the discussions: MOF concerned about public finance; various people concerned about the Anti-Monopoly Law; the prime minister and other top
politicians. And we started to talk about it at more of a macro level in
terms of which policy was best in a much broader context.[65]

The quote is long, but it summarizes very well the effects of the strategy
I have called participation expansion. Government agencies like MITI
adjust policy in areas like the LSL to reflect the balance of political forces
which are motivated to make their preferences known. Gaiatsu can thus
have a significant effect if it can motivate previously uninvolved actors
with less of a stake in the status quo to get involved in the policy process.

EXPANSION OF PARTICIPATION TO INCLUDE THE GENERAL PUBLIC

That said, I am not satisfied that elite politics can account by itself for the
shift in policy on this issue. We also have to consider the impact of public
opinion. It is, of course, difficult if not impossible to establish a clear
causal chain running from gaiatsu to public opinion and finally to policy
change. Opinion polls never ask the public *why* they take the positions
they do, so it is impossible to tell if a particular public opinion shift is
attributable to public statements by U.S. officials or related media coverage. It is also difficult to establish that public opinion affected policy since
this diffuse force leaves few footprints. To the extent it matters, public
opinion makes a difference only when it works its way through the *perceptions* of politicians and bureaucrats—when these elite actors perceive
that public opinion is shifting in ways that require them to adjust their
preferences to reflect this shift. In this case, however, we have some evidence that the shift in public attitudes was fostered by gaiatsu and that it
did play a role in influencing positions taken by various elite actors.

First, let's look at the link between U.S. pressure tactics and public
perceptions of the Large Store Law. Notably, it seems that most of the
public was unaware of the Large Store Law until the SII talks put a spotlight on the issue.[66] When they were made aware, the information most
consumers obtained about the law came from media reporting about the
Americans' complaints. While some of this reporting was critical, focus-

ing on such aspects of the dispute as the plight to the Niigata toy shops, much of it supported the U.S. position by informing the public about abuses of the law, the long delays, and MITI's disregard for the original purpose of the law. Simply by providing a "hook" for news articles and television news reports, gaiatsu fostered a broader awareness of the issue and motivated consumers to develop preferences where they previously had none.

Furthermore, journalists such as the NHK reporter quoted in chapter 4 used SII as the basis for a conscious campaign to force the government to take into account the interests of consumers and the general public in the range of policy areas targeted by the Americans. This media strategy was described in some detail in that earlier chapter, so I will not cover it again, but what needs to be emphasized here is that the campaign focused especially on the Large Store Law. Not only the *Asahi* (the most liberal of the major dailies) but also the *Nikkei* (the counterpart to America's *Wall Street Journal*) editorialized in favor of LSL liberalization.[67] In so doing, they helped shape public opinion and served as a voice for this opinion which could be heard in *Nagatachō* (Japan's Capitol Hill) and in *Kasumigaseki* (the bureaucrats' district).

The impact of gaiatsu and all of this media coverage can be measured by a *Nikkei* public opinion survey conducted in April 1990, just as the coverage of SII was peaking.[68] By that date, 74 percent of those polled reported that they knew about the Large Store Law. Of these, 76.7 percent agreed that "deregulation [of the LSL] would be a plus for my own life," surpassing by a huge margin the 10 percent who agreed that it would be a "minus" for their lives. Furthermore, the poll revealed that the American message that deregulation would lead to lower prices and increased choices for consumers was getting through. Of those who supported deregulation, 93 percent pointed to their expectation that prices would decline, and 97 percent emphasized the wider choice they expected would result from deregulation. Of all of these numbers, this last set probably came closest to proving that gaiatsu (and the associated media coverage) was behind the shift in public opinion on this issue. In this regard, it is interesting that small store interests blamed the Japanese media for fostering the public perception that deregulation would improve the lives of ordinary consumers.[69]

But did public opinion affect policy, and if so how? First, it needs to be emphasized that diffuse public support for LSL liberalization was not represented in the policy process by any significant public interest group. The consumers' groups were caught by surprise when the U.S. presented itself as an advocate for Japanese consumers, and many consumer groups insisted that the U.S. did not know what "true" consumer interests were. "Consumers have the impression that large stores offer lower prices," one consumer interest leader remarked, "but in many cases their prices are no different in areas like fish and produce."[70] Other leaders pointed out that consumers need more than low prices. As one argued, urban shoppers who do not own cars need neighborhood mom and pop shops for their convenience.[71] Recalling that the U.S. had in the past pressed Japan to import food products containing traces of pesticides banned in Japan, another consumer leader emphasized that lower prices do not help consumers if the products they buy are dangerous.[72] All of these comments, reflecting the skepticism of consumer groups about U.S. motives and their concerns for issues other than low prices, hampered the ability of these groups to work with the U.S. to advance the public's interest in LSL deregulation. If public opinion affected the policy process, it did not do so by way of the consumers' groups.[73]

It is my argument that public opinion influenced policy in the way at least some journalists had intended: by forcing politicians and bureaucrats to take into account the diffuse interests of the general public. Before SII, this issue was a complex regulatory issue of concern to only the affected groups, so both politicians and bureaucrats could ignore public opinion. Once the LSL was given extensive publicity, however, it became a factor both had to consider. Kaifu in particular seems to have deliberately calculated that he could improve his weak position in the Japanese political arena by playing to the general public on this issue. During the election, he had responded to the incentives of the electoral system by parroting the usual party line about the need to maintain the LSL regulatory regime. Once the election was over, however, his main interest was in his public approval rating, which, analysts repeatedly pointed out, was his only political asset. The best way to improve this rating was to push policies he perceived to be supported by the largest number of citizens. On the LSL, this meant pushing for a big symbolic policy change: the abolition of the law.[74]

While few other LDP politicians altered their policy positions to this extent, perhaps because none of them were as sensitive to public approval ratings, their behavior did change in tandem with the shift in public opinion. While there were still those who voiced support for small stores, several senior members of the party, as noted above, began to push for changes more radical than what MITI was proposing—a reversal of the roles the two actors had played up to that time.[75] Another measure of the shift in the way Dietmen viewed the politics of this issue was the number of LDP Diet members who showed up when they were invited to the rally called by interest groups opposed to LSL repeal: three.[76]

Public opinion also seems to have affected MITI bureaucrats. They responded, first, because the politicians were changing their policy preferences in response to gaiatsu and public opinion. Where previously their effort to implement the Vision proposals had been delayed because of LDP opposition, they were now dealing with politicians who in some cases wanted MITI to go further. It would be a mistake, however, to focus only on this indirect impact of public opinion, since Japanese bureaucrats seem to have their own antennae tuned to the public mood. In the case of MITI on this issue, these antennae told the officials that the public was ready for change. One official put it this way: "MITI is very sensitive to the social situation, and perceived that the situation was ripe for change in the distribution sector."[77] Another contrasted the "social consensus" in favor of restrictions on large store expansion before SII with a new consensus in favor of reform that emerged after the U.S. targeted the issue.[78] Both emphasized the role gaiatsu played in convincing interest groups that had previously resisted changes in the LSL regime that they could no longer resist. As one newspaper put it, these were the "it can't be avoided" (yamunashi) faction.[79] The SII demands and the sympathetic media attention they generated proved such a shock that previously stubborn opponents were forced to realize that they had no choice but to go to MITI and seek the best deal they could get.[80]

This last reference to a "deal" brings us to the last way in which gaiatsu, through participation expansion at both the elite and general public levels, helped bring about policy change in this case. It served as the impetus for a policy initiative providing side-payments to one sector of society (small stores), compensating them for sacrificing in the interests of other sectors of society (large stores, consumers, export-interests). In ordinary times, absent foreign pressure, such deals are very difficult to arrange in Japan because of its rigid system of vertically segmented administration (tatewari gyōsei). Each section of the bureaucracy, with its attendant interest groups, maintains a claim on a certain mix of policies and financial support, and the Ministry of Finance, dedicated to the concept of "balance," is loathe to authorize new subsidy programs.

All parties, however, recognize gaiatsu as a trigger for a cross-sector deal: from their previous experience with liberalization of agricultural markets, MOF officials knew that they would have to allow MITI a new program to help small stores adjust to the liberalized system; MITI officials knew they could extract such a deal; LDP zoku Dietmen knew they could take credit for arranging such a deal; and the interest groups opposed to liberalization knew they could extract resources from the state in compensation. Once it became clear that the foreign pressure over the LSL issue was too strong to resist, all that remained was for the parties to get together in MITI's offices and draw up the details. In the end, MITI was able to convince MOF to set aside a new budget line of 10 billion yen a year ($100 million) for the ministry's use in helping modernize the nation's shopping districts.[81]

It is interesting to note that most of the supposed losers in the LSL debate got something out of this deal. Shopping districts composed of small stores recognized that time was not on their side. The increasing use of automobiles was making it difficult for them to compete with a new generation of superstores offering vast selection, low prices, and parking lots. These districts needed government assistance to help them modernize to meet this challenge. As a result of the LSL, these shopping districts had a chance to compete for MITI grants for parking garages and other physical improvements designed to attract customers back to their neighborhood shops.[82]

It is also notable that a leading small merchant interest group was given a role in administering these new funds. Zenshinren, the National Association for the Promotion of Shopping Districts, is a government-founded organization charged with the task of promoting the revitalization of shopping districts. It has close ties with MITI and no doubt knew that it would be given a prominent role in administering any funds extracted from MOF as a result of an LSL deal. Not coincidentally, it was also the first small merchant group to break with the confrontational opposition tactics of groups like the Japan Federation of Specialty Store Associations. Instead, it went to MITI hat in hand to seek the best deal it could get.[83]

Finally, MITI (or at least those sections of the ministry most interested in modernizing the distribution sector) was perhaps the biggest winner. It was able to have its Vision proposals fully implemented, including the limits on local government regulations, and on top of that got an increase in its budget. Where previously it had only "soft" money for supporting shopping district events like town festivals, the new program gave it "hard" money for construction projects like parking structures. In cooperation with Zenshinren, it has used this money to promote the modernization of shopping districts and ameliorate opposition to new large store expansion. Compared to the pre-SII situation when MITI was hostage to local merchants who were often able to block all new development, the ministry now had much greater leverage over the retail sector.

THE LIMITS OF SYNERGISTIC STRATEGIES IN THIS CASE

This last section, while identifying yet another mechanism through which foreign pressure helped influence policy outcomes, also points to a critical limitation in this strategy. The U.S. may have brought LDP leaders into the process and helped force politicians and bureaucrats to take into account the interests of the general public, and it may also have moved policy generally in a more liberal direction; but in the end it had to leave it to MITI, the LDP commerce zoku, and the same old interest groups to craft the details of the policy change.

For American negotiators who work on trade negotiations with Japan, this is perhaps the biggest frustration. As a result of their efforts, U.S. firms often increase their market share, but the result is never genuinely open markets. Frequently, the deals worked out by bureaucrats and interest groups simply *manage* market opening in such a way that both benefit. The ministries get large budget increases and increased control of affected areas of the economy, and interest groups are given a share of these resources in one way or another. Market opening thus proceeds in a slow and haphazard fashion designed so that affected sectors of the Japanese economy are not unduly burdened.

Such results do not deny gaiatsu's power to influence Japanese policy but do testify to its limits. Foreign pressure is inevitably an indirect influence on the policy process. It can shift the general direction of policy under certain circumstances, but it cannot dictate the details. These are inevitably left to the elite actors mentioned above. In the LSL case, leaving the details to MITI, the zoku, and the interest groups meant that the outright abolition of the LSL was out of the question. Maintaining the law was crucial, in particular, for MITI's strategy of developing leverage over the retail sector. To go with its new carrot (the shopping district revitalization fund), it needed a *stick*. As we will see in examining the implementation of the LSL reforms, MITI has been faithful in allowing more liberal large store expansion—but has been careful to avoid carrying the process so far as to lose its influence on the retail sector.

Implementation of LSL Liberalization

Even before MITI began implementing its Large Store Law reforms, the impact of the impending policy shift began to become apparent. By the spring of 1990, retail chains were rushing to put together plans for opening new large stores in cities like Niigata (11 requests) and Matsumoto (5 requests) where all new store expansion had been frozen for years.[84] By the summer, after the first round of administrative reforms had been implemented, this initial rush had become a veritable stampede involving 376 plans submitted in just two months—50 percent more than had been submitted in all of 1988. In just one spot, around Kyoto station, four giant new stores were planned—and this in a place where new large stores had been frozen out since 1981.[85]

And these retail chains were not wrong in betting that this time MITI would have to follow through on its promise to liberalize the law. Once MITI signed off on the SII reports, the ministry had little room to deviate from its international commitments. The first set of reforms, implemented May 30 even before the final SII deal was struck, fully complied with the promises contained in the April interim report. Administrative guidance issued by the ministry limited the delay possible under the law to a maximum of 18 months and made it possible for stores to stay open an hour longer and more days each year without having to worry about local opposition.

MITI then set its advisory councils to work drawing up plans for revising the actual text of the LSL as provided for in Phase Two of the reform plan, and again, the results of this process were largely in line with Japan's SII commitments. In amendments passed in May 1991 and implemented on January 31, 1992, the delay under the law was shortened further to one year. In addition, the new law provided for "restraints" (yokusei) on local regulations, and, in the most far-reaching change, abolished the controversial Commercial Activities Adjustment Boards as well as the Prior Adjustment Boards—the organs which had until then done the real work of sorting out disputes between new and established stores. This step had not been specifically promised in the SII reports, but was taken in an effort to meet the vague promise to make the process "transparent." MITI officials considered keeping the CAABs and making their members quasi-government officials but ended up concluding that there was not enough time in a year for both these councils and the ministry's own Large Store Councils (Daitenshin) to conduct their reviews.[86]

The final step of the liberalization promised in the sii talks came to fruition in May 1994 with the passage of additional changes in the lsl. The government had promised to conduct a basic review of the law and take additional steps as necessary by this date, and had suggested in the interim sii report that this review might lead to exempting specified regions from the restrictions of the law. Already in June 1992, however, miti officials were telling me such a step was unlikely, and it did not get seriously considered in the basic review process. Instead, the latest reforms allow large stores to stay open one hour later (now until 8 p.m.) and close less frequently (24 days rather than 44 days). The most important change, however, affected medium-sized stores rather than large ones: stores under 1,000 square meters no longer are subject to lsl restrictions.

Overall, all of these changes complied with the letter of Japan's sii commitments. Even the lack of progress on exemptions for specified regions cannot be described as a violation of a promise since such a step was listed only as a possibility in the sii reports. The real test of whether all of this has resulted in liberalization, however, lies in the figures for retail store expansion. As noted earlier, these numbers had declined sharply in the 1980s. If the lsl liberalization was real, we ought to see a sharp increase.

Indeed, the numbers jumped sharply following the initial phase of liberalization, rising from an average of around 85 large store openings a year in the late 1980s to more than 200 in 1993 by the time the initial wave of proposals had been processed. Medium sized stores, also regulated by the lsl and stuck at a store opening rate of around 350 a year in the late 1980s, were opening at double that rate by 1992 and 1993[87] (see figure 6.3). The boost in numbers of store openings included, significantly, 16 new Toys 'R' Us stores by early 1994. Ten more were expected to open within a year.[88]

The impact of the renewed competitiveness of the retail sector can also be seen in the recent boom in discounting. Over the past few years, newspapers and magazines have been full of articles on the new surge in price-based competition, and imports have featured prominently in many of these stores' strategies.[89] As the U.S. negotiators hoped, large discount stores have developed direct and parallel importing operations which have brought retail prices for goods such as American cosmetics, British liquor, and imported business suits down. In the summer of 1994, supermarket chains even began competing on prices of beer and cola, both of which had been offered at uniform prices regardless of store size.

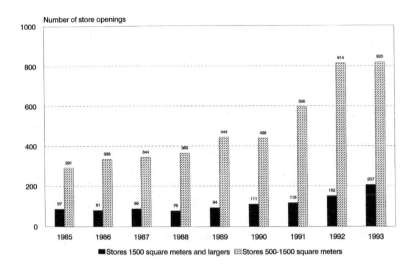

FIGURE 6.3   Large Store Openings, 1985–1993

Source: Tōyo keizai tokei geppō, (Tōyo Keizai Statistical Monthly), August 1994, p. 18.

While all of this testifies to the fact that LSL regulations have become more liberal since SII, it is clear that the law remains a barrier to large store expansion. The most disturbing reports have been those involving specific large store disputes which have resulted in MITI orders requiring developers to sharply reduce the size of their planned stores. In some cases, MITI's Large Store Councils have ordered cuts as large as 70 percent in floor space. Overall, according to *Nikkei shimbun*'s analysis of the data, the council ordered stores to cut back on their planned floor space by an average of 23 percent in 1992 and 39 percent in 1993.[90]

These results reflect the fact that the influence of local merchants has not disappeared with the elimination of the CAABs. The Large Store Councils still base their advice to the MITI minister on recommendations compiled by local chambers of commerce, and some have speculated that a shortage of MITI staff has forced the ministry to continue to depend heavily on these reports.[91] Because the regulatory regime no longer allows pressure for protection to be expressed in the form of delayed action, it is now being diverted to the only remaining area of MITI discretion: floor space.

Other evidence that the LSL remains a barrier can be found by examining retail store strategies. One rapidly growing discount apparel chain, for example, found the LSL burdensome enough that it chose to build each of its stores so that floor space totalled exactly 499 square meters, just under the threshold for the LSL—a strategy it dubbed "resistance by one square meter."[92] After the LSL was revised in 1994 to increase that threshold to 1,000 square meters, developers rushed to open stores just under this new level. If the LSL had truly been liberalized, stores would not be bothering to adjust their floor space figures to avoid the law. By 1994, Keidanren, the peak organization for big business, was frustrated enough with the way the post-SII reforms had gone that it was calling for the abolition of the law.[93]

Overall, the record of the government's implementation of the LSL reforms has to be described as mixed. The government complied with the letter of its SII commitments and introduced reforms that have eliminated the problem of delay. As a consequence, the number of new large store openings has increased sharply. However, the ministry continues to use the law to force reductions in floor space and otherwise create a continuing regulatory burden for large store developers. The best way to measure the net "liberalization" quotient may be to look at what the regulatory regime is costing those who want to open new stores. According to the *Nikkei*, store officials report that it costs them 3,000 to 4,000 yen per square meter in "aid" to local communities to open a new store. The figure again reflects the fact that the LSL continues to generate "rents" by limiting free competition, but it is notable that these same store officials report that this post-reform level of "aid" is half of what they used to have to pay.[94] Assuming that aid levels are proportional to the level of regulatory interference in the market, we can therefore extrapolate that the SII reforms resulted in a 50 percent liberalization of the LSL.

Conclusion

Regulation of retail store expansion continues to be a messy process in Japan, reflecting the persistent power of existing store interests and their ability to take advantage of a law that still allows MITI to exercise significant discretionary power. This does not mean, however, that foreign pressure "failed" in this case. On the contrary, a 50 percent reduction in regulatory interference, if this estimate is correct, still represents a significant departure from the direction in which government policy was headed prior to the SII talks. Until SII, one must remember, MITI had ended up stiffening retail regulation each time it attempted to reestablish order in the regime. In the end, the record of this case provides insights into both the potential and limits of foreign pressure.

Its potential is evidenced by the power of gaiatsu to alter policy outcomes by expanding levels of participation in the decisionmaking process. Before SII, in each of the episodes in which MITI attempted to reform the LSL, participation was limited to a tight circle of elite actors: the ministry, interests representing the various sectors of the retail business, and the LDP commerce zoku. As a result, MITI was forced to calibrate its regulatory policy to the balance of political power within this group—most of which had an interest in maintaining and stiffening regulations. Once the issue became the subject of U.S.-Japan talks, however, the circle grew much wider. LDP leaders and other elite actors with a stake in the overall U.S.-Japan relationship had an incentive to intervene. And the Japanese public, informed of the problem through media reporting on the U.S. complaints, for the first time forced the government to consider their interests. Given the opportunity to base its policy on a broader political base, MITI then fashioned a compromise that satisfied the minimum requirements of the affected interests but nevertheless moved policy in a significantly more liberal direction. As one newspaper reported at the time, government policy had shifted 180 degrees.[95]

Still, while pointing to the potential of gaiatsu, the LSL case also demonstrates its limitations. The U.S. could help create the conditions for reform, but it ultimately had to rely on MITI to design the details of the policy change. Consequently, the policy resulting from the U.S. intervention served that ministry's mix of interests as much as America's. Total liberalization would have deprived MITI of the ability to influence the development of the retail sector, so the ministry was not about to allow advocates of abolition to win the debate. The revised system allowed MITI to keep a somewhat smaller "stick," enabling it to respond to small store pressure by using threats of floor space reductions to encourage developers to create room for local merchants in their new complexes. At the same time, it provided the ministry with a new "carrot"—in the form of the new retail revitalization program it was able to extract from MOF—to support the ministry's efforts to modernize the retail sector without trampling on the "mom and pops."

By 1994, as the lingering post-bubble recession began to hit the retail sector, it was clear MITI was still using the LSL to "manage" the retail sector and avoid extreme disruptions. In being particularly tough on giant superstores planned for rural areas, it seemed to be trying to help Japan avoid the fate that has hurt American towns and cities so badly: the hollowing out of inner city shopping districts following the growth of giant malls.[96] If MITI has its way, and it probably will, the number of mom and pop shops will decline slowly over the next several decades, but tourists in the 21st century will still be able to find shopping districts with that distinctly Japanese atmosphere—revitalized with a new parking garage and arcade roof.

7 THE LAND POLICY ISSUE

With land prices spiraling upward in the late 1980s, this SII issue area was one where Japanese citizens had a clear stake in the outcome of the negotiations. In just four years, between 1986 and 1990, the price of a condominium in the Tokyo metropolitan area had risen from 4.5 times the income of an average household to 8.5 times annual income, pushing the dream of home ownership beyond the reach of middle-class workers.[1] Those still intent on purchasing homes were being forced to buy tiny units far out from the center city and endure daily commutes of more than 100 minutes each way. Even those fortunate enough to inherit property were increasingly being forced to sell the family home in order to pay inheritance taxes. Arguably, no set of Japanese government policies had more of an effect on the quality of life of ordinary citizens than those in this vaguely defined area of "land policy."

According to the American SII negotiators, however, Japanese land policy was also a problem for the U.S. By forcing residents in that country to save massive sums of money for downpayments, it contributed to the nation's savings surplus. At the same time, by making it extremely expensive for the government to acquire land for public works projects, it depressed investment. It therefore contributed adversely to the S-I balance on both sides of the ledger, adding to America's trade deficit through the same mechanism described in chapter 5. As if that weren't enough, high land prices also hurt the U.S. by making it expensive for American firms to invest in Japan and by giving their landowning Japanese competitors a huge advantage—most recently by allowing them to use their landholdings to raise capital at negative interest rates.

With both domestic and international pressure for reform, one might suppose that the land-issue area would have been the one to experience the most change as a result of the SII talks. In fact, as I will argue, the talks did help the government eliminate a loophole in the tax code that had contributed to the phenomenon of vegetable farms in the middle of prime residential areas, an important cause of the land-price problem which had nevertheless been immune to domestic reform initiatives for more than twenty years. Overall, however, change in this area was not as dramatic as it was in the two areas surveyed in chapters 5 and 6. Although land prices have come down sharply from the "bubble" years, economists generally agree that this price correction has been primarily the result of short-term macroeconomic policies. Because tax and regulatory policies continue to artificially constrain the supply of land, a renewed land-price spiral is likely when macroeconomic conditions like those of the mid- to late-1980s next arise.[2]

In terms of the present study, therefore, the puzzle presented by the results of the Americans' land-policy demands is twofold: first, in what way and to what degree did gaiatsu help close the urban agricultural land-tax loophole?; and second, why were the Americans less successful in forcing the Japanese to agree to broader concessions? As in the previous cases, the argument developed in this chapter emphasizes the relationship between domestic political conditions and foreign pressure tactics. In this case, the U.S. was generally less successful because the already-politicized environment of the land-policy debate in the late 1980s allowed it little room to influence the results through participation expansion, the strategy that had been the key to its successes in the first two issue areas surveyed. Because the Japanese were still debating which policy proposals should be adopted to deal with the crisis, however, the U.S. did have an opportunity to influence policy results through its intervention in "the idea stream." This intervention, for reasons articulated below, proved particularly critical in the case of urban agricultural land taxation.

Land Policy Before SII

"Land Policy" is too generous a term to apply to the set of policies affecting land use and prices that emerged in the postwar period. Encompassing a range of conflicting, uncoordinated policies pursued by

THE LAND POLICY ISSUE   183

a host of separate government agencies, the set of measures surveyed here is more aptly described as a "non-policy." Nevertheless, as we will see, this set of policies together came to have a powerful effect on land prices specifically and on the Japanese economy more generally.

The conventional wisdom is that Japan's high land prices are a natural result of its high population-density. As one Japanese delegate put it during the sii talks, "there is simply nothing we can do about the fact that Japan's land area is extremely small."[3] In fact, it's not that simple. As Noguchi Yukio and other critics of Japanese government policy have repeatedly pointed out, this simplistic view is belied by the existence of substantial idle and agricultural land in urban areas and by the continuing underutilization of already-developed property.[4] In a 1990 report, the Economic Planning Agency estimated that there were some 17,400 hectares (42,995 acres) of idle or underutilized land within 20 kilometers of the center of Tokyo, enough to accommodate 200,000 to 500,000 apartment units. Just beyond the 20-kilometer radius, still within an hour commute of central Tokyo, the Ministry of Construction estimated that some 45.4 percent of land was either agricultural or idle, a phenomenon one Japanese economist described as "unbelievably inefficient use of land."[5] Furthermore, much of Tokyo is low-rise, averaging just 2.5 stories area-wide.[6] If such property were developed to the extent similar urban areas are developed in New York, London, or Paris, Japan's land supply would be more than enough to accommodate its population in comfort. Japan suffers from high land prices, in other words, not because it is land-short but because land use is so inefficient.

Tax Policies

That so much urban property remains underutilized is a direct result of incentives arising from government tax and regulatory policies. In most advanced industrialized nations, land taxes serve the function of encouraging the efficient utilization of land. In New York, for example, the owner of a vacant lot in midtown Manhattan would quickly be forced to develop his land by the need to cover the cost of property taxes. In Japan, in contrast, effective property tax rates are so low in urban areas like Tokyo that they provide virtually no incentive to develop. According to Noguchi's calculations, the effective rate in Tokyo prior to sii was only 0.06 percent of actual land values, or $600 annually on a $1 million property.[7] At rates this low, firms and individuals literally had no incentive to sacrifice the liquidity of their land assets by developing them.

If this policy helps explain the abundance of *vacant* lots (and barely developed parking lots) in urban areas of Japan, the even more generous treatment of agricultural land explains the abundance of Tokyo *farmland*. Since the start of the postwar period, owners of urban agricultural land have enjoyed tax breaks that have allowed them to get away with paying only a fraction of the tax they would have to pay if the land were valued at the rate of surrounding residential land. By the 1980s, it was estimated that this break allowed urban agricultural land to be taxed at annual rates as low as 0.0002 percent—or $200 on a piece of property worth $100 million![8] Tax rates like this made even the most urbane Tokyo salaryman hold on to the ancestral farm.

Perhaps the strongest disincentive for development, however, did not arise from the policy on property taxes but from the policy on inheritance taxes. For farmland, inheritance taxes again were calculated at rates well below the market value of land, were deferred for 20 years for heirs planning to continue farming the land, and waived altogether for small farms—a system that often let the owners of farmed real estate in the priciest areas of Tokyo escape inheritance taxation all together. For agricultural landowners eager to pass their wealth on to their children, this system meant it would be crazy for them to develop their land.[9] While the system was not quite as kind to non-farmers, here too there was a major tax break for land assets relative to other forms of assets passed on to heirs at death. By the late 1980s, in many areas where land prices rose quickly, assessments for the purpose of inheritance taxation lagged way behind market values (as low as 30 percent). This meant individuals worried about how to pass on their wealth again had a crazy-to-ignore incentive to keep as much as possible of their assets in land even to the point of leveraging all their financial assets in order to borrow and buy more land.[10]

The final element of land-tax policy was its treatment of capital gains from land sales. Gains from land held for more than five years were taxed at 20 to 25 percent, with still higher rates applied to short-term (speculative) investments in land. For corporations in particular, the high rate of taxation on gains encouraged them to hold onto idle property. The National Land Agency estimated that corporations held land valued on the books at $537 billion which at market rates would be worth $3.4 tril-

lion for unrealized capital gains worth $2.9 trillion.[11] Given the low
effective property tax rate and the fact that they could use the *market*
value of the land as collateral for loans, it made little sense for firms to
part with their idle landholdings.

It doesn't take much knowledge of economics to see how the combination of all of the above tax incentives served to generate an artificial gap
between demand for land and its supply. To get the favorable tax treatment, everyone wanted as much land as they could buy, but those who
already had land had strong incentives to hold onto the land themselves.
The consequent shortage meant that land which did come onto the market tended to sell at a premium. In time, these structural incentives contributed to the "land myth"—the belief that land prices would always rise
at a rapid rate—which in turn propelled the land-price spiral even higher
as investors began to treat land as a financial instrument divorced from its
productive value. If you expected land prices to continue rising, it didn't
matter if a property investment produced only a small trickle of current
income since the real reason for the investment was the expected capital
gain.

The Land and House Lease Laws

The artificial demand for land as an asset, described above, would not
prove nearly as disruptive if Japanese policy provided more incentives for
landowners to lease their land to others for productive development.
Here again, however, the legal regime of the Land and House Lease Laws
has long served to discourage all but the feeble-minded from leasing out
their land. These laws, dating back to 1921 and last revised in 1941 during the war, effectively made it impossible for landlords to evict tenants
or sharply raise rents, even upon the termination of a lease.[12] These regulations have limited the efficient use of land, first, by discouraging owners of idle land from building rental units on their property (especially
dwellings large and comfortable enough that a family of tenants might
never leave).[13] Second, and perhaps more importantly, they have locked
up a great deal of existing urban land in a rent control regime that dis-
courages property redevelopment. In Tokyo, for example, 20 percent of
the city's households live in housing built on leased land, and 56 percent
live in leased housing covered under the Building Lease Law[14]—providing in many cases two layers of rent control that locks in land use patterns
that may have made sense fifty years ago but make no sense today (e.g.

two-story wooden houses a few blocks from Nihonbashi in downtown Tokyo). Many analysts argue that these lease laws represent a more important limit on the supply of land in Japan than the convoluted tax code described above.

CITY PLANNING REGULATIONS

While the land-price problem was partly a function of supply and demand, it can also be seen as a reflection of the government's failure to actively manage the process of land development through city planning. By helping to bring more housing onto the market at times of shortage and by strictly regulating land use so that residential land prices would be immune from forces pushing up commercial land values, the Japanese government could have slowed the land-price spiral. In both West Germany and Britain, active government involvement in the development of new suburban residential areas and strict zoning have prevented land-price inflation, even in areas of high population density.[15]

The Japanese government, in contrast, has been singularly ineffective in its land use planning efforts in the postwar period. One analyst describes the state of Japanese city planning through much of its postwar history:

> Japan's urbanization continued at a breakneck pace without deliberate, effective urban planning. Developers expanded residential areas rapidly but often without providing adequate roads, parks, or sewers. Factories and retail stores sprang up amid residential neighborhoods interspersed with patches of farmland to create widespread urban sprawl. This meant also that individual buyers of housing land had to compete in the same market with commercial and industrial bidders. Few resources were allocated for urban amenities.[16]

The contrast with the planned new towns of West Germany and the UK could hardly be more striking.

MONETARY POLICY

A final set of government policies impacting land prices were the macroeconomic policies and financial market regulations of the Ministry of Finance. Since land was seen by most Japanese primarily as a financial asset, it follows that the value of this investment would be significantly influenced by the policies MOF used to influence the value of other finan-

cial instruments. Early on, the land myth was fed by MOF policies limiting the interest rate banks could offer on savings accounts to an extremely
low level. Faced with a choice between a 2 percent nominal return on
passbook savings and a 20 percent return on investments in land,
Japanese households chose land.[17] Later, in the 1980s, the government
again fed the land-price spiral by simultaneously reducing the official discount rate, deregulating financial markets, and reducing government
borrowing. The first two steps lowered the cost of borrowing (from banks
and from equity markets) while the last reduced the quantity of government securities into which this money could flow. Together they had the
effect of sending a tremendous surge of investment capital into the land
market—serving as the immediate trigger for the runaway land-price
inflation of the "bubble" years.[18]

Previous Reform Initiatives and the Politics of Land Policy

Throughout the 1950s and for most of the 1960s, land policy was for all
intents and purposes a non-issue in Japan. The government sporadically
intervened to help industry acquire and develop land it needed for large-
scale projects, but there was no serious attempt to address the kinds of
problems just described.[19] From around 1968 to 1974, however, there
were a number of initiatives that aimed to introduce more systematic city
planning and to eliminate distortions in land-tax policy such as the preferential treatment of urban agricultural land. After another lull, the
period following the emergence of a new land-price spiral in the mid-
1980s saw a second attempt to deal with these same issues. In almost all
cases, however, reforms either petered out, were shot full of loopholes,
or proved to be counterproductive.

   The following discussion of reform initiatives during these two periods in this section demonstrates, by way of contrast, the significance of
the changes that followed in the wake of SII. In particular, it suggests that
since the urban farmland tax loophole survived all previous efforts to
close it, most likely it would have failed again had gaiatsu not been part of
the process after 1989. In addition, the discussion sketches out the politics of this issue area much as we did with the politics of fiscal and distribution policy in the previous two chapters. Just as policy segmentation
and particularism inhibited reform initiatives in those other areas, we will
see, they served to block reformers also in this issue area. The degree to

which gaiatsu would work during sɪɪ therefore depended on the way it interacted with these features of politics in the policy sphere.

Reform Initiatives in 1968–1974

Pressured by the success of the progressive parties in electing mayors in urban areas, the ʟᴅᴘ government in 1965 set up a Council for Land Price Policy, charging it with making land policy recommendations. Over the succeeding decade, a variety of legislative proposals made their way onto the agenda of the Diet, and some even passed; but none survived in a form that addressed the structural roots of the land problem.

The first law to pass was the New City Planning Law of 1968. Its fate is typical. Drawn up by the Ministry of Construction (ᴍᴏᴄ) as a means of increasing the government's authority to control and direct patterns of urban development and land use, its designation of Urbanization Promotion Areas (ᴜᴘᴀꜱ) for development and Urbanization Control Areas for preservation was critical to its success. Within the ᴜᴘᴀꜱ, farmland was to be freed up for residential development without prior permission, but in return the landowners were to be required to pay property taxes on the land at the same rate as surrounding residential land. Land was to be designated according to its proximity to existing residential areas and infrastructure.

Almost immediately, however, farmland owners who until this point had been paying property taxes discounted to reflect the agricultural productivity of their land objected to the prospect of having to pay higher taxes. If that was the deal, they would use their political influence to make sure their land was kept out of the new districts. Worried that such a boycott could gut the new city planning system, the ᴍᴏᴄ ended up agreeing to postpone the tax increase. This result, of course, provided farmland owners who got their land designated as ᴜᴘᴀꜱ with the best of both worlds: higher land values reflecting prospects for development without having to pay taxes on the increased value. Instead of objecting, farmers rushed to sign up their land—seeking political favors when necessary to get even relatively isolated farmland designated part of the new ᴜᴘᴀꜱ.[20]

The results of the compromise of 1968 created an agricultural land-tax regime with interesting parallels to the Large Store Law regime that emerged after 1974: both maximized the ability of ʟᴅᴘ politicians to direct political goods to narrow constituencies. In this case ʟᴅᴘ members—by dragging out the "postponement" of the tax increase—could offer a small group of urban farmland owners a financial windfall and extract their loyal support in return. At the same time, by using their influence with the MOC to get land rezoned as UPAS, they could offer individual landowners a piece of this action—again in exchange for generous support. The 1968 settlement made little sense in terms of the public good: it gave away tax revenue, while it kept farmland off the market and deprived urban salaried workers of more affordable housing closer to their workplaces. It made perfect sense, though, in terms of the Japanese political system with its bias toward particularism.[21]

There was one more parallel to the LSL story: the system turned out to be impossible to reform once it was put in place. In 1970–1971, the government made its first attempt to implement the tax increase on farmland in UPAS set out in the 1968 law. A compromise, providing for a phased implementation between 1972 and 1976, actually passed the Diet. When those years rolled around, however, the leading agricultural interest group, Nōkyō, repeatedly pressured the LDP to intervene to delay implementation. Finally, in 1981, the year the delaying tactics were supposed to end, the farm lobby convinced the LDP to "throw in the towel." Plots of farmland in UPAS larger than 990 square meters were to be taxed at agricultural rates as long as owners intended to farm them for the next 10 years.[22] By the late 1980s, this settlement was allowing 85 percent of the 43,000 hectares of agricultural land in the Urbanization Promotion Areas of the three largest metropolitan areas to avoid being taxed at the rate of surrounding residential land.[23]

The urban agricultural land-tax issue was only one aspect of the land-policy reform drive of the late 1960s and early 1970s. An attempt was made, in addition, to increase incentives for landowners to put their holdings on the market by lowering the tax on long-term capital gains from land transactions.[24] In the absence of concurrent changes in land-holding taxes, however, this change merely fueled land speculation. Those who owned land had a greater incentive to sell since they could keep more of their profits, but demand still outran supply since the landhold-ing costs faced by buyers remained minimal and also because the cut in the capital gains tax made land a more attractive long-term investment. Partly as a result of this half-reform, Japan soon found itself in the midst of the biggest land-price explosion it had ever seen. To cool it off, the government in 1976 once again raised the capital gains tax.[25]

Why didn't the government attempt a more comprehensive land-tax reform? How did it find itself in a position where effective landholding tax rates and inheritance taxes on land assets were so low? Part of the problem is policy segmentation. The MOF oversees capital gains and inheritance tax rates, but as a result of the postwar settlement, local governments and the Ministry of Home Affairs (MHA) in Tokyo have exclusive control of property taxes. As far as local governments are concerned, the land-price effects of their tax rates are much less of a concern than the tax revolts they would face if they actually tried to tax land at the nominal rate. The main reason effective property tax rates (in some cases under 0.1 percent) are so much lower than the nominal property tax rate (in general 1.4 percent) is because at times of land-price inflation local governments have pressured the MHA to let its property assessments lag behind the increase in market prices. By 1990, it was estimated that MHA assessments, on average, came to only about 25 percent of market land prices—with a great deal of variation depending on how fast local land prices were increasing. Regardless of the distortions this policy caused, local governments (and the MHA) were simply in no hurry to raise assessments as long as effective rates provided them with enough revenue to cover the cost of providing local services.[26]

An important reason why the government has failed to rationalize land-tax policy thus lies in the multijurisdictional nature of the policy, something the strictly segmented bureaucracy is not well equipped to handle. On the property tax, MOF has had difficulty getting the MHA and local governments to cooperate.[27] And on the urban agricultural land tax, MOF has actually had to work with the MOC (which oversees the UPAS) and the Ministry of Agriculture (which oversees farm policy) as well as the MHA (which oversees property taxes). By the late 1980s, having failed to reform the system after trying numerous times, MOF officials were not at all eager to take up the challenge one more time. Officials at the MHA didn't even want to talk about the issue.[28]

If jurisdictional battles have been a problem for land *tax* policy in the postwar period, they have been even more of one for reform initiatives in the area of land use planning and regulation. Prior to World War II, the Home Ministry (which held extensive powers over land use regulation) had actually been quite effective in this area, overseeing the development of what is now central Tokyo and managing the reconstruction after the Great Kanto Earthquake.[29] After the war, however, the old Home Ministry was dissolved, and its city planning powers were given to the Economic Planning Agency, a new and not very powerful player in the Japanese bureaucracy. As a result, a multitude of other agencies—the

THE LAND POLICY ISSUE   191

Ministries of Finance, Construction, Industry, Agriculture, and Transportation among them—gradually encroached on the EPA's turf, leaving no single agency with overall coordinating power.[30]

Over the succeeding years, each of these agencies worked to make sure its own interests were not sacrificed in the interest of rational land use. MITI worked to ensure that industry could acquire the land it needed for factories and industrial infrastructure; Agriculture worked to make sure farmers weren't pushed aside in the rapid expansion of cities; and Finance made sure it got a decent price when plots of public land were put up for sale. No agency, however, effectively represented the broader public interest in effective urban planning: in the provision of high-quality housing, zoning, adequate roads, parks, and other infrastructure. It was due largely to this structure of the system that, during Japan's high growth years, regulation of land use ended up being handled on a case by case basis.

It is notable, though, that this haphazard system again suited the political interests of the LDP quite well. As Calder put it in his study of land politics, "Most LDP politicians do not want systematic land use planning; case-by-case decision making is politically advantageous, and they cannot easily make concessions via planning to defuse political dissent."[31] Anchordoguy describes land as a "political resource" the LDP has found useful in catering to its clients.[32] By leaving administration of land use regulation divided, the LDP was able to give all of its relevant zoku a piece of the action.

When the government embarked on several attempts to reform and strengthen land use regulation in the 1968–1974 period, therefore, the turf battles and the lack of political will on the part of the LDP kept these initiatives from achieving their objectives. By the early 1970s, it was clear that the MOC's New City Planning Law had not solved the problem. Land prices were soaring, and urban salaried employees began to complain that they were being priced out of the housing market. Faced with a continuing erosion of support in Diet elections, the Tanaka government pushed through the National Land Use Planning Law, setting up a new government agency, the National Land Agency (NLA), and charging it with the task of reining in land speculation, coordinating land use regulation for the government as a whole, and representing the public interest in land policy.[33]

The law gave the government increased authority to intervene in the land market: prefectural governors were authorized to freeze land prices in areas where speculation was rampant and could even force owners of idle land to sell it if they refused to develop it themselves. The NLA was also to oversee sales of public land to make sure these served the public interest. As it turned out, however, the newly created NLA did not have the clout to bring order to land use policy. Its staffing arrangements, where by the 1980s some 450 employees were on loan from other agencies, did not promote coordination since the loaned staff tended to represent the interests of their own agency. Other ministries with data relevant to the NLA's mission often failed to share that information with the agency.[34] And when it came to sales of public land, the MOF and the LDP still dictated NLA policy such that maximizing revenue and serving the interests of political clients—rather than promoting land use in the public interest—remained the dominant concerns.[35]

REFORM INITIATIVES IN 1987–1989

The clearest indication of the failure of the reforms adopted during the speculative land-price bubble of the early 1970s was the recurrence of another even bigger one in the mid-1980s. Figure 7.1 shows the sudden emergence of this bubble, illustrating how it affected commercial real estate in Tokyo first, then spread to affect Tokyo land prices in general and

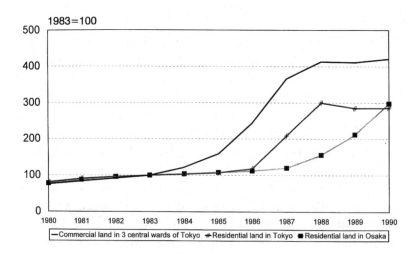

FIGURE 7.1 The Rise in Japanese Land Prices, 1980-90

Source: EPA, Nenji keizai hōkoku: heisel 3-nendo, 1991, pp. 450–451

finally land prices in other major urban centers. Just as in the early 1970s, this land-price explosion pushed the price of housing out of the reach of median-income earners, and also as in that earlier time, it sparked a vigorous debate filled with rhetoric about the need to reform land policy to serve the public interest. At least through 1989, however, it failed to yield any policy change addressing the root causes of the problem.

With Tokyo land prices shooting up at an annual rate of 75 percent, Prime Minister Nakasone took the first step toward land policy reform in August 1987 by establishing the Advisory Council on Land Policy (*Tochi rinchō*). At the same time, the government announced a set of measures designed to deal with the crisis, including a sharp increase in the tax on short-term capital gains from land sales (to 96 percent) and administrative guidance by the MOF aimed at discouraging banks from financing speculative land purchases. The government also amended the National Land Use Planning Act in order to increase monitoring of land transactions—an approach that was beefed up further after the interim report from the Advisory Council on Land Policy recommended government action to freeze and in some cases force reductions in negotiated prices.

Neither of these approaches, however, addressed the underlying causes of the land-price problem. The first set was designed to curb the flow of capital into the land market, the immediate cause of the "bubble." A similar logic underlay later moves by the financial authorities to impose even stricter administrative guidance and tighter monetary policy. Ultimately, the shift in monetary policy deflated the speculative bubble, but it did nothing to address the artificial shortage of land which made land seem like such a good bet whenever loose monetary policy left investors with ready credit. The second set of measures, the controls on land transactions, did even less to deal with the problem and were criticized for actually keeping land prices from falling once the "correction" phase of the bubble set in.[36] In short, these emergency measures did nothing to stop the reoccurrence of another land-price bubble.

Recognizing this fact, the members of the Advisory Council proceeded to discuss more far-reaching changes in land policy over the next several months. The majority group within the council, dominated by economists and representatives from the big business community, favored reforms geared at increasing the supply of land.[37] Among the steps they recommended most specifically were revisions in the Land and House Lease Laws designed to facilitate the development of leased property and the relaxation of local regulations such as those which restricted building height. The council also considered a proposal for a new one-percent landholding tax (rejecting it) and once again examined the idea of raising taxes on urban farmland (concluding its deliberations with a lukewarm endorsement).[38]

The Tochi rinchō received immense publicity and raised public expectations, particularly when it emphasized the "public" nature of land resources and called for improved housing and more efficient land use in its June 1988 final report, but in the end the effort produced a great deal of smoke and very little fire. Even its more specific recommendations on the Land and House Lease Laws and relaxed land use restrictions produced little change. The Lease Law reform, as with other land-policy changes discussed earlier, was a victim of the Japanese system's bias toward preserving policies that offered large benefits to narrow constituencies, in this case the lessees who had locked into low rent contracts many years earlier. Faced with their demands, the Ministry of Justice in its February 1989 draft amendments refused to change the system in such a way as to affect existing leases—meaning the change would do nothing to bring onto the market the inefficiently-developed land under their homes.[39]

The Advisory Council's other major initiative, its push for deregulation of land use, was the victim of the same vertically-segmented administrative structure that had earlier prevented effective city planning. While parts of the government pushed for deregulation to spur private development (*minkatsu*), other parts resisted this line and argued that the answer to land problems lay in more vigorous and restrictive city planning. The Tochi rinchō itself included representatives of five different government agencies, and in total eleven ministries and agencies sent representatives to testify before the council.[40] The report itself was muddled on the question of whether more or less regulation was required, rejecting the strict controls on land transactions and land use proposed by the National Land Agency, but also rejecting rapid decontrol advocated by real estate interests.

Finally, the period up through 1989 saw a replay of the political games that had delayed the elimination of the loopholes allowing urban agricultural land to avoid taxation at the rate of surrounding residential property. Once again, after the Advisory Council proposed the elimination of these loopholes, the LDP balked. Taking up the proposal in the fall of 1989, the LDP Tax Commission finally endorsed the idea of raising taxes, and even went so far as to set a date (1991), but it limited the change to just the central wards of Tokyo, affecting less than five percent of the urban agricultural land in the metropolitan area. Reporting on this decision made it clear that LDP politicians were once again being driven by their political calculus: they could not afford to lose the votes and political funds supplied by the well-organized urban farm lobby.[41] Furthermore, discussion during this period concentrated on raising *property taxes* on urban farmland, not *inheritance taxes*. After 20 years of continuing battles over the issue, the latter subject was considered to be a "taboo" issue, too politically volatile even to talk about.[42]

At the end of 1989, the government had produced only one piece of new legislation to deal with the land-price spiral: the Basic Land Law passed in December of that year. While this law boldly declared that the welfare of the general public should be given top priority in land policy, it did nothing to change the myriad of specific land policies which thwarted that interest. As Marie Anchordoguy puts it, the law "was merely a declaration of abstract ideas about public welfare and entirely void of concrete policies to alleviate the land problem."[43] We now return to the SII talks in order to examine whether the Americans had any more luck trying to squeeze change out of this lemon of a policy process.

The American Demands

In an unusual trade initiative, the land issue was probably the most unusual agenda item. With the Large Store Law and the Anti-Monopoly Law issues, one could at least relate the policies (indirectly) to real American products, and with the public investment issue, the macroeconomic logic was fairly straightforward once you bought into the idea that the trade balance was related to the Savings-Investment balance. With the land issue, however, one had neither an indirect link to products or a direct macroeconomic link. The economics behind the American demands was in fact so complicated that even the American delegate representing the Council of Economic Advisors, economist John Taylor, was unsure about the bottom line: the American demands on land policy could move the S-I balance (and the trade balance) either way.[44]

Publicly, American negotiators displayed no doubts. At the first two SII negotiating sessions in September and November, U.S. negotiators laid out the macroeconomic logic behind their land policy concerns with unabashed confidence. High land prices led to higher savings rates as families put a large portion of their income in the bank in an effort to accumulate enough funds for a down payment, small homes depressed consumption by leaving families with little room for bulky consumer durables, and the high cost of land acquisition put a damper on public and private investment. On all counts, the Americans argued, expensive land increased the gap between savings and investment and contributed to the corresponding current account imbalance.[45]

And up to a point, the data supported their arguments. The cost of purchasing a home in Japan *was* much higher than in other countries. Table 7.1 shows how the cost of purchasing a new condominium in the Tokyo metropolitan area stood at 7.5 times the average household income in 1988 compared to ratios of 3.4 to 4.6 in other advanced industrialized nations. As noted earlier, the Tokyo ratio had grown to 8.5 times average household income by 1990—and that was for a small unit of only 70 square meters (754 square feet). It was estimated that the average single-family house in the Tokyo area cost more than *17 times* the average annual household income![46] The main reason for the difference in the price of homes, not surprisingly, was the high cost of residential land in Japan relative to other nations. Residential land in Tokyo cost more than twice as much as land in Paris, the second most expensive city. Even in outlying Japanese cities, land cost more than ten times more than in San Francisco, a relatively high-cost U.S. city (see table 7.2).

TABLE 7.1
Comparison of New Home Prices

Country/Year	Currency	Average New Home Price (A)	Average Household Income (B)	Ratio A/B
Japan (1988) (Tokyo area)	Yen	50,853,000	6,822,000	7.5
W. Germany (1986)	Mark	249,777	53,992	4.6
Britain (1987)	Pound	51,290	11,648	4.4
U.S. (1987)	Dollar	104,500	30,853	3.4

TABLE 7.2
Comparison of Residential Land Prices (1987)

City	Price Per Square Meter
Tokyo	$7,200
Paris	3,240
Taipei	1.967
Tachikawa (Tokyo suburb)	1,667
Osaka/Kobe/Kyoto	1,513
Seoul	373
London	247
Sidney	140
San Francisco	135
Los Angeles	75

TABLE 7.3
Comparison of Residential Floor Space

Country	Square Feet of Floor Space Per House
Japan (1987)	854
U.S. (1987)	1,594
W. Germany (1986)	1,010
France (1984)	920
Sweeden (1987)	992

Source: Based on data in Takagi Shintaro, "Nihon no chika, jutaku kakaku wa takasugiru?" (Are Japanese Land and Housing Prices Too High?) Nihon keizai kenkyu 20 (May 1990), pp. 113, 116.

Japanese homes are also small. While it is not surprising that dwellings in densely populated Japan are smaller than those in the U.S., it is notable that they are smaller even than those in similarly crowded European countries[47] (table 7.3). And the size of new Japanese homes has actually *shrunk* over the past decade. As Figure 7.2 shows, while the size of new owned homes grew over the course of the 1980s, the size of new rental dwellings shrunk from a high of 55 square meters in 1979 to 45.8 square meters by 1989—only 493 square feet. The overall number fell too during this period by almost 15 square meters to 80.9 because rentals were smaller and because a much smaller proportion of the new homes being built were "owned homes"—a drop from 45 percent in 1978 to 30 percent in 1989.[48]

Citing statistics like these, the Americans could make the case that high land prices were squeezing the Japanese public. Within the American camp, however, there was significant dissension about whether the data supported the next step in their argument: that high land and housing prices increased the S-I imbalance. As C E A negotiator Taylor pointed out, Japanese families save a lot for houses when young but they also *dissave* a lot when they finally purchase a home—making the impact of high land prices on savings rates a wash. Citing an economic study by Jeffrey Sachs and Peter Boone, he argued that lowering Japanese land prices might

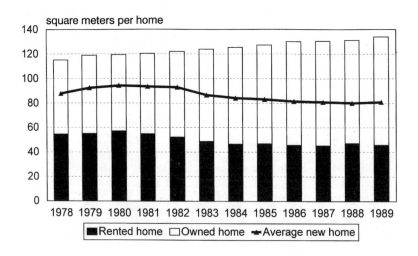

FIGURE 7.2 Average Size of New Homes in Japan, 1978-89

Source: MOC, Kensetsu hakusho: heisei 5-nendo, (Construction White Paper: 1993), p. 255

actually increase savings rates since Japanese see their investments in land as a way of accumulating assets. If land prices level off or fall, many Japanese will feel they need to save *more* in order to reach their economic goals.[49] Partly because the U.S. delegation disagreed about this line of argument, the Americans increasingly emphasized a new (non-macro) argument during later negotiating sessions, arguing that high land prices are a barrier to foreign investment.[50]

TABLE 7.4

The Americans' Land Policy Demands

1. Full Implementation of the Ministry of Construction's Plan for reforming taxation of urban agricultural land (raising both property taxes throughout the three largest metropolitan areas of Japan)—instead of limiting it to central wards of Tokyo as LDP has proposed.

2. Rationalization of land assessments so that they reflect market prices.

3. Reduce inheritance taxes overall instead of reducing the burden by allowing land assets to receive special treatment.

4. Reduce the capital gains tax (and reduce to one year the period one must hold land to qualify for lower rate).

5. Raise taxes on idle land.

6. Centralize the administration of land use regulations (perhaps in the National Land Agency) while relaxing regulations and delegating more authority to localities.

7. Identify under-utilized land in the Tokyo area and promote its use for such purposes as public housing.

8. Promote the conversion of urban farmland into housing.

9. Make it easier for localities to shift land from urbanization coordination areas to promotion areas and promote the development of this land.

10. Substantially reduce building standards such as those which limit the height and breadth of structures.

11. Provide authority and resources to local governments so that they can greatly expand infrastructure (sewers, roads) needed to support housing development.

12. Reduce the level of demands placed on private housing developers by local governments.

13. Revise the Land and House Lease Laws in order to promote the development of leased land.

14. Improve the mortgage market.

Source: Americans' List of 200 Demands

Throughout the year of negotiations, however, the Americans were consistent in their *prescription* for Japan's high land-price problem. Perhaps because the Treasury officials formulating the U.S. position were economists, they bought fully into the reform ideas of Japanese economists: raise land holding taxes (especially on urban farmland); cut the capital gains taxes to encourage land sales; and remove regulatory impediments to land development such as building standards and the Land and House Lease Law. Add to supply, reduce demand, and prices will fall. A more complete summary of the American demands in this issue area is provided in table 7.4.

Synergistic Strategies and the Deal on Land Policy

While at the start of the negotiations the Japanese responded to the American charges with throwaway lines ("Japan is a small island nation, so there is nothing we can do . . .") and spent most of their time defending government policies, by February they were offering some real concessions. In fact, going into the February session, newspapers were describing land as one of the few areas where the Japanese had come to an agreement on movement toward the American position: they were willing to raise taxes on urban farm land; they were willing to revise the Land and House Lease Law; and they were willing to devise a system to promote the utilization of idle urban land.[51] Recognizing the progress the Japanese were making (and also because of their continuing doubts about whether land policy had anything to do with the trade balance) the U.S. relaxed its pressure on this issue area during the end-game leading up to the interim and final reports.[52] Nevertheless the final sii land deal was full of "concessions."

Characterizing the results of the sii talks on land is not a simple matter. The standard for judging the effectiveness of gaiatsu, I noted in chapter 2, involves comparing what happened after international negotiations to "what would have happened" in the absence of U.S. involvement. On one issue, urban farmland taxation, I am confident in crediting sii with helping to produce policy change that would not have happened in its absence. In the April interim report, the government pledged to review and "address" the loopholes that allowed urban agricultural land to escape property and inheritance taxation at the rate of nearby residential land. While the final reform retained a smaller loophole (described below), it went much further than any previous initiative on this issue. Similar proposals had been defeated many times in the past, and the LDP was showing every sign of blocking meaningful reform as late as December 1989.

I have trouble, however, crediting SII with influence on most of the rest of the land policy "concessions," partly because many of these changes would have been adopted anyway and also because some of the promised reforms did not result in the kind of change the U.S. sought. First, given the prominence of the land issue on the domestic political agenda, the government was destined to pass some legislation on the issue regardless of whether or not the U.S. had intervened. A law improving the government's ability to identify and force development of idle land, and amendments to two other laws providing for the creation of special urban districts where city planning and building regulations would be relaxed to promote housing development, were touted in the SII deal but very likely would have been adopted anyway without gaiatsu.

On the other hand, the Japanese promises to reform land taxation more broadly (not just as it applied to urban farmland) and revise the Land and House Lease Laws produced such meager results that they cannot exactly be touted as major achievements. The government refused to lower the capital gains tax—essentially rejecting the American argument that land prices could be brought down by adding to the stock of land on the market. They also ended up doing very little to increase property taxes, creating a national land tax with an extremely low rate and adding so many exemptions that it affected only a tiny fraction of landholdings. Finally, the Land and House Lease Law revisions ended up going no further than the Ministry of Justice draft announced in February 1989— doing nothing to bring land governed by existing leases onto the market.

How then shall we evaluate the impact of gaiatsu on this issue area? As noted at the start of this chapter, I see these results as presenting us with two puzzles: (1) why didn't foreign pressure have more of an impact, overall, on this issue area?; and (2) how did it help produce more movement on the specific issue of urban farmland taxation? Both questions, I propose, can be answered by referring to the arguments developed in chapter 2.

PARTICIPATION EXPANSION

At a superficial level, the politics of land policy resembled those in the area of the Large Store Law. Here was a set of policies that benefited small groups (urban farmers, lessees who locked into contracts forty years ago, land speculators) but imposed huge costs on the general public which, as a result of government policy, had to pay exorbitant prices for cramped housing. As the sii talks came to a head, public opinion polls revealed that 40 percent of Japanese considered spiralling land prices to be the nation's *biggest* domestic problem.[53] If the politics were this similar, we might expect the U.S. to have been more successful in employing a strategy of participation expansion, as it had in the case of lsl, altering Japanese policy process by bringing added political actors into the game.

There were two problems with this scenario. First, this issue was already at the top of the political agenda before sii—unlike the lsl—such that the Americans had little ability to alter policy outcomes by adding new participants. A cabinet-level advisory council had been appointed specifically to recommend land policy changes two years before sii started, and ldp leaders starting with Nakasone had been involved personally in dealing with the issue. The Tochi rinchō, as noted above, included representatives of five ministries and heard from many more. All were intensely involved, even without sii. Even the general public, angered by intense media coverage of land-policy problems predating sii, were forcing the government to pay more attention to their concerns even before the Americans got involved.[54] A second related problem was that the distribution of *costs* of dealing with the land-policy problem were much more widely spread than in the case of the lsl. Recall that in the case of the lsl, almost all of the costs of reforming the regulatory regime were to be borne by existing retailers (especially small stores). The actors whom the U.S. succeeded in bringing into the game (other ministries, export interests within Keidanren, the general public) faced no costs and at least some diffuse benefits from backing up the U.S. position on the issue. In contrast, most elite actors and the general public faced clear costs as well as benefits from any attempt to reform Japanese land policy.

Take the example of Keidanren. In the long term, big business knew that it might benefit from more rational land policy, but in the short term, many of the federation's members faced high costs from proposed solutions to the problem. Raising taxes on land holding (a key component of any serious plan to deal with the artificial shortage of land) would hit heavy industries like steel, with their large factory sites, particularly hard. Many firms too had invested heavily in land assets during the bubble, leveraging these holdings in turn to raise cheap capital. If the government actually succeeded in bringing land prices down, they would face a huge paper loss and, in the case of a few especially vulnerable firms, potential bankruptcy. When it came time to take a position on land-tax reform following s11, therefore, Keidanren used all of its substantial muscle to block and water down proposed changes.[55]

What was true of big business was also true of the myriad of ministries involved in the land-policy debate: proposed solutions affected their "vital interests." MOF, never eager to cut taxes, was being asked to cut the capital gains tax on land—a major source of revenue during the bubble years. It also no doubt had mixed feelings about any remedy that might actually succeed in dramatically lowering land prices. Such a development, it knew, would threaten the stability of the numerous financial institutions that had become involved in financing land speculation, and leave MOF with the hard work of cleaning up the mess. Numerous other ministries were threatened by policy proposals that encroached on their turf—another "vital interest" for bureaucracies. The Ministry of Home Affairs, for example, was strongly opposed to a new national landholding tax since such a tax would compete with one of the few it controlled, the property tax.

Even in the case of the general public, however, proposed policy changes confronted households with visible costs as well as benefits. According to Economic Planning Agency data, even in the relatively high-priced Tokyo area, 64.3 percent of households own land, a home, or a condominium, and the number rises to 78 percent if you include those who expect to inherit property.[56] For these individuals, high land prices do not seem to be such a bad thing. Those who own property feel like they are getting wealthier every time they see land prices rise. Those who expect to inherit feel that eventually they will get their due. To these individuals, proposals to raise property-tax assessments and eliminate special treatment of land under the inheritance tax threaten to impose very visible costs even as the potential benefits (cheaper and larger homes) seem less tangible.

As Noguchi Yukio, one of the leading proponents of land-tax reform put it, the general public suffers from a "failure to understand the true nature of the problem and to recognize their true positions."[57] Higher property taxes offset by lower income taxes, he points out, would result in a lower overall tax burden for most salaried employees, and yet they don't see it. Closing loopholes on bequests of land would not affect most families, and yet they oppose the idea. "Although [most citizens] are not satisfied with the present situation, they do not accept radical reform." The task of educating the public to see their "true interests" was apparently beyond the capabilities of the Americans, and without public support, fundamental reform was doomed.[58]

If there was one issue where the distribution of costs most closely resembled that of the Large Store Law, however, it was that of urban agricultural land taxation. This was a case where the benefits of the existing policy (and the costs of changing it) accrued exclusively to a small group of urban agricultural landowners. Because benefits were concentrated and meshed with the particularistic bias of the Japanese political system, this issue (like the LSL) had long been immune to reform. But because other political actors faced few costs from changing it, it was also the easiest target once participation expanded beyond the small circle of elites with a stake in the status quo. This circle was already expanding before the Americans got involved, but the U.S. probably helped bring about more far-reaching change by making this issue a "U.S.-Japan" problem.

ALTERNATIVE SPECIFICATION

Also important in explaining why the urban agricultural land-tax issue saw more change, however, is the role of gaiatsu in influencing the "idea stream" within this issue area. As noted earlier, the land-price issue was already recognized as a major domestic "problem" long before the Americans entered the picture. Nevertheless, there was little agreement on which of the many proposed solutions would best address the problem. Many MOF officials felt administrative guidance of banks and higher capital gains taxes on land speculation would solve the problem. The NLA and some MOC officials felt the answer lay in stricter regulation of land sales and better city planning. The most radical proposals, however, came from a group of economists who called for far-reaching changes in land-tax policy designed to bring a market-based solution to the land-price problem.

The Americans, interested only in the bottom line of whether policies would bring land prices down or not, could have backed any of these proposals, but they ended up siding blatantly with the last group: the reform economists. At each of the SII negotiating sessions and in their list of 200 demands, the Americans always put land-tax policy first. The specifics of their proposals were drawn directly from books and articles by Noguchi,

Hasegawa Tokunosuke, and Miyao Takahiro, among others. U.S. officials from the embassy in Tokyo consulted with all of these economists at various points during the negotiating year, and U.S. Ambassador Armacost invited some of them to a reception he hosted for the Japanese delegation after the February bargaining session.[59] It is unclear why the Americans tilted so far in favor of this camp, but Shigeko Fukai has speculated that the U.S. officials who researched this issue naturally gravitated toward the market-based approach since it fit their own world view. The officials were mostly economists, and Treasury (with its extreme market-orientation) took the lead in laying out U.S. positions.[60]

By favoring the prescriptions of this group of economists, the U.S. got the government to pay much more attention to their radical reform proposals than it would have. As we saw in the discussion of Tochi rinchō, that group had deadlocked on many proposals for far-reaching change and was very tentative in its recommendations on land-tax reform. As late as the fall of 1989, MOF was still extremely hesitant to take up land-tax policy, afraid it was going to find itself in the middle of another losing battle with LDP-backed interest groups. With the Americans insisting that land-tax policy lay at the root of the problem, however, the ministry finally decided after the passage of the Basic Land Law in December that it was time to take another look at the issue.[61] When it set up a subcommittee of its Tax Commission to look at land taxes, not only were the ideas of the reform economists at the top of the agenda, but also both Hasegawa and Noguchi were named expert members. Both give the Americans a great deal of credit for getting the Japanese government to pay more attention to their ideas.[62]

That still leaves us, of course, with the question of why only *some* of the reform economists' ideas were enacted. Ultimately, as Kingdon describes in his book on American policymaking, the results depended on how the processes of problem recognition, the generation of policy proposals, and politics came together: change happened only when the three streams converged.[63] On the issue of agricultural land taxation, the Americans helped the three streams come together both by giving the economists' ideas an extra boost and by facilitating an expansion of participation beyond the group of vested interests. Once the conditions were favorable, MOF officials were then happy to use this opportunity to rid the tax system of one of its greatest inequities.

The circumstances were similar, if not quite so ideal, for the issue of a broader hike in property taxes. Again, the Americans helped give this idea

(which had been rejected out of hand during the Tochi rinchō deliberations) extra attention. The recognition of the land-price crisis also put the
issue on the agenda and gave the proposal some momentum. MOF officials, again, were eager to run with the ball once they received the hand-
off—this time because the proposal of a new national land tax promised
to allow the ministry to tap a source of revenue that had long been off
limits. While all of this was enough to see a new tax enacted in record
time, however, it wasn't enough to protect the proposal from being
watered down during the course of deliberations when conditions in the
political stream proved to be less than ideal. We will examine the fate of
this tax reform in more detail below.

Finally, to take an example of an idea advocated by the reform economists that went absolutely nowhere, consider the case of the capital gains
tax reduction. This reform, readers will recall, was designed to lower the
tax cost of putting land up for sale—the counterpart to the other tax
reforms designed to increase the tax cost of holding onto land. In combination, the reforms were designed to bring much more land onto the market and bid down high prices. Despite the specific American demand for
this kind of change, however, the Japanese government ended up doing
exactly the opposite! It actually *increased* capital gains taxes (up to 30 percent for land held five years or more) in order to reduce the profitability
of investing in land as an asset. This was on top of the 1987 revision which
had increased the tax on land held for less than two years to 96 percent.[64]

The main difference between this case and the other tax reform cases
discussed above: MOF was totally opposed to the American position. As
one official put it, "The Americans were totally backwards on how land
policy works here. They think you lower taxes and land prices come
down. Here things work in the opposite way. You lower taxes and land
prices rise. You need to keep high taxes to discourage speculation."[65]
MOF's position was based partly on experience. In the early 1970s, they
had tried lowering capital gains taxes and it had sparked a land-price
explosion. Land is so scarce in Japan, MOF officials believe, that marginally increasing supply will only feed speculation. The ministry's position
may also have reflected its interest in maximizing tax revenues. As noted
above, the capital gains tax on land had proved to be a lucrative source of
revenue, especially during the "bubble" years. Whatever the rationale, the
fate of this U.S. and reform economist proposal points to the limits of
gaiatsu's ability to influence policy by affecting ideas. When the politics
were not right, as in this case, ideas went nowhere.

Implementation

In the years since the initial sɪɪ land deal was negotiated, Japanese land prices have come way down. Most significantly, the price of a new Tokyo condominium has fallen from 8.5 times household income in 1990 to "just" five times household income by 1993.[66] Nationwide, commercial and residential land prices have also fallen, in some cases sharply (see figure 7.3). Those seeking a verdict on the sɪɪ's land policy demands would be misled, however, if they focused too much on these numbers. After the land-price explosion of the early 1970s, there was a similar period in which land prices stabilized, but this trend was rudely interrupted in the mid-1980s. We will not truly know that the reforms adopted in the wake of sɪɪ and the "bubble" have worked until a similar span of time has passed without another speculative explosion in prices. In the meantime, the best way to evaluate the impact of sɪɪ on land policy is to look at how commitments made in the 1990 sɪɪ reports were actually implemented.

REFORMS IN TAXATION OF URBAN FARMLAND

The most significant land policy reform adopted in the wake of sɪɪ was the change in the tax treatment of urban farmland. As a result of the

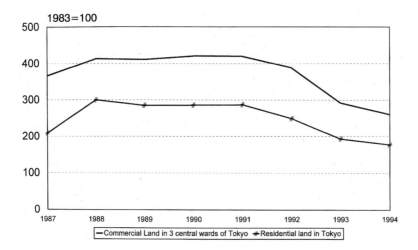

FIGURE 7.3 The Fall in Japanese Land Prices, 1987-94

Source: EPA, Nenji keizai hōkoku: heisei 3-nendo, (Annual Economic Report: 1991), pp. 450–451; and EPA, Nihon keizai no genkyō: heisei 6-nendo, (The Current Condition of the Japanese Economy: 1994), p.250.

reform, 69 percent of the urban farmland that had previously escaped taxation at the rate of surrounding residential land is now subject to being taxed at the higher rate. While this bottom line figure confirms that this reform went further than any of the repeated attempts to tackle the problem, a close look at how the reform has actually been implemented reveals that urban landowners did succeed in modifying the plan—providing further evidence of the ability of domestic political actors in Japan to reshape policy to suit their own needs even when gaiatsu works to alter overall policy outcomes.

In devising a program for revising the tax treatment of urban farms, the government never seriously considered raising taxes on *all* farmland in urbanization promotion areas. Some land designated for urbanization was actually not very suitable for conversion to residential use, and the government realized that it could not afford to build the infrastructure needed to develop all urban farmland at once. The MOC therefore proposed that some farmland be redesignated as "productive green areas" subject to lower tax rates even as the bulk of urban farmland was subjected to higher rates. Once a decision was made to raise taxes on urban farms, therefore, the political battle shifted to the question of how the rules for "productive green areas" would be written.[67]

As one might suspect, landowners hoped this new loophole would be as large as the old one: first, they wanted to be able to choose how to designate their land; and second, they hoped a designation as a "green area" would come with a minimum of restrictions on their freedom to cash out and/or develop their land at some date in the future. Significantly, on the latter count, they proved unable to alter the MOC's rules: those whose land is designated as a green area are not allowed to sell it at market rates for 30 years, and they are required to keep the land "green" for this entire period either by farming it or, in a deal with the local government, having it set aside as a vegetable-growing area for the public.[68] Since few landowners could count on living 30 years in order to cash out on the investment themselves, the deal looked attractive only to those who were most interested in keeping their taxes low while they held land for eventual bequest to their heirs.

On the question of who should decide which urban farmland was designated "green," however, the MOC was forced to give in to LDP pressure. The ministry had originally wanted to determine *itself* how land would be designated, hoping it would be able to integrate this process into the broader process of city planning. When it took its plan before the Diet, though, it encountered a storm of protest from Diet members insistent that property owners be given the right to decide how to designate their own land. Eventually, both houses of the Diet passed resolutions urging the MOC to respect the wishes of landowners. Having no choice, the ministry revised its rules to give landowners complete freedom to choose how to designate their land. Once it had done so, all it could do was wait to see what landowners would decide to do.

The results came in at the end of 1993, by which date landowners were required to decide how to designate their land. That the reforms were more than an empty shell became clear when 69 percent of urban farmland became subject to higher taxes and only 31 percent was designated to remain "green." In the Tokyo metropolitan area, this meant that 18,500 hectares of farmland would be subject to economic incentives encouraging landowners to develop their land at least enough to pay the higher tax bills.[69] Not all of this land is being converted immediately to housing. In fact, because property tax rates remain low even at residential rates, some landowners have found that they can pay the increased *property* tax by developing only part of their land.[70] According to the NLA, landowners have announced plans to convert approximately 11 percent of their rezoned land into housing—3,600 hectares in the three largest metropolitan areas.[71]

The key to the long-term impact of this tax reform, however, lies in the change in the *inheritance tax* treatment of the rezoned farmland.[72] Even if the current generation of landowners continue to hold off developing some of their farmland while they are still alive, most of this farmland will be developed when they die because few heirs will be able to pay residential-rate inheritance taxes on it without either selling or developing the land. Where previously heirs avoided inheritance taxation in many cases if they planned to continue farming land for 20 years, they will now be taxed at regular rates—which for large bequests reach 50 percent. With this giant loophole now gone, urban Japan can expect to add a steady stream of farmland to its stock of residential land over the next two decades.

While all of this testifies to the significance of the reform and the impact of gaiatsu on this particular policy, the politically motivated concession allowing landowners to choose for themselves how to designate their land has produced some strange distortions which, while benefiting landowners, will cost the state and the public a great deal in the long term. One distortion was apparent immediately when the government announced the breakdown for how land was designated across urban prefectures. Perversely, large proportions of the land closest to Tokyo have been designated "green" even as virtually all land in the more remote suburbs has been designated for conversion to housing.[73] Furthermore, many landowners divided their landholdings, designating part of it "green" and the rest for development—producing a crazy patchwork of land, some of it to be developed and others to be kept green for the next 30 years.[74] Both of these distortions will cost the state a great deal in extra expenditures on infrastructure. They will also cost the public, who—forced to buy homes farther out from their jobs—will continue to commute past undeveloped farms close in to Tokyo.[75]

New National Landholding Tax

In April 1991, when the Diet passed the legislation effecting the changes in urban farmland taxation discussed above, it also adopted a new national property tax. While the Japanese had not made any mention of such a tax in the sii reports just a year earlier, this step was designed to accomplish what the government said it would do when it pledged to raise local property taxes. Local governments and the Ministry of Home Affairs had strongly resisted pressure to raise their property tax assessments when mof and the Government Tax Commission began talking about the subject in the spring of 1990, and so mof had begun to push for a new *national* tax that would accomplish the same purpose. At one point, the Tax Commission had talked about a tax rate as high as 1 percent—a rate that clearly would have had a big impact given that effective local tax rates were often less than 0.1 percent. In the end, the Diet approved a new tax with a rate of 0.3 percent, with numerous exemptions.

That the government adopted this tax as quickly as it did is partly attributable, again, to sii. One mof official pointed out, by way of contrast, that it had taken his ministry more than a decade to get the Diet to approve the last totally new tax—the consumption tax.[76] Still, the low rate, and more importantly the huge exemptions, testify to the ability of domestic political forces in Japan to limit the impact of foreign pressure when the issue involves something as big and broad as this type of tax. Let us take a look at the fate of this tax reform initiative.[77]

When the Tax Commission first began talking about a new national landholding tax in the summer of 1990, it encountered a storm of protest. While MOF favored a broad tax, most other ministries (representing their client interests) opposed having the tax apply to *them*. Agriculture didn't want it to apply to farmland. MITI and big business organizations accused MOF of being interested in nothing more than a new revenue source. The Ministry of Home Affairs was particularly opposed, seeing MOF's proposal as a direct challenge to local governments' right to tap this source of revenue. Even the NLA opposed the idea of applying the new tax to *individual* property holdings, arguing instead that only corporate property should be subject to the tax. Meanwhile, with the list of interest groups coming out opposed to the tax looking like a "who's who" of LDP support groups, the party quietly began to pressure MOF to scale back its proposal.

When the new tax was finally adopted by the Diet, most agreed that it was "boneless" (*honenuki*), having been punched so full of holes that only 50,000 corporations and individuals would actually have to pay the tax. Whereas many members of the Government Tax Commission had favored a one percent tax applied to all landholdings valued over 500 million yen ($4 million), the final plan called for a mere 0.3 percent tax with the following exemptions: it would not apply to the first 1 billion yen of corporate landholdings or to the first 1.5 billion yen of individual or small firm holdings; it would not apply to property on which the owner lived or to land used for rental housing; it would not apply to parcels of land smaller than 1,000 square meters; and—perhaps most significantly—it would not apply to any land valued at less than 30,000 yen per square meter. This last loophole was particularly large since it exempted almost all land held by farmers and small merchants. Also notable were the categories of land-use that were exempted because of their "public nature": farms, pastures, forests, land for hospitals, nursing homes, drug stores, various types of schools, railways, ports, and warehouses.[78]

As Noguchi and others have pointed out, the final land-tax program offers a perfect illustration of how Japanese policymaking is based on a political calculus that rewards certain privileged groups. As he put it, "The LDP's tax plan thus perfectly matches the party's political needs, having been tailored to give big breaks to its biggest supporters: shopkeepers, farmers, and companies."[79] In this case, the impact of the proposed policy on vested interests was so great and affected so many of them that gaiatsu had no chance to alter policy outcomes by bringing in new actors. As a result, the political process played out its course in such a way that the final policy change served the public purpose of lowering prices hardly at all. According to Noguchi's calculations, the new tax would bring down land prices in Tokyo by only 0.4 to 2 percent—a tiny fraction of the impact he expected from the original proposal.[80]

OTHER SII-RELATED LAND POLICIES

The two land-tax reform policies discussed above were of course just the most prominent of those debated in the aftermath of SII. Many of the rest, however, encountered a fate similar to that of the national landholding tax. The proposal for a tax on the increased value of corporate landholdings (*fukumieki kazei*) was blocked by strong corporate opposition; so was the MOF proposal to create a new national tax on idle landholdings; and so was a proposal to make the existing special tax on idle land no longer tax deductible.[81] Likewise, the LDP in late 1992 forced a slowdown on a campaign by the Ministry of Home Affairs to raise its property tax assessments up from 20 percent to 70 percent of market values. After initially resisting MOF and American pressure to raise assessments, the MHA had announced in the fall of 1990 that it wanted local governments to work toward reaching this goal. While too late to stop MOF's push for a national land tax, this plan held the potential to raise the cost of landholding significantly and accomplish the purpose of reducing the supply-demand imbalance on the land market. Faced with pressure from local governments afraid of citizen complaints, however, the MHA had allowed localities to delay the increases and in December 1992 worked out a deal with the LDP such that localities would raise rates by just 2–3 percent a year, "far too slowly to bring landholding taxes up to a level where land will be forced onto the market."[82]

Finally, there is the issue of the Land and House Lease Laws. As noted above, the final reforms adopted by the Diet in 1991 were almost identical to the legislation drafted by the Ministry of Justice in February 1989, suggesting the SII had no impact on the *content* of the reform. Given that the Diet vote was close, it is possible that the government's SII pledge to revise the laws helped steady proponents of reform and tipped the balance in favor of *passage*.[83] Nevertheless, given the limited nature of the reform, it is hard to credit gaiatsu with much impact.

The revisions, which combined three separate laws into a single Land and House Lease Law, create a new category of lease called the "fixed term land lease" where the lessor no longer needs to show "just cause" not to renew the lease upon its expiration. Previously, this need to show "just cause" had robbed lessors of all control over their property once they signed a lease, greatly discouraging development of leased property. The requirement that leases of this new type extend for at least 50 years, however, promised to continue to dissuade many landowners who might have wanted to make their land available for development. Most such owners would be dead in 50 years! Furthermore, the new law did nothing to change the way the "just cause" provisions served to limit development of property already under existing contracts.[84]

Conclusion

In the two issue areas discussed in chapter 5 and 6, the U.S. gradually focused its demands to the point that they could be summed up in one headline each: "Japan agrees to spend 430 trillion yen on public investment" and "Japan agrees to shorten delay under Large Store Law to one year." The issues at stake in the land issue area were never that simple. The U.S. decided it wanted to see lower Japanese land prices, but the policies it sought as a means of bringing that result about involved complex combinations of tax increases and reductions, changes in legal protection for tenants, and much more. The complexity of the issue, we saw, provided an opportunity for foreign pressure to have some impact on policy outcomes by concentrating attention on specific proposals. This complexity was not conducive, however, to the strategies of participation expansion which were so effective in the two issue areas discussed earlier.

In a highly politicized policy debate where all of the Japanese actors had clearly conceived interests in policy outcomes, gaiatsu was a blunt instrument. It could demand action and present a long list of specific policy proposals, but it could not intervene with the dexterity necessary to solicit favorable action on all of its demands. Ultimately, the U.S. had to leave it to Japanese actors to pick and choose which of its proposals to pursue, and when it did, it lost the opportunity to fundamentally reform Japanese land policy. This was because the domestic actors best situated to "pick and choose" were Japanese bureaucrats, politicians, and "vested interests."

Of all of the U.S. demands in this issue area, the one the bureaucrats (especially MOF bureaucrats) had been working on the longest was the demand to eliminate the loophole that gave urban farmland owners a huge break on their taxes. Regardless of the impact on land prices, MOF officials were eager to eliminate a provision of their tax code that they saw as blantantly unfair. In contrast, bureaucrats (especially MOF officials) were much less interested in cutting capital gains taxes on land or liberalizing the House and Land Lease Law, and they were strongly divided on the new national landholding tax. The final results of the policy process reveal a striking correspondence to the preferences of Kasumigaseki (the Tokyo district home to the offices of Japanese ministries).

The results were also not inconsistent, however, with the interests of LDP politicians. Proposals that threatened business interests were almost uniformly watered down—especially the new national landholding tax. Even the urban farmland tax reform, which asked a loyal LDP constituency to take a hit, was revised to allow landowners to divide up their landholding to maximize their financial advantage even as it forced taxpayers and home-buyers to suffer continuing inefficiencies. Furthermore, as in the case of the LSL, gaiatsu gave the LDP the cover it needed to revise a policy that, while benefiting a small but loyal group of voters, was proving to be increasingly unpopular with the general public. Gaiatsu once again played its well-rehearsed role as the "necessary evil" able to correct the extreme bias of the LDP regime toward particularistic policies.

Ironically, given that land policy was probably the SII issue of greatest importance to the Japanese general public, gaiatsu was not able in this case to tap into this political force as an ally on the side of broad change. Given that the public proved to be a key ally in the case of the LSL and to some extent on public investment as well, it is curious why foreign pressure was not able in this case to take advantage of a similar strategy. The problem was that the policies at stake in the land debate promised to impose costs on the public (especially the majority landowning public) even as it promised long-term benefits. As Noguchi has argued, the Japanese public does not seem to understand its own interests in land policy. America, it seems, was not in a position to re-educate them.

8 Competition Policy Issues

The final two issue areas covered during the SII talks both dealt with Japan's "competition policies"—policies aimed at fostering free and fair competition among firms within Japan's national boundaries. Under the heading "exclusionary business practices," the U.S. urged the Japanese to strengthen their enforcement of the Anti-Monopoly Law (AML), the statute at the heart of Japan's competition policy. According to the Americans, the administration of this law by the Japanese Fair Trade Commission (JFTC) was so lax that it allowed price cartels, group boycotts, and other collusive practices to go virtually unpunished. Undeterred, firms were free to conspire in ways that kept closed markets that were nominally open to competitive imports.

At the same time, under the heading "*keiretsu* business groups," the U.S. called on Japan to supplement its traditional antitrust enforcement with regulatory reforms designed to foster greater openness and accountability in the management of firms. Shareholders, the theory went, are a natural ally of competition policy since they value profits, and profitability often suffers when firms engage in practices like boycotts of cheap imports. Empower shareholders, the U.S. argued, and firms engaged in such practices will be forced to adjust their behavior.

This set of issues was in many ways a "natural" for the SII talks. Not only were U.S. Trade Representative Carla Hills and her deputy Linn Williams both lawyers with extensive experience with antitrust issues, but also the topics covered were ones that emerged repeatedly in sectoral trade talks with Japan. During talks on the public-sector construction market, U.S. negotiators had learned that Japanese firms typically participated in a system of rigged bidding (*dangō*) where all contractors who were part of the process had a turn at winning bids. U.S. engineering firms, because they were cut out of these deals, were effectively excluded from the market. Similar problems with cartels and refusals to deal were identified in complaints by U.S. firms in sectors as diverse as soda ash, flat glass, paper, and amorphous metals.

The problems caused by the Japanese keiretsu business groups were likewise frequently identified as barriers to U.S. exports. The MOSS talks on semiconductors and auto parts had focused, for example, on how U.S. market share was limited by vertical keiretsu arrangements wherein Japanese manufacturers discriminated against foreign firms in favor of domestic suppliers with which they had long business dealings. Similarly, horizontal keiretsu arrangements of the kind represented by the giant Mitsui, Mitsubishi, and Sumitomo groups had been cited as barriers by U.S. firms in sectors like insurance and financial services. Firms associated with these groups tended to purchase such services exclusively from fellow group members, often without even opening up the bidding process to outside competition.

In many ways, the two sets of competition policy issues were the quintessential "structural impediment" that the members of Congress who wrote the Super 301 legislation and government officials who conceived of SII had in mind when they pushed U.S. trade policy in this new direction. Rather than dealing with competition policy problems over and over in separate sectoral talks with Japan, they felt, the U.S. should address the fundamental structural problem by talking with the Japanese about their competition policy as a whole.

It should be noted, however, that the Americans' goals in this issue area went beyond the aim of opening up specific sectors to U.S. exports. Ultimately, the U.S. hoped, freer competition within the Japanese market would eliminate the windfall Japanese firms earned by maintaining artificially high prices in their domestic market—reducing the ability of these firms to continually invest in new equipment and simultaneously "dump" products in the U.S. At the same time, greater shareholder power promised to make Japanese firms pay more attention to short-term profits, forcing them to end their relentless focus on market share at any cost. In short, the U.S. hoped to reduce trade tension by making Japan more like itself—more consumer-oriented and less producer-oriented, more profit-oriented and less market-share-oriented.

However, while the link between this set of American demands and U.S. trade policy goals was thus clearer than in most of the other sii issue areas, the results were relatively meager. The Japanese agreed to stiffen penalty levels under the AML, and the JFTC has pursued a few more cases, but important types of collusive behavior continue to go unpunished. The government of Japan, furthermore, said "absolutely not" to the key American demand calling for restrictions on cross-shareholding—the main practice that shelters Japanese management from shareholder pressure. It is the primary aim of this chapter to explain why gaiatsu was less effective in bringing about policy change in this issue area than it was in the other areas surveyed in Chapters 5–7. A subsidiary purpose is to explain why, within this issue area, the U.S. was somewhat more successful in winning support for stiffer antitrust penalties than it was for the rest of its agenda.

Competition Policy Before SII

For most of the postwar period, Japanese competition policy has been in retreat from the tough standards established during the U.S. occupation. The Anti-Monopoly Law, based on antitrust laws in the U.S., was initially pushed through under heavy pressure from the Americans in 1947. In its original form, it banned all holding companies and horizontal restraints on price and output—regardless of whether the practice had a proven impact on the level of competition within an industry. It also placed strong restrictions on cross-shareholding and mergers.[1] This initiative was extremely ambitious since, as a variety of analysts have noted, Japan lacked a native tradition of competition policy.[2] In fact, the government had actively encouraged the formation of cartels before and during the war, seeing them as a way of fostering the development of industries that would not have developed in a freely competitive market.[3]

Thus, almost as soon as the ink on the new law was dry, Japanese officials and businessmen began to conspire to weaken it. In 1949, they succeeded in relaxing restrictions on mergers and cross-shareholding. The more serious challenge to the integrity of the law, however, came in 1953—shortly after the Americans had packed their bags and gone home. The set of amendments pushed through at this time further reduced limits on cross-shareholding (allowing the practice as long as "the

results would not be a substantial restraint of competition in any particular field of trade"); allowed depression and rationalization cartels as long
as they were authorized by the JFTC; required proof that horizontal
agreements on price and output had a real impact on competition; and
authorized resale price maintenance in some cases.[4] To top it off, the
JFTC's staff was slashed from 305 to 241.[5]

The next two decades were tough times for the JFTC. In 1957, MITI
had declared competition to be "an impediment to the rational development of a nation's economy."[6] While it failed in a 1958 attempt to push
through another set of amendments that would have all but abolished the
AML, the ministry proceeded with a campaign to exempt as many sectors
as possible from the AML's restrictions. As Iyori Hiroshi, a JFTC staffer in
those days, recalls, his agency constantly found its efforts thwarted by its
more powerful ministerial rival: "If we even began an investigation of a
price cartel, MITI would quickly work to get the industry exempted from
the AML—as if it had been waiting for us."[7] By 1965, the number of cartels exempted from the law had increased to 1,079.[8]

Simultaneously, MITI was also working to encourage firms to trade
stock and develop extensive cross-shareholding networks. Although the
ministry had been pushing firms in this direction for some time, its
efforts acquired a new sense of urgency in the mid-1960s as Japan's entry
into the OECD obliged it to begin removing its restrictions on foreign
investment. Once it removed these restrictions, MITI worried, foreign
firms would rush in and buy up their undercapitalized Japanese competitors. To prevent that from happening, the ministry encouraged firms,
most of which already had networks of "stable shareholders," to further
expand these networks. By the 1980s, this system had grown to the
extent that stable shareholders accounted for an estimated 60 to 80 percent of the shares listed on the Tokyo Stock Exchange.[9]

While there was little in all of this history to offer any encouragement,
the JFTC nevertheless attempted to assert itself for the first time in the
late 1960s and early 1970s. First, in 1969, the agency went to court to
challenge a MITI-backed merger in the steel sector. MITI, still worried
about the challenge of foreign firms as trade and capital liberalization
progressed, was intent on creating a giant new steel firm by bringing
together the Yawata and Fuji steelworks, but the JFTC, worried about the
anticompetitive effects of this merger, insisted that the two firms sell off
some of their subsidiaries as a condition for the agency's approval of the
merger.[10] Then, in 1973, the JFTC filed *criminal* charges, in a rare use of

this authority, against oil firms who had coordinated price hikes under administrative guidance from MITI.[11] Finally, encouraged by the popular support it gained for its pursuit of the oil cartel cases, the agency sought to win Diet approval of amendments to the AML which were designed to vastly increase JFTC power.

None of these initiatives, however, succeeded in significantly reversing the trend toward weaker competition policy which had been established in the first two decades after the occupation. The steel merger went through, albeit with a requirement that each steel firm sell one of its factories to a competitor; the JFTC gave up using criminal sanctions; and MITI and the LDP prevented the agency from making full use of the new powers granted to it under the watered-down amendments passed in 1977. A close look at the actual state of Japanese competition policy in the 1980s, leading up to the start of the SII talks, confirms that the JFTC, despite its efforts, failed to create anything approaching the level of competition policy found in the United States and Europe.

TENDENCY TOWARD INFORMAL ENFORCEMENT

Under the AML, as revised in 1977, the JFTC has a wide variety of means through which to enforce the law. First, as in the oil cartel cases, it can pursue *criminal charges* against violators of the law, which, if resulting in a conviction, can lead to prison sentences and/or fines for the individuals involved and additional fines for their firms. Second, the JFTC has the option of pursuing administrative remedies. In these cases, the JFTC itself acts as investigator, prosecutor, and judge, conducting either a summary investigation or a formal investigation and issuing one of the following depending on the severity of the offense: (1) a formal *recommendation* requiring the offending parties to cease practices the JFTC found to be a violation of the law; (2) a *warning* calling on the parties to end activities which are of dubious legality under the law; (3) a *caution*; (4) a dismissal.

Of these administrative remedies, the recommendation is the most formal. Like an American cease and desist order, it legally requires compliance; it can serve as the basis for private damage litigation; and it comes with public disclosure of the offending firms' names. In addition, since the 1977 amendments, this type of decision in cases involving price and output cartels results in a mandatory *surcharge*. Warnings and cautions, because they do not come with surcharges or publicity and foreclose the possibility of civil suits under the AML (which can be initiated only when the JFTC takes formal action against a firm), are much less serious.

Nevertheless, it is the last two types of remedies that the JFTC pursued most commonly in the 1980s. As can be seen in table 8.1, the JFTC had not (as of 1989) pursued *any* criminal charges since the oil cartel cases of the early 1970s. Furthermore, the number of cases in which it issued formal recommendations dropped from an average of 24.7 in 1973–1983 to an average of 6.8 between 1984 and 1989. In almost all cases, the JFTC issued only warnings and cautions. The statistics for 1989 are especially striking. In that year, the JFTC found evidence of illegal activity in some 122 cases, but took formal action in just 7, choosing merely to issue warnings in the other 115.

TABLE 8.1

Type of Fair Trade Commission Action in Anti-Monopoly Law Cases, 1973–89 (number of cases, not firms)

Year	criminal action	formal recommendation	(surcharge)*	warning	caution**
1973	2	66	–	47	–
1974	0	58	–	55	–
1975	0	30	–	52	–
1976	0	31	–	63	–
1977	0	10	–	78	–
1978	0	6	1	26	–
1979	0	16	5	22	–
1980	0	14	12	39	–
1981	0	11	6	91	–
1982	0	19	8	151	–
1983	0	11	10	118	60
1984	0	6	2	94	66
1985	0	10	4	80	62
1986	0	8	4	88	37
1987	0	4	6	84	28
1988	0	6	3	65	17
1989	0	7	6	115	28

* cases resulting in surcharges are a *subtotal* of those resulting in formal recommendations; this system did not come into effect until 1978.

* the FTC did not report statistics for cautions until 1983.

Source: Issues of FTC, *Kosei Torihiki Iinkai Nenji Hokoku—Dokusen Kinshi Hakusho* (Fair Trade Commission Annual Report—The Anti-Monopoly White Paper).

The contrast between the JFTC's preference for informality and the approaches of the U.S. and European Community are striking. In the U.S., which has an antitrust system based primarily on criminal sanctions, the government typically pursues 100 cases a year.[12] In Europe, with a system relying purely on administrative sanctions, the European Commission took formal action in an average of 16 cases a year during the 1980s with additional cases pursued in each of the EC member nations.[13]

LAX SANCTIONS

Another striking feature of Japanese competition policy, going into the SII talks, were the extremely low limits placed on the sanctions available to the JFTC. Criminal fines were limited to a *maximum* of 5 million yen ($40,000)—regardless of the severity of the offense. In contrast, in the U.S., violators of antitrust laws faced fines ranging up to a maximum of $10 million for firms and $350,000 for individuals and *averaging* $224,000 in the years 1985 to 1988.[14] The surcharges, furthermore, were limited to 0.5 to 2 percent of the turnover of goods or services subject to the cartel for the period during which the cartel was in effect.[15] While the JFTC has been able to collect fines ranging up to 1.1 billion yen ($4.6 million at $1 = 240 yen) even at this low rate,[16] the method of calculation guaranteed firms participating in cartels that they could profit from collusion—even if they were fined—as long as they could boost prices at a rate higher than 2 percent. In Europe, where firms are subject to fines of 10 percent on *all* goods they produce, fines exercise much more of a deterrent effect. It is important to note, furthermore, that the JFTC could impose surcharges only in cases involving price and output cartels. This meant, given the JFTC's reluctance to use criminal sanctions, that firms violating AML prohibitions on refusals to deal or resale price maintenance, for example, faced no risk of financial penalty. Should they engage in illegal activity, the worst they could expect was a recommendation that they stop the offensive behavior.

LEGAL BARRIERS TO EFFECTIVE ENFORCEMENT

Another problem facing JFTC officials intent on enforcing the AML is the variety of limits on their investigative powers. First, unlike their American counterparts, JFTC officials cannot rely on wiretapping to gather evidence of a conspiracy such as a cartel. Wiretapping is illegal and tapes are rarely admissible in court. Second, when seeking access to company records (discovery), the JFTC is forced to compile a complete list of the documents it is seeking prior to its raid—something it cannot do unless is has the cooperation of an insider. Third, the JFTC cannot prosecute executives for obstruction if they get wind of an agency plan to raid their offices and proceed to remove incriminating evidence. In the U.S., the threat of a charge of this sort serves as a powerful aid in investigations of white collar crimes. Finally, the JFTC on its own cannot get witnesses to cooperate by detaining suspects for long periods as do the Japanese police.[17]

Part of the explanation for why the JFTC prefers to issue "warnings" instead of taking formal actions can be traced to this set of legal restrictions. Lacking many of the tools needed for effective investigations, and also short on staff, the JFTC has a great deal of difficulty gathering the evidence it needs to make formal charges stick. If it makes a formal recommendation, the party charged with a violation of the AML has the option to demand a hearing. Even if a hearing confirms the JFTC charge, the party can appeal to the Tokyo High Court.[18] Fearing court challenges, the JFTC has tended to back down when firms threaten to fight. As one former JFTC official put it, "JFTC lawyers are too timid. They lack self-confidence. If it looks like their target is going to fight them in court, they settle for a warning because, they figure, at least this will get them to stop the offensive behavior. This kind of attitude has been there for a long time."[19]

Gaps in AML Coverage of Anticompetitive Practices

Adding to the above barriers to effective enforcement of the AML, going into the SII talks, were several important gaps in the law's coverage. First, large numbers of cartels were exempted from the AML's anti-cartel provisions. While the number of exempted cartels peaked at more than 1,000 in 1965, as noted above, in 1988 there were still 310 such cartels.[20] Many of these had no significant impact on imports or import-competing sectors, but some—such as those that protected small textile firms and coal mines—did.[21] As recently as 1978 and 1983, the government had set up *new* legal cartels in sectors ranging from aluminum-smelting to shipbuilding to steel.[22] Again, the legal authorizations for these cartels had expired by 1988, but Mark Tilton found, in his detailed investigation of the cartels in basic materials industries, that many continued to have de facto exemptions from the AML through deals worked out between MITI and JFTC officials.[23]

As Tilton's findings indicate, the gaps in the AML's coverage were much larger than the list of officially exempted cartels. The Japanese construction industry, for example, was and is officially covered by the AML's provisions. Nevertheless, the JFTC has rarely taken action against this politically influential sector. When it did, in 1982, it faced such a backlash from LDP Diet members that it was forced to issue a special set of "Guidelines" for the construction industry telling the industry exactly what steps to avoid in order not to be considered a cartel under the AML.[24]

The relationship between dangō and Japan's competition policy is complex but important to understand. First, the problems in this sector are typical of those characterizing other heavily regulated sectors of the economy. Although the bidding process has been reformed to some extent in recent years, at the time the SII talks were underway government officials at the national and local levels were involved in the dangō process from start to finish. They made collusion possible by limiting the number of construction firms authorized to bid on public projects. Then they facilitated the process by: (1) establishing an (officially secret) "ceiling price" and regularly leaking this information to cartel firms; (2) making known the amount of all bids so as to assist the cartel in punishing firms that submitted "improper" bids; and (3) punishing dangō-busting bidders by leaving them off the designated bidder list for future contracts. That the dangō functioned as intended is suggested by the large number of bids that came in just below the "secret" MOC ceiling price.[25]

The Ministry of Construction (MOC), in particular, used this system, not just because LDP politicians saw it as a way to gather political funds, but because the ministry viewed it as an integral part of its efforts to nurture a healthy construction industry where public projects were well-built and small contractors as well as the big engineering firms could all thrive. By regulating firm entry and prices, it prevented the excessive competition that would lead to cost-cutting (potentially dangerous if building standards were compromised) and bankruptcy for industry firms. A similar philosophy underlies the efforts of many other Japanese ministries to nurture their sectors. In some sectors, such as finance and securities, special industry laws allow ministries to strictly regulate prices and firm entry without regard to the AML.[26] In others, such as Tilton's basic materials industries and construction, the exemption from the AML has to be negotiated with the JFTC (bureaucratically or politically). In all of these cases, however, the industries are broadly exempt from rules restricting horizontal restraints on competition.

The second reason why understanding the construction dangō is critical for an understanding of Japanese competition policy is because collusion in this sector makes possible collusion in so many others. One of the reasons why intermediate goods cartels are supposed to be unstable, according to economists, is because downstream market competition forces buyers to relentlessly search for lower prices. Auto firms, for example, will not put up with a price-fixing steel cartel if they are having to compete with auto firms who have access to lower-priced steel. This strong market pressure does not operate, however, when downstream sectors are insulated to some degree from price competition—as in the construction industry. In such cases, all the industries along the chain of intermediate goods-suppliers will more willingly accept price-fixing as long as they themselves can collude to pass along the added cost to the end-user—in this case, the taxpayer who foots the bill for public sector construction projects inflated, according to various estimates, by 30–50 percent.[27] Because the construction industry, itself accounting for 18.2 percent of the Japanese economy, consumes all of Japanese cement, half its steel, and a large proportion of its glass, the insulation of this sector from competition policy has the effect of reducing market pressure on a whole host of supplier industries and thus making cartels easier to maintain in those sectors as well.[28]

While the discussion of gaps in Japanese competition policy has focused thus far on *horizontal* restraints, the holes were arguably greater when it came to *vertical* restrictions. At least with horizontal collusion, the JFTC and Japanese courts were on the record as finding such practices in principle illegal under the AML. Going into the SII talks, however, the courts and the JFTC had generally failed to see such practices as exclusive dealerships (where a manufacturer prohibits its dealers from handling competing products) and exclusive supplier relationships as contravening the AML.[29] The vertical keiretsu, in other words, were viewed as being outside the jurisdiction of the AML and the JFTC. Significantly, economists and legal scholars (in the U.S. as well as Japan) are much more divided in their opinions about the effects of vertical restraints on competition than they are about the effects of horizontal restraints, and many other nations maintain antitrust laws which are quite permissive of such practices.[30] Still, the pervasiveness of vertical restraints in Japan—where in some sectors the *entire* distribution network is dominated by a small group of Japanese firms—generated anticompetitive effects that arguably should have been the subject of JFTC scrutiny.

The final "gap" in the JFTC's enforcement of competition policy going into the SII talks was the agency's lax policy with regard to cross-shareholding among members of horizontal keiretsu such as the Mitsui, Mitsubishi, and Sumitomo groups.[31] The JFTC's own studies had found that in 1985 an average of 30 percent of the outstanding stock of firms that were part of these groups were owned by other group members.[32] Others have noted that when one looks only at the *leading* stockholders of the keiretsu, the cross-shareholding ratio ranges from 55 to 74 percent for these three groups.[33] Going into the SII talks, however, the JFTC had never forced any keiretsu firms to divest themselves of group shares.[34] The law allows the JFTC to limit practices such as cross-shareholding, but only when they serve to "substantially" restrain competition. Current levels of cross-shareholding, according to the agency, are not a significant barrier to competition. While the weakness of Japanese competition policy in this respect is arguably a "gap" in the Japanese context, however, it is important to note that U.S. antitrust law places no limits on cross-shareholding. Neither does it ban holding companies as does the Japanese AML.

A Dysfunctional Private Damage Remedy System

Japan is known for its nonlitigious culture, but as leading legal scholars point out, it is important to recognize that this nonlitigiousness is enhanced by a variety of legal rules that make it unprofitable for potential plaintiffs to sue.[35] The impact of these rules is especially pronounced in the case of private damage action under antitrust law. Those suffering losses due to anticompetitive practices can only file under the AML if the JFTC first makes a formal recommendation against a defendant,[36] can file for single damages only (no treble damages as in the U.S.), cannot file class action suits, and face a burden of proof which in several respects is much more difficult to meet than in the U.S.

The clearest evidence that the system is stacked against those who might sue under the AML is the scarcity of cases. As of 1985, when Mark Ramseyer surveyed the record of private antitrust suits, there had been only seven such suits filed in the almost four decades since the AML first established the private damage system. Two of these cases were settled out of court for small sums, but none of those litigated to the finish resulted in positive verdicts for the plaintiffs.[37] Typically, Ramseyer found, plaintiffs found it impossible to meet the court-established burden of proof on the issue of *damages*: even when they succeeded in proving that a group of firms colluded to set prices, they had trouble proving that this action resulted in an increase in the prices they paid (several steps down the distribution chain) over what the price would have been without collusion. This burden of proof is especially difficult to meet given restrictive rules of discovery that make it difficult for plaintiffs to acquire the information needed to demonstrate, for example, what prices would have been without the cartel.[38]

The main reason there have been so few cases, however, is because legal rules greatly restrict the sum of money plaintiffs have a chance of winning under the AML. In the U.S., plaintiffs and their lawyers have the opportunity to win huge sums of money by suing on behalf of a large class of injured parties and claiming treble damages. In Japan, only those plaintiffs who are party to a suit can claim damages, and they can recover only what they can prove to have lost. As a result, the amounts of money at issue in the handful of cases litigated under the AML in Japan were minimal (ranging from \$370 to \$19,000). Sums like these, clearly, were not going to encourage many plaintiffs to sue. At the same time, they were not going to do anything to discourage firms from engaging in anticompetitive practices.[39]

The Politics of Competition Policy

As the above discussion makes clear, the competition policy problems at issue during the SII talks were complex. To make a real difference, the Americans during SII would have to convince the Japanese to move forward with reforms in all of these areas: higher penalties without narrowing gaps in the AML's coverage, for example, would have minimal effects. Yet, in almost all cases, Japanese policy on these issues was subject to stringent domestic political constraints that would make reform extremely difficult. On many issues, the Americans had no allies within the Japanese political system. On others, their only ally was the JFTC, a relatively weak player in the game of bureaucratic politics. In the realm of "ideas," where U.S. demands made some difference on land policy, the situation was no better: the Japanese view of the role competition policy should play within the economy has long been distinct from the predominant view in the U.S.

A look at the politics of competition policy, leading up to the SII talks, sets the stage for the analysis of why American pressure proved to be generally ineffective in this area as well as for the analysis of why there was more movement on some sub-issues than others.

The JFTC, as noted above, had tried to address some competition policy problems during its reform initiative of the 1970s. By looking at the shape and fate of this purely domestic reform initiative, we can begin to map out who stood where in Japanese politics on a variety of competition policy issues. First, it is important to make a note of later American reform proposals that were *not* part of the JFTC's proposals—for these would likely be the proposals enjoying the least support within Japan. The JFTC made no attempt to facilitate private damage suits under the AML; it made no proposals to toughen the AML's coverage of vertical restraints; and it sought only minor changes in cross-shareholding rules.[40]

Instead, the main JFTC proposals were designed to beef up the ability of the agency to police anticompetitive behavior aimed at *raising prices*. It was through the 1977 amendments that the JFTC fought for and gained the opportunity to impose administrative surcharges on price and output cartels. The agency also won the power to force firms in a given industry to report and justify price increases when they raised their prices in tandem.[41] The emphasis on price cartels in both of these policy changes is reflective of the JFTC's (and Japan's) primary concern with this aspect of competition policy. As former JFTC official Iyori put it, the reason his agency has devoted most of its anti-cartel efforts to *price* cartels rather than other types (like group boycotts) "is that Japanese antitrust policy has developed since 1960 in the context of anti-inflation and consumer protection policies. Concern for free competition as an ultimate objective and for diffusion of economic power has been rather weak in Japan, and thus opposition to concentrations of economic power, which underlies traditional American antitrust policy, has also been weak."[42]

The fate of the other primary JFTC reform proposal in the 1970s testifies to the nation's lack of concern with concentrations of economic power in and of themselves. The agency had proposed, as the centerpiece of its 1974 reform package, that it be given the power to force the breakup of large firms in monopolistic markets. In the final version of the 1977 amendments, the JFTC *is* given the power to break up firms when one controls over 50 percent of the market or two control over 75 percent—but only after "consulting" with the minister in the relevant area and abiding by a number of other restrictive conditions. Given that MITI and the other ministries were likely in most cases to strongly oppose JFTC-ordered breakups, the inclusion of these conditions essentially emasculated the provision. The JFTC, in the years since, has yet to use this provision of the law even though there are numerous sectors (e.g. flat glass, beer, photographic film) where such market structures exist.[43]

The JFTC's lack of success with its deconcentration proposal serves as one example of how Japanese ideas about competition policy constrained reform before SII. More critical with respect to the American demands during the talks, however, were Japanese attitudes toward *cartels*. Despite the concern with price cartels on the part of the JFTC, Japanese have tended not to see cartels in and of themselves as a problem. As noted above, MITI for many years sought to exempt and emasculate the AML's anti-cartel provisions. For MITI, cartels were a tool of industrial policy crucial to helping it nurture vital industries. The problem was not too little competition, but *excessive competition*.[44] For most of the postwar period, even the JFTC went along with this view, tolerating cartels (even those without official exemptions) as long as they did not seek to raise prices. The idea was that cartels, supervised by MITI and the JFTC, would help firms survive the low points in the business cycle—allowing them to coordinate cutbacks in productions and invest in new products—but would not be allowed to raise prices during upswings.

By the 1970s, this consensus was starting to come apart, with the JFTC increasingly articulating the view that cartels, despite MITI's efforts, were causing more problems than they were worth. MITI, however, retained faith in its ability to manage cartels and, as noted above, even set up new ones. When the JFTC proposed new anti-cartel enforcement powers for itself in the 1970s, therefore, MITI took the lead in fighting the reform. The ministry, representing equally concerned voices in the business community, was especially worried that the JFTC's proposed surcharge system would allow it (a mere administrative organ) to impose fines. While it finally agreed to the surcharge system, MITI (along with the MOF and the Ministry of Justice) insisted that the fine level be set very low. According to retired JFTC officials, the level of the fine—though ostensibly set at the level necessary to recoup a cartel's ill-gotten gains— was lowered substantially in deference to bureaucratic opposition.[45]

By the time SII started, MITI's defensiveness on cartels had mellowed to some degree. According to the JFTC's Iyori, "the most recent change in MITI's industrial policy has been to place central emphasis on the operation of market forces, at least in principle."[46] A MITI official in the ministry's industrial policy bureau confirmed this shift. His agency, he said, was interested even before SII in reducing the number of AML exemptions—"in principle."[47] As the repeated use of the phrase "in principle" suggests, however, the conversion of MITI on this issue could not be described as wholehearted. MITI's attitudes had certainly not changed to the point that it would be an *ally* of U.S. demands for stronger anti-cartel enforcement.

If attitudes on the part of MITI bureaucrats and big business were not supportive of competition policy reform, the attitudes of LDP Diet members were even more hostile. For reasons similar to those behind LDP opposition to Large Store Law liberalization and agricultural land tax reform, Dietmen representing key LDP constituencies (especially construction) strongly opposed JFTC efforts to strengthen the AML in the 1970s and to make use of its new powers in the 1980s. The sensitivity of LDP Diet members to construction interests, once again, can be traced partly to the structure of Japanese political institutions. In medium-sized electoral districts where LDP candidates needed dependable personal votes and funds to operate their expensive *kōenkai*, construction interests were a critical constituency. They provided district offices for LDP candidates, loaned them staff during campaigns, and funneled huge sums of money to the LDP (half the total, according to one estimate)—most of it to faction bosses and other top LDP politicians where it bought the most influence.[48]

The reason construction interests and their LDP allies would be threatened by JFTC efforts to strengthen antitrust enforcement should be obvious given the discussion of dangō above. These bid-rigging arrangement were critical to maintaining the profitability of the construction sector. They in turn provided a brokering and coordinating role for LDP politicians, for which individual Dietmen were rewarded with campaign funds.[49] Were the JFTC ever to attempt to end bid-rigging by applying the AML in this sector, the whole system would come apart.

Thus, when the JFTC pushed for reform in the mid-1970s, LDP Diet members repeatedly tried to sabotage the legislation. First, when the relatively liberal and "clean" Prime Minister Miki—who took power after Prime Minister Tanaka was implicated in a scandal—embraced the legislation, his LDP opponents arranged for the legislation to be killed in the Upper House after first allowing it to pass in the Lower House. Although the popularity of the JFTC-proposed revisions eventually led Miki's successor, Fukuda, to try again with the legislation, the version he pushed through in 1977 had been seriously weakened. In particular, back bench opposition to the new surcharge system helped force JFTC to set fines at a very low level.[50] Even after the 1977 amendments were passed, however, relations between the JFTC and the LDP remained strained. Worried about a backlash on the part of the party, JFTC official Iyori reports that his agency decided "we shouldn't push too far."[51] Still, over the next several years, the JFTC pursued a growing number of cases and imposed a rapidly growing volume of fines—finally going so far as to take on a small construction dangō in Shizuoka Prefecture in 1982.[52] This move, it turned out, was too much for many LDP Diet members. The way in which the LDP uproar forced the JFTC to issue weaker guidelines for the construction industry was described above. Even more threatening to the JFTC, though, were the calls from some LDP members for legislation aimed at once again weakening the AML. "After that," retired JFTC official Kikuchi Gen'ichi reports, "the agency became an incredibly timid organization which relied almost entirely on administrative guidance."[53] Indeed, as the statistics in table 8.1 show, the number of formal actions taken by the JFTC declined sharply after 1983. This atmosphere, according to the man who was JFTC head during the SII talks, was just beginning to dissipate by the late 1980s.[54]

The domestic politics of competition policy going into the SII talks, the above recounting shows, was not very favorable for the Americans. On some issues where the JFTC had never even tried to push for change, the U.S. had no allies. On others, powerful ministries like MITI and MOF as well as the LDP were opposed to (or at least unenthusiastic about) reform. Virtually the only ally the U.S. had—and even then on just some issues—was the JFTC, and it was not a heavyweight player.

The JFTC, organized under the Prime Minister's Office, is one of the few "independent commissions" in Japan. Its personnel system belies its status, however, for four out of the five commissioners that run the agency are sent to the JFTC from other ministries: the commission chair is almost always from the Ministry of Finance and other seats usually go to MITI, MOF, and Justice. One, at most, is drawn from within the ranks of the career JFTC staff. Some of the rest of the staff, furthermore, are also drawn from other ministries—all complicating any effort by the JFTC to establish its own direction.[55] The JFTC head, being a civil servant rather than a politician, does not have cabinet rank. Because the commission does not have cabinet status, it does not have the authority on its own to draft legislation (as all ministries do). Instead, it has to work out of the Prime Minister's Office in cooperation with other concerned parts of the bureaucracy such as the Industrial Organization Section of MITI. Similarly, because the LDP does not have a separate PARC division for the JFTC, all legislation (such as proposals to strengthen the AML) has to go through the party's Commerce Division before being considered at higher levels within the party. The only JFTC constituencies, it seems, were consumers and—starting in the 1980s—the Americans.

The American Demands

While the Americans had been involved in imposing the AML on the Japanese during the Occupation, the U.S. government largely lost interest in Japanese competition policy until the 1980s when, under the Reagan Administration, the U.S. began to take a closer look at how lax competition policy in Japan might be robbing the U.S. of export opportunities. The original impetus for this renewed interest was a complaint from U.S. producers of soda ash, a commodity used heavily in the manufacture of glass, detergents, and other industrial processes. Because this initial encounter with Japanese competition policy played an important role in shaping American demands on this issue during SII, it is worth taking a moment to examine how this complaint was "resolved."

In the early 1970s, as part of Japan's effort to remove formal trade barriers, the government officially opened up the nation's market for soda ash. This move made economic sense since Japan had no competitive advantage in this market, relying totally on the synthetic production of a commodity that could be supplied much more cheaply by North American firms with access to natural deposits. Ten years later, however, U.S. firms had made only small inroads into the market. It seems the Japanese firms had conspired to cap import levels by: (1) controlling an import terminal that served as the sole point of entry into the Japanese market; (2) signing up almost all of Japan's major trading companies in a scheme that gave them all a piece of the action but paid them a set fee regardless of the volume of imports they handled; and (3) pressuring potential customers of American firms not to import ash outside this neat arrangement.[56]

Appalled at the blatant violations of Japan's AML, U.S. firms complained to the U.S. government which in turn brought the matter to the attention of the JFTC. Still, while the JFTC acted quickly on the complaint, U.S. firms received only marginal help. The JFTC confirmed that violations of the AML had taken place and issued a formal recommendation calling on the Japanese firms concerned to cease a variety of exclusionary business practices, but it did not impose any fines or other penalties.[57] While American exports of soda ash did increase for a few years after the JFTC's 1983 decision, they soon leveled off at around 18 percent of the market.

After another round of American complaints, the JFTC conducted a second survey of industry conditions in 1987. This time, it only warned the Japanese firms, finding that while certain industry practices "could be problematic," there was not enough evidence to take formal action. Again, American exports increased, only to level off again. Meanwhile, the Japanese firms invested in more efficient methods for artificially producing soda ash and bought into American producers of natural ash. By 1992, according to the head of one American soda ash firm's Asian operations, the Japanese market looked much less attractive than it once had.[58]

Both the American soda ash firms and U.S. trade officials were clearly frustrated with this experience. They saw Japanese firms merely slapped on the wrists in 1983 (there was no fine) and felt the JFTC had failed to address some of the mechanisms through which Japanese firms colluded to cap their market share. They were also frustrated that the JFTC had not dealt with this cartel, which had existed since 1974, until the U.S. made a complaint. Compounding the concern on the part of trade officials were similar complaints from U.S. firms in additional sectors such as glass and paper. During the SII talks, therefore, the U.S. sought to force the JFTC to be more aggressive in pursuing these types of cases, to take formal actions instead of relying on warnings, to use its surcharge system, and to increase the levels of its penalties.

Two other episodes in U.S.-Japan relations played particular roles in shaping U.S. demands. The first was the Navy's encounter with a construction dangō. The U.S. government had been made aware of the dangō system during the course of bilateral talks aimed at opening the public sector construction market. U.S. officials never guessed, however, that the construction firms would be bold enough to rip off *American* taxpayers. This is exactly what they did, though, over a series of years at the Yokosuka Naval Yards. Again prodded by U.S. complaints, the JFTC overcame its aversion to acting against the construction industry and actually fined a group of 70 firms 290 million yen ($3.3 million) in December 1988. The episode merely confirmed for U.S. officials that dangō was a widespread practice, so when Carla Hills announced the sii talks in May 1989, this issue got specific mention.

The other experience shaping U.S. demands was the frustration officials felt over their struggle to help American auto parts firms gain access to the Japanese market. During the moss talks, U.S. officials had made this market a priority. When these officials told the Japanese that keiretsu ties between auto makers and their suppliers were an important problem, however, miti officials refused to offer any help, insisting the barriers were "in the private sector." Enter T. Boone Pickens, an unlikely hero, who then focused a spotlight on these keiretsu ties when he bought 26 percent of Koito, a supplier of headlights to Toyota. Although he had more shares than Toyota, Pickens was denied a seat on the board and access to company books. Having acquired almost all of the Koito shares not held by "stable shareholders," he was also prevented from reaching the threshold needed to take control of the company (51 percent). The cross-shareholding network had held its ground.[59] While Pickens, with his reputation for greenmailing, was hardly the ideal spokesperson for American-style capitalism, his experience led the U.S. to focus its keiretsu demands on opening up opportunities for mergers and acquisitions, increasing shareholder rights, and limiting cross-shareholding.

Over the course of 1989, as the sii talks got underway, U.S. officials from the ustr and the Justice Department (working together on antitrust issues) and the Treasury Department (taking the lead on keiretsu) compiled an extensive list of reform demands that together constituted a call for what one observer termed the "Americanization" of Japanese-style capitalism.[60] The U.S. called on Japan to increase both civil and criminal penalties under the aml, to increase staffing and funding of the jftc, to remove impediments to the effective functioning of the private damage remedy system, to pursue more formal and aggressive antitrust actions, to target the dangō, and to clarify which vertical restraints were illegal under the aml—especially in relation to distribution networks. In addition, the U.S. called for tougher limits on cross-shareholding, more liberal rules on mergers and acquisitions as well as foreign direct investment, and a variety of improvements in stockholder rights. (See table 8.2)

TABLE 8.2
The Americans' Competition Policy Demands

1. Increase FTC staffing and funding.

2. Announce that FTC policy will be to pursue formal remedies when violations of AML are found.

3. Announce intention to prosecute AML violators under criminal law and improve coordination between FTC and the Ministry of Justice in order to facilitate such prosecution of AML violators.

4. Strengthen AML guidelines for the construction industry and put in place administrative procedures designed to increase cooperation between FTC and other ministries aimed at stopping unfair bidding procedures. Revise law so that criminal penalty for such violations is increased.

5. Revise the AML in order to substantially increase administrative penalties (surcharge rates).

6.Revise the AML so that surcharges can be imposed in cases of group boycotts [rather than just in cases of price cartels].

7. Revise the AML in order to increase levels of criminal fines for firms and individuals.

8. Facilitate private damage suits through FTC encouragement, hand-over of FTC-collected evidence, easing the burden of proof on plaintiffs in several specified ways, allowing class action suits, and lowering court fees.

9. Release the names of all firms and individuals subject to FTC action (including warnings).

10. Improve the transparency of Japanese government administrative guidance and end its use for protectionist purposes.

11. Promote the adoption of guidelines for non-discriminatory procurement by Japanese firms and trade associations and set up a monitoring system to ascertain the degree to which competitive foreign goods and services are being procured. Publicize the findings of this research.

12. Reduce patent delays and other patent reforms.

13. Announce official AML guidelines for distribution specifying exactly which kinds of practices constitute violations of the law. These guidelines should prohibit firms with market power from preventing its dealers from handling competing products; and otherwise imposing anti-competitive conditions on distributors. The full force of AML penalties should be employed to enforce these guidelines.

14. End resale price maintenance exemption for cosmetics.

15. Announce government policy statement recognizing the negative effects of *keiretsu* on the competitiveness of Japanese markets as well as intention to promote a weakening of *keiretsu* ties and an increase in foreign direct investment.

16. Bring disclosure rules (obligating firms to disclose related-party transactions) into line

with U.S. standards—in particular lowering disclosure threshold from 10 percent to 5 percent.

17. Limit cross-shareholding in the following ways: by lowering limit on bank holdings of any given firm with which is does business from 5 percent to 2 percent; by putting explicit limits (or even a ban) on holdings by trading companies; by tightening limits on holdings by large firms and by parent companies in affiliates.

18. Study by FTC of the effects on competition of keiretsu practices such as monthly meetings of member firm heads and cross-shareholding and use of penalties to deal with any of these practices found to have anti-competitive effects.

19. Eliminate regulations which, by limiting competition, allow *keiretsu* to continue inefficient practices.

20. Eliminate requirement that foreign firms notify MOF 30 days in advance of foreign direct investments. Relax other rules which require prior notification of take-over bids (not just for foreign firms).

21. Eliminate bureaucracy's wide latitude to restrict on national security grounds any case of foreign direct investment.

22. Revision of Company Law to authorize derivative law suits by stockholders (against firm management); reduce percentage of a firm's shares one must hold before one can demand to see its books from 10 percent to 1 percent; etc.

Source: Americans' List of 200 Demands

Synergistic Strategies and the Deal on Competition Policy Issues

As with the negotiations over the other three SII issues, those over the U.S. competition policy demands were heated, with tempers reaching a boiling point by the spring of 1990. Whenever the Americans raised the issue of cross-shareholding, MOF delegate Utsumi Makoto turned "various shades of the rainbow," refusing even to discuss the issue.[61] As late as January of 1990, JFTC chief Umezawa—representing the agency that was supposed to be the Americans' ally on these issues—was giving interviews in which he insisted that there was no need to revise the AML. "As far as we're concerned," he stated, "the current level of fines offers an adequate deterrent effect."[62]

Similar hard bargaining over the other issue areas, however, had not prevented the Japanese from moving significantly toward the American demands over the final month of the talks. The difference was that this time they refused to blink. Where the Americans had demanded concrete changes in rules limiting cross-shareholding among keiretsu firms, the government of Japan agreed only to study whether this practice was limiting competition. Its agreements to "raise" penalty levels and pursue "more" formal actions were almost as vague—leaving substantial wriggle room for an JFTC nervous about opposition from the agency's critics within the LDP and other ministries. On some demands, such as the U.S. call for more JFTC staff and funding, the Japanese were willing to go along with the full extent of the U.S. proposals. The net effect of all of their promises, however, was not nearly enough to significantly ameliorate the exclusionary effects of Japan's lax competition policy.

How can we explain this set of results? As in the previous chapters, the argument developed here is that Japan yielded only when the conditions supporting the effective use of specific pressure tactics were operative. On many of the U.S. competition policy demands, the conditions were simply not supportive. To the extent gaiatsu did force some change, it was only in areas closest to the JFTC's inflation-fighting mission and most removed from the core concerns of powerful domestic actors such as LDP politicians, construction interests, big business, MITI, MOF, and the Ministry of Justice. As with the LSL and other policies surveyed in earlier chapters, gaiatsu served as a diffuse force that could be molded to suit the interests of powerful Japanese actors. Because fewer of these domestic actors sympathized with the core concerns of the Americans, however, U.S. pressure in this issue area produced much more meager results than in cases like the LSL.

PARTICIPATION EXPANSION AT THE ELITE LEVEL

Whereas there was at least some policy debate within Japan—even before SII—about the American demands surveyed in the last three chapters, there was virtually *no* prior discussion of the American demands in this issue area. No one, other than a few academics, was talking about once again pursuing criminal charges under the AML; no one was talking about raising surcharge levels; and all of the talk about keiretsu, among economists, government officials, and big business leaders, was about the *virtues* of this system of business organization. The climate, clearly, was hardly ideal for the strategy of expanding participation at the elite level, the tactic which overall proved to be the most effective during the SII talks in extracting policy concessions from the Japanese.

On some of the American demands, such as the demand for tighter limits on cross-shareholding, there was literally *no* elite support. The mainstream view among the Japanese elite, echoed in countless scholarly and popular publications, is that cross-shareholding serves a useful purpose by buffering Japanese firms from the short-term profit-maximizing demands of exit-threatening shareholders under American-style capitalism. This system is seen as something that distinguishes Japanese-style capitalism from the American variety and makes it *superior*.[63] Neither was there any support for the American demand that the JFTC use the AML to force vertical keiretsu like Toyota to open up their procurement process. Even career JFTC official Iyori, who on the whole is critical of his agency's failure to pursue a more aggressive antitrust policy, waxes eloquent about the virtues of his nation's manufacturing keiretsu. As long as the core firms in these groups are competing against each other, he argues, such practices are not problematic from the point of view of antitrust law. This system, he pointed out, is one American firms are trying to copy![64]

Not surprisingly, given this dearth of support among elites, the Japanese gave no ground on this set of demands. They insisted, in fact, that the U.S. agree to add a line to the start of the keiretsu section of the SII report recognizing "certain aspects of economic rationality of keiretsu relationships." On cross-shareholding, they promised only that the JFTC would "strengthen its monitoring of transactions among keiretsu firms." The agency would impose new limits on cross-shareholding *only if* it found evidence that cross-shareholding served as "a substantial restraint on competition."[65] Everyone knew at the time that this promised JFTC study would be no more critical of cross-shareholding than were previous agency surveys. As it happened, the JFTC found that levels of cross-shareholding had actually declined from rates it had declared innocuous in the 1980s. In the years since, the JFTC has actually *relaxed* limits on cross-shareholding.

On keiretsu procurement, the Japanese promised little more. The JFTC would draft guidelines clarifying what manner of intra-group dealings would be considered illegal under the AML and the agency would conduct a "close analysis of various aspects of keiretsu groups" every two years. As Kozo Yamamura has noted, statements like these were so vague as to be virtually meaningless. He found them to be among the "most disappointing" in the entire SII report.[66]

Other American demands, such as the call for a more effective private damage remedy under the AML and a crackdown on closed distribution networks, provoked less hostility but nevertheless failed to find sympathizers among even an expanded elite. These proposals had not been part of the JFTC's reform initiative in the 1970s, an absence demonstrating that the agency did not see them as a priority.

Japanese government officials, even those in the JFTC, almost without exception find American-style civil antitrust suits "unsuitable" for Japan, so their lack of support for this SII demand was no surprise.[67] The Ministry of Justice, in particular, was unwilling to change laws under its jurisdiction (such as those disallowing class action suits) merely to appease the U.S. The final SII deal on this issue reflected the lack of elite support. The JFTC promised to take a more active role in assisting private parties seeking to recover damages under the AML by turning over evidence collected in its investigations, but there was no mention of the American demand for specific reforms designed to ease the burden of proof confronting plaintiffs in these cases and no concession on the U.S. call for reforms designed to allow class action suits or treble damages in antitrust cases.[68]

The American demands for stricter controls on exclusionary distribution networks likewise sparked little enthusiasm. The JFTC had surveyed these practices in 1980 and had found some reason for concern.[69] The agency was fundamentally conflicted, though, about how far it could go in applying the AML to such cases. Iyori, for example, points to the U.S. Supreme Court decision which found GTE-Sylvania's system of exclusive dealers to be legal under American antitrust law to defend his own agency's timidity in using formal actions against such practices.[70] If the JFTC was unsure, the rest of the Japanese establishment—especially the numerous powerful firms who had invested heavily in their networks of wholesalers and retailers—were not: they wanted to make certain any change in policy would be minimal. The final SII compromise, under which the JFTC agreed to draw up a set of "guidelines" for distribution practices, was worded vaguely enough (including a list of *possible* restrictions) to reassure manufacturers that change would not go too far.[71]

That the JFTC was not enthusiastic about *some* of the American demands did not mean, however, that it was indifferent to the entire U.S. agenda. In fact, the agency saw quite quickly that the SII talks represented a rare opportunity for it to push through a few long-stymied reforms. Remember that during the 1970s, the agency had been forced to set surcharge levels extremely low in order to appease opponents. Officials were quietly excited that the SII talks might give them an opportunity to raise these levels. They were also eager to use SII to move beyond the agency's cautious and informal approach to antitrust enforcement, a tendency that dated back in particular to the JFTC's confrontation with the LDP over construction dangō in 1983. Obviously, they also didn't mind at all the American call for a boost in the agency's staff and budget.[72]

To the extent the Americans won any concessions in the area of competition policy, it was in these areas where it enjoyed real support within the JFTC. Just as MITI's willingness to carry the ball for the Americans on the Large Store Law had led to reforms on that issue, the JFTC's willingness to champion U.S. calls for tougher penalties and more formal actions within government policy circles made possible the limited changes that did result due to SII. Where these reforms had been blocked entirely as long as the debate was dominated by the narrow circle of interests most concerned about antitrust issues (construction interests and LDP sympathizers; MITI; the MOJ), the "internationalization" of these issues allowed the JFTC to appeal to senior LDP leaders and other elites concerned about the U.S.-Japan relationship—bringing about some change where there had previously been none.

Even on those issues where the U.S. enjoyed JFTC support, however, the strategy of participation expansion brought about only limited change—for two reasons. First, because the JFTC (relative to MITI on the LSL, for example) was a feeble ally. The institutional weakness of the JFTC was discussed above. On issues like penalty levels, the agency was operating, moreover, largely without a constituency. Where MITI had large retail chains and, to some extent, Keidanren, on its side in the LSL debate, the JFTC had no powerful interest group backing it up.

Lacking such a base, the JFTC was forced to proceed with extreme caution in its effort to use SII to increase penalty levels under the AML. Even as the U.S. and Japan were meeting for their first formal SII negotiating session, the JFTC set up a study group to look into how the agency ought to respond to the pressure they expected to face.[73] Already, officials like commission member Iyori were pushing, in internal discussions, for the agency to use the opportunity to increase surcharge levels. Some even favored using SII to restart criminal prosecutions. Still, the agency could not come out publicly in favor of such American demands. To do so would have been to expose the agency to the charge that it was nothing more than an American tool—a charge to which it had to be extremely sensitive due to its lack of a domestic base.[74] Publicly, therefore, JFTC chief Umezawa maintained the position that penalty levels were already high enough.

Forced to pretend that it was making grudging concessions to the U.S., the JFTC was in a poor position to respond when—in the final months of negotiations—LDP Diet members began to express misgivings about the JFTC's apparent willingness to revise the AML in order to increase penalty levels. Although the Japanese had agreed in the April interim report to put specific figures for the increase in penalty levels into the June ("final") report, the JFTC was unable to forge a consensus in time to meet this deadline. The final report merely promised, therefore, to "raise" surcharges, and "consider increasing" criminal fines. There was no promise to increase the range of actions subject to surcharges as demanded by the U.S., but the Japanese did agree to begin once again employing criminal sanctions in "vicious and serious cases."[75] As we will see in the discussion of the implementation of competition policy reforms below, the JFTC's institutional weakness continued to hamper its ability to deliver meaningful change during that stage of the process.

The other reason the Americans' strategy of participation expansion yielded only limited results even when the JFTC seemed to be on its side was because the agency's interests diverged in subtle but important ways from those of the U.S. In chapter 5, we noted how the divergence in interests between MITI and the U.S. led LSL reforms to be structured in ways that were not exactly in line with American interests. Similarly, the JFTC's primary focus on inflation-fighting led it to bias its response to U.S. pressure during the talks (and later during implementation) in ways that limited the impact of reforms on the kinds of anticompetitive practices of greatest concern to the U.S.

One reason why the JFTC was most sympathetic to the American call for higher penalty levels was because such changes would allow it to employ more muscle to deter *price cartels*—the kinds of anticompetitive practices officials were most concerned about and the type of antitrust action that enjoyed the broadest support among other Japanese elites. The JFTC's emphasis on fighting price cartels dated back, as noted above, to its anti-inflation campaigns in the 1960s and 1970s, but it was reinforced over the years through the agency's interaction with other ministry officials. MITI officials, for example, had come to distinguish between "good" cartels (where firms "cooperate" to avoid problems of excessive competition, especially during times of recession) and "bad" ones which engage in price-gouging. They don't mind when the agency goes after the bad ones.[76] Similarly, prosecutors with the Ministry of Justice are willing to go after "bad" dangō (where firms use political influence to profiteer off the government) but are hesitant to punish "good" dangō which maintain "order" in the construction market in accordance with MOC guidance.[77] JFTC officials maintain publicly that *all* cartels are illegal under the AML and insist that they pursue all such cases with equal vigor, but the political reality is such that the JFTC has tended to engage in selective enforcement—a policy that SII, with its emphasis on higher penalty levels, did little to change.[78]

Why is this a problem? Because price cartels were not the anticompetitive practice that was causing U.S. firms the most trouble. As John Haley has argued, price cartels may in fact serve to *increase* opportunities for foreign penetration by maintaining high domestic prices that provide new market entrants with the prospect of enticing profits.[79] The anticompetitive practices that create the biggest problem for American firms, as seen in the discussion of the soda ash and construction cases above, were (and are) group boycotts, use of refusals to deal to force distributors not to deal with foreigners, and government bidding procedures and other regulations limiting market entry. The Americans could hope that busting up price cartels might lead firms in some sectors to procure foreign products in an effort to get an edge in the enhanced price competition, but without action aimed at eliminating the anticompetitive practices with more of a direct bearing on foreign market entry, it was unlikely that price competition alone would bring about the desired result.

The way in which one side-issue in the SII negotiations was resolved illustrates how the JFTC's focus on inflation-fighting took it in a direction which was really of no direct interest to the U.S. One of the American demands (14 on the list in table 8.2) called on the JFTC to eliminate exemptions allowing Japanese cosmetics firms to engage in resale price maintenance, the practice of requiring retailers to sell brand-name products at a certain price. Such practices, by firms like Shiseidō, are one reason why Japanese pay prices for items like lipstick that are several times those in the U.S. By bringing about retail price competition, the elimination of the exemption for cosmetics promised to lower prices for Japanese consumers. It is unclear what benefit American firms might derive from this change, however. In fact, U.S. firms like Amway, which had been expanding market share rapidly in Japan by offering much lower prices and bypassing traditional retail outlets, could be expected to *suffer* as a result of the drop in Japanese cosmetic prices.

Nevertheless, this demand made it onto the American list, according to JFTC officials, because they urged U.S. officials to put it there. The JFTC had attempted to eliminate RPM exemptions in the 1970s (when the U.S. and European government were doing so) but had failed. They hoped to use sɪɪ to achieve this objective.[80] Having planted the demand, the jftc of course made sure the final sɪɪ report contained a promise to meet it. As we will see, the broader pattern of jftc enforcement of the aml since the sɪɪ has followed a similar pattern: gaiatsu was used by the jftc to toughen up enforcement in the areas *it* was most concerned about, with a continuing neglect of areas of greater interest to the U.S.

Participation Expansion at the General Public Level

If the Japanese elite were not sympathetic enough, why wasn't the U.S. able to take advantage of potential support from Japanese consumers as it had, again, in the case of the Large Store Law? As in that other case, the Japanese public should have been sympathetic to the American demands in the area of competition policy—at least to those which urged the Japanese government to beef up antitrust enforcement. Such a policy, the U.S. argued, would lead to lower consumer prices. The U.S. could have pointed out too that an end to collusive construction bidding held the potential to lower the cost of public works projects—meaning Japanese could get either a tax break or more projects for their tax money.

As ustr delegate Linn Williams acknowledges, however, this strategy didn't work as well on antitrust issues. It was too difficult to get consumers to see the link between the aml and their interests.[81] While consumers could relate directly to the prospect of large discount stores offering lower prices, they had more trouble understanding how collusion among soda ash firms or steelmakers, several steps removed from the retail level, affected the prices they paid. If it was difficult to appeal to consumers on antitrust, it was even more so on the keiretsu issue where issues concerned topics like cross-shareholding and shareholder rights which the general public had difficulty comprehending, much less getting excited about. To top it off, Williams feels that his team did a poor job of articulating the U.S. position on keiretsu: "We just didn't present it well," he says.[82]

Especially on antitrust this strategy held some potential. During the 1970s, public support had been critical to the jftc's success in pushing through the first strengthening amendments ever added to the aml. The ldp had killed the legislation once in 1976, only to reverse itself and push the amendments through once it discovered how popular the issue was with the general public.[83] The U.S. might have been able to generate similar enthusiasm for a stricter competition policy if its campaign had been more focused on this issue. With the barrage of issues covered during sɪɪ, however, it seems the American message on this issue got lost—or at least took too much time to germinate. Public awareness has increased, probably even more so in the years since the SII talks, but this increase has not been sufficient to bring significant pressure to bear on an elite generally happy enough with existing Japanese competition policy.

OTHER GAIATSU STRATEGIES

That the above strategies were not extremely effective does not preclude others—gaiatsu as threats and linkage, for example—from having more of an impact. As I argued in chapter 4, gaiatsu as threats promised to have some impact on most cases involving Japan because U.S. pressure had come to be seen as a "necessary evil" that had to be accommodated to some degree. Similarly, gaiatsu as target nation linkage promised to provide the U.S. with some support on most issues as ministerial rivals worked to make sure each compromised a "fair share" in multijurisdictional trade negotiations like the SII talks. These strategies can indeed be credited with getting the Japanese to agree to at least some commitment on almost every one of their demands—in some cases, even when there was absolutely no domestic constituency.

The Japanese agreed, for example, to remove the requirement that foreign firms notify the MOF 30 days in advance of foreign direct investments and to narrow national security restrictions on FDI (demands 20 and 21 on the list in table 8.2) even though these changes affected only foreign firms. Similarly, it agreed to relax takeover-bid rules; enhance disclosure requirements; and "reexamine the Company Law," all steps with relatively little support within Japan.[84]

What limited the effectiveness of these gaiatsu strategies, though, was their inability to force the Japanese to compromise on core issues. Threats could not force compromise on cross-shareholding, and without this change, changes in rules governing direct foreign investment and takeover-bid rules were not going to have much impact. Most firms would still be unavailable because loyal shareholders would continue to hold the majority of their shares. As one member of the American SII delegation put it, these were "marginal issues."[85] Japan was willing to compromise on these and give the Americans just enough to avoid a breakdown in U.S.-Japan relations. Since both U.S. and Japanese negotiators had domestic political interests in wrapping up the talks and declaring them a success, Japan could pick and choose—giving in first on those demands where there was some domestic support for change and second where the reform promised to have little impact. It could respond to gaiatsu as threats and as target-nation issue linkage without giving in on core issues like cross-shareholding.

Implementation

Looking back at what has happened since the 1990 SII deal, it is clear that there has been some change in Japanese competition policy. In June 1990, in perhaps the most important policy shift, the JFTC announced that it was going to start pursuing *criminal* sanctions under the AML— reversing a de facto policy that had forgone criminal sanctions in favor of the administrative surcharge system since the mid-1970s. Since that time, the agency (in a new cooperative relationship with the prosecutors' office) has pressed criminal charges against two cartels. The government has also revised the AML, as promised, to raise surcharge and criminal fine rates; has increased the number of cases in which it has pursued formal action; has imposed a record sum of fines; and has followed through with most of its promises to change laws governing foreign investment, takeover bids, and stockholder rights.

A close look at the pattern of implementation in these cases, however, reveals that the impact of gaiatsu in terms of actual policy change has been limited in much the same manner as was the negotiated SII settlement in this issue area. Legal changes have been compromised to protect vested interests, and enforcement has been beefed up only in selective areas: those of greatest concern to the JFTC. Areas of particular concern to the U.S., such as the construction dangō, vertical restraints, and group boycotts, have not seen significant enforcement activity.

THE USE OF CRIMINAL SANCTIONS

According to a variety of analysts, this policy shift held the greatest potential to bring about change in the behavior of Japanese firms. While businesses intent on colluding could work around higher surcharge rates by making sure a cartel generated enough extra profits to pay the fines, they would have more trouble getting managers to risk the personal shame of a criminal trial.[86] Indeed, it seems that the threat of criminal sanctions was a major force behind Keidanren's push to have Japanese firms draw up internal guidelines clarifying for their staff what they could and could not do under the AML when making procurement and pricing decisions.

The impact of this initial pronouncement has been weakened, however, by the JFTC's failure to pursue criminal charges against large and politically influential industries: especially the notoriously collusive construction industry. Relative to the construction sector, the two sectors targeted for criminal action by the JFTC since its 1990 policy shift have involved "small fish." The first charges, brought in November 1991 against eight firms operating a cartel in the commercial food-packaging wrap business, involved an industry with annual sales of only 40 billion yen— compared to the 80 *trillion* yen at stake in the construction industry.[87] The second, brought in February 1993, involved four printing companies charged with rigging bids on a relatively small contract for adhesive seals used by the Social Insurance Agency.

Executives of the the wrap firms especially—the first subjects of criminal prosecution under the AML in 17 years—complained that they were being thrown to the wolves to appease the Americans. Why, they asked, was the JFTC picking on such a small and weak industry?[88] Their sense of frustration was even greater, one can be sure, when in the same month in which they were convicted (May 1992) the JFTC decided to forgo the use of criminal sanctions in its case against 66 construction firms charged with operating a dangō in Saitama Prefecture, a rapidly growing suburban district outside of Tokyo. That the JFTC and Prosecutors' Office were building a case against the Saitama dangō was widely reported during the spring of 1992, and those with an interest in antitrust policy (including the SII follow-up team) had awaited this decision with eager anticipation.

In announcing that the JFTC would pursue formal administrative action rather than criminal sanctions, Commission Chief Umezawa explained that his agency had failed to find enough evidence to prosecute. The case, involving so many firms and contracts, was just too complicated to allow the agency to identify specific individuals for prosecution.[89] The press quite freely speculated, however, that this decision reflected the political influence of the construction sector. The JFTC needed the LDP's support to get a bill raising criminal fines under the AML through the Diet (see below), and the theory was that the JFTC had been forced to back off on the Saitama dangō as a price for that support.[90] Though Umezawa denied that the LDP influenced the JFTC's decision at the time, it has subsequently become known that one of the LDP's leading construction Dietmen, Nakamura Kishirō, then the Minister of Construction, personally visited Umezawa on a number of occasions in the spring of 1992.

Nakamura had accepted large political donations from construction firms and in 1994 was arrested under bribery statutes for his role in attempting to force the JFTC to back down in this case.[91]

While it therefore seems likely that the LDP's connections to the construction industry had something to do with the JFTC's hesitance to employ criminal sanctions in this case, JFTC officials I interviewed claim that the decision not to prosecute also reflected the attitudes of prosecutors in the Ministry of Justice. Prosecutors, according to my informants, insisted that they needed to determine whether or not the Saitama dangō was "bad" before going through with a criminal prosecution. While the law (and the JFTC) care only about whether or not collusion took place, the prosecutors wanted to know whether this collusion had resulted in excess profits for certain firms—something the JFTC had trouble proving. Prosecutors displayed similar attitudes, these officials reported, in deciding not to use the AML against construction firms during what became known as the *Zenekon* (or General Contractor) Scandal of 1993. While the acquiescence of the entire dangō was necessary for certain firms to secure the contracts they sought by bribing local officials, the prosecutors chose to go only after the top managers of firms that *won* contracts. In both cases, the JFTC official pointed out, the prosecutors betrayed a lack of support for the basic premise of antitrust policy: that horizontal collusion in and of itself is illegal.[92] Prosecutors, in other words, continued to act according to the philosophy that there are "good" cartels (that serve state interests in things like maintaining a healthy construction industry) as well as "bad" ones. As long as such attitudes persist, one can be sure that criminal sanctions will be used only sparingly and mostly in cases where the main problem is raising prices, not keeping out imports.

INCREASES IN AML PENALTIES

Both the administrative surcharge rate and the maximum level of criminal fines have been raised since the SII deal in 1990. The effect of these changes, however, has again been compromised by political and bureaucratic opposition which limited the rate of the increase, especially in the case of the criminal fine.

The increase in surcharges actually went fairly smoothly. The JFTC sought a hike from 0.5–2 percent of annual sales under the old statute to a new maximum of 6 percent, and this is what was ultimately adopted in April 1991. The U.S. had pushed for a rate of 10 percent, arguing that only a rate of this level would prevent cartels from simply adjusting their prices to reflect the possibility of fines. The JFTC, however, insisted that it could not raise rates higher than 6 percent since Japanese law prohibited an administrative unit from imposing *punitive* remedies. Six percent would allow the JFTC to take colluding firms' ill-gotten gains, but any more than that would constitute a punishment. Given that the government had rationalized the original rates with the argument that *2 percent* was the maximum surcharge the JFTC could impose without violating the prohibition against punitive administrative remedies, it was odd to see the government use the same argument now to defend 6 percent. In fact, no one knows how much "excess profits" cartels earn, and quite a range of numbers could have been defended.[93] The best explanation for how the JFTC arrived a 6 percent is political: the rate was high enough to satisfy the Americans without offending the LDP.

That the JFTC needed to be careful not to push the LDP too far in raising penalty levels became clear when the agency began to discuss how much to raise *criminal* fines. The JFTC, it seems, wanted to raise the fine rate for corporations from its absurdly low level of 5 million yen ($40,000 at 125 yen/dollar) to 300 million yen ($2.4 million)—an increase of 60 times. But when the JFTC advisory panel studying the question attempted to publish its report calling for an increase to "several hundred million yen" in December 1991, it encountered such stiff resistance from LDP politicians that it was forced to delay the issuance of its report until March. When legislation was finally prepared, it called for an increase to just 100 million yen ($800,000).[94] Though the law was ultimately passed in December 1992, the episode once again reveals how the implementation of competition policy reforms after the SII deal continued to be constrained by domestic politics.

Were penalty levels raised high enough? The administrative surcharge level of 6 percent remains significantly lower than the level in Europe where a punitive sanction of 10 percent is imposed. The maximum criminal fine of $800,000 is also low compared to other nations like the U.S. and Canada where fines can be as high as $10 million. While Japanese officials respond to such criticism by pointing out that Japan (unlike Europe, the U.S., or Canada) employs *both* the surcharge and criminal fine systems, the fact is that Japanese officials employ just one of the two sanctions in any one case. That the new surcharge rate of 6 percent may very well have been set too low is suggested by the fact that four of the firms that were subjected to the new rate in 1992 apparently were not deterred by the experience. In 1993, the JFTC accused the same firms of operating another cartel—but this time employed criminal sanctions.[95]

The debate about whether penalty levels are high enough, though, may ultimately be "academic" since the real impact of any change in Japanese competition policy would rest on whether or not the JFTC actually *enforced* the AML (with the new penalty levels) more vigorously and consistently. It is to this question that we turn next.

More Formal Antitrust Actions

In the 1990 deal, the Japanese government promised to take formal antitrust action more often, and indeed it has. As table 8.3 shows, the number of "formal recommendations" has increased markedly since 1989, rising from 7 in that year to 34 in 1992. Because formal recommendations come with an automatic surcharge in cases that involve price cartels, there has naturally been a corresponding increase in the number of cases where firms were fined: from 6 in 1989 to 17 in 1992. Some of these cases, furthermore, have involved large numbers of firms and massive fines, the largest being a 1990 case involving a group of firms charged with operating regional cement cartels. In total, these firms were fined 12 billion yen ($96 million), an amount that by itself exceeded the sum total of *all* of the fines the JFTC had levied since 1978.[96]

TABLE 8.3

Type of Fair Trade Commission Action in Anti-Monopoly Law Cases, 1985–93 (number of cases, not firms)

Year	criminal action	formal recommendation	(surcharge)*	warning	caution
1985	0	10	4	80	62
1986	0	8	4	88	37
1987	0	4	6	84	28
1988	0	6	3	65	17
1989	0	7	6	115	28
1990	0	22	11	60	85
1991	1	30	10	24	88
1992	1	34	17	21	73
1993	0	31	21	25	79

* cases resulting in surcharges are a subtotal of those resulting in formal recommendations.

Source: Issues of FTC, *Kosei Torihiki Iinkai Nenji Hokoku-Dokusen Kinshi Hakusho* (Fair Trade Commission Annual Report—The Anti-Monopoly White Paper).

Does this increase in the number of cases being pursued by the JFTC add up to the more vigorous enforcement the U.S. had sought? Undeniably there has been marginal improvement; but a close look at the JFTC's record since 1990 shows that important gaps remain in the agency's antitrust enforcement. First, another look at table 8.3 shows the agency's continuing preference for informality. In the 1990 SII deal, the JFTC agreed to increase transparency by publishing the names of firms that were subject to "warnings." The immediate result of this shift, however, has been a marked reduction in the number of cases subject to "warnings" (from 115 in 1989 to 24 in 1991) accompanied by a sharp increase in the number of "cautions" (from 28 to 88 over the same period). The JFTC does not publish the names of firms subject to "cautions."

Second, increased JFTC enforcement activity, while aimed at forcing firms to stop colluding to set prices and rig bids, has by and large failed to address the anticompetitive practices that exclude newcomers from the market. An example is the cement cartel case cited above. While the JFTC punished the firms severely for colluding to raise prices, it did nothing to force these firms to stop harassing construction firms and distributors that handle non-cartel (e.g. Korean) cement, practices that have been widely reported in the press. As Mark Tilton notes in his in-depth study of this industry, it is through these practices (including a trade association boycott of firms buying imported cement, attempts to leverage the cartel's control of distribution facilities, and threats of physical violence) that the cement cartel has been able to maintain prices 68 percent above import prices.[97] The fact that this gap between import and domestic prices has continued long after the JFTC took action against the price cartel suggests that the JFTC is still getting at only part of the problem. It may have reduced the ability of the established firms to collude to raise prices (they've fallen 2 percent), but it hasn't affected their ability to keep out new competition.

This failure is critical from the point of view of the U.S. because it is the *latter* competition policy problem that is the real concern for American firms. U.S. firms don't mind if Japanese prices are high. In fact, as noted above, high prices actually give them an added incentive to invest to get into the market. That the JFTC is attacking price cartels is well and good from the point of view of helping Japanese consumers, but it won't by itself help U.S. firms get into the Japanese market. What U.S. firms need is for the JFTC to go after practices such as the cement trade association's group boycott, and the JFTC has not taken this step.

The U.S. government, in the years since sii, has pressured the jftc to investigate and act against similar problems in flat glass, paper, and autos. Distributors of each of these products have reportedly been threatened by their major suppliers with a boycott if they handle imported goods.[98] The jftc investigated each of the industries, but it chose not to take formal action in any of these cases. This record of what *hasn't* happened in Japanese antitrust enforcement suggests that in the areas most important to U.S. interests, little has changed since the days of the soda ash cases.[99]

Changes in Policy Toward Vertical Restraints

While the jftc could have addressed problems such as those discussed above by using its prohibitions against *horizontal* restraints (group boycotts are a horizontal restraint), it also could have dealt with them by toughening its restrictions on *vertical* restraints. One reason the cement cartel (and firms in flat glass, paper, etc.) are able to enforce group boycotts is because each firm has tight control over distribution facilities and networks. It was for this reason that the U.S. pressured the jftc during sii to toughen up its policies in this area. As noted above, however, the final deal in this area was merely a vague statement promising that the jftc would issue a new set of guidelines for distribution.

In July 1991, the jftc issued these guidelines, touching on manufacturer relations with both distributors and suppliers. The jftc's disposition of a number of cases since that time suggests, however, that little has changed. Pressed by the Americans, the jftc conducted surveys of trade practices in flat glass, passenger car, auto parts, and paper industries in 1992–1993 and published reports in June 1993. It found in flat glass, for example, that 357 out of 381 wholesalers were "de facto exclusive agents" of one of the three firms in this monopolistic market, and that no agents were distributing imported products that were available from their primary supplier (despite a 20–30 percent price advantage).[100] Yet, it concluded, there were no violations of the aml in either this or any of the other three surveyed sectors. While it called for firms to discontinue certain questionable practices like rebate systems based on achievement of sales targets, it did not act to force any firm to divest itself of stock-ownership in its distributors/suppliers or otherwise weaken the ties that make it difficult for firms up and down the distribution chain to venture out of their exclusive relationships.[101]

OTHER COMPETITION POLICY REFORMS

The Japanese government's implementation of reforms in most of the rest of the competition policy areas complied by and large with the commitments it made in 1990. JFTC investigative staff was increased by 40 percent between 1989 and 1992, and the JFTC's budget is also up.[102] Exemptions from the AML have been sharply reduced, from 261 in 1989 to 68 as of January 1, 1994.[103] Most of the rest of the SII-inspired reforms, though, were destined to have minimal impact because of the failure of U.S. officials to extract more far-reaching commitments during the negotiation process.

In the case of the private damage remedy, for example, the JFTC announced a new policy promising to aid litigants by turning over to them evidence collected in the course of agency investigations. Court fees were also lowered from 5 percent to 2 percent of the claim. Because other rules reducing the payoff for potential litigants (such as those dealing with class action suits, burden of proof, and treble damages) were not addressed in the SII deal, however, these few changes have done little to increase the number of private antitrust suits.[104]

Likewise, reforms that have made it easier for foreigners to invest in Japan, eliminating prior notification rules in almost all cases and modifying the takeover-bid rules, were destined to have almost no impact as long as cross-shareholding—which was untouched in the SII deal—effectively closed the possibility of obtaining controlling interest in most Japanese firms. Stockholder rights too have been increased by lowering the threshold for access to books from 10 percent to 3 percent, tightening disclosure rules, and lowering court fees for derivative lawsuits by shareholders, but again the impact of these changes will be minimal as long as the system of cross-shareholding protects managers from real shareholder scrutiny. The idea is that shareholders, now more able to see the cost of management's preferential procurement decisions, will take managers to court, but thus far none of the derivative lawsuits filed in Tokyo has challenged managers for sticking with their keiretsu suppliers.[105]

Conclusion

This chapter has argued two points. First, it asserts that the Japanese concessions on competition policy, though including a large number of nominal changes, do not add up to meaningful reform. Second, it argues that the pattern of Japan's response (the nation's acceptance of marginal concessions in some areas even as it held fast against fundamental change) reflects the contours of Japanese domestic politics which American pressure encountered.

While the detailed analysis of JFTC cases that were pursued and those that weren't in the last section of the chapter serves to support my contention that fundamental reform has not yet happened, the best indicator of whether or not the U.S. succeeded in bringing about real change in competition policy is the repeated reemergence of this issue in U.S.-Japan trade talks in the years since the SII talks. Throughout the SII Follow-Up process, the antitrust and keiretsu issues were the ones that generated the greatest American criticism.[106] By 1992, Bush Administration officials were so frustrated with the pace of competition policy reform in Japan that the Justice Department revised its guidelines for *U.S.* antitrust law, allowing it to be applied extraterritorially to cover the actions of Japanese firms in Japan.[107] By that time, competition policy issues were also at the heart of a growing number of American sectoral trade disputes with Japan—most notably including auto parts, paper, and flat glass.

The Clinton Administration's focus on "objective criteria" as well as the priority it placed on the insurance market, autos, and auto parts, also reflected American frustration with the inability of SII to transform Japanese competition policy. As will be discussed in more detail in the next chapter, the Clinton team basically concluded that SII—especially in the areas of antitrust and keiretsu—was a failure. Recognizing that it was impossible to get the Japanese to change anticompetitive practices that went to the heart of the nation's economic system, the new administration proposed to address the Japan problem in a new way, by negotiating "results" instead of "rules."

The other argument advanced in this chapter is that this quite obvious failure of SII to fundamentally reform Japanese competition policy, except in certain limited areas, can be explained in terms of the two-level game approach. The basic reason for SII's failure in this issue area was grasped by the incoming Clinton team: Japan didn't agree to real reform on antitrust and keiretsu because these issues went to the heart of the Japanese system. Many Japanese believed that keiretsu forms of organization and cartels designed to ameliorate the effects of "excess competition" made Japanese-style capitalism superior to the American variety. There were no significant interest groups or government ministries that

favored the American demands. The political calculus facing LDP politicians, furthermore, made them especially sensitive to the concerns of the
construction industry which was openly hostile to the idea of a more vigorous antitrust policy. The only ally the U.S. had, and even then only on
some of its demands, was the JFTC, and this agency was a 100-pound
weakling in a ring full of giant sumo wrestlers. The strategy of participation expansion which had worked on other SII issues therefore wasn't
going to work here.

   The shape of Japan's competition policy coming out of SII clearly
reflects the limits imposed by the topography of Japanese domestic politics. The JFTC was eager to use American pressure to boost its budget and
staff, raise penalty levels, and pursue a few more high-profile cases. It was
forced to compromise, however, whenever it ran up against the interests
of Japanese politicians or bureaucrats: it was forced to compromise on
surcharge and criminal fine levels; it was forced to abandon its efforts to
employ criminal sanctions against the Saitama dangō; and it was forced
(to a large extent by its own timidity) to go only part way in its challenges
to Japanese cartels—taking them to task for colluding to raise prices but
doing little to address the structures that allowed these firms to keep out
newcomers.

   Given that it was this set of structures blocking market entry (and not
collusion to raise prices) that really bothered American firms, it was
inevitable that competition policy issues would once again become a bone
of contention in U.S.-Japan trade talks with the inauguration of the new
Clinton Administration. U.S. firms hoping to break into or expand their
share of the Japanese market in areas like autos, auto parts, flat glass, and
insurance were all back in Washington pressing the government to renew
pressure on Japan. This time their approach would be different, with a
focus on "results," but as we will see, the outcome was the same.

9 THE CLINTON FRAMEWORK TALKS

On June 28, 1995, President Clinton announced that the U.S. and Japan, after going to the brink of a trade war, had reached an agreement on autos and auto parts. The deal, Clinton claimed, was "a great victory for the American people" and "a major breakthrough toward free trade throughout the world."[1] Nine months earlier, administration officials had greeted a batch of deals in the areas of insurance and government procurement—also negotiated under the Framework Talks—with similar enthusiasm. What Clinton and other administration officials claimed to be "breakthroughs," however, fell well short of what they had been demanding over two long years of contentious talks.

Throughout the Framework Talks, these officials had insisted that their most critical concern was to make sure all deals included Japanese government commitments to "objective criteria" in the text of agreements. Without such criteria for assessing the implementation of accords, they repeatedly said, the Japanese could not be trusted to truly open up the nation's markets. It was especially important to include numbers in the deal on autos, U.S. officials insisted, because the barriers at issue (in particular the keiretsu system linking Japan's automakers with their suppliers and dealers) were so opaque.

When the Framework deals were announced, however, none of them included concrete numbers in the text of the agreements. In the case of the government procurement accords, there was only a vague reference to a "significant increase in access and sales" over the "medium term." The

Bush administration, with much less bluster, had managed to get similar language included in earlier accords on computers and paper. Moreover, in the auto accords the U.S. could not get the Japanese government to commit to *any* "objective criteria" that indicated change would occur in a particular amount or even direction. The government, Japanese officials insisted, had no influence over private-sector decisions such as those having to do with parts purchases and dealership networks.

In the end, therefore, the U.S. was forced to provide its own estimates of the "results" it expected from the accord, based loosely (in some cases *very* loosely) on "voluntary plans" announced by the Japanese automakers. The Japanese government, the deal made clear, had nothing to do with these estimates, and the U.S. agreed that the numbers were "not commitments and are not subject to the trade remedy laws of either country." While administration officials insisted that the voluntary plans issued by the automakers were specific and formal enough to allow the U.S. government to monitor and enforce the deal, they were actually much vaguer and more heavily hedged than the plans Bush had extracted from the Japanese in 1992.

Writing in 1995 just after the auto accords were reached, it is impossible to offer a definitive evaluation of the Framework Talks. We do not have the benefit of five years of hindsight as we did with the sii talks. An examination of the text of the deal and the voluntary plans of the automakers, however, suggests that the Clinton administration (or its successor) is likely to be extremely frustrated with this deal. The Japanese government does not see itself as having any responsibility to produce the "results" that are forecast in the plans. Japanese firms, meanwhile, offer only very vague forecasts and have hedged their plans with references to market conditions. Clinton officials knew that vague and voluntary plans without government backing would not be enough to dent the nation's keiretsu ties, and that is why they sought more formal commitments to "results." *But they could not get them*—even after two years of constant and intense pressure including, in the leadup to the auto accords, a threat to impose prohibitive tariffs on $5.9 billion in Japanese luxury cars.

Why didn't gaiatsu work more effectively for Clinton? Is it a problem of the administration having chosen the wrong *demands*—as would be suggested by the analysis of sii cases? Or has something in the *context* of bilateral negotiations changed so much that the effectiveness of American pressure—regardless of the specific nature of demands—has been compromised? My answers to the latter two questions are "yes" and "maybe."

The fact that Clinton's core demand for a "results-oriented" deal was unsupported by anyone within Japan made his job very difficult, preventing him from being able to use a strategy of participation expansion. In two subsidiary cases in which Clinton did choose demands with domestic allies, the 1994 cellular phone case and on the issue of relaxing government regulation of automobile inspections, gaiatsu proved more successful. These results, of course, are perfectly consistent with the pattern we saw in the SII talks.

There is some evidence, however, that Clinton's difficulties may have gone beyond the problem of unpopular demands. Despite wide support for a delayed-offset income tax cut at a time of prolonged recession, Japanese policy in this area was *not* affected in any meaningful way by Clinton's demands—suggesting that the tactic of participation expansion may no longer work as well as it did before. Similarly, Clinton's failure to extract "results-oriented" deals through threats when Reagan and Bush had managed to obtain such deals on semiconductors in 1986 and auto parts in 1992 suggests that gaiatsu-as-threats may also have lost some of its punch. These results suggest that recent changes in the domestic and international context of U.S.-Japan relations (the end of the Cold War, the creation of the World Trade Organization, and the end of the LDP regime) may be degrading the impact of gaiatsu across the board—regardless of the specific demands.

It is likely that *both* Clinton's choice of demands *and* recent changes in the context of negotiations contributed to his failure to achieve his negotiating objectives. Social scientifically, because of a phenomenon known as "overdetermination," it is impossible to know which problem was more important. Looking closely at each source of Clinton's difficulty, however, suggests that both limited the effectiveness of foreign pressure by impinging on synergistic strategies that worked in the past—confirming the utility of the framework employed in this book and providing us with a better understanding of the conditions that limit the effectiveness of American pressure.

The first section of this chapter looks at Clinton's choice of format and demands for the Framework Talks, contrasting the administration's approach with that of the Bush administration and emphasizing the role of "two-level logic" in shaping trade policy. The second section, recounting the administration's failure to make significant headway with its core demand for "results-oriented" deals, emphasizes how Clinton's choice of demands made his job very difficult. The final section then examines the question of whether Clinton's limited success can be seen as a reflection of changes in the context of the negotiations and considers how the end of the Cold War, the new World Trade Organization (WTO), and recent changes in the Japanese political system may be degrading the effectiveness of gaiatsu.

American Politics and the Birth of the Framework

The objective situation facing the Clinton administration as it set out to devise its Japan policy in 1993 was not that different from the one that had faced the Bush administration four years earlier. The trade deficit with Japan was growing again, rising back to 1989 levels by 1992. (See figure 9.1) U.S. government forecasts, furthermore, pointed toward further rising deficits as Japanese imports were slowed by weakening domestic demand. Finally, on many of the indices of market openness discussed in chapter 3, Japan had shown only a little progress—suggesting that the nation remained an "adversarial," or at least "unequal" trader.[2] The U.S. still had a "Japan Problem" not too different from the one Bush had faced.

Confronted with a similar situation, however, Clinton consciously rejected the approach chosen by his predecessor. Where Bush had sought

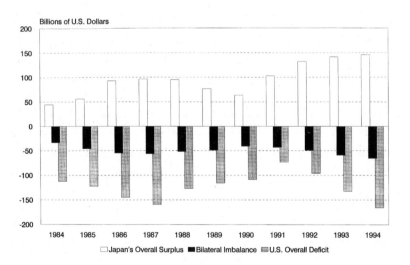

FIGURE 9.1   U.S.-Japan Balance of Trade, 1984-94

Sources: Bank of Japan for Japan's surpluses; U.S. Department of Commerce for U.S. deficits and bilateral balances.

through sii to prove that "managed trade" of the type represented by the Semiconductor Accords was unnecessary, the new Clinton team saw the 1986 Accords as a model. Belittling sii as a foolish and futile attempt to change the entire Japanese economic system, the administration embraced instead a "results-oriented" approach to the Japan Problem: give the Japanese a target and let them figure out how to reach it. As Commerce Secretary Ron Brown put it during one of his early visits to Tokyo, "Removal of barriers will not be the ultimate measure of success but rather, sales will be. . . . Markets will be considered open not when rules and regulations and arrangements change, but when we see that American products, successful all over the world, have equal success in Japan."[3] By chance, just as the administration was beginning its discussion of how to deal with Japan, it was announced that the Japanese had finally reached the 20 percent foreign market share established in the Semiconductor Accords—reinforcing the new group's conviction that a results-oriented approach was the best one.

In the time since, the Clinton administration has remained committed to this particular approach. In July 1993, it allowed the negotiations over the format for the new round of talks to drag on for the duration of the G-7 summit in Tokyo, pushing them to the brink of failure before the Japanese agreed that future assessments of trade deals would be based "upon sets of objective criteria, either qualitative or quantitative or both as appropriate"—in other words "results."[4] Then, in February 1994, Clinton let his summit meeting with Prime Minister Hosokawa end without an agreement on the set of Framework issues which were due to be settled by that date—specifically because the Japanese had refused to agree to results-oriented deals. Quoting directly from the part of the July agreement in which the Japanese had promised that future deals would include "objective criteria," Clinton insisted that proposals from the Japanese side "simply did not meet the standards agreed to in Tokyo."[5] In the summer of 1995, the Clinton administration was still sticking to its guns, allowing the dispute to escalate to a trade war over auto issues.

Why did the Clinton administration commit so completely to a results-oriented approach to the Japan Problem? Can this decision, in contrast with the Bush administration's decision to concentrate its demands on structural barriers under similar circumstances, be explained by models of foreign policy formation that emphasize international structural forces? Or can it be better understood as a product of domestic politics? The argument developed here, following closely the one developed in chapter 3 to explain the Bush administration's policy, emphasizes the role of domestic ideas and institutions in filtering the mixed incentives emanating from the international system. It also stresses the process through which policy is refined to reflect what I called "two level logic."

The Impact of International Variables

The analysis of how the international system influenced the Bush administration's choice of a Japan policy emphasized the *mixed* nature of these incentives. The "adversarial" pattern of Japanese trade and the challenge posed by Japanese exports to key sectors of the U.S. economy created incentives for the U.S. to adopt a tougher trade policy toward Japan, but common interests in preserving the world trading system and maintaining cooperative security relations pushed policy toward moderation. Four years later, there was only one change at the international level with the potential to cut through these mixed signals and generate sufficient force to shape policy: the post-Cold War world order which was just "emerging" in 1989 had fully emerged by 1993. The Berlin Wall fell and the Soviet Union disintegrated in the interim—substantially eliminating the Soviet threat which had tied the U.S. and Japan together since the end of World War II.

At first glance, this development might seem to explain the Clinton administration's more aggressive trade policy. Perhaps the new administration got tough simply because the U.S. no longer needed to soften its economic demands to preserve security cooperation.[6] A closer look at the actual change in the strategic environment suggests, however, that the end of the Cold War did not eliminate the need for security cooperation as definitively as this version of the story presumes. Even with the de facto elimination of the Soviet threat, threats to regional instability remained: North Korea was known to be working on a nuclear bomb and China was rapidly modernizing its military forces. The U.S. would not be able to deal with these threats alone. Furthermore, the end of the Cold War made the American public less willing to shoulder alone the burden of maintaining peace and stability across the globe, increasing U.S. reliance on Japanese support for international ventures outside the immediate region: from Cambodia to the Persian Gulf. U.S. officials have continued to insist regularly throughout the Clinton administration that the bilateral security alliance remains something which the government considers vital for American interests.[7]

Given that the U.S. had good reasons to continue to value its alliance with Japan, it is not at all clear that the end of the Cold War significantly simplified the incentives emanating from the international level. Those incentives remained mixed, as they had been for Bush, and once again their impact would depend on how they were mediated by domestic ideas and institutions.

Mediation by Ideas and Institutions

It was argued in chapter 3 that ideas, especially those that are institutionalized, can play an important role in shaping trade policy—especially when the incentives coming from the international system are mixed.[8] In the U.S., I argued, the emerging economic power and challenge of Japan did not result in the immediate adoption of an aggressive trade policy toward that nation because institutions—built up after the Great Depression delegitimized protectionism and after the Cold War privileged security concerns—got in the way. When Clinton arrived in Washington, these ideas and institutions were still in place, and their continuing impact can be seen, for example, in the administration's decision to embrace the North American Free Trade Agreement (NAFTA).

They did not prevent Clinton from adopting a more aggressive Japan policy, however, for two reasons: first, because the end of the Cold War and perceived failure of Reagan/Bush trade policies provided enough of a "shock" to open the door to new ideas and reconstituted institutions; and second, because Clinton's domestic political coalition encouraged him to be open to this new thinking. Goldstein, the most prominent proponent of the argument that ideas shape trade policy, emphasizes the importance of "shocks":

> In the case of economic policymaking, three factors are of great importance: exogenous shocks, such as wars or international depressions, demographic changes, and the failure of current economic policies to generate desirable economic outcomes, all motivate political leaders to examine current policy. Fundamentally, it is the perception, whether warranted or not, of failure in current policy or political institutions or both that creates the incentive for political elites to change. Such moments create political space, windows of time, and political entrepreneurs begin to search out and try new policy prescriptions.[9]

Clinton was such an entrepreneur. "Revisionists" had been arguing since the mid-1980s that the economic challenge from Japan was at least as much of a threat to U.S. interests as the Soviet Union, but their views had little impact in the face of dominant liberal and Cold War ideas and institutions. The persistence of giant trade deficits with Japan after seven years of Republican trade initiatives delegitimized the rule-oriented approach, however, and the end of the Cold War made it possible to question foreign policy institutions which valued security interests at the expense of economic concerns. The combination made it possible for Clinton, when he came to Washington, to adopt a significantly different trade policy than that of his predecessor.

Taking advantage of this opportunity, Clinton has consistently supported new thinking about American foreign policy interests. Throughout the campaign and at his Little Rock economic summit after the election, he emphasized the need for the United States to pursue its *economic* interests. His advisers on Japan policy during the campaign included Glen Fukushima, Mike Mochizuki, and Derek Shearer, all advocates of a results-oriented approach.[10] As he began to staff his cabinet, Clinton emphasized the shift in thinking by picking Laura D'Andrea Tyson, author of the revisionist tome *Who's Bashing Whom*, as head of his Council of Economic Advisors. Nothing better indicated the power of new ideas in the Clinton administration than his selection of this advocate of managed trade policy as chief of an agency that, since its establishment, had been a bastion of neoclassical economists who supported free trade policy down the line.

But Clinton did more than choose advocates of new thinking as his advisers and officials. He also reformed institutions. Where the White House foreign policy apparatus had previously been dominated by the National Security Council, Clinton emphasized his commitment to pursuing America's economic interests by creating a new National Economic Council (NEC) charged with coordinating the positions of government agencies involved in the formation of foreign economic policy. When it came time to devise the administration's trade policy toward Japan, the president put W. Bowman Cutter, the deputy head of the NEC, in charge.

What is interesting about this process, in contrast to that of the Bush administration in 1989, is the way in which Clinton consciously sought to separate America's economic policy toward Japan from its security policy. In the early months, there were actually two separate "policy reviews" headed by Cutter and NSC deputy Sandy Berger, respectively. The parts of the government that in the past had pushed for a more moderate trade

policy out of concern about the bilateral alliance, including the heads of
the East Asia sections of the State Department and NSC as well as the
Regional Affairs section of the Defense Department, were all isolated
within the security policy group. Meanwhile, the USTR and Commerce
were each given prominent roles in the economic policy group, along
with CEA, State, and Treasury officials in charge of international economic issues.[11]

"Two Level Logic"

This new institutional structure, combined with the influence of revisionists within the administration, clearly facilitated agreement on a
more aggressive trade policy. Before crediting revisionist ideas with too
much power, however, we need to reflect on the other source of this new
and different Japan policy. As I suggested above, we also need to recognize how Clinton's decision to embrace this new approach fit in with his
domestic political calculations. Recall that in Goldstein's formulation,
she uses the metaphor of an open window to describe the impact of
exogenous shocks on the policy process. The end of the Cold War and
persistent trade deficits may have opened a window, but these events did
not force Clinton to take advantage of this situation and articulate a new
vision of American interests.

To fully understand why Clinton chose an approach so different from
Bush's, we need to recognize how his "international" policy fit in with the
other level in our two-level game. Because the incentives emanating from
the international level were mixed, and because there were competing
ideas about how to deal with Japan, Clinton had a choice, and his decision
to adopt a results-oriented approach can be attributed at least in part to
his judgment that a get-tough-with-Japan policy would help him solidify
his domestic political base and draw voters away from the Republican and
Perot camps.

The domestic incentives to adopt an aggressive trade policy toward
Japan were particularly pronounced after the administration decided to
back NAFTA. That decision alienated core Democratic constituencies and
aggravated Perot backers.[12] Clinton perceived that he could assuage ill
feelings on the part of organized labor and appeal to at least some Perot
voters by getting tough with Japan—long the target of attacks by protec-
tionists and economic nationalists. He also saw his Japan policy as part of
a broader initiative—spearheaded by Ron Brown at Commerce—

designed to win the support of an American business community usually loyal to Republicans by demonstrating that the aggressive pursuit of American economic interests abroad could yield material benefits for specific firms. The Big Three automakers, glass manufacturers, and Motorola, among others, could all expect to gain one way or another from a get-tough-with-Japan policy, and Clinton hoped that their gratitude would translate into critical political support. It is interesting in this regard that Clinton seemed to reaffirm this strategic calculation in 1995, much later in the Framework game, when he decided to go ahead with sanction threats timed so that he would be able to continue playing the tough guy with Japan as his reelection campaign got underway.

The combination of international incentives, mediated by ideas and institutions and refined by domestic political calculations, produced by April 1993 a surprising degree of consensus behind the decision to insist on "results" in future trade deals with Japan. Only by insisting that future agreements included concrete goals and time lines for progress, the group of deputies involved in the economic policy review concluded, would the administration be able to hold the Japanese accountable for their promises.[13] As consultations with Japanese officials began, Clinton officials thus insisted that the two sides agree to include "benchmarks" in their sectoral trade deals. In addition, the administration sought to have Tokyo commit to a specific reduction in its current account surplus (down from 3.2 percent 1992 to somewhere in the range of 1 to 2 percent within three years) and a specific increase in the ratio of manufactured imports to GDP (up by one-third, also over a three-year period).[14] The results of the Clinton initiative have to be judged against this initial formulation of America's demands.

The Results—or the Lack Thereof

Despite the centrality of "benchmarks" in the administration's new Japan initiative, the U.S. found it impossible to convince the Japanese to put meaningful "results" in the Framework agreements. The Americans gave up on their aim of getting Japan to commit to macroeconomic targets even before the Framework talks got officially underway. They were more stubborn in insisting on results in the talks on insurance, telecommunications, and medical technology, but agreements reached October 1, 1994, offered no assurance of "annual progress," much less specific and enforceable numbers. In the auto deal the U.S. was forced, in effect, to issue its own estimates of the increased sales it hoped the accord would produce. This section of the chapter summarizes and evaluates the fruits of Clinton's demands for "results" and points to the complete lack of domestic support for this demand within Japan as an important reason for the failure of gaiatsu in this case.

Macro Targets

The first "targets" to be jettisoned were those in the macroeconomic area. As it had during the sii talks, the U.S. sought to narrow the trade imbalance by attacking the savings-investment gap in Japan. Rather than talk about public investment levels, however, the U.S. this time attempted to force the Japanese to commit to a specific reduction in its current account surplus (the "result"), leaving it to the Japanese to decide how to achieve this target through fiscal policy or other means. The most intense bargaining on this point actually took place between April 1993, when the demands were formulated as described above, and July 1993, when Clinton's visit to Tokyo for the G-7 Summit coincided with the final negotiations on the terms for the Framework talks.

Not surprisingly, the MOF strongly objected to U.S. demands, and the Americans were soon forced to back down.[15] The July Framework document committed Japan only to a vaguely worded "highly significant decrease in its current account surplus" over the "medium term," and made no specific mention of manufactured imports. Since this agreement, the Clinton administration has made no further efforts to get the Japanese to agree to specific macroeconomic "results." Instead, U.S. officials have been reduced to arguing with the Japanese about tax and budget policy in a manner not too different from earlier administrations. (More on this in the next section.)

The First Year

The U.S. was able to hold out a little longer with its demand for "results" in sectoral agreements, managing to get the Japanese to agree in the text of the July 1993 Framework document that subsequent deals would include "objective criteria" for assessing the implementation of commitments.[16] While the Japanese insisted that this term meant something different from "benchmarks," the U.S. for the next two years continued to demand that concrete goals and time lines for progress be included in sectoral deals. The July document also established the more specific negotiating agenda. The two sides would talk about government procurement in a variety of specific areas, regulatory reform and competitiveness, the auto and auto parts sector, economic harmonization, and the implementation of existing arrangements and measures. Of these, four topics would get priority attention aimed at reaching agreement within just six months: (1) government procurement of medical technology; (2) government procurement of telecommunications; (3) regulatory reform, in the insurance sector; (4) a variety of issues in the automotive sector. While agreements were eventually reached in other areas, I concentrate here on the fate of the administration's demands in these priority sectors.

During the fall of 1993, the two sides met several times and made some progress on procedural issues, but the Japanese stubbornly resisted American demands to include quantitative criteria in agreements. Particularly contentious was the American suggestion that the two sides use foreign market share numbers for other countries as a basis against which to measure Japanese market-opening progress. In all of the targeted areas, figures produced by the American negotiators showed that the gap was quite large: U.S. firms had 40–75 percent of the markets for medical technology in Europe, Australia, and Canada, but only 20 percent of Japan's market; foreign market share in insurance stood at only 2 percent for Japan compared to a range of 10–33 percent in other G-7 countries; while foreign market shares for telecom equipment stood at 5 percent for Japan compared to a range of 11–38 percent in the rest of the G-7.[17] The Japanese, the U.S. proposed, should commit to working toward foreign market share numbers in other developed nations over a period of three to four years.[18]

This attempt by the Americans to use market share numbers as "objective criteria" was vigorously resisted by Japanese officials. They insisted they would never accept such "targets," arguing that the American demands were tantamount to "managed trade." At the negotiating sessions, they disputed all of the American numbers—pointing out, for example, that numbers for *government procurement* of telecom and medical technology showed Japan to be more open than the U.S.[19] They also proposed their own "objective criteria," focusing on the efforts of foreign firms to get into the Japanese market (e.g. how much did U.S. automakers spend on advertising? how many of their offerings were tailored to Japan's market?), in an attempt to divert attention to what they considered to be the reason for the lack of U.S. market share in the targeted sectors: too little effort.[20] Outside the negotiations, the Japanese government launched a public relations campaign characterizing the American demands as "managed trade" and urging other governments to register their protests against the U.S. demands. Even as the date of the Clinton-Hosokawa Summit approached, confronting both sides with the deadline by which they had pledged to reach agreement on priority sectors, Japanese officials steadfastly refused to accept what they called "targets."

Fast forward to the summer of 1994. The U.S. and Japan were talking again, having agreed to restart their negotiations after a three-month hiatus following the failure of the Clinton-Hosokawa Summit. The arguments being made by the two sides, however, were essentially the same. The Americans, though having officially forsworn "numerical targets" in an effort to get the talks back on track in May, were still calling for criteria that would allow the two sides to measure future progress. Japanese officials, however, continued to insist that such "forward-looking indicators" were the same thing as "targets" and were consequently unacceptable.[21] Unable to bridge this gap, the two sides let a series of deadlines pass without a deal before confronting a final deadline which, the U.S. insisted, could not be postponed.[22]

September 30 was the date by which the U.S. government was required to determine whether or not to target Japan under the Super 301 provision of U.S. trade law which had been reinstated by Clinton in March. It was also the date on which sanctions were to go into effect under an ongoing Title VII investigation of unfair government procurement practices unless the disputes over medical technology and telecommunications were resolved. Leading up to the deadline, the two sides held their ground, with the Americans proposing as their bottom line the inclusion of passages calling for "annual progress" in foreign access and sales, and the Japanese insisting that they could not promise that sales of foreign goods would increase every year. Finally, after negotiating through the final night, USTR Kantor and his Japanese counterparts came to an agreement covering all issues except autos and auto parts. After the deal, both sides claimed victory.

An assessment of the effectiveness of gaiatsu under Clinton depends very much on whether you believe the American or Japanese characterizations of these deals. U.S. officials pointed to sections of each deal on government procurement which referred to "a significant increase in access and sales of competitive foreign [medical technology/telecommunications] products and services" over the "medium term" and listed "recent trends in the value, rate of growth and share" of foreign procurement as one of the ten objective criteria for evaluating progress. Japanese officials, on the other hand, insisted they had resisted all U.S. demands for "targets." Where the Americans had once sought to include foreign market shares in other countries as a reference point for evaluating market-opening progress, the Japanese had resisted even the much weaker American demand that such progress be evaluated according to whether there was "annual progress" in the value and share of foreign goods and services.

Who gave in? It is my evaluation that the Clinton team failed to achieve its most critical aim of securing a Japanese commitment to "results" which would be explicit enough to allow the U.S. to hold the Japanese government accountable under U.S. trade law. The inclusion of specific numbers in the semiconductor accords and 1992 auto pact had allowed the U.S. to hold Section 301 of U.S. trade law, with its provisions providing for the U.S. to retaliate when nations fail to live up to negotiated agreements, over the heads of the Japanese. The agreements reached October 1, in contrast, contained no specific numbers. Even the more innocuous phrase "annual progress in the value and share" of foreign procurements, which could have been interpreted as having committed the government to guaranteeing at least some increase every year, was excised. The final language, with multiple words requiring an element of interpretation, simply fell short of what the U.S. needed in order to hold Japan accountable.[23]

It is true that these agreements included some real Japanese concessions on procedural issues. In the insurance deal, the Japanese government agreed not to deregulate "third sector" insurance markets in which U.S. firms were strong prior to the deregulation of life and casualty insurance markets where Japanese firms were predominant, a MOF plan that had threatened to discriminate against foreign insurers.[24] In the government procurement deals, the government agreed to provide more advanced notice and more opportunities for consultations about technical standards. It also agreed to introduce new bid evaluation systems which would allow purchasing agents to take into account factors other than just price—such as the more advanced technology of American medical equipment. It would be difficult to proclaim the Clinton Framework a success based on these procedural concessions, however, for the administration had been saying from the beginning that changes in rules alone would not make a difference. The U.S. needed Japan to commit to "results." By this standard, set by the Clinton administration itself, the October 1 agreements could not be described as a success.

THE SECOND YEAR

The settlement of three out of four priority Framework issues by October 1, however, still left the largest and most contentious issue—autos and auto parts—unresolved. On this issue, the kind of language on which the others had been settled was unsatisfactory to both sides. Here, the U.S. was firm in insisting that it really needed specific numbers. It wanted a renewal of the voluntary parts purchase plans (the most recent of which had provided for purchases of $19 billion worth of foreign-made auto parts by the Japanese makers during the fiscal year ending in March 1995) by Japanese automakers, this time backed more explicitly by the government. It also wanted quantitative criteria for evaluating progress toward opening up the auto dealership networks affiliated with the Japanese automakers. The Japanese, on the other hand, drew a distinction between the auto issues and the government procurement deals, emphasizing that while the former necessarily involved the government, the latter concerned arrangements in the private sector that were totally beyond government control.

Having failed to bridge this gap in time for the September 30 deadline, the Clinton administration decided to up the ante by initiating Section 301 proceedings against the Japanese. While the specific charge, that Japanese government regulation of the auto parts *aftermarket* discriminated against foreign partsmakers, was relatively narrow—certainly more narrow than the alternative of "naming Japan" under Super 301—this move enabled U.S. officials to step up pressure in a way which they deemed would be less inflammatory. Section 301, like Super 301, provided deadlines for settling issues and would allow the U.S. to impose sanctions if a satisfactory deal was not reached, but it was less of a target of foreign criticism than the better-known Super 301.

Another six months of talking, however, still did not lead to a narrowing of the gap between the two sides, and so in May 1995, the Clinton Administration announced that it would impose tariffs on $5.9 billion worth of Japanese luxury autos unless the dispute were settled by June 28. When the Japanese threatened to complain to the World Trade Organization if the U.S. resorted to unilateral sanctions, the Americans added their own threat to appeal to the WTO with a case challenging "the continuing discrimination against U.S. products in the market for automobiles and automotive parts in Japan."[25] After a flurry of negotiations lasting, again, right up to the eve of a sanctions deadline, the two sides finally managed to reach an agreement.

Who won this time? As indicated by the discussion of the auto accords at the start of this chapter, the "unilateral estimates" in the deal were a far cry from the explicit commitment to "results" sought by the Clinton administration.[26] First, explicit language qualifying the numbers given in the joint statement announcing the deal made it clear these were not "commitments," were not in any way the responsibility of the government of Japan, and could not be enforced under U.S. trade law. MITI Minister Hashimoto Ryūtarō, in his written comments, put it this way: "The Government of Japan has had no involvement in this forecast because it is beyond the scope and responsibility of the government. . . . Ambassador Kantor's estimates are his own and neither shared by the Minister himself nor the Government of Japan."[27]

At least as significant as the Japanese government's abdication of responsibility for the numbers in the deal, however, was the weakness of the Japanese automakers' commitments. They too had held out in the face of almost $6 billion in sanctions and resisted U.S. demands that they make explicit commitments. Toyota's only commitments related to their dealership networks, for example, were to "send out a letter . . . stating once again that the handling of foreign makers' vehicles are not subject to prior consultation with Toyota, and that they are free to handle them" and to "consider establishing an internal 'grievance body' to handle questions and concerns on handling foreign makers' cars."[28] With little more than such promises from Japan's automakers (to do again what they had already done), Kantor announced that the U.S. expected that the Big Three automakers would create 200 new sales outlets by 1996 and 1,000 by the end of the century.[29]

The U.S. estimate that the auto accord would generate an additional $2.4 billion in parts sales in the Japanese market was based on similarly vague language in the automakers' plans. Again, the Toyota plan said only that the firm would work "to increase opportunities for business by seeking out new suppliers" and "to increase clarity, improve accessibility, and assure objectivity and fairness in the procurement process." It would also produce a "guidebook" explaining Toyota's procurement system and establish a "Global Optimized Purchase System" aimed at selecting "the most competitive suppliers." Notice that these passages do not say anything explicitly about foreign suppliers, much less about the quantity of parts Toyota might purchase from them.[30] How the U.S. came up with the number of $2.4 billion based on voluntary plans such as this one is unclear.

The vagueness of the automakers' plans for the Japanese market is especially striking when one considers that these same firms had announced more explicit plans in this area in 1992. At that time, they had announced plans to buy $4 billion in foreign-made parts for the Japanese market by fiscal year 1994.[31] They had had difficulty delivering on these plans, however, because of the slowdown in the Japanese auto market and the auto firms' loyalty to their networks of domestic suppliers. It was in order to force the automakers to deliver on their plans for their Japanese operations and to break down these networks that Clinton had pressed so hard for Japan to make firmer pledges in this area. The fact that the new voluntary plans were *less* specific in this area, more than anything else about the auto deal, signaled the administration's failure to achieve its objectives.

The only sections in the automakers' forecasts that were at all specific were those that referred to their plans for their U.S. operations. Even these, however, went little beyond previously announced plans and were heavily couched with conditional language. Toyota, for example, had earlier announced plans to build minivans in the U.S. starting in 1998, but in its plan released the day of the auto pact said only that such a move would be "considered." Its reference to the option of constructing a new auto plant, with initial production of 100,000 units, in North America said only that such a plan would be "studied." As if these sentences were not conditioned enough already, Toyota added an extra escape clause at the end of its forecast indicating that "the numerical figures raised in this business plan may change depending on economic circumstances such as the exchange rate and market conditions."[32]

Honda's statement also went little further than what it had announced months before. Its plan to increase its production in the U.S. to 720,000 by 1998, for example, had been made public almost a year earlier.[33] Few of these plans included specific information about the firms' intentions to purchase foreign-made parts other than to say they expected new vehicles to meet NAFTA local-content rules. Nevertheless, despite all of the qualifiers, the U.S. government was able to extrapolate that the Japanese automakers ought to be buying an additional $6.75 billion of foreign parts for their U.S. operations by 1998.

Explaining the Lack of "Results"

As the above citations of specific automaker plans make clear, the U.S. failed to extract commitments to "results" not only from the Japanese government but also from the automakers. When viewed alongside the administration's failure to extract commitments to meaningful goals in the October 1994 package of Framework deals, this lack of "results" raises an obvious question: why was the administration unable to use gaiatsu to achieve its core objective?

A big part of the explanation had to do with the complete lack of support within Japan for "results-oriented" trade deals. In the discussion of SII, we saw that American pressure tended to be most effective when it was able to bring into the policy process latent supporters of U.S. demands who had previously been excluded. This was the key to the achievement of U.S. demands in the areas of the Large Store Law, public investment, and agricultural land taxation. In the case of the Framework talks, however, there was absolutely no support within Japan—latent or otherwise—for the American position on "objective criteria."

This opposition was clear from the time when administration officials first announced that they wanted future U.S.-Japan deals to include "benchmarks." This term, it quickly became clear, sounded too much like "numerical targets" to Japanese bureaucrats whose experience with the Semiconductor Accords and 1992 auto parts pact had left them sour on the idea of trade agreements with numbers. The 20 percent market share number in the 1986 Semiconductor Accords had been intended, MITI officials claimed, as a goal to aim for—not a commitment. And yet the Americans had insisted ever since that Japanese officials deliver steady progress toward this number, forcing MITI to scramble every year to get Japanese electronics firms to buy American.

Similarly, Japanese officials had been told by Bush officials in 1992 that the numbers included in the auto parts deal—mentioned only in a Japanese auto industry press release stapled to the formal agreement—would be treated as voluntary private sector "plans" and not government commitments.[34] And yet Kantor and Brown had delivered a letter to the Japanese government in the early months of the Clinton administration pointing out that the Japanese were behind their purchasing plans and calling on the automakers to live up to their "pledge."[35]

Japanese bureaucrats came away from these experiences firm in their

resolve never again to accept American demands to include specific numbers in trade deals. As one MITI official put it during these early months,
"We have learned a lesson. Once reference is made in a trade agreement
to numerical figures, then those figures will get a life of their own. So we
will never repeat this type of thing, to avoid misunderstandings and managed trade."[36] MITI, MOFA, and MOF officials, as well as leading Japanese
politicians, repeated such statements throughout the Framework talks.
Even Economic Planning Agency (EPA) officials, some of whom
expressed guarded support for putting *macro* targets into the Framework
agreement (setting a goal for reducing the size of the Japanese trade surplus relative to its GNP), drew the line at micro or sectoral numbers.[37]

The Americans' isolation during the Framework Talks can also be seen
in the reaction of the Japanese media. Recall that during the SII talks,
newspapers wrote dozens of editorials supporting American demands.
Asahi shimbun, for example, wrote six editorials supportive of the
American position in the month leading up to the April 1990 deal on SII.
During the Framework talks, in contrast, the *Asahi* ran only one editorial
about the Clinton talks in the month leading up to the February 1994
deadline for settling priority issues, and it largely parroted MITI criticism
of the U.S. demands: to agree to the American demands for "numerical
targets," it said, would be to increase government regulation of the economy. "The government," the *Asahi* argued, "should frankly explain the limits to what it can do."[38] After Hosokawa stood up and said "no" to the
Americans, the same newspaper editorialized in support of that position.[39] Such media attitudes, reflected in print and TV news reporting as
well as editorials, was the rule throughout the two-year standoff over
"objective criteria."

With the bureaucrats, the media, and other opinion leaders uniformly
against the Clinton demands, there was little incentive for political leaders to intervene to broker a deal—as Kaifu had done during SII. The key
politicians during the Framework, Prime Minister Hosokawa in the leadup to February 1994 and MITI minister Hashimoto since the summer of
1994, both earned accolades, not by smoothing out relations with the
Americans but by refusing to give in. As the deadline for luxury auto sanctions approached in June of 1995, for example, Hashimoto thrived by
playing the role of "tough guy" who would stand up to the Americans, thus
boosting his approval ratings to the point that he stood 10 points ahead of
his nearest rival in the race to succeed Prime Minister Murayama.[40]

All of the above demonstrates how unfavorable Japanese politics was to the effective use of a strategy of participation expansion in pursuit of Clinton's core demand for "results." Just as Bush had found it difficult to extract concessions on the keiretsu and antitrust issues where conditions did not favor use of this strategy, Clinton too was frustrated by his lack of domestic allies. Though he and Bush had sought to challenge vertical restraints like dealership networks and long-term supplier networks in different ways, one by attacking structures and one by asking for "results," both ultimately ran into the same problem: they had no allies within Japan.

A FEW SUCCESSES

It is interesting in this regard that the Clinton administration had more success in achieving its objectives when it *did* have allies inside Japan. The first example of such an issue is the case of the American demands for a relaxation in Japanese regulations governing automobile inspections and repairs. These rules, limiting the number of garages qualified to do inspections and make certain repairs, were subjected to domestic criticism even before the U.S. brought up the issue. Just as a variety of big business groups and government agencies had questioned the Large Store Law in advance of SII, a number of groups and agencies had criticized the Ministry of Transportation's strict rules in this area.[41] Before the Framework, however, the MOT had succeeded in resisting most proposals for reform.

The American charge was that regulations limiting the number of "designated" garages (the only ones allowed to perform required periodic inspections) and "certified" garages (the only ones allowed to perform repairs involving "critical parts" without a separate inspection by an MOT official) were unnecessarily strict. Both of these types of garages, the U.S. pointed out, tended to stock only "genuine" parts—those coming via the Japanese automakers from their networks of suppliers. In effect, the U.S. charged, these rules gave garages tied to Japanese automakers a monopoly of the safety inspection business—alone accounting for 40 percent of automotive repair and maintenance business in Japan—and of the business involving critical parts. In the process, they locked competitive foreign parts makers out of the lucrative parts aftermarket. The U.S. called on the MOT to relax its rules so that garages less tied to Japanese automakers and more willing to stock foreign parts would be allowed into the game.[42]

The MOT strongly resisted these demands, claiming American proposals threatened automotive safety and the environment. Even as late as May 1995, when Clinton threatened sanctions, they had refused to accept the main American demands. In the final days of negotiations, however, MITI emerged as a vocal ally of the U.S., pressuring MOT to accept most of the American demands.[43] Whether it did so because it sympathized with U.S. demands or because it did not want "its" industry (the automakers) to suffer sanctions due to the MOT's intransigence is unclear, but regardless it seems its support helped make this the one area of the 1995 auto pact where the government committed to meaningful policy change. The MOT agreed to make changes in its rules which would allow an estimated 7,000–8,000 more garages into the inspection business and others, which would greatly expand the number of certified garages qualified to deal with "critical parts."

Another issue where gaiatsu proved more effective was the case of cellular phones which came to a head in March 1994 just after the failed Clinton-Hosokawa Summit. In this highly publicized case, the American firm Motorola was having difficulty convincing its Japanese "partner" IDO to invest in building the base stations needed to make a Motorola system known as TACS fully operational in the lucrative Tokyo-Nagoya corridor. Until IDO built the stations, Motorola was not going to be able to sell many of its phones.[44] IDO was hesitant, however, because it had already invested in base stations for the system it had licensed from Motorola's rival, NTT, and because some of its top officials (including the vice president) were retired from the Ministry of Posts and Telecommunications, NTT's bureaucratic patron. Despite this conflict of interest, however, there were many executives inside IDO who wanted to invest in TACS, recognizing that the firm could gain market-share by operating this system. Such Japanese firms as Toshiba, Kyocera, and Matsushita also quietly supported Motorola's position since they too made phones for the TACS system and hoped to gain ground on rivals who built primarily for NTT. Without pressure from the American government, however, these Motorola allies could not overcome resistance from the MPT and that ministry's Old Boys within IDO.[45]

After the failure of the Clinton-Hosokawa Summit, Motorola therefore embarked on a concerted campaign to bring U.S. government pressure to bear on IDO, convincing the USTR to issue a decision finding the Japanese government in violation of the 1989 cellular phone agreement and threatening to impose sanctions unless a deal was made by March 10. Faced with this pressure, IDO consented to Motorola's demands and agreed to step up its investment in the TACS system, pledging to make it fully operational by September 1995. With IDO meeting this commitment without any difficulties, Motorola official Robert Orr reported that the U.S. firm's relations with IDO had become much more harmonious.[46] Just as gaiatsu had worked in cases where America had Japanese allies during SII, it worked for Clinton too under these circumstances (at least some of the time).

Is Gaiatsu Losing Its Punch?

The two cases profiled briefly at the end of the last section make it clear that American pressure retains the ability to extract concessions from Japan when conditions are particularly favorable. A further review of the Clinton administration's experiences suggests, however, that gaiatsu strategies that worked in the past may be losing some of their effectiveness at the margins. This section examines the evidence behind the "gaiatsu is dead" argument and considers how several recent changes in the international and domestic context of bilateral negotiations (the end of the Cold War, the establishment of the WTO, and the end of the LDP regime) may be limiting the effectiveness of American pressure on Japan.[47]

THE EVIDENCE

Showing that Clinton had less success with his demands for "results-oriented" trade deals than Bush did with his demands for increased public investment does *not* prove that foreign pressure has become less effective over time. Bush too had trouble achieving his objectives when he chose demands that were unsupported by allies within Japan. The best way to get at the question of whether gaiatsu has lost some of its "punch" is to compare cases, across time, that involved *similar U.S. demands*. Fortunately, both administrations made a variety of demands on Japan, and it is possible to compare and contrast similar pairs.

The first contrast, implicitly considered in the previous section, is between the "results-oriented" initiatives of the Reagan/Bush era and those of the Clinton administration. Both the Republican administrations extracted deals, the Semiconductor Accords of 1986 and 1991 and the auto parts deal of 1992, which called on Japan to attain specific foreign market shares and import volumes. These deals did not enjoy support within Japan, they all challenged to some degree the cozy ties between Japanese manufacturers and their networks of suppliers, and they all called on the Japanese government to influence private sector procurement practices. Nevertheless, Japan agreed to them because it faced strong pressure backed by threats of sanctions. In these cases, gaiatsu worked not "softly" by taking advantage of allies within the target country as in the SII cases but more roughly by threatening to impose costs on Japan high enough to offset the advantages of resisting the pressure.[48]

The Clinton administration clearly hoped that it would be able to extract similar (and even better) results-oriented deals through gaiatsu-as-threats. Initially, administration officials avoided making the threats explicit, putting off a decision on whether or not to reinstate Super 301. After the failure of the February 1994 summit, however, they moved to increase their leverage. First, in March, the administration reinstated Super 301, giving itself until September 30 before deciding whether to rename Japan under the provisions of that statute.[49] Then, after even this deadline passed without a deal on auto issues, the administration initiated Section 301 proceedings against Japan for barriers in the auto parts aftermarket—a step that set the stage for the decision to actually publish a retaliation hit-list in May 1995.

The hit-list was, in many respects, brilliantly designed—meeting most of the conditions for an effective threat as outlined in chapter 2. First, the costs it threatened to impose fell on exactly those actors within Japan who were in a position to deliver the concessions sought by the Clinton administration: the biggest Japanese automakers. Targeted were 13 luxury autos made by Toyota, Nissan, Honda, Mitsubishi, and Mazda—firms with annual exports of 200,000 high-profit vehicles at stake.[50] These enterprises were therefore forced to weigh the prospect of losing this business for a year or more (while the two nations fought about the sanctions before the WTO) against the costs of locking themselves into voluntary import expansion deals. Second, the threat was relatively credible since the *direct* costs of imposing it fell on a small group of luxury import auto dealers. While these dealers launched an aggressive campaign drawing attention to the likelihood that many would go out of business, their influence hardly compared with that of the Big Three auto firms and unions which were likely to gain from the sanctions threats.

That even this threat failed to extract more meaningful concessions from the Japanese automakers and government suggests that something in the broader context of the bilateral negotiations may be reducing the ability of the U.S. to make effective use of threats. The credibility of U.S. threats rested, not just on the *direct* costs and benefits at stake in the auto dispute, but also on the wider costs and benefits at issue: the costs both nations faced if the dispute spilled over to involve other areas of their relationship (security cooperation, other economic sectors, and the maintenance of the international trade order); and the benefits both nations might expect if a tough stand on the auto issue set precedents for other trading relationships. The results of the auto negotiations suggest that when these elements are factored in, the U.S. now has less leverage.

While we will come back to the question of how recent changes in contextual factors may be impeding the ability of the U.S. to use gaiatsu-as-threats, we first need to consider another pairing of similar demands which suggests that even the trusty strategy of participation expansion may not be working as well as it used to. During the sii talks, one area where this strategy worked well was on the issue of public investment—because politicians and spending bureaucrats were happy to use gaiatsu to expand their budgets and because the idea of expanded sewers and housing infrastructure appealed to the general public. Yet, when Clinton pressured Japan to adopt a bigger and delayed-offset income tax—an issue with similar appeal—he was largely unable to influence the Japanese policy process. If anything, the circumstances surrounding these issues should have favored Clinton. The fact that the Japanese economy was in a deep recession at the time Clinton was making his demands while it had still been booming when Bush was pushing for his public investment increase ought to have made Clinton's job easier. But the outcome was actually the reverse.

Treasury Department officials were pressuring the Japanese to adopt bigger and better fiscal stimulus packages from Day One of the Clinton Administration, but by the fall of 1993, their efforts were concentrated on a more specific goal: getting the government to move beyond public works projects to incorporate income tax cuts into the government's stimulus packages. Toward this end, Clinton wrote Hosokawa—in a letter timed to influence the deliberations of the Government Tax Commission—urging him to adopt a tax cut much larger than the 5–6 trillion yen cut that was then being discussed in the council. While Clinton did not recommend a specific figure, the administration reportedly was seeking a cut on the order of 10 trillion yen. In addition, Clinton urged Hosokawa to delay by three to four years any increase in the consumption tax designed to finance the tax cut—a move that would rob the income tax cut of its stimulative effect.[51]

While the government ultimately did adopt an income tax cut, its size and the manner in which it was implemented left it without much punch. The initial cut, announced by Hosokawa in February 1994, amounted to just 5.5 trillion yen and was limited to just one year after Hosokawa stumbled in his attempt (encouraged by MOF) to announce simultaneously a plan to increase the consumption tax to 7 percent. As Treasury Undersecretary Lawrence Summers pointed out during Congressional testimony, governments have found that income tax cuts that are just temporary tend to be saved rather than spent, providing less stimulus than cuts that are permanent. As a result, he predicted the Hosokawa cut would provide only "limited" stimulus.[52] Over the remaining months of 1994 (crucial months given that the economy was already three years into recession), the MOF held permanent income tax cuts hostage to its cherished aim of increasing the consumption tax rate.

Amazingly, the MOF managed to hold up approval of a permanent tax cut even after the Murayama cabinet, featuring leading advocates of an early and unconditional permanent tax cut, took over in June 1994. Takemura Masayoshi, the new Finance Minister, had broken with Hosokawa over his deference to MOF on the consumption tax, and he was intent on showing career officials in that ministry that he was the boss. Nevertheless, it took the new cabinet three months to come up with its tax plan, another two to push it through the Diet, and the plan ended up not very different from the one proposed by MOF officials at the start of the year. It still provided a cut of only 5.5 trillion yen, required Diet action to extend it beyond another year, and linked the income tax cut to a two-point hike in the consumption tax (from 3 to 5 percent) in 1997. It was estimated that this hike would completely offset the income tax cut once it went into effect.[53]

Given the small size of the cut, the delays, and the linkage to a consumption tax increase, it is difficult to credit American pressure with having done anything significant to bolster fiscal policy. Throughout the debate, MOF made every effort to limit American involvement, vetoing a visit by Treasury Undersecretary Summers to talk about the income tax cut in the fall of 1993 and making Ambassador Mondale wait a day before allowing him to set up a visit by Treasury Secretary Bentsen in the spring of 1994.[54] MOF made it clear throughout the process that it did not consider the tax cut a subject of international negotiations. By the end of the process, when the cabinet was debating alternatives and the Diet was passing the bills, few news articles even mentioned the U.S. position on the issue—in sharp contrast with the 430 trillion yen public works commitment coming out of sii where the press always made note of how the 10-year plan was the result of U.S. pressure.

Clinton's difficulty on this issue, compared to Bush's success on the public investment issue, signals that the strategy of participation expansion, like that of threats, is not working the way it used to. We now turn to an examination of how changes in the context of bilateral negotiations may be degrading the impact of foreign pressure across the board.

THE BILATERAL BALANCE OF POWER AND THE END OF THE COLD WAR

The first set of contextual factors we need to consider are those at the international level. As summarized in chapter 2, realists emphasize the importance of relative power in explaining the outcome of negotiations—suggesting that the Clinton team's difficulties compared to those of the Bush administration could be explained by changes over time in the two nations' relative power positions. Japan may have been able to stand up to the U.S. more often under Clinton simply because the U.S. has less leverage over Japan now than it did before. The rhetoric used by Japanese leaders in explaining their new-found eagerness to stand up to the U.S. certainly lends credence to this interpretation. Hosokawa, for example, pointed to the "maturing" relationship between the U.S. and Japan in his press conference comments after saying "no" to Clinton. Japan could now politely disagree with the U.S., he suggested, because it had matured from being a child to being a fellow "grown-up" on equal footing with the U.S.[55]

Careful reflection on the sources of American leverage and how these changed in the four-year interval between the Bush and Clinton initiatives provides us with some insights into why gaiatsu seems to have worked less effectively over time. Analysts of U.S.-Japan relations have long pointed to two sources of America's leverage over Japan: Japan's asymmetric interdependence on the U.S. export market and its similarly unbalanced dependence on the U.S. for protection from the Soviet military threat. Both of these sources of U.S. leverage have been affected by recent changes in the international system. My analysis below suggests, however, that changes in the "raw" power balance have been marginal at best, especially if one considers just the Bush-Clinton interval. To account for the seemingly abrupt decline in the effectiveness of U.S. pressure, we need to think in a more sophisticated way about how recent changes at the international level have affected U.S.-Japan negotiations—something the two-level game approach is better able to help us do.

Changes in the economic balance of power have been dramatic when measured over a period of decades. In 1970, Japan's exports to the U.S. accounted for 3 percent of its GNP at a time when American exports to Japan represented a barely noticed fraction of the U.S. economy (0.46 percent)—meaning that Japan's dependence on the U.S. market exceeded the inverse by a factor of 6.5. By 1990, however, America's exports to Japan had grown to 0.74 percent of the U.S. economy and the ratio of Japan's dependence to that of the U.S. had shrunk to just 3.5. This is just one measure of what Hosokawa was thinking of when he spoke of Japan having "grown up."

TABLE 9.1

Japanese and American Dependence on Bilateral Exports

Date	Japanese Exports to U.S. as share of Japan's GDP	Exports to Japan as share of U.S. GDP	Ratio
1983	3.1%	0.54%	5.7
1984	4.0	0.53	7.5
1985	4.2	0.48	8.8
1986	3.5	0.53	5.7
1987	3.0	0.53	5.7
1988	2.6	0.65	4.0
1989	2.7	0.72	3.8
1990	2.6	0.74	3.5
1991	2.3	0.71	3.2
1992	2.2	0.67	3.3
1993	2.1	0.64	3.3

Sources: Calculated based on OECD data.

The change over the interval between the Bush and Clinton administrations, however, has not been that significant. In the six years since 1988, the asymmetry ratio has declined just a few points, from 4.0 to 3.3. U.S. export dependence on Japan has remained fairly steady over this same period, ranging between 0.64 and 0.74 percent of U.S. GDP, while Japanese export dependence has declined only a little, from 2.6 percent of Japan's GDP in 1988 to 2.1 percent in 1993 (see table 9.1). These shifts are not large enough to account for the Clinton administration's difficulties.[56]

As noted earlier, shifts in asymmetries on the security side in the years between Bush and Clinton are potentially more dramatic given the sudden disappearance of the Soviet threat. One seeking to explain Japan's greater ability to refuse American demands might therefore point to how this change in the security environment has taken away one of the main reasons why Japan used to listen to the U.S. Because the Russians are less of a threat, Japan doesn't have to worry as much as it used to about whether the Americans will remove their security guarantee. Being less dependent on the U.S., it can afford to refuse American trade demands.

If it were true that the reduced Soviet threat to Japan was the only change in the equation, the above logic might explain the contrast between the results of the Bush and Clinton trade initiatives. A full accounting of how the asymmetries in the security relationship have changed suggests, however, that the power shifts in this area have been no more significant than those in the economic realm. First, one must remember that during the Cold War Japan depended on the U.S. not just for protection from the Soviets, but also for defense of the sea lanes that connect Japan to its sources of raw materials and for the maintenance of regional stability. Only one of these threats has been (largely) removed. The vulnerability of sea lanes remains a Japanese concern, especially after the Gulf War showed Japan that the end of the Cold War may only have increased the chance that similar regional wars could cut off its supplies of raw materials. Likewise, the recent standoff with North Korea over its nuclear program as well as the recent heating up of a regional arms race have reminded Japan that the end of the Cold War has only served to increase the potential for regional instability in Asia, leaving Japan still very dependent on the U.S.-Japan Security Treaty as its best defense against uncertain developments.[57] Japan may be somewhat less dependent on the U.S. than it was during the Cold War, but it remains very dependent.[58]

Second, one must remember that the U.S. too gained some room to maneuver as a result of the end of the Cold War. As long as the communist threat remained, the U.S. was forced to moderate its demands on Japan—the power derived from Japan's dependence on the U.S. was largely offset by its own dependence on Japan. Today, it retains important reasons to value Japan as an ally, but the "dependencies" that concern U.S. policymakers are a far cry from those that worried American Cold Warriors in the 1950s and 1960s when the "loss" of Japan was seen as something that had to be avoided at all costs.

Overall, it is probably true that *both* sides of the U.S.-Japan alliance no longer need the other as much as they used to. The continuing dependencies flowing both ways across a wide range of security and political issues makes it difficult, however, to support a conclusion that on balance the end of the Cold War has reduced the dependency of one side more than the other. As in the economic area, the shifts in "raw" power here have not been large enough to account for the recent decline in Japan's responsiveness to U.S. pressure.

That said, I am now going to argue that the end of the Cold War *has* contributed to the apparent decline in the effectiveness of U.S. pressure on Japan—not through shifts in "raw" power balances but through *the differing ways in which these events have been processed through the domestic politics of the two nations*. The two-level game approach emphasizes how even threats—though reliant on the ability of one nation to impose costs on another ("power")—are conditioned in important ways by politics at the domestic level. Threats will not be effective if officials in the target country perceive that they will not be ratified within the domestic arena of the issuing country. Likewise, the impact of threats depends on the degree to which those in the target nation perceive them to be "legitimate," as coming from an important ally on an issue which they see as "fair game."[59] Clinton's difficulties, I propose, derive in part from the ways in which the end of the Cold War has limited the impact of American threats through these "two-level" channels.

In the U.S., as noted earlier in this chapter, the end of the Cold War led Clinton to put more emphasis on America's foreign economic interests and to reorganize foreign policy institutions toward this end. Nevertheless, the political-security institutions privileged during the long Cold War proved remarkably resilient, intruding on economic officials' efforts to get tough with Japan at several points during the Framework negotiations and preventing *any* attempt to play the "security card" in an effort to extract a better trade deal.

We can see how American institutions biased the way security "interdependence" was translated into bargaining leverage by looking first at how the North Korean nuclear threat influenced the course of the Framework negotiations. Because the threat posed by this development

to the region's stability concerned both the U.S. and Japan, the two countries had taken pains to separate it from the Framework talks during most
of the first year of talks. On the same day the Clinton-Hosokawa summit
failed in February, the two leaders announced that they had agreed that
they would cooperate in efforts to force the North Koreans to accept
IAEA inspections of their nuclear sites.[60] By May, however, American officials in the State and Defense Departments had begun to worry that continued pressure on the Japanese would affect their willingness to stand
firm on economic sanctions against North Korea. Compared to the
strategic issues at stake in North Korea, one official reportedly
exclaimed, the economic issues at stake in the Framework talks were
"peanuts."[61] When the U.S. subsequently signed off on a statement for-
swearing "numerical targets" in an effort to jump start the talks, the
apparent softening of the U.S. position was partly attributed to these
American concerns about Japanese willingness to cooperate on North
Korea.[62]

Interestingly, there were no corresponding worries by the Japanese
that *U.S.* willingness to cooperate on North Korea would somehow be
affected by whether or not they chose to compromise in their trade talks.
Why not? Because American institutions, despite Clinton's modifica-
tions, allowed linkage to work in only one direction. Economic policy
might sometimes be compromised to maintain good security relations,
but security policy would never be used to extract concessions on economic issues. Japanese confidence that security leverage would not be
brought to bear on economic conflicts was only confirmed by what came
to be known as "the Nye initiative."

Starting in the fall of 1994, at a time when the auto talks were stale-
mated, Assistant Secretary of Defense Joseph Nye embarked on a campaign to repair what he and others in the political-security establishment
perceived to be an erosion in the bilateral security relationship. An advisory report written for the Japanese government had recommended that
the nation begin to think about building up its autonomous military capabilities and engaging more actively in multilateral peacekeeping operations as a hedge against a decline in U.S. willingness to maintain its security guarantee, and Nye saw this hedging strategy as potentially destabilizing. Japan needed to be reassured about the American commitment.[63]
He thus oversaw the production of a report outlining the Clinton administration's security strategy for East Asia in which the U.S. government
reversed its previous plan to reduce the number of American troops sta-

tioned in the region and committed to retaining "the existing level of about 100,000 troops, for the foreseeable future."[64] While the initiative succeeded in reassuring Tokyo about the U.S. security commitment to Japan, it simultaneously signalled the nation's trade negotiators that the U.S. was "unilaterally giving up its only real bit of leverage in dealing with its ruinous trade deficits."[65]

Reassured by the Nye Report and other evidence that linkage continued to operate only one way, even under Clinton, Japanese officials were able to discount U.S. threats. While administration officials on the economic side (Kantor and company) were saying that the U.S. would impose sanctions unless the Japanese agreed to put reference points like G-7 market shares and specific future auto part sales into trade agreements, Japanese officials could be confident that they could get the Americans to settle for deals without such firm "results" because administration officials on the political-security side would urge moderation. Despite the end of the Cold War, American institutions functioned in such a way as to prevent the U.S. from taking advantage of the increased room it may have had to pursue its economic interests with Japan.

In Japan, in contrast, the end of the Cold War was translated much more thoroughly into a new willingness on the part of Japan's bureaucrats and politicians to stand up to U.S. pressure. The political elite in Japan saw the Cold War as having frozen in place an attitude of deference toward the U.S. which was born at a time when the U.S. was very much the dominant partner. While Japan's economic power had grown in the interim, its attitude toward the U.S. remained largely unchanged. For many Japanese, especially the younger generation of bureaucrats and politicians, the end of the Cold War marked the end of an era: a time for Japan to assert its independence.

Ozawa Ichirō, the kingmaker behind both the Hosokawa and Hata cabinets, is typical of other younger-generation politicians in the way he emphasizes the significance of the end of the Cold War. The Cold War, he argued in an influential book published in 1993, stunted Japan's growth as a nation. Now that it was over, Japan needed to assert itself as a "normal nation." Among the specific artifacts of the Cold War that Ozawa urged abandoning was Japan's reliance on gaiatsu. "Normal nations," he asserted, do not "take action unwillingly as a result of 'international pressure.' "[66] Younger bureaucrats in ministries like MITI similarly saw the end of the Cold War as providing Japan with an opportunity to break its habit of always giving in to U.S. pressure.[67]

As in the U.S., there were elements on the Japanese side as well that saw how Japan continued to need the U.S. and thus urged moderation. When Clinton called on Japan to accept its proposals for "results-oriented" Framework talks in the summer of 1993, for example, MITI hardliners were overruled by Prime Minister Miyazawa and Ministry of Foreign Affairs officials who stepped in to support the compromise term "objective criteria."[68] Once talks began on separate issues like autos that were firmly within MITI's jurisdiction, however, MOFA had little ability to intervene and MITI hardliners held sway. In a political system oriented around the goal of rapid economic growth, MOFA had always had less influence than MITI. The end of the Cold War only marginalized the ministry even more and allowed MITI officials to take full advantage of the new latitude Japan had to redefine its relations with the U.S.

With institutions in Japan facilitating a shift in attitudes as a result of the end of the Cold War, American threats sparked more of a backlash than they had before. Gaiatsu from Japan's most important ally had been tolerated during the Cold War as something that could not be avoided. Absent that framework, however, U.S. pressure seemed much more grating, especially when the specific demands the U.S. was making were seen as a selfish attempt to use American political muscle to buy U.S. firms extra business. With the Cold War over, U.S. threats started to be seen in Japan more like they have long been seen in Europe—as bullying by the big kid on the block. Even big threats therefore made less of an impact on Japan than they would have earlier.

THE ESTABLISHMENT OF THE WORLD TRADE ORGANIZATION

Not only the international power balance but also the international rules changed in the interval between the Republican Japan initiatives and those of the Clinton administration. Most importantly, the nations of the world finally brought the Uruguay Round to a close in December 1993 and set up a new international institution: the WTO. Hard core realists would have us believe that institutions do not significantly influence the behavior of nation states,[69] but scholars in the neoliberal tradition point to a number of ways in which international institutions can alter how states pursue their interests: they can lengthen their time horizons and create iterated games; they can alter transaction costs (making cooperative moves less costly and uncooperative ones more so); they can create linkages between issues; and they can provide information.[70] If these neoliberals are right, something like the establishment of the WTO should have affected the outcome of U.S.-Japan bargaining. But how? The brief analysis of this question here suggests that changes in international rules too worked to limit the leverage of the United States under the Clinton administration—especially on the auto issue.

The change in rules arising out of the creation of the WTO that was of greatest relevance here was the adoption of new dispute settlement rules. Under the old GATT rules, any nation that didn't want another country to take a matter to GATT could indefinitely delay the establishment of a dispute panel. Furthermore, a nation that allowed a dispute settlement panel to be established but was not happy with a ruling could block the finding on appeal.[71] As a result, an American government that felt Japan had "nullified and impaired" its trade rights could not be sure Japan would allow a panel decision through the appeal process. Likewise, a Japanese government upset at the use of GATT-illegal unilateral sanctions would worry that the U.S. might block a dispute settlement ruling against it. The uncertainty involved in the process forced Japan to put up with American threats of sanctions and led the U.S. to rely on aggressive unilateral trade diplomacy to make Japan respect what it saw as its trade rights.

The new system that went into force with the establishment of the WTO in January 1995 eliminates the possibility of indefinite delay by setting up a strict timetable for the establishment of a dispute settlement panel once a nation makes a complaint. More importantly, it prevents the loser in a panel finding from blocking a ruling on appeal. Under the new rules, only a *consensus* of those on the appellate body can keep a panel finding from going into force. The WTO still cannot force nations to change their laws to bring them into line with panel rulings, but it can authorize the party whose trade rights are being violated to impose WTO-*legal* sanctions to compensate for its loss and force the offending party to modify its behavior.[72]

These changes, once they were agreed in December 1993, changed the way both the U.S. and Japan calculated the costs and benefits at stake in their disputes. On the Japanese side, the new dispute settlement rules created extra reasons to stand tough in the face of American sanction threats. The nation now had an opportunity, if the U.S. actually imposed sanctions, of taking the matter to the WTO and winning a ruling against America's unilateral trade laws.[73] This advantage was widely trumpeted by MITI officials at the time the Uruguay Round settlement was announced in December 1993. One official, for example, claimed that "unilateral U.S. actions using these laws [Section 301 and Super 301] will now be impossible where multilateral rules are established." He added that the new rules would make it "morally difficult" for the U.S. and Japan to reach results-oriented deals.[74]

As the Framework Talks bogged down, Japanese officials maneuvered to bring the new WTO rules to bear on the negotiations. After Clinton reinstated Super 301 in March 1994 (and even before the WTO was formally established), the Japanese announced that they would appeal to the WTO if the U.S. were to use unilateral trade laws like Super 301 to impose sanctions on Japan.[75] As the prospect that the Americans would actually impose sanctions grew in the spring of 1995, MITI officials visited WTO headquarters in Geneva to prepare the groundwork for a case against the U.S. and to determine exactly how quickly Japan could get the body to rule on the legality of American sanctions.[76] Finally, after Clinton announced his luxury auto sanctions threat, the Japanese government followed through with its promise, filing a formal complaint with the WTO and forcing the U.S. to conduct the remaining negotiating sessions in Geneva under WTO auspices.

Japan, however, was not the only party whose options were affected by the adoption of new international rules. The U.S. too now had improved prospects of winning a "nullification and impairment" case against Japanese practices that deprived it of trade rights granted when the nation lowered its tariffs. While the Clinton administration did not move as quickly as the Japanese to bring the WTO rules to bear on the negotiations, it did seek to counter Japanese plans to appeal to the WTO in May 1995 by announcing that the U.S. too would launch a case. The same day Clinton announced that the U.S. would be preparing a sanctions hit-list, Kantor notified WTO head Renato Ruggiero of U.S. plans to charge Japan with "actions and inactions with respect to the automotive sector" depriving it of its trade rights.[77] A few trade experts predicted that the U.S. might actually win this case.[78]

With both sides seeking advantage under a new and untested WTO dispute settlement process, there was already plenty of uncertainty about which side was advantaged by this change in the international rules. Yet another complicating factor, however, was the worry on both sides (and on the part of third parties) that forcing the WTO to deal with their high-stakes dispute when it was just getting established might damage the new international organization, preventing it from evolving into an effective means of enforcing liberal trading rules. Japan had to worry that if it was too successful—winning verdicts against U.S. unilateral sanctions and beating back American complaints about unfair trade practices—the U.S. might ignore WTO rulings and undermine the new institution's credibility.[79] Such an outcome would do nothing to stop U.S. unilateral aggression, the Japanese objective, and would risk undermining the carefully constructed Uruguay Round settlement. Even by winning, Japan might lose.[80] The U.S., however, also had reason to be concerned about such an outcome. Even if the WTO limited the nation's ability to employ its trade laws unilaterally, it had the potential to be an effective means of opening up a wide variety of markets where governments blatantly contravened world trading rules.

And finally, there were the third parties. With the future of the WTO at stake and the possibility that the U.S. and Japan might make a "results-oriented" deal at their expense, other nations—particularly those in Europe—could not sit idly by.[81] Led by EU trade commissioner Leon Brittan, these nations weighed in against America's unilateral sanctions and demands for "results," insisting that these tactics risked undermining the world trade order. When Japan and the U.S. met in Geneva for their final rounds of talks before the auto deal, Europe had a seat at the table. In addition, the WTO itself could not be considered a passive actor. The body, and its leader Ruggiero, wanted to preserve its influence and build its legitimacy, and given the difficulty of satisfying both parties in this dispute, that meant it wanted to avoid having to deal with a huge U.S.-Japan dispute in its first year.[82] Toward this end, Ruggiero used his discretion to propose that the American and Japanese complaints be handled simultaneously and over the maximum time allotted under WTO rules.

The intensity of activity surrounding the WTO in the endgame leading up to the auto dispute suggests that the new international institution did matter. Both sides, however, faced costs as well as benefits from pursuing the WTO option—along with a great deal of uncertainty. Japan might have a strong legal case, but it knew it could "lose by winning." It also faced added short-term costs due to Ruggiero's strategy of prolonging the dispute settlement process, and had to worry that the WTO might tailor a ruling in such a way as to avoid antagonizing the U.S.—perhaps by strongly criticizing informal barriers in the Japanese market.[83] The U.S. had to worry that it might lose its case, especially with the Europeans taking the Japanese side. Overall, my reading of the WTO impact is that the high degree of uncertainly and risk of damaging the institution acted to encourage both Japan and the U.S. to seek a negotiated settlement ahead of the sanctions deadline. This probably worked slightly in Japan's favor since it reduced the impact of U.S. threats. Japan had made it clear that it would take the U.S. to the WTO if it followed through on its threats—regardless of any damage this might do to the WTO. Japan knew that the U.S., faced with this choice, would seek a negotiated settlement. It therefore discounted the American threats, forcing the U.S. to accept a deal without meaningful "results."

THE END OF THE LDP REGIME

In chapter 4, extensive attention was devoted to the advantages gaiatsu enjoyed under the LDP regime. Due to the multimember electoral system, LDP backbenchers had unusually strong incentives to cater to particularistic interests, and so they organized themselves into zoku to protect policies that favored their clients. Compounding this tendency were the stable relations developed between turf-conscious ministries and the zoku in their jurisdiction over the long period of LDP rule. Although particularistic/protectionist policies hurt Japanese consumers and created friction with Japan's trading partners, LDP leaders and internationally oriented ministries were unable to modify such policies absent a "crisis" created by strong pressure from abroad. Gaiatsu-as-threats encountered less resistance from the Japanese because many elites recognized it was a "necessary evil" the system could not work without. The segmented structure of the system also made it well-suited to U.S. strategies of gaiatsu-as-participation expansion.

Given the advantages American pressure enjoyed under stable LDP rule, we are naturally led to ask whether changes that have taken place within Japanese politics since the summer of 1993 have influenced the degree to which old pressure tactics work on Japan. First, let us briefly review the changes. In June 1993, Prime Minister Miyazawa lost a vote of confidence in the Diet after a group of Dietmen from his own party deserted him. These deserters promptly established their own parties which, together with other opposition parties, deprived the LDP of a majority in the general election held the following month. From August 1993 to June 1994, Japan was then ruled by an anti-LDP coalition. While the LDP came back to power as part of a new ruling coalition that month, it continued for the duration of the Framework talks to rely on votes from its two coalition partners (including its long-time rival, the Socialists) to stay in power.

In the meantime, Japan also adopted a new electoral system and campaign finance reforms. In place of the old multimember system, Lower House Diet members are henceforth to be elected under a system that combines single-member districts (300 seats) with proportional representation (200 seats). At the same time, individual Dietmen will rely less on their own fund-raising efforts as the new system for public financing of parties goes into effect (along with some limits on corporate campaign donations to individual Diet members).

The combination of these institutional reforms with the end of stable LDP rule has clearly altered some of the fundamental features of the LDP regime. Although the LDP returned to office in 1994, no one took it for granted any longer that it would be able to hold onto power. The electoral reforms raised the uncertainty level by promising to magnify (in the single seat-districts) the impact of any future swing in party support. Absent the old assumption that the LDP would remain indefinitely in office, interest groups have begun to recognize that they have alternatives to that party.[84]

At the same time, incentives are now in place that encourage politicians to discard the old particularistic approach of catering to special-interest groups in an effort to solicit personal campaign funds and personal votes. In the single-member districts, they now need to win a plurality—not just the 15–20% that won them seats under the old system. Winning that many votes in the old way, with appeals to special interests and careful tending of the kōenkai, promises to be extremely expensive, and at least some politicians are likely to learn that they can much more cheaply appeal for votes with programmatic platforms catering to a broader cross-section of the public.[85] In addition, limits on corporate funding combined with public financing through the party headquarters reduce incentives for Diet members to cater to monied interests (at least relative to the incentives in place under the old regime).

These changes in the Japanese political system reduced the effectiveness of gaiatsu, first, by disrupting old routines that relied on participation expansion to widen Japanese win-sets. As noted above, the LDP regime (with its segmented policymaking process reliant on gaiatsu to offset its centrifugal tendencies) was perfectly suited to this strategy. U.S. officials had established relations with LDP bosses whom they could call on at the last minute to intervene with subgovernmental opponents of change to produce the concessions needed for a deal. The recent political changes meant, first, that many of these old contacts in the LDP were now out of the government, and second, that those who were in the government were often stretched too thin to devote time to resolving U.S.-Japan frictions. Just when U.S. Embassy was starting to get to know the new players in the summer of 1994, the Ozawa camp was thrown out of power.

During crucial stages of the Framework Talks, such as the month leading up to the February summit, the Americans tried to expand participation in the talks to include political bosses. As one U.S. negotiator
explained, "We had to get the negotiations out of the hands of the bureaucrats and into the hands of some senior politicians. The difficulty was:
which politicians, and how?"[86] My own interviews with U.S. officials
involved in the talks confirm that the Americans were largely frustrated
in their efforts to get politicians involved. Without the old, stable LDP
hierarchy of policy specialists and bosses, they could not identify which
Diet member had the power to intervene in specific sectors. In many
cases, there simply were no specialists or bosses to call upon. Part of the
explanation for the failure of the Clinton talks must therefore be ascribed
to such short-term difficulties created by political transition.

There is some evidence, however, that changes in the political system
may also have limited the effectiveness of the Clinton administration's
pressure tactics through their impact on *attitudes* toward gaiatsu. Part of
the reason why threats and persuasion worked on Japan in the past, I
argued above, derived from the old system's inability to generate policy
change *internally*, a characteristic that made gaiatsu a legitimate "necessary evil." While the new system had not yet produced significant internally generated policy change during the period of the Clinton talks,
there was in the immediate post-1993 period widespread optimism that
such self-reform was finally *possible*. No longer bound to a zoku-domi-
nated policymaking apparatus that attempted to maintain ties to the full
range of special-interest groups, new forces calling for across-the-board
deregulation, market liberalization, and a more visible role of Japan in
world affairs had sought to assert themselves—not by taking advantage of
gaiatsu but by seeking power and influence within a more fluid Japanese
political system.

At the center of all of this (again) was Ozawa, the man whose views
on the meaning of the end the Cold War were cited above. Because the
end of the Cold War made gaiatsu no longer appropriate as a crutch,
Ozawa argued, Japan needed political reforms so that the nation could
deal with its policy problems on its own.[87] Very much as I argued in
chapter 4, Ozawa claimed that the old electoral system was largely to
blame for the corruption and special-interest orientation of Japanese
politics which left the policy process so immobile. Electoral reform, he
proposed, would encourage parties to compete through programmatic
appeals to broad public interests, restoring "responsibility" to Japanese

politics and making real policy change a possibility. Regardless of whether electoral reform really *is* changing Japanese politics as Ozawa predicted, at the height of the reform movement, when Clinton was attempting to use gaiatsu the old fashioned way, many Japanese believed the rhetoric and felt that Japan really *could* deal with its problems on its own. Ozawa himself succeeded in riding this wave to the point where he was able to realize his vision of unifying the ragtag group of LDP splinter groups and old opposition parties into *Shinshintō*, a party large enough to challenge the LDP.

What matters when it comes to attitudes toward gaiatsu, I propose, is expectations, and at least during the 1993–1995 period when the Clinton Framework Talks were under way, expectations about what the Japanese political system could accomplish on its own had begun to change. As old assumptions about the impossibility of overcoming the opposition of protected special interests without foreign pressure began to fade, there was a corresponding decline in the legitimacy of American pressure. Evidence that gaiatsu had lost some of its legitimacy comes in the form of reports emanating from both camps about the attitudes of Japanese officials during the Framework Talks. Negotiators with experience in previous rounds of trade talks reported that Ministry of Foreign Affairs officials, for example, took a much harder line than they had in the past—when they often welcomed foreign pressure. As one MOFA official told me, "the day of gaiatsu has past. The rice issue was really the last issue where we really needed to use gaiatsu. The rest we can deal with on our own."[88]

With Japanese officials adopting such positions, it should come as no surprise that U.S. pressure tactics relying on threats did not produce concessions the way they had in the past. The reinstatement of Super 301 in March 1994, the threat to initiate sanctions procedures over the government procurement issue in July of that year, and the threat of the largest sanctions ever imposed under U.S. trade law in the leadup to the auto deal, barely budged the Japanese from the negotiating positions they started with in early 1993.

Conclusion

At this point readers who have waded through the entire chapter are probably shaking their heads and saying, "no wonder Clinton failed." First the President chose as his core negotiating objective a demand for "results-oriented" trade deals, which had absolutely no support within Japan, ruling out from the start the use of a strategy of participation expansion that had worked on some issues for the Bush administration. Compounding his difficulties, he had to operate in an international environment which, because of the end of the Cold War and creation of the WTO, was less suited to the old strategy of unilateral threats. Finally, both tactics worked less well because of disruptions and changed attitudes accompanying domestic political reforms inside Japan. To this list we should probably add one other factor. Clinton suffered from having to make his pitch for "results" *after* previous administrations (and his own) had turned Japanese off to this approach by trying to turn "goals" and "voluntary plans" into iron-clad market-share and sales guarantees.

The length of this list is not well-suited to the purpose of sorting out *which* of these factors was most important. The whole exercise would have been much simpler (and, in some ways, fit in better with the arguments developed in the SII chapters) if *only* the Clinton administration's demands had been different. As it is, the administration's failure is way overdetermined. That the biggest and most recent attempt to employ gaiatsu to force Japan to accept U.S. demands doesn't generate the neatest social scientific results should not, however, keep us from reflecting on how the full variety of factors determining the effectiveness of foreign pressure operated in this case.

What the analysis in this chapter adds to that in the previous ones is a stress on the importance of *contextual* factors—as well as *issue-specific* ones—in determining the effectiveness of pressure tactics. That the domestic politics of specific issues is important in determining which demands (within a given bilateral relationship) succeed should not blind us to the fact that changes in international power balances, in international institutions, and domestic political systems can affect the way pressure works across a wide range of cases involving the same two parties. The results of the Clinton talks suggest: (1) that the end of the Cold War has led Japanese to change the way they look at American threats— reducing the effectiveness of this tactic across the board; (2) that the establishment of the WTO has improved Japan's "no agreement" options somewhat by giving it an opportunity to appeal to a dispute settlement panel if it is subject to sanctions—again reducing the impact of unilateral threats across the range of issues covered by WTO rules; and (3) that the end of the LDP regime and accompanying political reforms gave Japanese enough confidence in their ability to generate policy change internally that they no longer viewed gaiatsu as a "necessary evil" like they used to—reducing the impact of both threats and participation expansion. While it is impossible to definitively rank order these factors in terms of their impact, my reading of the evidence ranks them first, second, and third as listed above.

While directing us to think about factors other than issue politics when analyzing the politics of international bargaining, my analysis of how recent changes in the domestic and international context of the U.S.-Japan relationship seems to be limiting the efficacy of gaiatsu also has important practical implications. The Clinton administration should not have assumed that tactics that worked in the past (as when the Reagan administration came up with the Semiconductor Accords) would work again. The context had changed. Similarly, when thinking about the "lessons" we draw from the Bush and Clinton administration's Japan initiatives, we need to be sensitive to the fact that the world is changing and that it will continue to change. We will turn to that task in the next chapter.

10 CONCLUSIONS

As indicated by its subtitle, this book has aimed to answer one straightforward question: what American pressure on Japan can and cannot do. In order to answer this question, we first drew on insights from Putnam's two-level game approach for clues as to which pressure tactics under what conditions were likely to be most effective. Then, in seven empirical chapters, we examined the major Japan initiatives of the last two American administrations. Now it is time to reflect on what the empirical record of successful and failed American attempts to extract concessions from Japan tells us about the utility of the approach we employed and what "theory" and practice combined tell us about the practical question that motivated this book. Once we have an answer to the question of what American pressure *can* do, we will turn to the more normative question of what America *should* do.

Insights into the Nature of International Negotiations

If the theoretical assumptions that guide policy are flawed, I argued in chapter 1, it is useful to question not just the policy but the theory that unlies it as well. Most works offering advice on how America should deal with the "Japan Problem" do not explicitly deal with the question of whether the trade deals they recommend can actually be negotiated, but those that do generally assume Japan will act as a unitary rational actor and that therefore it can be induced to accept American demands if only the threats are strong and credible enough. This certainly seems to be the guiding philosophy behind Congressional demands for new and better trade laws employed in an ever more forceful manner.

Rather than accepting this logic, however, this book began by questioning whether realism, with its assumptions that states can be expected to act "as if" they are unitary rational actors and that relative power considerations motivate and determine the outcome of negotiations, is really very useful in explaining the results of real-world negotiations and offering guidance to real-world policymakers.[1] Finding reasons to doubt the utility of realism, I drew instead on the negotiation-analytic approach in general and especially Robert Putnam's two-level game metaphor for international negotiations in order to construct a more complex framework for understanding when and how foreign pressure is likely to be effective in extracting unilateral concessions. The record of U.S. attempts to pressure Japan during the Bush and Clinton administrations, surveyed in the empirical chapters, confirms the superiority of this approach in explaining the actual results of bilateral bargaining and thus suggests that it is likely to be more useful in guiding policymakers.

In the sections that follow, I highlight the ways in which the case studies of the SII and Framework Talks confirm the insights of the modified Putnam approach while introducing for the first time additional evidence, some drawn from studies of U.S. attempts to pressure countries *other than Japan*, that reinforces the importance of recognizing how negotiations work as "two-level games."

Raw Power has Little to do with the Outcome of Negotiations. The selection of the SII talks as the primary focus of this book prejudiced us toward a finding that power by itself does not tell us much about whether pressure will result in concessions in any given case. As noted from the beginning of this book, these talks involved the same two nations negotiating at the same time over five issues which produced markedly different degrees of Japanese concessions—telling us right away that, with relative power as a constant, realism was not going to be of much use in explaining the significant variation in negotiating outcomes over this set of cases. The empirical chapters on specific SII issues reinforced this message by detailing how similar American pressure was picked up and "used" in some cases, resulting in meaningful policy change, while it was firmly resisted in others.

The consideration of U.S.-Japan cases separated by a period of a few years in chapter 9 offered us more of an opportunity to see whether changes in relative power balances over time might tell us something about negotiating outcomes, but the conclusion that neither economic nor security-dependence-derived power balances had changed enough in the interim to account for the apparent decline in gaiatsu effectiveness led us once again to focus on other issue-specific and contextual factors to account for the variation. The end of the Cold War affected relative bargaining power, we concluded, but not by enhancing one side's "raw" power by making it significantly less dependent on the other. Instead, the critical role was played by domestic institutions in the two nations that processed the end of the Cold War differently.

Given the lack of meaningful variation in "raw power" over the cases surveyed in this volume, critics will no doubt object that it did not really test whether this factor—though clearly not explaining all of the variation in negotiating outcomes—might not still account for some degree of variation *when power balances vary more markedly*. In fact, a comprehensive survey of U.S. attempts to pressure a wide variety of nations (including Japan) through the use of Section 301 of U.S. trade law concluded that raw power as measured by the target nation's dependence on the U.S. export market *does* emerge as a "significant" explanatory factor. In cases where American pressure proved successful in achieving U.S. objectives, nations depended on exports to the U.S. for an average of 7.5 percent of their GNP, while in unsuccessful cases nations depended on the U.S. market for only 4.3 percent of their GNP—a difference that proved significant to the 95 percent level in the authors' regression analysis.[2]

While the findings of this study by Thomas Bayard and Kimberly Ann Elliott provide evidence that raw power does skew results of negotiations in the predicted direction, their study also offers substantial support for the argument that negotiating outcomes depend on much more than just this factor. Table 10.1 reports the authors' evaluation of the degree to which the U.S. was successful in achieving its negotiating objectives in 301 cases involving some of America's most important trading partners.[3] Notably, outcomes of U.S. negotiations varied significantly for each bilateral relationship, much as in the SII cases, even though in each bilateral relationship "raw power" was by and large constant over the cases. U.S. pressure on Europe, for example, produced no or only nominal success 13 out of 20 times, but proved to be largely successful in two cases and resulted in partial success five times. Cases with Canada also ranged from no success at all to largely successful.[4] That the effectiveness of U.S. pressure varied widely for all of these trading partners suggests that factors other than raw power (such as those emphasized in this book) greatly influence the outcome of negotiations in any given case.

TABLE 10.1
Outcomes of U.S. Pressure as Evaluated by Bayard & Elliott

Cases involving *Japan*	Degree to Which U.S. Objective Achieved
Thrown silk (1977–78)	Largely successful
Leather (1977–85)	Partially successful
Cigars (1979–81)	Nominally successful
Pipe tobacco (1979–81)	Nominally successful
Semiconductors (1985–91)	Nominally successful
Cigarettes (1985–86)	Largely successful
Citrus (1988)	Largely successful
Construction (1988–91)	Partially successful
Satellites (1989–90)	Largely successful
Supercomputers (1989–90)	Partially successful
Wood products (1989–90)	Partially successful

Cases involving *E.C.*	Degree to Which U.S. Objective Achieved
Egg albumin (1975–80)	Partially successful
Canned fruit and vegetables (1975–79)	Nominally successful
Malt (1975–80)	Not at all successful
Wheat flour (1975–83)	Not at all successful
Canned fruit (1976–80)	Nominally successful
Soybeans and soy meal (1976–79)	Nominally successful
Citrus (1976–86)	Partially successful
Wheat (1978–80)	Nominally successful
Sugar (1981–82)	Not at all successful
Poultry (1981–84)	Nominally successful
Pasta (1981–87)	Partially successful
Canned fruit and raisins (1981–85)	Nominally successful
Corn, sorghum, oilseeds (1986–87)	Largely successful
Meatpacking (1987–89)	Not at all successful
Beef (1987–89)	Not at all successful
Soybeans (1987–90)	Nominally successful
Fabricated copper (1988–90)	Largely successful
Canned fruit (1989)	Partially successful
Corn, sorghum, oilseeds (1990)	Partially successful
Meatpacking (1990–93)	Nominally successful

Cases involving *Canada*	Degree to Which U.S. Objective Achieved
Eggs (1975–76)	Largely successful
Broadcasting (1978–84)	Not at all successful
Fish (1986–90)	Partially successful
Beer (1990–93)	Nominally successful

Cases involving *Brazil*	Degree to Which U.S. Objective Achieved
Footwear (1982–85)	Partially successful
Soybean oil and meal (1983–85)	Partially successful
Informatics (1985–89)	Partially successful
Pharmaceuticals (1987–90)	Nominally successful
Import licensing (1989–90)	Largely successful
Intellectual property (1993–94)	Nominally successful

Cases involving *Argentina*	Degree to Which U.S. Objective Achieved
Marine insurance (1979–80)	Nominally successful
Leather (1981–82)	Not at all successful
Air couriers (1983–89)	Partially successful
Soy bean oil and meal (1986–88)	Partially successful
Pharmaceuticals (1988–89)	Nominally successful

Cases involving *Korea*	Degree to Which U.S. Objective Achieved
Insurance (1979–80)	Nominally successful
Footwear (1982–85)	Partially successful
Insurance (1985–86)	Partially successful
Intellectual property (1985–86)	Nominally successful
Cigarettes (1988)	Partially successful
Beef (1988–90)	Partially successful
Wine (1988–89)	Partially successful

Cases involving *Taiwan*	Degree to Which U.S. Objective Achieved
Home appliances (1976–77)	Largely successful
Rice (1983–84)	Partially successful
Motion picture films (1983–84)	Partially successful
Customs valuation (1986)	Partially successful
Beer, wine, tobacco (1986)	Partially successful
Intellectual property (1992)	Nominally successful

Cases involving *India*	Degree to Which U.S. Objective Achieved
Almonds (1987–88)	Partially successful
Investment (1989–90)	Not at all successful
Insurance (1989–90)	Not at all successful
Intellectual property (1991–92)	Not at all successful

Source: Bayard and Elliott, *Reciprocity and Retaliation in U.S. Trade Policy.*

Bayard and Elliott's data also show how the responsiveness of *nations* varies in ways that cannot be explained by "raw power." As figure 10.1 shows, the responsiveness of many nations lies well off the regression line which plots where it "should" be based on the level of its dependence on the U.S. export market. Canada, while it relies on the U.S. export market for 14.7 percent of its GDP, is only a little more responsive than the European Community, which relies on U.S. exports for only 1.6 percent of its GDP. Japan, on the other hand, shows up as the major outlier on the responsive side, giving in most often to U.S. pressure even though its export dependence (3.55 percent) was much lower than several of America's other major trading partners. This figure suggests again that factors other than raw power (such as cross-national variation in domes-

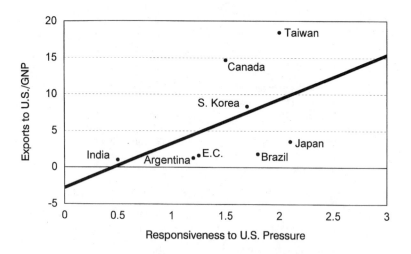

FIGURE 10.1 Responsiveness to U.S. Pressure of Major Trading Partners

Note: Responsiveness Index constructed on scale of 0 to 3 using data in Table 10.1 with "not at all successful" cases weighted as "0" up through "largely successful cases weighted as "3". Export to GNP ratio is based on OECD and CIA World Factbook data.

tic political systems and attitudes toward U.S. pressure) also influence the outcome of negotiations.[5]

Bayard and Elliott thus confirm this book's finding that realist "power" explains only a little of the variation in the outcomes of international bargaining. As we will see, they also offer corroboration of some of this study's conclusions about how strategy and domestic politics have much more to tell us about how negotiations will turn out.

Pressure works best when conditions support the use of one or more synergistic strategies. In chapter 2, I hypothesized that it is synergy and not brute force that gets nations to respond to pressure. The record of U.S. attempts to pressure Japan during the SII and Framework talks confirms this prediction. In terms of brute force, it is hard to conceive of a sanction threat much more brutish than Clinton's threat to impose prohibitive tariffs on $5.9 billion worth of Japanese luxury cars. Yet, as we saw in chapter 9, this threat produced no real concession toward the main U.S. demand for a "results-oriented" deal. In contrast, when the Americans made demands that worked well with Japanese politics, as in the case of some SII issues, pressure produced greater movement toward U.S. negotiating objectives.

One tactic that worked especially well for the U.S. when its demands enjoyed latent support within Japan was *participation expansion*. In chapter 4, I argued that the Japanese political system—at least as it operated under stable LDP rule—was particularly well suited to this strategy. The system suffered from a tendency toward immobilism that made LDP leaders and others who recognized the need for economic liberalization reliant on gaiatsu to provide the excuse they needed to confront defenders of the status quo within the party and its support coalition. When the U.S. made demands, domestic actors who supported the U.S. position for their own reasons were able to use foreign pressure to secure for themselves a place in a policymaking process from which they had previously been excluded.

During SII, the U.S. government consciously set out to choose demands that enjoyed support within Japan, and this strategy bore fruit on the Large Store Law, public investment, and to a degree on the issue of agricultural land tax reform. In each case, domestic actors (MITI and the large stores on the LSL; LDP politicians and the spending ministries on public investment; MOF on the land tax) supported the U.S. demands and were successfully able to assert their influence once gaiatsu gave them an excuse to get involved. With the media generally sympathetic to

American demands in these areas, gaiatsu also increased the awareness of the unorganized general public and gave political leaders like Prime Minister Kaifu reason to assert themselves on their behalf.

This tactic did not work as consistently for Clinton, we noted in chapter 9, but it did continue to work to some degree. The U.S. cause was assisted during the cellular phones dispute, I argued, by support from influential firms like Toshiba and Matsushita while MITI once again proved to be an ally on liberalizing regulation of the auto parts aftermarket.

In contrast, U.S. pressure was largely ineffective—however forceful its demands—when America had no allies. On the keiretsu issue during SII and on "quantiative criteria" during the Clinton talks, the U.S. had literally no support within Japan, and in both cases Japan was able to hold out completely in the face of American pressure. Similarly, the weakness of the one U.S. ally on the antitrust issue (the JFTC) prevented the Americans from extracting meaningful concessions on this issue as well.

We did not encounter many examples of the strategy I called *alternative specification*, but the case of land policy during SII suggested its potential. In this case, Japan had a clear problem in search of a solution, and the U.S. was able to influence to some degree the way in which policy ideas already being considered in expert policy communities within Japan were linked together and to this recognized problem. When the U.S. proposed policies that were not even being considered within Japanese policy communities and were addressed at no recognized "problem" (e.g. limits on cross-shareholding; a strong private damage remedy under the AML), U.S. pressure proved totally unsuccessful.

Finally, in chapter 2 we hypothesized that even *threats* had to "work well" with domestic politics. Indeed, the Japanese political system under the LDP and during the Cold War was unusually well-suited to this strategy as well. The reliance of the LDP-dominated system on gaiatsu led many elites to regard it as a "necessary evil" and the extended Cold War nurtured deferential attitudes on the part of Japanese officials toward their Superpower patron—both giving U.S. threats enough "legitimacy" to minimize the backlash similar threats would encounter when targeted at other nations. When U.S. threats met other conditions specified in chapter 2 (when they were credible because Japanese perceived that they would be ratified within U.S. politics; when the costs they threatened to impose fell on actors within Japan that were able to deliver the concessions at issue), they were able to extract concessions from Japan even when U.S. demands enjoyed little support within Japan. Though these deals were only briefly discussed in this book, the 1986 semiconductor accords and 1992 auto deal are examples of how gaiatsu-as-threats worked with Japan.

That threats don't work when they lack synergy was shown by the example of Clinton's auto sanctions. Even though the administration's hit list was constructed to maximize the costs imposed on Japanese actors able to deliver concessions and minimize costs imposed on U.S. actors able to block sanctions, the threat failed to yield meaningful concessions. This lack of "results" stemmed, I argued, from new attitudes toward gaiatsu in Japan resulting from changes in the international and domestic context (the end of the Cold War; the establishment of the WTO; and the end of the LDP regime) that made unilateral American threats less legitimate in the eyes of Japanese and prevented them from working as they had in the past.

Given that the analysis in this book was based exclusively on U.S.-Japan cases, critics may question whether its finding that synergy is more important than brute force was biased by the narrow sample. Again, the recent study of Bayard and Elliott offers evidence confirming the insights of this book and suggesting its broader relevance. Examining the results of America's 301 cases against the full range of trading partners, the authors repeatedly emphasize that "a vocal constituency for change in the target country" is a critical factor determining whether pressure will be successful in a given case.[6] "*Positive* participation expansion" of the kind I describe in this book, they find, tends to be a very effective strategy. They actually cite my earlier published work on the SII talks in developing this argument.[7] In contrast, when they test for the impact of what they call "*negative* participation expansion" (which relies on sanctions "hit lists" to mobilize constituencies in the target country), they find such tactics produce no improvement in the terms of trade deals.[8]

While Bayard and Elliott emphasize domestic-issue politics much as I do in this book, they do not consider why some *nations* are more responsive than they "should" be (see figure 10.1 above) or how attitudes toward foreign pressure and domestic political institutions play an important role in determining the overall responsiveness of a given nation. My analysis of U.S.-Japan cases, by emphasizing how politics under the old LDP regime was especially suited to the exercise of U.S. pressure, explains Japan's unusual responsiveness as seen in their data but left unexplained in their analysis. In this sense, my study offers a deeper understanding of the conditions that make pressure more or less effective. While we can only speculate at this point, it may be that similar domestic political and attitudinal factors explain why Canada and Brazil are located well off the regression line.[9]

Domestic political actors can manipulate and use international negotiations for their own purposes. If international negotiations truly operate like a two-level game, we noted in chapter 2, players at the domestic level— and not just government negotiators—ought to have strategic options. Since this implication of Putnam's two-level game has been little studied, we set out in this book to use our case studies to determine if domestic actors really *do* reach across international boundaries and seek to use foreign pressure to secure domestic objectives. The answer is a resounding yes. Furthermore, my analysis of how pressure was translated into policy change in the specific SII issue areas demonstrates how this kind of behavior can significantly distort the way foreign pressure operates.

In chapter 3, we saw how Japanese officials in specific ministries and even executives in specific firms began maneuvering even before the SII talks got underway to influence the U.S. negotiating agenda to make sure pressure would serve their domestic purposes. Then, as talks progressed, actors in every SII issue area set out to twist foreign pressure to their own ends. The JFTC convinced American negotiators to include on their list of demands such objectives as a reduction in exemptions from resale price maintenance restrictions which, as argued in chapter 8, did not serve U.S. objectives at all. MITI officials similarly conspired to use the pressure they faced on the LSL to get a deal that would allow them to secure funds for revitalizing shopping districts while simultaneously increasing their ability to use the law as a "stick" to encourage shōtengai to modernize.

The problem was that America's "allies" on all of these issues had goals that differed in subtle but nevertheless important ways from those of the U.S. In the area of competition policy, the JFTC wanted to strengthen its ability to fight price cartels, but it wasn't that interested in going after the kinds of vertical restraints that were the most important barrier to foreign imports. On land tax policy, MOF didn't mind using foreign pressure as an extra excuse to establish new sources of revenue and close tax loopholes, but it didn't really care if these changes went far enough to eliminate market distortions. On the Large Store Law, MITI cared more about modernization than it did about liberalization. And on public investment, the politicians and spending bureaucrats were happy to use pressure to extract extra resources from MOF, but they didn't care whether these funds came from bonds (the U.S. preference) or tax revenue (MOF's choice).

Especially at the implementation stage after SII deals had been struck, differences between American goals and those of the Japanese ministries were critical. U.S. officials, though still involved in monitoring the deal, had less leverage, so Japanese bureaucrats were able to twist policy further to favor their own objectives. By diverting pressure to serve their own aims, domestic actors drained American pressure of some of its impact—even as they were helping the U.S. win concessions.

By confirming that domestic actors too act strategically, the empirical material in this book offers additional proof that real-world international negotiations operate more like two-level games than like the realist game of billiards. States, the U.S.-Japan cases considered in this book make clear, *do not* act "as if" they are unitary or rational. More importantly, the cases show how the two-level game approach, by relaxing these assumptions, is better able to recognize the host of ways in which the *nonunitary* nature of states conditions the effectiveness of cross-level strategies— strategies that in turn do much to determine the distributional terms of negotiations. On some issues, domestic divisions create *opportunities* for strategies like participation expansion—such that pressure will produce *more* of a response than a realist approach would predict. At other times, domestic politics will *constrain* the effectiveness of foreign pressure by producing more of a backlash—such that pressure will produce much *less* of a response than a realist would predict. Only an approach that takes domestic politics out of the black box and examines how it conditions the effectiveness of pressure tactics can provide the kind of guidance policymakers need when trying to figure out what they can and cannot achieve through pressure.

What American Pressure on Japan Can and Cannot Do

Much of this book has been devoted to identifying what U.S. pressure *cannot* do. Both the two-level game approach and the experiences of the Bush and Clinton administrations demonstrate how U.S. pressure tactics are constrained. Participation expansion will not work when U.S. demands lack domestic support inside Japan. Alternative specification will not work when there is no recognized domestic "problem" in search of a solution. And threats—even when coming from a more "powerful" nation—will not work if they are perceived to be illegitimate and/or if they are judged unlikely to be ratified.

The frustrating experience of the Clinton administration, in particular, points to the limits of gaiatsu. Clinton chose as his most important demand one that had no support inside Japan. On top of this, he had to contend with changes in the context of U.S.-Japan negotiations that made the environment more hostile to the use of unilateral American pressure: the end of the Cold War led the Japanese to rethink their habit of giving in to the U.S.; the establishment of the WTO gave Japanese officials the opportunity to challenge American threats under the strengthened dispute settlement mechanism; and post-1993 reforms in domestic political institutions led to increasing confidence on the part of the Japanese that the nation could deal with its own problems without gaiatsu. All of these changes made continuing American attempts to extract concessions the old-fashioned way seem illegitimate and stiffened the resolve of Japanese negotiators to the point that they were able to stare down repeated sanctions threats and force the U.S. to settle for mediocre deals without meaningful "results."

That Japan has begun to stand up to U.S. threats should not have come as a surprise to Clinton administration officials. The changes in the context of U.S.-Japan negotiations, they should have noticed, made Japan much more like other nations. And other nations (as we saw in figure 10.1) are generally much less responsive to unilateral U.S. pressure. If it is true, as Clinton's experience suggests, that Japan is becoming more of a "normal" country, this means it is likely to be less and less responsive to U.S. pressure—making this study's conclusions about the *constraints* on the effective use of foreign pressure more relevant than ever.

But what about the study's "positive" lessons about conditions that create *opportunities* for the use of pressure? If anything, the likelihood that Japan will be less responsive to gaiatsu means U.S. officials will need to be more selective in choosing their demands, thinking more than ever about how best to frame and present their demands so that they will "work well" with domestic politics. Unilateral threats in particular are least likely to produce results, and so policymakers will need to consider other alternatives. Below I summarize the lessons we can draw about what American pressure still *can* do for each of the major strategies discussed in this book, based on the two-level game approach and the experience of the last two American administrations.

THREATS

Threats will work, the two-level game approach tells us, if they promise to impose high enough costs on the right domestic actors in the target country, are seen as ratifiable and otherwise credible, and are perceived as legitimate. Meeting all of these conditions for the effective use of threats with Japan, the Clinton administration found, was not easy—especially given how recent changes in the international and domestic context of the relationship have changed the way Japanese look at unilateral American bullying. Rather than suggesting that America give up entirely on threats, however, this experience signals a need for the U.S. to shift tactics from aggressive *unilateralism* to what is being termed "aggressive *multilateralism*." By working *through* rather than against the WTO dispute settlement mechanism, the U.S. should be able to continue to use threats as a viable bargaining tactic with Japan.[10]

The main reason why threats made through the WTO process are likely to be more effective with Japan is because they will enjoy much greater legitimacy. Clinton's auto sanctions were viewed as illegitimate partly because they were being imposed by the U.S. outside the WTO process. The U.S. had insisted throughout the Uruguay Round that its aggressive use of Section 301 and Super 301 was necessary to enforce America's trade rights because the GATT did not have an effective multilateral process. While making such complaints, the U.S. had pushed hard for the new and stronger multilateral procedures, offering its trading partners an implicit bargain: if they would agree to a stronger *multilateral* dispute settlement mechanism, the U.S. would limit its use of *unilateral* pressure.[11] That the U.S. was still using its trade laws to make unilateral threats even after the WTO procedures went into effect was for Japanese officials a sign of American duplicity. It was completely unacceptable.

Threats made through the WTO, in contrast, would not encounter such a visceral reaction. On the contrary, having pressured the U.S. to work through the WTO, Japanese officials would be under strong moral pressure to comply with the ruling of any WTO dispute panel. Being "neutral," such panels would be seen as fairer in Japan—unlike the situation under unilateral U.S. trade laws where the U.S. presented itself as both prosecutor and judge. Finally, American pressure exerted through the WTO would gain added legitimacy to the extent the U.S. itself submitted to WTO rulings. The legitimacy advantage of switching from aggressive unilateralism to aggressive multilateralism would completely "turn around" a factor that had been a disadvantage for Clinton during the auto dispute. It would also go some way toward substituting for the lost legitimacy American gaiatsu used to enjoy during the Cold War and under the LDP regime.

While I emphasize the "legitimacy advantage" of a multilateral approach here, it is also important to recognize the other ways in which such an approach would augment the impact of threats. While the new WTO dispute settlement process made it possible for Japan to challenge unilateral U.S. sanctions during the auto dispute, they do not allow Japan to challenge sanctions authorized through the formal WTO process.[12] Though Japan could still counter-retaliate against WTO-authorized U.S. sanctions, it would be very unlikely to do so given the damage such action would do not only to U.S.-Japan relations but to Japan's standing in the world and the stability of the liberal trading order. The fact that counter-retaliation would be much less likely would enhance the credibility of U.S. threats and make them more effective. Furthermore, credibility would also be enhanced because the U.S. (if it succeeds in winning WTO authorization for sanctions) would be under strong pressure from domestic forces to pursue its advantage and impose the authorized sanctions unless the Japanese agreed to acceptable concessions.[13]

While threats made through the WTO are likely to have more impact for all of the above reasons, they cannot be seen as *the* solution to the "Japan Problem." If readers get one message from this book, it should be the pessimistic one that there is *no* easy solution. First, given that a WTO-imposed solution would still be accepted by Japan under duress, there is every likelihood that bureaucrats in that nation would divert and distort the actual implemented policy change at least as much as they did with the SII issues. Second, the U.S. will only be able to use multilateral gaiatsu to challenge Japanese trade barriers that are covered under WTO rules. If the U.S. can prove that the Japanese government contravened rules against non-tariff barriers like subsidies or discriminatory health and safety standards, it is very likely to win Japanese concessions without even pressing matters to the point of sanctions. But if it tries to target informal barriers like keiretsu networks or closed distribution systems that are not covered under WTO rules, Japan is no more likely to yield than it would be under unilateral pressure. Finally, the U.S. will not be able to press its advantage too far even in areas that *are* covered by WTO rules lest its aggressiveness worry too many of its trading partners (the EC and the big developing nations, for example) to the point that this puts the WTO at risk. Because a strategy relying on multilateral threats, for all of these reasons, is likely to prove effective only on some issues, the U.S. will have to employ other strategies as well.

PARTICIPATION EXPANSION

This tactic can make a difference, the two-level game approach and our cases show, when pressure is able to bring into the policy process previously excluded domestic actors who support U.S. demands for their own reasons. As we saw with the SII talks, the strategy proved largely successful in helping the U.S. achieve its negotiating objectives in the areas of public investment and the Large Store Law. It also worked on occasion for the Clinton administration (as in the cellular phones case) even though it wasn't really trying to tap into domestic sources of support in the way its predecessor had.

Despite the evidence that Clinton had some difficulties making this strategy work on other issues (like income tax cuts), there are good reasons to expect that the U.S. will have opportunities to pursue this tactic with a moderate degree of success in the future. During the period of the Clinton talks, the preoccupation of leading politicians with political reforms (which made them unavailable as allies) and the post-1993 optimism that Japan would now be able to reform inefficient and particularistic policy on its own (which made Japanese less willing to rely on gaiatsu) both got in the way of efforts to use this tactic. As of this writing in early 1996, however, it is clear that the post-reform euphoria has been replaced by widespread politicial apathy and frustration with bureaucratic inertia. The LDP is back in power; its politicians seem to cater more than ever to moneyed special interests; and no political party has developed the broad programmatic appeal to public interests that the electoral reforms were supposed to foster.

With socioeconomic changes in Japan continuing to generate demands for policy reform faster than the still-rigid system can deal with them, there is once again an opening for an SII-style campaign aimed at mobilizing support for liberalization and policy change within Japan. Business leaders weighed down by government regulations that add to their costs at a time when the high yen and slow economy demand cost-cutting are calling for "deregulation" in a wide array of areas.[14] The aging of the workforces in long-protected areas like farming and small-scale retailing, furthermore, has created room for reforms designed to liberalize markets and enhance efficiency. Finally, the continuing internationalization of the Japanese economy creates more and more cases in which certain firms (with ties to foreign firms, with foreign operations, with needs for cheaper imports or foreign technology) favor liberalization. As long as such changes outpace the ability of the domestic political system to respond on its own, there will be domestic actors inside Japan willing and eager to use gaiatsu to push the process along.

As in the case of multilateral threats, however, this tactic should not be seen as a magic bullet. Given what happened in the *real* s ΙΙ talks, it is unlikely a new s ΙΙ-style initiative would have much more luck finding "latent support" for tougher limits on cross-shareholding or tougher A M L enforcement aimed at opening up supplier and distribution networks. Some of the barriers that matter most to U.S. firms are thus going to be out of reach of this tactic. Furthermore, the divergence in interests between the U.S. and its domestic allies would likely mean that in many cases reforms might be implemented in such a way as to benefit Japanese firms more than American ones.

ALTERNATIVE SPECIFICATION

This tactic can work, the two-level game approach and our cases showed, when Japan has a big and recognized policy problem in search of proposals that can be packaged as a "solution." As of early 1996, the obvious "big and recognized problem" was Japan's lingering recession which at that point had produced zero or negative growth for four consecutive years. If the U.S. could make a convincing case to the Japanese public that the package of proposals it was pushing (in another s ΙΙ type initiative) would address this problem, and if it could link up with Japanese economists in the policy community who were making similar arguments, it might be able to influence policy outcomes in this way as well.

MAKING NEGOTIATIONS A TWO-OR-MORE-WAY STREET

In this book, I have focused attention on efforts by the U.S. to use a variety of strategies to extract one-way concessions. Most U.S.-Japan trade talks have been of this type. Even the s ΙΙ talks, which had a superficial two-way gloss, did not involve the kind of tradeoffs one expects in real two-way negotiations. Neither Japan nor the Americans took seriously the Japanese calls on the U.S. to place limits on the number of credit cards that could be issued to Americans or speed the adoption of the metric system. The Japanese demands, moreover, were generally of the type where it was urging the U.S. to increase its competitiveness (e.g. Japan urged the U.S. to improve its education system)—hardly the kind of "concession" that would stimulate tradeoffs and side-payments.[15]

This study's findings about the limited ability of one-way negotiations to extract Japanese concessions suggest that the U.S. ought to consider engaging in more genuine two-way or multilateral bargaining. Japan might actually give up something valuable if the U.S. offered something of value to it as well.[16] One possible way in which such bargaining could be conducted would be through bilateral or multilateral talks on structural harmonization where the U.S. as well as other nations would be called upon to adjust policies toward foreign direct investment, competition policies, and/or their environmental and labor standards. These could be held bilaterally, regionally (under the Asian Pacific Economic Cooperation forum), or multilaterally (under the WTO or OECD).[17] Talks on macroeconomic policy coordination already held on a regular basis by G-7 finance officials also provide opportunities for greater two-way and multilateral bargaining as an alternative to one-way pressure.

What America Should and Shouldn't Do

Throughout this book, I have tried to maintain as much social scientific detachment as possible on the question of whether the demands the U.S. has made on Japan were "good" or in America's "national interest." Given the politically heated debate in the U.S. over how to deal with Japan, maintaining such detachment has not been easy and my efforts to do so have no doubt frustrated readers who have strong feelings one way or another. "How can he talk about American 'success' on land policy when the issue has so little to do with U.S.-Japan trade problems?" readers partial to a revisionist approach no doubt were thinking. Others on the opposite side of the political spectrum probably questioned how I could write in a neutral tone about the Clinton administration's "outrageous demands for numerical targets."

I have maintained this detachment, however, because I believe it is possible to address the question of what American pressure *can* achieve separately from the question of what America *should* do with its pressure. The former question, which bargaining theory and case study analysis can help us answer in an objective way, narrows down for American policymakers the range of realistic negotiating strategies and demands the U.S. has to choose from. From this list of options, policymakers then need to choose those strategies and demands that promise the most benefit for U.S. "interests"—a list that ought to be much shorter and more focused than the universe of demands that *can* be negotiated. Having tried to stay on the fence on this latter question this long, however, I am now going to step down and tackle the more contentious questions of whether Bush and Clinton trade demands served U.S. "interests" and what strategy and kinds of demands the U.S. should emphasize in the future.

Evaluating the worth of trade demands immediately forces one to specify exactly where U.S. "interests" lie. In my view, the U.S. has two broad interests at stake in its relationship with Japan. First, its interest lies in continuing bilateral cooperation, which serves common interests in maintaining regional peace and stability and in maintaining a liberal world trading regime. And second, its interest lies in assuring that Japan does not continue to gain disproportionate benefits from the world trading system by taking advantage of open markets elsewhere while maintaining informal and "strategic" barriers at home.[18] Reducing the size of the bilateral trade imbalance should *not* be an end in itself, though it probably does need to be addressed through macroeconomic policy adjustments on both sides in order to maintain public support for a liberal and moderate trade policy in the U.S.

By this standard, some of the SII demands clearly fell short. As I noted in my chapter on land policy, key Bush administration officials had strong doubts about whether bringing Japanese land prices down would have any impact on the bilateral trade balance. Looking back now after land prices have dropped sharply, it is clear lower land prices have not stimulated consumer spending or otherwise reduced the savings-investment imbalance. In the short term at least the recession brought on partly by the drop in land prices and dragged out by the overhang of bad property loans has *increased* macroeconomic imbalances—contributing to the largest monthly bilateral trade gaps ever. It is also doubtful that the land price drop has encouraged more U.S. direct investment in Japan (which was supposed to increase U.S. exports). Foreign investment in Japan has actually decreased since the fall in land prices, and U.S. firms continue to pull out of Tokyo, giving high prices due to the high yen and low profits due to the recession as their excuse.[19]

Some Bush administration demands in the area of competition policy had equally little connection to U.S. interests. U.S. demands for an end to resale price maintenance exemptions and tougher sanctions against price cartels, for example, only promised to lower prices in Japan without necessarily increasing foreign access to the market. In fact, since lower prices imply lower profits, such reforms (to the extent they have been implemented) reduced incentives for foreign firms to invest in the Japanese marketplace and thus may have aggravated the trade imbalance.

Finally, there is the issue of whether U.S. pressure really serves American interests when the foreign products that gain access to the Japanese market are not "Made in the USA." Most of the cellular phones Motorola has sold in Japan after the Clinton administration's intervention on its behalf are made in Malaysia. Very few of the toys sold in Toys 'R' Us stores set up in Japan after the U.S. pressed for liberalization of the Large Store Law are imported from the U.S.. And much of the "foreign market share" generated by the 1986 Semiconductor Accords actually went to chips made by firms like Texas Instruments in factories located in Japan. An argument can be made that by helping U.S. firms the American government ultimately serves American interests regardless of where the firms locate production, but there are definite limits to such logic.

While many other U.S. demands discussed in this book could be challenged on similar grounds, these examples suffice to illustrate the need for policymakers to "shorten and focus" their list of demands beyond the point of eliminating unwinnable cases—which has been the main focus of this book. Gaiatsu should be used only in cases where pressure is likely to win concessions *and* the demands at issue promise to make a serious dent in barriers to U.S. goods and services. Because the barriers that matter most to U.S. firms are often the ones that are least likely to be vulnerable to U.S. pressure tactics, the final list should be short indeed. Rather than target a wide range of Japanese barriers with a scatter shot approach, the U.S. should target the most important ones with a coordinated strategy making use of the entire array of effective negotiating tactics as outlined above.

In my view, the most important Japanese barriers include: government regulations and procurement practices, such as those in the telecommunications, construction, and insurance sectors, that exclude competitive foreign goods and services; and distribution networks such as those in autos, flat glass, and paper that are controlled (or at least intimidated) by small groups of Japanese firms. Many of these barriers were subject to pressure by the Bush or Clinton administrations in one way or another and the difficulties encountered by both administrations have been documented in excruciating detail in this book. Addressing them will not be easy, but the American government has to make the best effort possible. What follows is my recommended course of action.

Lay the Groundwork

Whatever administration is sworn in on January 20, 1997 should start by declaring that the U.S. is giving up attempts to negotiate voluntary import expansion agreements of the type represented by the 1986 Semiconductor Accords and that it will henceforth impose sanctions under Section 301 of its trade law only when the WTO has authorized it to do so. Instead, the U.S. will begin a coordinated campaign involving the WTO, bilateral talks, and multilateral dialogue aimed at liberalizing the Japanese market for the benefit of U.S. firms, third-country firms, and Japanese consumers. Giving up VIES and unilateral Section 301 threats will aggravate some trade hawks in the U.S., but it will cost the U.S. very little in terms of lost leverage (since, as this book has shown, these tools have not proved at all effective for the Clinton administration). Meanwhile, making this announcement will help lay the groundwork for a new campaign drawing on third-country and Japanese public support for the new initiative.

Simultaneously, the U.S. should send officials to Europe and Asian capitals and to Tokyo to consult with and involve a wide array of actors in planning for the initiative. Europeans and Asians, impressed at the American willingness to work through the WTO, should shift from being mostly opposed to U.S. efforts (as they were during the Clinton talks) to being useful allies. Given the centrality of the WTO in this new strategy, open support for U.S. objectives from a wide array of third countries will help increase the likelihood that Japan will expect dispute panels to rule against them and so will make the nation more likely to offer concessions ahead of the actual imposition of sanctions.

The U.S. officials sent to Japan should consult widely with their Japanese counterparts (especially at places like the JFTC and EPA), Japanese businessmen, politicians, and reporters. Involving all at an early stage will increase the likelihood that they will support the new U.S. strategy. To further increase the likelihood of their support, stress should be placed on how the U.S. objective is to help the Japanese address sources of inefficiency in the Japanese market resulting from excessive state involvement and collusive business practices—both of which have proven to be a drag on the nation's attempts to emerge from a prolonged recession. Consultations should be designed not only to develop support for the U.S. strategy but also to solicit specific suggestions about the kinds of regulations and practices that most concern domestic actors in Japan.

Coordinated Launching of WTO Cases

The U.S. needs leverage to get Japan's attention, and the most effective source of leverage today, I have argued, is the WTO. The U.S. should launch cases where its evidence is strongest, targeting relatively clear WTO violations in areas like government regulations and procurement. It should also launch cases that highlight the exclusionary impact of weak antitrust enforcement. Though WTO rules do not cover competition policy, the U.S. might be able to win a case if it can show government complicity in encouraging collusive behavior aimed at "nullifying and impairing" U.S. trade rights. Even if these cases are weaker, they will serve as an opportunity to publicize the prevalence and costs of such behavior in such a way as to support parallel campaigns to deal with these issues in bilateral and multilateral fora.

Cases should be brought, to the extent evidence is available, in areas such as those listed above: telecommunications, insurance, construction, autos, flat glass, and paper. For maximum impact, as many cases as possible should be launched at the same time. The U.S. might coordinate its filings with other nations for additional impact. Korea, for example, might launch a case on cement and Europe, a case on liquor. To the extent the U.S. and other nations make strong legal cases, Japan should respond to WTO-sanctioned pressure fairly smoothly.

Bilateral Talks

Given the limitation of the WTO as noted above, however, it would be a grave mistake for the U.S. to count on the international institution by itself to open up Japan's market. The WTO mandates bilateral consultations at early stages of the dispute process, and the U.S. should coordinate and use these in order to press for broader changes in the Japanese market, holding open the possibility that the nation will drop some or all of its WTO cases if Japan agrees to a variety of reforms. The specific list of U.S. demands should be short since it ought to include only ones that have support within Japan, promise to significantly open up the Japanese market to U.S. goods and services, and are related closely to the issues highlighted in WTO cases. Possibilities include significant liberalization of the telecommunications and insurance sectors, both of which are already being discussed in Japan and enjoy the support of some domestic actors, and more vigorous enforcement of the AML aimed at anticompetitive use of market power by large firms designed to exclude new market entry by controlling distributors and downstream processors.

Getting real policy change on this latter demand will not be easy, as the discussion of the Bush administration's efforts in chapter 8 suggests. By focusing pressure more narrowly on the types of collusive practices that matter most to U.S. firms and conducting a better public relations campaign, however, the U.S. should be able to bring about some change. The key is to raise public awareness of how producer domination of distribution networks contribute to higher costs for a wide array of consumer goods and tax-funded government purchases. To increase public and elite support, the U.S. also needs to make it clear that it is not asking the JFTC (this time) to use the Anti-Monopoly Law to attack horizontal keiretsu or supplier networks. Support for these systems of business organization remains too high in Japan, such that any attempt to target these will only reduce support for demands that *do* have the potential of winning Japanese allies. The kinds of barriers I propose the U.S. should target impose costs on distributors, downstream processors, Japanese firms that are locked out of distribution channels, and consumers—all of which (along with the media) are potential allies if the U.S. can make a strong case.

MULTILATERAL FORUMS

The U.S. should press for multilateral talks, under APEC, the OECD, or possibly as part of a new round of WTO talks, focusing on harmonizing competition policy and certain types of government regulations (health and safety) and standards (telecommunications). These talks should be of the give and take variety where the U.S. as well as other parties are required to adjust their policies. Because they are give and take, there will be more opportunities for tradeoffs across issues that might induce Japan to offer concessions (say on competition policy) in return for U.S. concessions in another area.

American pressure on Japan to adjust its macroeconomic policy should similarly be coordinated through the multilateral G-7 process. The U.S. succeeded once, during SII, in convincing the MOF to talk about macro issues in a bilateral context and using this opportunity to draw on support from other Japanese domestic actors sympathetic to

U.S. demands. The MOF had such a terrible experience with SII, though, that it will not allow that to happen again. If the U.S. wants Japan to adjust its macro policy, it will need to use the G-7 process to get other members of the group (especially Germany) to cooperate in pressuring Japan and/or offer its own concessions in exchange for Japanese policy adjustment.

Some readers no doubt will object that the above course of action is too lax on Japan. "It doesn't address keiretsu!" some will cry. "Toyota will still buy from its network of suppliers, and Mitsubishi employees will drink only Kirin beer!" I am not arguing that business practices such as these do not represent a barrier to U.S. exports. The main lesson drawn in this book from bargaining theory and the record of the last two administrations, though, is that *no* amount of trade pressure is going to *force* Japanese firms to abandon these practices. Just like the Cold North Wind in Aesop's fable about competition between the wind and the sun to make a traveler take off his coat, gaiatsu aimed at these targets is only going to lead Japanese business to pull the Keiretsu Coat more tightly around itself.

The lesson I draw from the theory and practice surveyed in this book is that American pressure will succeed only when it works *with* domestic politics in Japan, when it works like the Sun in the same fable by turning up the heat and getting the Japanese government and business to assist in the process of taking the coat off. Some government policies are more amenable to changing in this way because domestic politics is predisposed to "work well" with the pressure. Even in the case of the troublesome keiretsu barriers, however, an effective campaign aimed at opening finished goods markets and distribution systems—combined with investments in time and money by U.S. private firms—may eventually succeed in inducing Japanese firms to relax their stable business ties and begin to buy more foreign goods. Competition with finished goods made by firms that are not burdened with keiretsu obligations will force Japanese firms to abandon their least efficient ties.

As a Cold Wind or a Hot Sun, gaiatsu will remain a fixture of U.S. policy toward Japan as long as the two nations remain economic competitors. If so, the U.S. government would do well, as former USTR negotiator Glen Fukushima put it, to figure out "where, when, and how much pressure should be applied to achieve the maximum result while minimizing Japanese resentment."[20] This book sought to answer these questions by focusing critically on what social science theory has to tell us about when and how nations can draw one-way concessions from each other and by looking closely at the real world records of the last two administrations. Most of the book addressed the question of what American pressure *can* and *cannot* do, but as summarized in the last few pages, the answer to this question has direct implications for what America *should* do. If my model of domestic politics dominating trade policymaking is right, the "ideas" expressed in this book will probably have no impact. But then I may be wrong.

NOTES

1. INTRODUCTION

1. These issues and the relevant economic literature are discussed in detail in chapter 3.

2. One of the most influential of these studies is the book by Laura D'Andrea Tyson, Chair of the Council of Economic Advisors under Clinton, *Who's Bashing Whom? Trade Conflict in High-Technology Industries* (Washington, D.C.: Institute for International Economics, 1992). Tyson argues that, under certain conditions, voluntary import expansion agreements such as the one that set market share targets for the Japanese semiconductor sector are preferable to the "manipulated trade" that exists in the absence of such agreements (pp. 133–136). Nowhere in the book, however, does she address the question of what the U.S. should do if threats fail to convince Japan to agree to targets in additional sectors. See also Clyde V. Prestowitz, *Trading Places: How We Are Giving Our Future to Japan and How to Reclaim It* (New York: Basic Books, 1988); James Fallows, "Containing Japan," *Atlantic*, May 1989, pp. 40–54; and Rudiger Dornbusch, "Policy Options for Freer Trade: The Case for Bilateralism," in Robert Z. Lawrence and Charles L. Schultze, eds., *An American Trade Strategy: Options for the 1990s* (Washington, D.C.: Brookings, 1990).

3. ACTPN, *Analysis of the U.S.-Japan Trade Problem*, February 1989, p. 108.

4. Clinton administration officials repeatedly insisted that they were not asking for "market share targets," but throughout the Framework Talks, they called on the Japanese to accept market share figures in third countries as a reference point for evaluating "progress," and in the auto talk in particular insisted on commitments to a specific increase in sales. Despite the strong pressure on Japan to accept these "results," the government steadfastly refused to agree to any commitment that would promise measurable sales or share growth. The automakers as well refused to issue

"voluntary" plans that included the kinds of specific commitments the Clinton administration was seeking. See chapter 9.

5. One recent (nonrevisionist) study that pays more attention to how domestic politics influences the outcome of aggressive American trade initiatives is Thomas O. Bayard and Kimberly Ann Elliott's *Reciprocity and Retaliation in U.S. Trade Policy* (Washington, D.C.: Institute for International Economics, 1994).

6. Aurelia George, "Japan's America Problem: The Japanese Response to U.S. Pressure," *The Washington Quarterly* 14:3 (Summer 1991), p. 18.

7. On gaiatsu and foreign aid, see Robert M. Orr, Jr., *The Emergence of Japan's Foreign Aid Power* (New York: Columbia University Press, 1990), chapter 5; on macroeconomic policy, see Yoichi Funabashi, *Managing the Dollar: From the Plaza to the Louvre*, 2nd ed. (Washington, D.C.: Institute for International Economics, 1989), pp. 104–107; on Gulf War policy, see Edward J. Lincoln, *Japan's New Global Role* (Washington, D.C.: Brookings Institution, 1993), pp. 219–238.

8. Glen Fukushima, "*Gaiatsu* Has Outlived Its Usefulness," *Japan Times Weekly*, November 16, 1991; George, "Japan's America Problem," pp. 5–19; Sasaki Takeshi, "Nichibei kōzō kyōgi: 'motareai' no kiken," (The SII Talks: The Danger of "Reliance") *Ekonomisuto*, November 7, 1989, p. 105.

9. See for example Kenneth Pyle, *The Japanese Question* (Washington, D.C.: AEI Press, 1992), pp. 112–113 and 128–139.

10. The best of these studies are the multi-case volumes I. M. Destler, Hideo Sato, Priscilla Clapp, and Haruhiro Fukui, *Managing an Alliance: The Politics of U.S.-Japan Relations* (Washington, D.C.: Brookings, 1976); and I. M. Destler and Hideo Sato, eds., *Coping with U.S.-Japanese Economic Conflicts* (Lexington, Mass.: D.C. Heath And Co., 1982). These two works are discussed further at the beginning of chapter 2 (and in footnote 1 of that chapter).

11. Robert Putnam, "Diplomacy and Domestic Politics: The Logic of Two-Level Games," *International Organization* 42 (Summer 1988), pp. 427–460; and Peter Evans, Harold K. Jacobson, and Robert Putnam, eds., *Double Edged Diplomacy: International Bargaining and Domestic Politics* (Berkeley: University of California Press, 1993).

12. For the concept of "nested games," see George Tsebelis, *Nested Games: Rational Choice in Comparative Politics* (Berkeley: University of California Press, 1990).

13. Note that I am not arguing that the Japan policy revisionists are all hard-core neorealists. In fact, a core argument in the revisionist literature (that Japan's foreign policy is shaped by a domestic political structure that is dominated by bureaucrats) is inconsistent with the neorealist view that foreign policy is shaped primarily by a nation's position in the international system. Nevertheless, revisionist works that do give thought to the question of *how* the results-oriented deals they favor can be extracted from the Japanese (such as the ACTPN Report quoted above) seem to fall back on a realist models of international bargaining. It is this often implicit faith of the revisionists in realist theory that, I propose, needs to be challenged.

14. Harry Eckstein, "Case Study and Theory in Political Science," in Fred Greenstein and Nelson Polsby, eds., *Handbook of Political Science*, vol. 7 (Reading,

Mass.: Addison-Wesley, 1975), pp. 79–138. See also Gary King, Robert O. Keohane, and Sidney Verba, *Designing Social Inquiry: Scientific Inference in Qualitative Research* (Princeton: Princeton University Press, 1994), especially pp. 128–149.

15. In addition, the U.S. criticized the operation of the price mechanism in Japan. As negotiations proceeded on this topic, however, it became clear that the problem of price differentials between Japan and foreign markets was more a result of other structural barriers than a cause in and of itself. The SII talks on this subject therefore concerned monitoring of price differentials as a way to measure progress. Given that substantive policy changes were not at issue in this case, it is not treated here as a separate case.

16. Noirio Naka has disputed my claim that the SII issues were given "essentially equal billing" and attributes part of the variation in SII negotiating outcomes across issues to what he describes as real differences in the degree to which issues were pushed—*Predicting Outcomes in United States-Japan Trade Negotiations: The Political Process of the Structural Impediments Initiative* (Westport, CT: Quorum Books, 1996), pp. 79–81. See my discussion in chapter 4, explaining how the American team consciously chose to push all SII issues at the same speed in the fall of 1989. While attention eventually came to be focused on a subset of the 240 demands, this process was shaped by the Japanese media and American negotiators' sense of where they could win concessions and so cannot be treated as an "independent" explanation of the negotiating outcome.

17. S. Linn Williams, "Kagami no naka no nichibei kōzō kyōgi: 3," (Looking in the Mirror at the SII Talks: Part 3) *Shūkan daiyamondo*, March 28, 1992, p. 94. See also Glen Fukushima, *Nichibei keizai masatsu no seijigaku* (The Political Science of U.S.-Japan Economic Disputes) (Tokyo: Asahi Shimbunsha, 1992), pp. 202–203.

18. Kensetsu Daijin Kambō Seisakuka, *Nichibei kōzō mondai kyōgi to kensetsu gyōsei* (The U.S.-Japan SII Talks and Construction Administration) (Tokyo: Taisei Shuppansha, 1990), p. 62. In actuality, this rate had increased to a much higher level by 1994 (see chapter 5).

19. *Wall Street Journal*, April 9, 1990.

20. See the coverage in the *Wall Street Journal*, April 9, 1990; most of the criticisms of SII referred to in this paragraph are drawn from the writings of Glen Fukushima, a former trade negotiator who was working in the USTR when SII started. See his book *Nichibei keizai masatsu no seijigaku*, pp. 197–218. See also Chalmers Johnson, "Trade, Revisionism, and the Future of Japanese-American Relations," in Kozo Yamamura, ed., *Japan's Economic Structure: Should it Change?* (Seattle: Society for Japanese Studies, 1990), pp. 105–136.

21. Tyson, *Who's Bashing Whom?*, pp. 106–133.

22. *JEI Report* 22B, June 18, 1993, pp. 7–8.

23. *New York Times*, October 2, 1994, p. 1, and October 3, 1994, p. D1.

24. The 1991 agreement on government procurement of computers, for example, included a range of quantitative measures. The 1992 paper agreement included a commitment to "substantially increase market access for foreign firms exporting paper products to Japan." See Merit E. Janow, "Trading With an Ally: Progress and

342 1. INTRODUCTION

Discontent in U.S.-Japan Trade Relations," in Gerald L. Curtis, ed., *The United States, Japan, and Asia: Challenges for U.S. Policy* (New York: W. W. Norton, 1994), pp. 60–65.

2. GAIATSU IN A TWO-LEVEL GAME

1. I.M. Destler and Hideo Sato, eds., *Coping with U.S.-Japanese Economic Conflicts* (Lexington, Mass: D.C. Heath and Company, 1982). For their comments on gaiatsu, see especially pp. 279–283. The authors conclude that foreign pressure should be applied much less often and much more selectively, but they do not attempt (as I do here) to identify when and how it *can* be used effectively. See also an earlier study by these authors: Destler, Sato, Pricilla Clapp, and Haruhiro Fukui, *Managing an Alliance: The Politics of U.S.-Japan Relations* (Washington, D.C.: Brookings, 1976). Though the book's use of a bureaucratic politics approach allows it to offer more of a unified perspective, the authors are less concerned with how the U.S. might improve the terms of its relationship with Japan than they are with how the two nations can avoid problems in their relations.

2. Prisoners' Dilemma and the other most common games used to fashion models of international bargaining limit their players to a binary choice: cooperate or defect. The main problem is a market failure, and research focuses on the conditions and the institutions that will give the players confidence they will both be better off it they choose to cooperate. Two of the most prominent studies employing game theory are Robert Keohane, *After Hegemony: Cooperation and Discord in the World Political Economy* (Princeton: Princeton University Press, 1984); and Robert Axelrod, *The Evolution of Cooperation* (New York: Basic Books, 1984).

3. The payoff structure in U.S.-Japan trade talks may resemble a Battle of the Sexes where both parties recognize that they need to cooperate but disagree as to the *terms* of the cooperative deal. For a discussion of how the recent surge in work examining problems of market failure in international relations has failed to deal with situations such as this where the distributional terms of a deal are of critical importance, see Stephen Krasner, "Global Communications and National Power: Life on the Pareto Frontier," *World Politics* 43:3 (April 1991), pp. 362–366; and James K. Sebenius, "Challenging Conventional Explanations of International Cooperation: Negotiation Analysis and the Case of Epistemic Communities," *International Organization* 46:1 (Winter 1992), pp. 326–328.

4. One could literally "quantify" the Japanese concession along the lines suggested here by attaching the number zero to "what would have happened" and 100 to the American demand, with corresponding numbers for points in between. Given the fuzziness of issues involved, however, I have chosen not to go that far. I should also recognize here that the reliance on "what the American's demanded" has some shortcomings as a yardstick for measuring the effectiveness of gaiatsu, primarily because the original American demands may, in specific cases, be either deflated or inflated versions of what the U.S. really wanted. They may be deflated if the U.S. scales back its demands even before negotiations in anticipation of a negative Japanese response. They may be inflated if the U.S. is seeking to force greater con-

cessions from Japan by making exaggerated demands at first and settling for lesser but still high concessions. While one must be aware of these distortions, in the absence of any reason to suspect that there is a systematic difference in the degree to which demands are inflated or deflated across policy areas, they can be treated as "noise"—making the original American demands a reasonable yardstick for evaluating the final terms.

5. Waltz distinguishes his "neorealism," which starts from the assumption that states pursue security and that power is often a means toward this end, from the classical realism of scholars like Hans Morgenthau, which sees states as power-maximizers. See his *Theory of International Politics* (Reading, Mass.: Addison-Wesley, 1979), especially p. 126. This debate has a long and noble history, but the distinction between classical and neorealism is not something we need to resolve here.

6. Krasner, "Global Communications and National Power."

7. Waltz, *Theory of International Politics.*

8. Albert O. Hirschman, *National Power and the Structure of Foreign Trade* (Berkeley: University of California Press, 1945); David Baldwin, "Interdependence and Power: A Conceptual Analysis," *International Organization* 34:4 (Autumn 1980), pp. 471–506; Klauss Knorr, *The Power of Nations* (New York: Basic Books, 1975). For a critique of the view that asymmetrical economic relations provide the less dependent nation with a source of bargaining power, see R. Harrison Wagner, "Economic Interdependence, Bargaining Power, and Political Influence," *International Organization* 42:3 (Summer 1988), pp. 461–483.

9. Robert O. Keohane and Joseph S. Nye, *Power and Interdependence*, 2nd ed. (Glenville, IL: Scott, Foresman, 1989), pp. 30–32.

10. See especially Keohane and Nye, *Power and Interdependence.*

11. John Burton, *World Society* (Cambridge: Cambridge University Press, 1972).

12. Pat Choate, *Agents of Influence* (New York: Alfred A. Knopf, 1990), pp. 7–11. Similar opposition has arisen when the U.S. has sought to put anti-dumping duties on critical imports from Japan. See the discussion of Laura D'Andrea Tyson, *Who's Bashing Whom? Trade Conflict in High-Technology Industries* (Washington, D.C.: Institute for International Economics, 1992), pp. 140–143.

13. Odell found that American computer firms with investments inside Brazil opposed the U.S. government's aggressive pressure tactics, thus making it possible for Brazil to resist making concessions—"International Threats and Internal Politics: Brazil, the European Community, and the United States, 1985–1987," in Peter B. Evans, Harold K. Jacobson, and Robert D. Putnam, eds., *Double-Edged Diplomacy: International Bargaining and Domestic Politics* (Berkeley: University of California Press, 1993), pp. 238–241.

14. Michael Mastanduno tests a similar hypothesis in his article looking at the selection of *targets* for U.S. trade pressure. He finds that the U.S. does choose, in general but not always, to apply pressure in support of strategic industries—which arguably serve to increase (or maintain) America's relative power position. His findings do not address, however, the question of whether the pattern of negotiating *outcomes* conforms with America's national interest. See "Do Relative Gains Matter?

America's Response to Japanese Industrial Policy," *International Security* 16:1 (Summer 1991), pp. 73–113.

15. My bottom line on the role of power is not greatly different from that of Keohane and Nye in *Power and Interdependence*, pp. 11, 18–19.

16. Thomas Schelling, *The Strategy of Conflict* (Cambridge: Harvard University Press, 1960); Richard Walton and Robert McKersie, *A Behavioral Theory of Labor Negotiations* (New York: McGraw-Hill, 1965); David Lax and James K. Sebenius, *Manager as Negotiator* (New York: The Free Press, 1986); Howard Raiffa, *The Art and Science of Negotiation* (Cambridge: Harvard University Press, 1984); and Evans, Jacobson, and Putnam, eds., *Double-Edged Diplomacy*. Some readers may wonder why this list does not include such familiar tactics as "issue-redefinition" and "internal side-payments" (aimed at one's own constituents). These are not discussed because both of these tactics, though important tools for negotiators seeking to facilitate domestic support for cooperative international agreements, are not used to *improve the terms* of bargains—which is what we are focusing on here. For specific discussion of these tactics, see H. Richard Friman, "Side-Payments Versus Security Cards: Domestic Bargaining Tactics in International Economic Negotiations," *International Organization* 47:3 (Summer 1993), pp. 387–410; and Frederick W. Mayer, "Managing Domestic Differences in International Negotiations: The Strategic Use of Internal Side-Payments," *International Organization* 46:4 (Autumn 1992), pp. 793–818.

17. James K. Sebenius, "Negotiation Arithmetic: Adding and Subtracting Issues and Parties," *International Organization* 37:2 (Spring 1983), p. 286. See various studies of attempts by the U.S. and U.N. to use economic coercion to force relatively powerless nations to comply with demands: Johan Galtung, "On the Effects of International Economic Sanctions, With Examples from the Case of Rhodesia," *World Politics* 19 (April 1967), pp. 378–416; and R. S. Olson, "Economic Coercion in World Politics: With A Focus on North-South Relations," *World Politics* 31:4 (July 1979), pp. 471–494.

18. For an interesting discussion contrasting the realist treatment of "power" with the way the concept is treated in the negotiation-analytic approach, see Sebenius, "Challenging Conventional Explanations of International Cooperation," pp. 339–344.

19. The negotiation-analytic approach was formalized in these terms in Lax and Sebenius, *Manager as Negotiator*, and Raiffa, *The Art and Science of Negotiation*.

20. Schelling, *Strategy of Conflict*; Lax and Sebenius, *Manager as Negotiator*, p. 248, 252–253; and Raiffa, *The Art and Science of Negotiation*.

21. Sebenius, "Negotiation Arithmetic," pp. 283–307.

22. James K. Sebenius, *Negotiating the Law of the Sea: Lessons in the Art and Science of Reaching Agreement* (Cambridge: Harvard University Press, 1984).

23. Robert Putnam, "Diplomacy and Domestic Politics: The Logic of Two-Level Games," *International Organization* 42:3 (Summer 1988), pp. 427–460. Putnam's work draws heavily on Walton and McKersie, *A Behavioral Theory of Labor Negotiations*. See also Raiffa, *The Art and Science of Negotiation*; and Lax and Sebenius, *The Manager*

as Negotiator, pp. 306–313. Even Schelling anticipated the "two level game" approach in his discussion of negotiating through agents—*The Strategy of Conflict*, p. 29.

24. Andrew Moravcsik similarly emphasizes this aspect of Putnam's approach, arguing that the main advantage of the two-level game framework over other approaches that have tried to combine domestic and international factors is that Putnam's model captures how the two levels simultaneously interact while the other approaches treat one level or the other as primary and then "add" the influence of the second level. See his "Introduction: Integrating International and Domestic Theories of International Bargaining," in Evans, Jacobson, and Putnam, eds., *Double-Edged Diplomacy*, p. 17.

25. Keisuke Iida, "When and How Do Domestic Constraints Matter?: Two-Level Games With Uncertainty," *Journal of Conflict Resolution* 37:3 (September 1993), pp. 403–426.

26. Putnam, "Diplomacy and Domestic Politics," pp. 442–450.

27. Graham T. Allison, *Essence of Decision: Explaining the Cuban Missile Crisis* (Boston: Little, Brown and Company, 1971). The theory of domestic politics employed in this book thus rejects the argument, commonly made in recent work in the "rational choice" school, that bureaucrats merely serve as the "agents" of elected politicians. In my view, bureaucrats may sometimes be constrained by politicians and act as their "agents," but it is also possible that politicians sometimes are constrained by bureaucrats and act as *their* agents. For an elaboration of this argument, see Junko Kato, *The Problem of Bureaucratic Rationality: Tax Politics in Japan* (Princeton: Princeton University Press, 1994). See also the analysis of Japanese politics in chapter 4 of this book.

28. Mancur Olson, *The Logic of Collective Action* (Cambridge: Harvard University Press, 1965); Russell Hardin, *Collective Action* (Baltimore: Johns Hopkins University Press and Resources for the Future, 1982).

29. Peter Hall, *Governing the Economy: Politics of State Intervention in Britain and France* (New York: Oxford University Press, 1986), p. 277. This basic observation, of course, is the bedrock of "rational choice" adherents in a range of disciplines and can therefore be found in a wide array of sources, but the basic argument is often traced to R. H. Coase, "The Problem of Social Cost," *Journal of Law and Economics* 3 (1960), pp. 1–44.

30. John W. Kingdon, *Agendas, Alternatives, and Public Policies* (Glenview, IL: Scott, Foresman and Company, 1984), pp. 20–21.

31. Although it does not draw explicitly on Kingdon's work or use the terminology of "policy communities," work by Peter Haas and others who emphasize the role of "epistemic communities" in fostering international cooperation similarly emphasize the power of ideas. See the special issue on epistemic communities, *International Organization* 46:1 (Winter 1992).

32. Putnam, "Diplomacy and Domestic Politics," p. 455.

33. Peter Evans, in his concluding chapter of the collaborative project, identifies nine hypotheses as the primary contributions of the book, but only three of those address the issue of when synergistic strategies are likely to be successful. Two

emphasize that certain strategies ("tying hands" and misleading the partner about the size of one's win-set) are rarely likely to work, while one argues that collusion between chief negotiators is more likely to work when a negotiator is a "dove" in relation to his domestic constituents. See Evans, "Building an Integrative Approach to International and Domestic Politics: Reflections and Projections," in Evans, Jacobson, and Putnam, eds., *Double-Edged Diplomacy*, pp. 402–412.

34. Putnam, "Diplomacy and Domestic Politics," pp. 444, 455.

35. Ibid., p. 456.

36. Wagner, "Economic Interdependence," p. 464.

37. The argument that threats need to work synergistically is made briefly by Putnam ("Diplomacy and Domestic Politics," p. 451) and is developed in more detail in the collaborative volume (Moravcsik, "Introduction," pp. 29–30). The basic argument here has also been made without the explicit two-level language in other works on international bargaining. See Galtung, "On the Effects of International Economic Sanctions,"; and Olson, "Economic Coercion in World Politics."

38. Odell, "International Threats and Internal Politics," pp. 245.

39. Putnam and the authors of the collaborative volume similarly link their arguments about when threats are likely to work to their theories of domestic politics, arguing that threats work best when they are "targeted" in a way that maximizes the policy response to the threat. See Putnam and Moravcsik citations above.

40. Kenneth Oye reminds us that threats themselves can transform unorganized or disinterested groups into organized and interested ones by threatening to impose concentrated costs. See his *Economic Discrimination and Political Exchange: World Political Economy in the 1930s and 1980s* (Princeton: Princeton University Press, 1992), especially pp. 51–67.

41. Moravcsik, "Introduction," p. 26; Odell, "International Threats and Internal Politics," p. 234. The authors in the collaborative volume put emphasis primarily the question of whether the costs imposed on groups are concentrated.

42. Olson, "Economic Coercion in World Politics, p. 479.

43. "Sidepayments" aimed at one's counterpart's domestic arena are sometimes discussed as a separate negotiating strategy (and were listed separately in the list of tactics at the start of the negotiation-analytic section above). They are not discussed separately here, however, because the way in which they operate and the conditions that determine whether or not they are likely to be successful are identical to those of the "mutually advantageous linkage" strategy discussed here. Such linkage is, after all, a sidepayment where the payment is made in the form of concessions on a linked issue. As Richard Friman notes, the literature is inconsistent as to whether these two tactics should be treated as separate or as variations on the same idea. See his "Side-payments versus Security Cards," p. 398.

44. Robert D. Tollison and Thomas D. Willett, "An Economic Theory of Mutually Advantageous Issue Linkages in International Negotiations," *International Organization* 33:4 (Autumn 1979), pp. 425–449. A similar approach to linkage can be found in Sebenius, "Negotiation Arithmetic."

45. Tollison and Willett, after relaxing the unitary actor assumption upon which

they base their core conclusions, admit that bureaucratic politics is likely to get in the way of cross-issue tradeoffs—"An Economic Theory of Mutually Advantageous Issue Linkages," p. 445. See also Friman, "Side-Payments versus Security Cards," pp. 398–399.

46. Putnam, "Diplomacy and Domestic Politics," pp. 445–448. This deal satisfied the condition outlined above for domestic ratification of the tradeoff because (on the U.S. side) some of the opponents of oil decontrol were concerned about more than just their issue area. They valued as well the job-creation benefits promised by macroeconomic stimulation abroad and were thus willing to switch their votes. If oil decontrol opponents had been exclusively concerned about "their" issue, the tradeoff would not have been ratified and the strategy would have failed.

47. Putnam, "Diplomacy and Domestic Politics," p. 446–447.

48. He actually confuses the issue with an Edgeworth Box analysis illustrating the tradeoff of votes across two issues for each nation. This analysis assumes that the group of actors involved in domestic ratification is a constant, contradicting Putnam's implicit recognition that the process of linking two previously separate issues *changes* who participates: where the actors with the most at stake dominated the process before linkage, they lose some of their dominance when international negotiations link "their" issue to another. See my analysis that follows.

49. One question remains: why would the target nation consent to linkage in a case such as this? It could have escaped without making any concessions but ends up making concessions on both issues after linkage. While a unitary rational state clearly would not agree to linkage in a case like this, a divided state might—especially if the decision on whether or not to link were made by a part of the state other than those which had a direct stake in each issue area.

50. The logic behind this hypothesis is similar to that which has been developed to support the argument that institutions promote cooperation in Prisoners' Dilemma situations. In this case, the beef and orange interests are in a PD situation since, if they both hold out and refuse to call for the other to make concessions, they should both be able to avoid making any. But each has an incentive to "defect" and mobilize in support of a demand that the other side make concessions since it wants to avoid the "sucker's payoff" where only the other side mobilizes in this way. If the institutional links between beef and orange interests are dense enough, they may manage to cooperate and avoid infighting, but if the institutional links are less dense (if policymaking is highly segmented) they are more likely to defect and start the process which leads both of them to mobilize in favor of the other side making all of the concessions. On the PD game, see Keohane, *After Hegemony*.

51. Sebenius, "Negotiation Arithmetic," pp. 307–314.

52. Kenneth Oye similarly emphasizes how changes in participation levels due to international pressure can change the way target nations define their negotiating positions. What he emphasizes, however, is the role of threats in imposing concentrated costs on specific groups that then emerge as allies of the pressuring country merely because they want to avoid the sanctions. See footnote 40 above. Thomas

Bayard and Kimberly Ann Elliott (in *Reciprocity and Retaliation in U.S. Trade Policy* (Washington: Institute for International Economics, 1994), p. 85) have called Oye's variety of participation expansion "negative participation expansion" to distinguish it from a tactic discussed in this section which they call "positive participation expansion." The difference is that in the case of the strategy discussed here, the parties support foreign demands *for their own reasons*. Pressure may give these groups an excuse to get involved, and it may also give them an extra reason to mobilize, but this tactic does not rely on changing the positions of these groups by imposing costs.

53. See for example Iida, "When and How Do Domestic Constraints Matter?" See my discussion of Iida's approach in footnote 25 above.

54. Putnam, "Diplomacy and Domestic Politics," p. 445. Putnam cites only one example where a negotiator sought to improve prospects for an international deal by expanding participation levels, Woodrow Wilson's campaign for the Versailles Treaty, but notes that it was unsuccessful.

55. E. E. Schattschneider, *The Semisovereign People: A Realist View of Democracy in America* (New York: Holt, 1960), p. 2.

56. Sebenius, "Challenging Conventional Explanation of International Cooperation," p. 341; Schattschneider, *The Semisovereign People*, p. 66.

57. Schelling, *Strategy of Conflict*, pp. 24–27.

58. Sebenius, "Challenging Conventional Explanations of International Cooperation," p. 336.

59. I have qualified this hypothesis with the line "to the extent this is an accurate description of how policy proposals are generated in a given issue area" because there are clearly many issues in international negotiations which are not complicated enough to be significantly influenced by experts (e.g. where to draw the border, or how high to set the tariff rate). There are, however, many other international issues where experts are much more involved (e.g. macroeconomic policy coordination, or international environmental cooperation). On these issues, the degree to which a negotiator's policy proposals resonate with the ongoing discussions going on in domestic policy communities is likely to be of greater importance.

60. The strategy of "tying hands" was also described in the work of Schelling (*Strategy of Conflict*) and its two-level implications are explored in the collaborative volume (Evans, "Building an Integrative Approach to International and Domestic Politics," pp. 402–403). A closely related strategy is the tactic of *misleading the partner* into believing that one's win-set is smaller than it is, a tactic that relies not on shrinking the win-set but on making one's partner *think* it is smaller than it is. The two-level implications of this strategy are given significant attention in the collaborative volume as well (Evans, "Building an Integrative Approach to International and Domestic Politics," pp. 408–412). It is not considered separately here because the analysis in the collaborative volume raises significant doubts as to whether there are meaningful differences in levels of "asymmetrical information"—the key variable likely to affect a negotiator's ability to mislead his partner about the size of his win-set—even across widely differing political systems. Given that the cases considered in this book all deal with the same two countries, it is even more doubtful we would

find enough cross-issue variation in "asymmetrical information" to warrant the effort.

61. Putnam refers to a negotiator's attitude toward the size of his own win-set as "sweet and sour"—"Diplomacy and Domestic Politics," p. 440.

62. The authors of the collaborative volume derive this hypothesis deductively based on a number of case studies, but it can also be posited based on the structure of the game as done here. See Evans, "Building an Integrative Approach to International and Domestic Politics," pp. 402–403.

63. Moravcsik, "Introduction," p. 31. One study in the collaborative volume which does note that domestic actors seek to take advantage of foreign pressure is, interestingly, a study of U.S.-Japan trade disputes. See Ellis Krauss, "U.S.-Japan Negotiations on Construction and Semiconductors, 1985–88: Building Friction and Relation-chips," pp. 265–299. The bias toward the strategic opportunities available to statesmen can be seen, however, in most other published studies employing the two-level game model, including Mayer, "Managing Domestic Differences in International Negotiations"; Howard P. Lehman and Jennifer L. McCoy, "The Dynamics of the Two-Level Bargaining Game: The 1988 Debt Negotiations," World Politics 44:4 (July 1992), pp. 600–644; and in my own study, "Two-Level Games and Bargaining Outcomes: Why Gaiatsu Succeeds in Japan in Some Cases But Not Others," International Organization 47:3 (Summer 1993), pp. 353–386.

64. Jeffrey W. Knopf, "Beyond Two-Level Games: Domestic-International Interaction in the Intermediate-Range Nuclear Forces Negotiations," International Organization 47:4 (Autumn 1993), pp. 599–628.

65. Knopf's tale of how German groups influenced the American negotiating position looks even less like a case of "cross-level" strategy when one looks at the U.S.-German negotiations as a subgame in the primary negotiations between the U.S. and Soviets over INF force reductions. Knopf himself admits that the latter talks were the "principal" negotiations. In terms of these negotiations, the story Knopf tells about how domestic groups in Germany limited the options available to U.S. negotiators is actually little different from the story of how domestic interests in general define their own state's win-set. German groups were able to influence the American strategy because, although they were located in another state, they had the power to veto American negotiating positions they didn't like. They were not actually reaching "cross-level" (which would have meant reaching out to the Soviets) but were simply defining the win-set for their own side in the principal negotiations between the Western alliance and the Soviet Union.

3. American Politics and the Birth of SII

1. Washington Times, March 30, 1990, p. C3; April 5, 1990, p. C1; June 26, 1990, C1; and seven other articles between 1989 and 1992. The term "strategic" was used often in the Cold War negotiations with the Soviets, in the Strategic Arms Limitation Treaty (SALT) and the Strategic Arms Reduction Treaty (START). The Times may also

have been confusing sɪɪ with the similar acronym sᴅɪ (Strategic Defense Initiative) which was of course another product of the Cold War era.

2. Dan Caldwell, *The Dynamics of Domestic Politics and Arms Control* (Columbia, SC: University of South Carolina, 1991); David Skidmore, "The Politics of National Security Policy: Interest Groups, Coalitions, and the SALT II Debate," in David Skidmore and Valerie M. Hudson, eds., *The Limits of State Autonomy* (Boulder: Westview Press, 1993), pp. 205–233; Lloyd Jensen, *Bargaining for National Security* (Columbia, SC: University of South Carolina, 1988); Strobe Talbott, *Endgame: The Inside Story of SALT II* (New York: Harper & Row, 1979).

3. On "homogeneous" and "heterogeneous" preferences, see Robert D. Putnam, "Diplomacy and Domestic Politics: the Logic of Two-Level Games," *International Organization* 42:3 (Summer 1988), pp. 444–445.

4. Judith Goldstein, *Ideas, Interests, and American Trade Policy* (Ithaca: Cornell University Press, 1993); I. M. Destler, *American Trade Politics: System Under Stress* (Washington, D.C.: Institute for International Economics, 1986); Robert A. Pastor, *Congress and the Politics of Foreign Economic Policy* (Berkeley: University of California Press, 1980); Gilbert R. Winham, *International Trade and the Tokyo Round Negotiations* (Princeton: Princeton University Press, 1986).

5. Japanese makers' share of U.S. market figures are from Ward's, reproduced in Keizai Koho Center, *Japan 1981: An International Comparison* (Japan: Keizai Koho Center, 1981), p. 20. Figures for Japanese auto exports are from the American Automobile Manufacturers' Association, *Facts and Figures '94*.

6. Auto parts figures are from *JEI Report* 15A (April 23, 1993), p. 6—reporting data from the Department of Commerce, International Trade Administration, Office of Automotive Affairs. Other data from various issues of ᴏᴇᴄᴅ, *Foreign Trade by Commodities*.

7. Destler, *American Trade Politics*, p. 160. See also Alan V. Deardorff and Robert M. Stern, "American Labor's Stake in International Trade," in Adam S. Walter, ed., *Tariffs, Quotas and Trade: The Politics of Protectionism* (San Francisco: Institute for Contemporary Studies, 1979).

8. Ibid., pp. 159–160.

9. E. E. Schattschneider, *Politics, Pressures, and the Tariff* (New York: Prentice-Hall, 1935). For more recent and more formal arguments that emphasize the same basic dynamic, see Stephen P. Magee and Leslie Young, "Endogenous Protection in the United States, 1900–1984," in Robert M. Stern, ed., *U.S. Trade Policies in a Changing World Economy* (Cambridge: MIT Press, 1987), pp. 145–195; and Robert E. Baldwin, *The Political Economy of U.S. Import Policy* (Cambridge: MIT Press, 1985).

10. Edward Mansfield and Joanne Gowa have emphasized how the "security externalities" of trade with allies motivate free trade policies in cases such as this. See Mansfield, "Alliances, Preferential Trading Arrangements and Sanctions," *Journal of International Affairs* 48:1 (Summer 1994), pp. 119–139; and Gowa, *Allies, Adversaries and International Trade* (Princeton: Princeton University Press, 1994).

11. Stephen Krasner calculated that if Japan and the U.S. maintained their ɢᴅᴘ growth rates of 1970–1982, Japan's economy would be larger than America's within

50 years (2032)—see his "Japan and the United States: Prospects for Stability," in Takashi Inoguchi and Daniel Okimoto, eds., *The Political Economy of Japan, Vol. 2: The Changing International Context* (Stanford: Stanford University Press, 1988), p. 391. More recently, C. Fred Bergsten and Marcus Noland calculated that the Japanese economy would surpass the American one in absolute size by "early in the 20th Century" if they maintained rates of the past two decades. The main reason the more recent forecast has Japan catching up at an earlier date: exchange rate shifts since 1985 which have doubled the size of the Japanese economy in dollar terms—see their *Reconcilable Differences?: United States-Japan Economic Conflict* (Washington, D.C.: Institute for International Economics, 1993), p. 9.

12. See Clyde V. Prestowitz, *Trading Places: How We Are Giving Our Future to Japan and How to Reclaim It* (New York: Basic Books, 1988).

13. Peter Drucker, "Japan's Choices," *Foreign Affairs* 65:5 (Summer 1987), pp. 923–941; Edward J. Lincoln, *Japan's Unequal Trade* (Washington, D.C.: Brookings, 1990); Karel van Wolferen, "The Japan Problem," *Foreign Affairs* 65:2 (Winter 1986/87), pp. 288–303; James Fallows, "Containing Japan," *The Atlantic Monthly*, May 1989, pp. 40–54.

14. See for example C. Fred Bergsten and William R. Cline, *The United States-Japan Economic Problem* (Washington, D.C.: Institute for International Economics, 1987), pp. 4–8.

15. The 40 percent number comes from Robert Z. Lawrence, "Imports in Japan: Closed Markets or Closed Minds?" *Brookings Papers on Economic Activity* 2 (1987), pp. 517–548, but other studies have yielded similar findings. See Bergsten and Cline, *The United-States-Japan Economic Problem*. The leading dissident from this view, arguing that Japanese manufactured import levels (taking into account comparative advantage) are not low, is Gary R. Saxonhouse. See his "Comparative Advantage, Structural Adaptation, and Japanese Performance," in Inoguchi and Okimoto, eds., *The Political Economy of Japan, Vol. 2*, pp. 225–248. For a comprehensive discussion of this issue and a review of a range of studies, see Lincoln, *Japan's Unequal Trade*, pp. 18–25; and Bergsten and Noland, *Reconcilable Differences?*, pp. 179–190.

16. Lincoln, *Japan's Unequal Trade*, pp. 46–59.

17. *JEI Report* No. 35A (September 20, 1991), p. 7. The imbalance has actually grown in the years since 1989, reaching 20.5 times in 1990. See also the analysis of Edward J. Lincoln, *Japan's New Global Role* (Washington, D.C.: Brookings, 1993), pp. 70–77.

18. Dennis J. Encarnation, *Rivals Beyond Trade: America Versus Japan in Global Competition* (Ithaca: Cornell University Press, 1992).

19. Robert Z. Lawrence, "Efficient or Exclusionist? The Import Behavior of Japanese Corporate Groups," *Brookings Papers on Economic Activity* 1 (1991), pp. 327–328; and Lawrence, "How Open is Japan?" in Paul Krugman, ed., *Trade With Japan: Has the Door Opened Wider?* (Chicago: University of Chicago Press), pp. 25–30.

20. The four classic revisionist texts are: Chalmers Johnson, *MITI and the Japanese Miracle: The Growth of Industrial Policy, 1925–1975* (Stanford: Stanford University Press, 1982); Prestowitz, *Trading Places*; Karel van Wolferen, *The Enigma of Japanese*

Power (New York: Knopf, 1989); and James Fallows, "Containing Japan." See also Johnson, "How to Think About Economic Competition From Japan," in Kenneth Pyle, ed., *The Trade Crisis: How Will Japan Respond?* (Seattle: Society for Japanese Studies, 1987), pp. 71–83; Charles Ferguson, "America's High Tech Decline," *Foreign Policy* 74 (1989), pp. 123–144; Laura d'Andrea Tyson and John Zysman, "Developmental Strategy and Production Innovation in Japan," in Chalmers Johnson, Tyson, and Zysman, eds., *Politics and Productivity* (New York: HarperBusiness, 1989), pp. 59–140; and Laura Tyson, *Who's Bashing Whom? Trade Conflict in High-Technology Industries* (Washington, D.C.: Institute for International Economics, 1992).

21. Fallows, "Containing Japan,," p. 41.

22. Stephen D. Krasner, "Trade Conflicts and the Common Defense: the United States and Japan," *Political Science Quarterly* 101:5 (1986), pp. 787–805.

23. See Joseph Grieco, *Cooperation Among Nations: Europe, America, and Non-Tariff Barriers to Trade* (Ithaca: Cornell University Press, 1990).

24. Michael Mastanduno formulates the realist prediction for American policy toward Japan in this way. See his article, "Do Relative Gains Matter? America's Response to Japanese Industrial Policy," *International Security* 16:1 (Summer 1991), pp. 73–113. The expectation that the U.S. would start to care more about relative gains as it lost its hegemony is of course based on the realist model known as "hegemonic stability theory." See Charles Kindleberger, *The World in Depression* (Berkeley: University of California Press, 1973); Robert Gilpin, *U.S. Power and the Multinational Corporation* (New York: Basic Books, 1975); and Stephen D. Krasner, "State Power and the Structure of International Trade," *World Politics* 28 (April 1976), pp. 317–347.

25. *JEI Report* No. 34A (September 13, 1991), pp. 41–43—reporting Department of Commerce data.

26. Fred Bergsten describes the dynamic this way: "Understandably, the response in Japan is often to co-opt the complaining foreign firms, to minimize disruption to the status quo. This often suits the interests of the new entrants, since they too come to enjoy the benefits of Japan's cartelized markets. This sets up a dynamic in which the US government is used as a lever to gain market entry, but as soon as entry is achieved, the government is encouraged to cease its liberalization pressures."— *Reconcilable Differences*, p. 60. That this is often the way the process works was confirmed in interviews with American executives in Tokyo.

27. Interviews with business executives in Tokyo. Note that John Odell identifies a similar dynamic at work in U.S. trade relations with Brazil. In the case he examines, he found that IBM led the forces *against* an aggressive trade policy designed to open up the Brazilian computer market because it already had a lucrative niche there which would be threatened by adverse relations between the U.S. and Brazil. See Odell, "International Threats and Internal Politics: Brazil, the European Community, and the United States, 1985–1987," in Peter B. Evans, Harold K. Jacobson, and Robert D. Putnam, eds., *Double Edged Diplomacy: International Bargaining and Domestic Politics* (Berkeley: University of California Press, 1993), pp. 238–241.

28. *JEI Report* 35A (September 20, 1991), p. 4—based on Ministry of Finance figures.

29. Helen Milner, *Resisting Protectionism: Global Industries and the Politics of International Trade* (Princeton: Princeton University Press, 1988); and I. M. Destler and John S. Odell, *Anti-Protection: Changing Forces in United States Trade Politics* (Washington, D.C.: Institute for International Economics, 1987).

30. Pat Choate, *Agents of Influence* (New York: Knopf, 1990), pp. 7–11. Note that Choate's book, while polemical, is basically about how U.S.-Japan economic interdependence creates interests in the U.S. which, with concentrated costs and benefits riding on good bilateral relations, have an incentive to mobilize in favor of moderation in U.S. trade policy.

31. Joseph Nye, "Coping with Japan," *Foreign Policy* 89 (Winter 92/93), pp. 96–115.

32. Michael W. Chinworth and Dean Cheng, "The United States and Asia in the Post-Cold War World," *SAIS Review* 11:1 (Winter-Spring 1991), pp. 73–91.

33. David Lake, "Beneath the Commerce of Nations: A Theory of International Economic Structures," *International Studies Quarterly* 28 (1984), pp. 143–170. Duncan Snidal arrives at a similar conclusion (that several powers can cooperate and maintain an open trading system despite relative gains concerns) by different means in "The Limits of Hegemonic Stability Theory," *International Organization* 39:4 (Autumn 1985), pp. 579–614. While Lake assigns only a minor role to regimes, others have placed greater emphasis on their role in fostering cooperation. See especially Robert O. Keohane, *After Hegemony: Cooperation and Discord in the World Political Economy* (Princeton: Princeton University Press, 1984).

34. Inoguchi Takashi employs Lake's construct and argues that indeed "Japan's economic size and productivity will perforce place Japan in the role of supporter." See his "Japan's Images and Options: Not a Challenger, but a Supporter," *Journal of Japanese Studies* 12:1 (Winter 1986), pp. 95–119.

35. Judith Goldstein, *Ideas, Interests, and American Trade Policy* puts particular emphasis on ideas as they are codified in laws and institutions. The argument that institutions bias the way political markets process societal inputs is of course a core assumption across the range of literature grouped under the rubric "new institutionalism." See such works as Douglass C. North, *Institutions, Institutional Change, and Economic Performance* (New York: Cambridge University Press, 1990); G. John Ikenberry, David A. Lake, and Michael Mastanduno, eds., *The State and American Foreign Economic Policy* (Ithaca: Cornell University Press, 1988); and Peter Hall, *Governing the Economy: The Politics of State Intervention in Britain and France* (New York: Oxford University Press, 1986).

36. Ellis S. Krauss and Simon Reich, "Ideology, Interests, and the American Executive: Toward a Theory of Foreign Competition and Manufacturing Trade Policy," *International Organization* 46:4 (Autumn 1992), pp. 857–897.

37. Schattschneider, *Politics, Pressures and the Tariff*.

38. Destler, *American Trade Politics*, p. 3.

39. Destler, *American Trade Politics*, pp. 12–30; Goldstein, *Ideas, Interests, and American Trade Policy*; Pastor, *Congress and the Politics of U.S. Foreign Economic Policy*.

40. Destler, *American Trade Politics*.

41. Goldstein, *Ideas, Interests, and American Trade Policy*.

42. One example of how these departments were institutionally privileged even in the waning years of the Cold War is the way the Commerce Department was kept deliberately in the dark by the Defense Department during the early stages of the U.S.-Japan negotiations over technology transfers related to the Japanese FSX fighter project—see Prestowitz's account in *Trading Places*, pp. 1–58.

43. Krauss and Reich, "Ideology, Interests, and the American Executive."

44. Krauss and Reich, "Ideology, Interests, and the American Executive," pp. 875–880, 882–886; Destler, *American Trade Politics*, pp. 69–72, 133–135.

45. Tyson, *Who's Bashing Whom: Trade Conflict in High-Technology Industries*, pp. 58–66; Lincoln, *Japan's Unequal Trade*, pp. 148–153; Prestowitz, *Trading Places*, pp. 480–485.

46. Judith Hippler Bello and Alan F. Holmer, "The Heart of the 1988 Trade Act: A Legislative History of the Amendments to Section 301," in Jagdish Bhagwati and Hugh T. Patrick, eds., *Aggressive Unilateralism: America's 301 Trade Policy and the World Trading System* (Ann Arbor: University of Michigan Press, 1990), p. 49. One other measure of Congressional activism was the increase in the number of hearings. According to Kusano Atsushi's count, the number of hearings on Japan-related topics rose from an average of 33 a year in the 1970s to 60 a year during the next decade—calculated from data presented in *Amerika gikai to nichibei kankei* (The U.S. Congress and U.S.-Japan Relations) (Tokyo: Chūkō Sōsho, 1991), p. 25.

47. The bill was not reconciled with Senate legislation, however, and so did not become law. See I. M. Destler, *American Trade Politics* 2nd ed. (Washington, D.C.: Institute for International Economics, 1992), pp. 89–90; Helen Milner, "The Political Economy of U.S. Trade Policy: A Study of the Super 301 Provision," in Bhagwati and Patrick, *Aggressive Unilateralism*, pp. 166–167; and Bello and Holmer, "The Heart of the 1988 Trade Act," pp. 77–80.

48. Yoichi Funabashi, *Managing the Dollar: From the Plaza to the Louvre* 2nd ed. (Washington, D.C.: Institute for International Economics, 1989).

49. Ibid., p. 16.

50. Prestowitz, *Trading Places*, pp. 159–173; Laura d'Andrea Tyson, *Who's Bashing Whom*, pp. 106–110.

51. At about the same time the administration was pushing hard for a semiconductor deal, Commerce was in the middle of a similarly aggressive push to open up the Japanese public sector construction market. This set of negotiations was intense as well, and resulted in an agreement to open up a limited number of mega-projects to bidding by foreign firms. See Ellis S. Krauss and Elizabeth Coles, "Built-in Impediments: The Political Economy of the U.S.-Japan Construction Dispute," in Kozo Yamamura, ed., *Japan's Economic Structure: Should It Change* (Seattle: Society for Japanese Studies, 1990), pp. 333–358; and Ellis Krauss, "U.S.-Japan Negotiations on Construction and Semiconductors, 1985–1988: Building Friction and Relation-chips," in Evans, Jacobson and Putnam, eds., *Double-Edged Diplomacy*, pp. 265–299.

52. Reconstruction of interagency arguments by one of the participants in the

debate, Counsellor for Japan Affairs to the Secretary of Commerce, Clyde Prestowitz. See his *Trading Places*, p. 164.

53. On the latter, see Helen V. Milner and David B. Yoffie, "Between Free Trade and Protectionism: Strategic Trade Policy and a Theory of Corporate Trade Demands," *International Organization* 43:2 (Spring 1989), pp. 239–272.

54. Bello and Holmer, "The Heart of the 1988 Trade Act"; Milner, "The Political Economy of U.S. Trade Policy"; and Destler, *American Trade Politics* 2nd ed., pp. 91–97.

55. Baucus told Hills she would be "cutting the heart out" of the Super 301 bill if she didn't name Japan.

56. S. Linn Williams, "Kagami no naka no nichibei kōzō kyōgi: #2," (Looking in the Mirror at the SII Talks: Part 2) *Shūkan Daiyamondo*, March 21, 1992, p. 110.

57. ACTPN, *Analysis of the U.S.-Japan Trade Problem*, February 1989, p. xvii.

58. For accounts of how the ideological environment was viewed by the Bush administration, see Amelia Porges, "U.S.-Japan Trade Negotiations: Paradigms Lost," in Paul Krugman, ed., *Trade With Japan*, pp. 306–307, 321; and Merit E. Janow, "Trading with an Ally: Progress and Discontent in U.S.-Japan Trade Relations," in Gerald Curtis, ed., *The United States, Japan, and Asia: Challenges for U.S. Policy* (New York, W. W. Norton, 1994), pp. 55–57.

59. Tyson, *Who's Bashing Whom*, pp. 44–45.

60. See Stephen S. Cohen and John Zysman, *Manufacturing Matters: The Myth of the Post-Industrial Economy* (New York: Basic Books, 1987); and Johnson, Tyson, and Zysman, *Politics and Productivity*.

61. Prestowitz, *Trading Places*; Fukushima, *Nichibei keizai masatsu no seijigaku* (The Political Science of U.S.-Japan Economic Disputes) (Tokyo: Asahi Shimbunsha, 1992).

62. Prestowitz, *Trading Places*, pp. 1–58; Richard Samuels, *"Rich Nation Strong Army": National Security and the Technological Transformation of Japan* (Ithaca: Cornell University Press, 1994), pp. 231–244;

63. Prestowitz, *Trading Places*, pp. 150–173, 480.

64. Interview with Williams, August 3, 1993.

65. Michael Mastanduno, "Framing the Japan Problem: the Bush Administration and the Structural Impediments Initiative," *International Journal*, 47:2 (Spring 1992), p. 242; *JEI Report* 22B (June 9, 1989), pp. 9–11.

66. Various Treasury officials have emphasized the Yen-Dollar-moss-Plaza-SII lineage. Mulford, for example, emphasizes that Treasury was worried that the adjustment process brought about (partly) by his department's previous efforts to engineer Plaza and the '87 fiscal package was about to peter out. See his testimony in U.S. Congress, Senate Committee on Finance, *United States-Japan Structural Impediments Initiative* (SII: Hearings before the Subcommittee on International Trade), 101st Congress, 1st sess., July 20, 1989, p. 22–23.

67. Treasury Deputy Assistant Secretary for International Affairs Charles Dallara, interviewed in NHK, *Nichibei no shōtotsu* (The U.S.-Japan Collision) (Tokyo: NHK, 1990), p. 71 (my translation of their translation). This concern with the lack of pass

through of lower import prices in Japan was similarly emphasized in other interviews I conducted and is cited by the USTR's Williams as a primary motivation for the Treasury Department's interest in SII in "Kagami no naka no nichibei kōzō kyōgi: #4," (Looking in the Mirror at the SII Talks: Part 4) *Shūkan daiyamondo*, April 4, 1992, p. 113. For evidence of the lack of pass through of lower import prices, see OECD, *OECD Economic Surveys 1986/87: Japan* (Paris: OECD, 1986), pp. 57–61.

68. Robert Fauver and Susan Creane authored a memo advocating a structural initiative early in 1988. Though initially the memo was largely ignored, Dallara and Mulford picked up on this idea when it was recirculated in early 1989—interview with U.S. official, September 8, 1993; numerous other sources trace the origins of SII to Treasury. See NHK, *Nichibei no shōtotsu*, pp. 65–66; Fukushima, *Nichibei keizai masatsu no seijigaku*, pp. 198–199; Williams, "Kagami no naka no nichibei kōzō kyōgi: #4," p. 113; and Mastanduno, "Framing the Japan problem," pp. 243.

69. Fukushima, *Nichibei keizai masatsu no seijigaku*, p. 48.

70. Mastanduno, "Framing the Japan Problem," p. 243. Mastanduno bases his description of the memo on interviews he conducted in July 1990, but he himself was on the staff of USTR at the time.

71. *JEI Report* 22B, June 9, 1989, p. 10. USTR's Williams confirmed in an interview, August 3, 1993, this account of the positions taken by the principals at the meeting.

72. Interview with Williams, August 3, 1993. Hills, in her press conference comments after announcing the proposed SII talks on May 25, articulated the administration's hope that SII would serve as a "constructive" complement to Super 301—text of press conference reprinted in *Asahi shimbun*, May 25, 1989, p. 2.

73. Text of Hill's announcement, *Nihon keizai shimbun*, May 26, 1989, p. 2. Partial text reprinted in Chalmers Johnson, "Trade, Revisionism, and the Future of Japanese-American Relations," in Yamamura, ed., *Japan's Economic Structure*, p. 106. For an analysis of the administration's selection of Super 301 targets, see Michael Mastanduno, "Setting Market Access Priorities: The Use of Super 301 in US Trade with Japan," *World Economy* 15:6 (November 1992), pp. 729–753.

74. Porges, "U.S.-Japan Trade Negotiations," p. 322.

75. Interview with retired Congressman William Frenzel, August 3, 1993.

76. Cited in Glen Fukushima, *Nichibei keizai masatsu no seijigaku*, p. 203.

77. S. Linn Williams, "Kagami no naka no nichibei kōzō kyōgi: #5," (Looking in the Mirror at the SII Talks: Part 5) *Shūkan daiyamondo*, April 11, 1992, p. 92.

78. Fukushima, *Nichibei keizai masatsu no seijigaku*, p. 200.

79. David A. Lax and James K. Sebenius, *The Manager as Negotiator: Bargaining for Cooperation and Competitive Gain* (New York: Free Press, 1986), p. 246.

80. Krauss and Reich, "Ideology, interests, and the American executive."

81. On the ties between Clinton and the business community, see Thomas Ferguson, *Golden Rule: The Investment Theory of Party Competition and the Logic of Money-Driven Political Systems* (Chicago: University of Chicago Press, 1995), p. 4.

82. A range of participants in the decisionmaking that led to the decision to go with SII argued in personal interviews that, while the decision on Super 301 was

heavily conditioned by pressure from Congress, sii itself was not motivated that much by Congressional pressure. Congress really didn't give the administration credit for this initiative and was mostly concerned about whether or not the administration would "name practices as well as Japan" under Super 301. As Williams put it, sii "gave us a chance to articulate a vision of the U.S.-Japan trading relationship that I thought was more constructive."—interview, June 22, 1993. See also Carla Hills' comment at her press conference on May 25 (note 72 above).

83. Williams, "Kagami no naka no nichibei kōzō kyōgi: #5," p. 90.

84. Interview with U.S. official, August 3, 1993. As this official put it, Treasury's purpose was to bring new ministries "into previously inaccessible territory. . . . , bringing domestic pressure to bear on issues."

85. Williams, "Kagami no naka no nichibei kōzō kyōgi: #5," p. 91.

86. Interview with U.S. official, June 16, 1992.

87. Note that Mulford, in congressional testimony, went out of his way to differentiate sii from the earlier Structural Dialogue, in sii Hearings of July 20, 1989, p. 22. This earlier round of talks was designed to provide an opportunity for an exchange of views on structural issues. See William H. Cooper, "Japan-U.S. Trade: The Structural Impediments Initiative," *Current Politics and Economics of Japan* 1:1 (1991), pp. 75–76.

88. Rather than contacting miti's man at the Japanese embassy in Washington, ustr used its standard "back door" route to approach miti, contacting the ministry's senior representative at the jetro office in New York. The embassy route was perceived as being unsecured since the Japanese Ministry of Foreign Affairs was very likely to be suspicious of any ustr communication with the miti official there, and because once mofa found out, the State Department was bound to find out as well—interview with Williams, June 22, 1993.

89. In the event, State's participation turned out not to present the feared problem of diluting American resolve, not only because State officials too were starting to perceive a need for a firmer line with Japan but also because of some timely personnel moves that blurred departmental lines. James Baker, who had moved over from Treasury to become Secretary of State in 1988, recruited two of his assistants from his years at Treasury (Robert Zoellick and Robert Fauver) to join him. Both were hawkish relative to most State officials on Japan issues and Fauver had been involved in drawing up the original concept for sii while still at Treasury.

90. This decision was reached at a U.S. delegation retreat held in December at the Airlie House in rural Virginia. The team had by this time compiled numerous position papers and faced a decision about which demands to emphasize. Instead of choosing, the group decided to "push all items at the same speed."—interview with Williams, August 3, 1993.

91. Mastanduno has noted how the U.S. delegation made no efforts to set priorities and ascribes it to the administration decision to frame the "Japan problem" as one of "loss avoidance"—see "Framing the Japan Problem," pp. 250–251.

92. Dallara, the Deputy Assistant Secretary who had been involved in sii from the beginning, insisted that he should serve as chair with the secretariat also located

at Treasury, but McCormack insisted that his rank (Undersecretary) and his depart-ment's status dictated that State should head the delegation. The issue was not resolved until Bush was brought in to personally mediate the dispute.

93. In the bureaucratic politics that led to sii, this mission seems to have served as the catalyst that led Treasury to make its big push for a structural initiative. State proposed the initiative in January, and the reaction at Treasury was immediate: "State doesn't know what it's doing; They're going to do another Structural Dialogue." To prevent State from taking charge of the Japan initiative, Treasury approached usTR with its own proposal for an a structural initiative and started the process that led to sii—interview with U.S. official, September 8, 1993.

94. Interview with Williams, August 3, 1993, and other U.S. officials; Mastanduno, "Framing the Japan Problem," p. 245.

95. Interview with Williams, June 22, 1993.

96. The U.S. side was actually very open about the fact that many of their demands were taken from the unimplemented reform proposals of Japanese gov-ernment agencies. U.S. Ambassador Michael Armacost in particular repeatedly referred to how U.S. demands were drawn from the Maekawa Reports. See Sasaki Takeshi, *Seiji wa doko e mukaunoka* (Where is Politics Headed?) (Tokyo: Chūkō Shinsho, 1992), p. 34. The Maekawa Commission was appointed as a private advi-sory commission by Nakasone in October 1985 to study the problem of economic restructuring. The group was known formally as the Advisory Group on Economic Structural Adjustment for International Harmony but, because it was headed by Maekawa Haruo, the former Governor of the Bank of Japan, it is generally known by the shorter name used here. The group issued its first report on April 7, 1986, and another on May 14, 1987. Its list of recommendations looks remarkably similar to the list of American sii demands, especially in the areas of public investment, dis-tribution, and land policy. Among other reform proposals, the council called for "extraordinary and urgent fiscal measures" to stimulate domestic demand-led eco-nomic growth, deregulation in the distribution sector, and land policy reforms such as increased taxes on urban agricultural land. See Ministry of Foreign Affairs, *Documents on Japan's Economic Structural Adjustment*, June 1987.

97. Interview with Williams, August 3, 1993.

98. Shigeko Fukai, "The Role of *Gaiatsu* in Japan's Land Policymaking," paper pre-sented at the APSA annual meeting in Chicago, September 3–6, 1992.

99. Interview with Shimizu, June 10, 1992.

100. Interview with Unno, May 25, 1992.

101. Glen Fukushima, *Nichibei keizai masatsu no seijigaku*, pp. 217–218.

102. See Funabashi, *Managing the Dollar*.

103. The Japanese made this demand almost immediately after Hills publicly pro-posed the structural initiative on May 25. See *JEI Report* 22B (June 9, 1989), p. 11. Williams insists that the U.S. anticipated this objection and had no problem with it—Interview, August 3, 1993.

104. Although the sii talks were therefore two-way, I do not devote any atten-tion in this book to the Japanese demands because neither side treated them with

anything like the seriousness with which the American demands were treated. My failure to incorporate an analysis of the Japanese demands into the study would be problematic if there were tradeoffs across the two nations' agendas, but other than on a few specific issues like intellectual property rights (see note 16 in chapter 10) there was no meaningful give and take. As Michael Mastanduno put it, "the United States and Japanese agendas proceeded on separate tracks. . . . No effort was made to relate the two agendas to one another or to make trade-offs across them (for example, 'we'll reduce our budget deficit if you increase your spending'). The SII was, in effect, two negotiations rather than one."—"Framing the Japan Problem," p. 249.

105. Two other issues were also settled at this prenegotiation stage. First, the Americans agreed to a Japanese demand that the SII deal not be treated as actionable under Section 301 of U.S. trade law. The Japanese were worried that some of the things they were likely to be asked to agree to (opening up keiretsu, for example) were likely to be largely beyond their control. The U.S. recognized that they were unlikely to be able to extract meaningful concessions if the Japanese were held under the Section 301 gun. The two sides thus agreed to this language: "These talks are not intended to seek an agreement that forms the basis for Section 301 proceedings. In the same vein, the assessment and joint press release [in the spring of 1990] will not be regarded as an agreement in the context of the U.S. trade act."—text of "U.S.-Japan Note on SII" agreed prior to July 14 joint communique. The second issue concerned the name for the talks. The U.S. had proposed "Structural Impediments Initiative," but there was some resistance on the Japanese side to admitting their were barriers of any kind already in the title of the talks. The Japanese relented, however, when the Americans began pressing them to call the talks "negotiations." That was even less acceptable since the Japanese refused to "negotiate" about matters they considered to be purely domestic. The talks therefore kept the name SII, instead of being renamed SIN. Interview with Williams, August 3, 1993; Fukushima, *Nichibei keizai masatsu no seijigaku*, pp. 205–207.

4. JAPANESE POLITICS AND THE SII NEGOTIATIONS

1. *JEI Report* 26B (July 6, 1990), pp. 11–12.

2. Robert M. Orr, Jr., *The Emergence of Japan's Foreign Aid Power* (New York: Columbia University Press, 1990); Edward J. Lincoln, *Japan's New Global Role* (Washington, D. C.: Brookings, 1993); Amelia Porges, "U. S.-Japan Trade Negotiations: Paradigms Lost," in Paul Krugman, ed., *Trade With Japan: Has the Door Opened Wider?* (Chicago: University of Chicago Press, 1991), pp. 305–327.

3. NHK, *Nichibei no shōtotsu* (The U. S.-Japan Collision) (Tokyo: NHK, 1990), pp. 248–304. The Japanese public television network, NHK, obtained detailed notes taken by one of the Japanese delegates at the supposedly closed SII negotiating sessions and published them, providing us with an opportunity to see how the various sides made their arguments.

4. The list was the product of the American delegation's December retreat at the Airlie House in Virginia. Because it contained so many specific demands on issues previously considered "purely domestic," it was controversial, and the way it was handled reflected this controversy. When the U. S. first attempted to hand over the list, the Japanese delegates refused to accept it. According to one of the Japanese, his delegation was shocked that the Americans were calling for such far-reaching changes. They were demanding reforms on a scale not seen since the American occupation!—NHK, *Nichibei no shōtotsu*, p. 100. They were worried in particular about what would happen if the list were to leak. The Japanese did look the list over, though, and the two sides arranged to have the list faxed to the Ministry of Foreign Affairs as "reference material" just prior to the next negotiating session—Interview with Williams, August 3, 1993, and NHK, *Nichibei no shōtotsu*, p. 102. MOFA, which took charge of the list, was still so worried about what would happen if it were to leak, however, that it divided it up and sent most other ministries only the parts of the document relevant to them. Almost immediately, it leaked anyway.

5. The list was eventually published in full by *Asahi Jaanaru* in a series running from April 20 to May 18, 1990. The summary of demands in this chapter focuses only on the most notable ones. More detailed lists are contained in each of the issue-specific chapters.

6. The Japanese general government deficit in 1979 amounted to over 4 percent of GNP, but after a decade of fiscal austerity the deficit had been turned into a surplus amounting to 1 percent of GNP in 1988. See OECD, *1988/89 OECD Economic Surveys: Japan* (Paris: OECD, 1989), p. 45. A variety of econometric studies have pointed to Japanese fiscal policy (along with America's mirror-image deficit spending fiscal policy) as the main sources of the U. S.-Japan current account imbalances of the 1980s. See Warwick McKibbin, Nouriel Roubini, and Jeffrey D. Sachs, "Correcting Global Imbalances: A Simulation Approach," in Robert M. Stern, ed., *Trade and Investment Relations Among the United States, Canada, and Japan* (Chicago: University of Chicago Press, 1989), pp. 379–424.

7. See calculations in chapter 5.

8. See figure 6.3.

9. Testimony of Dallara, U. S. Congress, Senate Committee on Finance, *United States-Japan Structural Impediments Initiative (SII): Hearings before the Subcommittee on International Trade*, 101st Congress, 2nd sess., March 5, 1990, (hereafter *SII Hearings of 5 March 1990*), p. 45.

10. Examples of the vagueness of promises are discussed in chapter 8.

11. *Washington Post*, May 23, 1991, p. B18. See also "Comments of U. S. Delegation," in the "First Annual Report of the SSI Followup," p. 7.

12. Dallara, *SII Hearings of 5 March 1990*, p. 46.

13. *New York Times*, March 16, 1991, p. A1; and Imai Ken'ichi, "The Legitimacy of Japan's Corporate Groups," *Japan Echo* 17 (Autumn 1990), pp. 23–28.

14. Fair Trade Commission Executive Office, *The Outline of the Report on the Actual Conditions of the Six Major Corporate Groups*, February 1992, p. 19.

15. Testimony of R. K. Morris, NAM director for international trade, in U.S.

Congress, Senate Committee on Finance, *Super 301: Effectiveness in Opening Foreign Markets: Hearings Before the Subcommittee on International Trade*, 101st Congress, 2d sess., April 27, 1990, pp. 79–80.

16. This alternative explanation was also suggested by one of the referees who read the manuscript for Columbia University Press.

17. Other hypotheses were generated as well, but these are the ones I focus on in this chapter.

18. Michio Muramatsu and Ellis Krauss, "The Conservative Policy Line and the Development of Patterned Pluralism," in Kozo Yamamura and Yasukichi Yasuba, eds., *The Political Economy of Japan, vol 1: The Domestic Transformation* (Stanford: Stanford University Press, 1987), pp. 517–554; Michio Muramatsu, "Patterned Pluralism Under Challenge: The Policies of the 1980s," in Gary D. Allinson and Yasunori Sone, eds., *Political Dynamics in Contemporary Japan* (Ithaca: Cornell University Press, 1993), pp. 50–71. On zoku, see Satō Seizaburō and Matsuzaki Tetsuhisa, *Jimintō seiken* (LDP Rule) (Tokyo: Chūō Koronsha, 1986); Inoguchi Takashi and Iwai Tomoaki, *'Zoku giin' no kenkyū* (Research on Policy Tribes) (Tokyo: Nihon Keizai Shimbunsha, 1987); Gerald Curtis, *The Japanese Way of Politics* (New York: Columbia University Press, 1988); and Leonard Schoppa, "*Zoku* power and LDP power: A Case Study of the *Zoku* Role in Education Policy," *Journal of Japanese Studies* 17:1 (Winter 1991), pp. 79–106.

19. Randall B. Ripley and Grace A. Franklin, *Congress, the Bureaucracy, and Public Policy* (Homewood, Ill.: The Dorsey Press, 1976). A large body of more recent work has shown how delegation creates rigidities similar to those described here in the U.S. For a survey of the literature, see D. Roderick Kiewiet and Matthew D. McCubbins, *The Logic of Delegation: Congressional Parties and the Appropriations Process* (Chicago: University of Chicago Press, 1991). In this literature, delegation is described as creating "agency loss." When the U. S. Congress as a whole delegates specialized tasks to committees and bureaucratic agencies, it achieves "efficiency gains," but in the process it risks losing some control of its agents who, inevitably, have their own interests to pursue. Among other problems created by delegation is the difficulty of achieving cross-issue linkage once responsibilities have been delegated to specialized units. Congress as a whole has the authority to intervene to achieve these cross-issue deals, but it is not likely to do so often since a primary reason for delegation in the first place was to avoid these responsibilities.

20. John Campbell, "Policy Conflict and its Resolution within the Governmental System," in Ellis Krauss, Thomas Rohlen, and Patricia Steinhoff, eds., *Conflict in Japan* (Honolulu: University of Hawaii Press, 1984), pp. 294–334.

21. For a study of how the subgovernmental system under the LDP contributed to "immobilism" in a non-trade-related sector, see Leonard Schoppa, *Education Reform in Japan* (London: Routledge, 1991).

22. See J. Mark Ramseyer and Frances M. Rosenbluth, *Japan's Political Marketplace* (Cambridge: Harvard University Press, 1993), especially pp. 16–37. For similar arguments, see Peter Cowey, "Domestic Institutions and the Credibility of International Commitments: Japan and the United States," *International Organization*

47:2 (Spring 1993), especially pp. 316–318; and Brian Woodall, *Japan Under Construction: Corruption, Politics, and Public Works* (Berkeley: University of California Press, 1996), pp. 96–99.

23. Ramseyer and Rosenbluth, *Japan's Political Marketplace*, p. 12.

24. Ramseyer and Rosenbluth, *Japan's Political Marketplace*, pp. 50–57.

25. Margaret McKean, "State Strength and the Public Interest," in Allinson and Sone, eds., *Political Dynamics in Contemporary Japan*, pp. 96–104.

26. The image of a "truncated pyramid" comes from Karel van Wolferen, *The Enigma of Japanese Power: People and Politics in a Stateless Nation* (New York: Vantage Books, 1989), p. 5. Another similar image, employed by Ozawa Ichirō, is that of a political structure with "hands and feet" but with no "brain" to govern them. See Ozawa, *Blueprint for a New Japan* (Tokyo: Kōdansha International, 1994), p. 24. The argument here is similar to those advanced by both of these critics of the LDP regime.

27. Note that I am referring here to a particular kind of "crisis," one where the threat to continued LDP rule came from excessively particularistic policies. Kent Calder, in *Crisis and Compensation: Public Policy and Political Stability in Japan* (Princeton: Princeton University Press, 1988), also looks at the LDP's reaction to crises, but focuses especially on crises caused by *not enough* particularism: hence the tendency of the LDP to "compensate" its clients during such periods. It seems that crises during the 1970s and before were of the Calder variety. Since that time, however, LDP "crises" (including the one that cost the party its hold on power in 1993) have arisen due to excessive particularism and the party's difficulty in reining in its compensatory policies.

28. Statistic on the share of bonds in revised total budgets comes from *JEI Report No. 16A* (April 24, 1992), p. 10.

29. For a similar argument, see Kent E. Calder, "Japanese Foreign Economic Policy: Explaining the Reactive State," *World Politics* 40:4 (July 1988), pp. 518–541.

30. Glen Fukushima, *Nichibei keizai masatsu no seijigaku* (The Political Science of U. S.-Japan Economic Disputes) (Tokyo: Asahi Shimbunsha, 1992), p. 114. An excellent example of how the press creates the mood necessary for the Japanese to concede comes from a *Japan Economic Journal* story during the 1988 beef and citrus talks: "A feeling of desperation was already widespread in Tokyo, with most people taking the view that the Japanese would eventually have to accept the American demands."—April 9, 1988, p. 1.

31. Schoppa, "Two Level Games and Bargaining Outcomes," p. 380.

32. Others have pointed out how gaiatsu plays this role. See Kenneth Pyle, *The Japanese Question* (Washington, D. C.: AEI Press, 1992), pp. 111–113; and Calder, "Japanese Foreign Economic Policy: Explaining the Reactive State."

33. See Glen Fukushima, "The Nature of United States-Japan Government Negotiations," in Valerie Kusuda-Smick, ed., *United States / Japan Commercial Law and Trade* (Transnational Juris Publications, 1990), p. 667; and Sasaki Takeshi, "Nichibei kōzō kyōgi: 'motareai' no kiken," (The SII Talks: The Danger of "Reliance") *Ekonomisuto*, November 7, 1989, p. 105.

34. The references to centrifugal and centripetal forces refer to work by T. J. Pempel, "The Unbundling of 'Japan, Inc.': The Changing Dynamics of Japanese Policy Formation," *Journal of Japanese Studies* 13:2 (1987), pp. 271–306.

35. Pyle, *The Japanese Question*, pp. 20–41.

36. The MOF had not always held such a tight rein on fiscal policy. As one would expect given the particularistic bias of the LDP regime described above, the MOF has frequently had difficulty resisting spending pressure from LDP Diet members eager to provide pork for their constituents. By the early 1980s, this bias of the system had helped create a situation where over 35 percent of central government spending was funded by borrowing. In the years after this fiscal "crisis" was recognized, however, the MOF had been much more successful in bringing the deficit under control and holding out against pressures for fiscal stimulus—even when MITI, LDP leaders, and the business community pressed it to do so during the post-Plaza slowdown of 1986–1987. It took strong gaiatsu to break through MOF's defenses and expand participation to include these supporters of increased public investment. For more details, see chapter 5.

37. NHK, *Nichibei no shōtotsu*, pp. 248–270.

38. Interview with Unno, May 25, 1992.

39. On Ambassador Armacost's role in this process during the SII talks, see Michael H. Armacost, *Friends or Rivals? The Insider's Account of U.S.-Japan Relations* (New York: Columbia University Press, 1996), pp. 51–55. Amelia Porges describes such efforts as standard procedure for the U.S. See her "U.S.-Japan Trade Negotiations," pp. 311–312. Interestingly, she notes that zoku veterans were often instrumental as brokers of trade liberalization deals, something that may seem to contradict my description of how zoku politicians in general were defenders of particularistic policies. The role of these zoku veterans can nevertheless be accounted for within the framework I propose by recognizing that these veterans behaved in this way partly to demonstrate that they could break free of sectional interest—something they needed to demonstrate if they wanted to advance their careers from being just zoku leaders to being *party* leaders. Their activism also often reflected the fact that trade liberalization accords typically provided zoku brokers with opportunities to request special compensating programs (aid to affected industries) which they could use in the traditional particularistic way to advance their careers. For an example of zoku leaders playing this role, see discussion in chapter 6 of LDP Dietman Mutō Kabun's role in brokering a settlement of the Large Store Law issue.

40. *Nikkei shimbun*, February 22, 1990; *Asahi shimbun*, February 23, 1990, p. 5; NHK, *Nichibei no shōtotsu*, pp. 292–304.

41. *Nikkei shimbun*, February 24, 1990, p. 3.

42. *JEI Report* 10B (March 9, 1990), p. 12.

43. *JEI Report*, 12B (March 23, 1990), pp. 11–12.

44. Comment of Dietman Aso Taro at party meeting, quoted in *Nikkei shimbun*, March 29, 1990, p. 2.

45. *Asahi shimbun*, March 14, 1990, p. 1 and p. 2.

46. On Brady-Hashimoto meetings, see *New York Times*, March 22, 1990.

Mosbacher met with MITI minister Mutō, LDP secretary general Ozawa, and power-broker Kanemaru during his visit to Tokyo in mid-March. *Nikkei shimbun*, March 15, 1990, p. 5; and same, March 30, 1990, p. 3.

47. A particularly prominent example of a previous attempt to take advantage of bureaucratic rivalry was the Reagan administration's effort to enlist MITI as an ally in an effort to open up the telecommunications market (regulated by the Ministry of Posts and Telecommunications). See Chalmers Johnson, "MITI, MPT, and the Telecom Wars: How Japan Makes Policy for High Technology," in Chalmers Johnson, Laura D'Andrea Tyson, and John Zysman, eds., *Politics and Productivity: How Japan's Development Strategy Works* (New York: Harper Business, 1989), pp. 177–240.

48. That Williams and his fellow U.S. negotiators had this tactic in mind even as they were framing the SII agenda was noted in chapter 3. The first step was Williams' decision, shortly after coming on board at USTR, to commission a survey of Japanese consumer attitudes. The U.S. did not, however, contact Japanese consumer organizations, instead preferring to draw from Japanese public opinion surveys. Because they had not been contacted, Japanese consumer organizations reacted with surprise when Williams began to present himself as an ally of the consumer at his September press conference. See *Asahi shimbun*, September 6, 1989.

49. *The Japan Economic Journal*, September 16, 1989, p. 2. Williams also spent extensive time meeting in small groups and one-on-one with Japanese reporters—interview with Williams, August 3, 1993. According to U.S. embassy sources, the U.S. side drew up an explicit public relations plan designed to help the delegates emphasize points that would reverberate with the Japanese public.

50. Ibid.

51. *Asahi shimbun*, March 5, 1990, p. 5.

52. *Asahi shimbun*, March 11, 1990, p. 5.

53. *Asahi shimbun*, March 16, 1990, p. 5.

54. *Asahi shimbun*, March 18, 1990, p. 5.

55. *Asahi shimbun*, March 29, 1990, p. 5.

56. *Asahi shimbun*, March 29, 1990, p. 5. Almost the same point is made in a *Yomiuri shimbun* editorial, April 2, 1990, p. 3. For another evaluation of the Japanese media's coverage of SII which emphasizes the generally positive tone, see Takeuchi Yasuo, "Tackling the Impediments to Trade," *Japan Echo* 17:3 (Autumn 1990), pp. 6–7.

57. The four are the *Nikkei*, the *Yomiuri*, the *Mainichi*, and the *Sankei*. On the press club system, see Taketoshi Yamamoto, "The Press Clubs of Japan," *Journal of Japanese Studies* 15:2 (Summer 1989), pp. 371–388; and Nathaniel B. Thayer, "Competition and Conformity: An Inquiry into the Structure of Japanese Newspapers," in Ezra F. Vogel, ed., *Modern Japanese Organization and Decision-Making* (Berkeley: University of California Press, 1975), pp. 284–303.

58. Interviews with NHK reporters in Washington D. C. and Tokyo. Studies of the media's impact on public opinion in the U.S. suggest that elite opinion of the type represented by these NHK reporters play an important role in shaping the views of the general public. See John R. Zaller, *The Nature and Origins of Mass Opinion* (Cambridge: Cambridge University Press, 1992).

59. Search conducted by the author at the Diet Library using the Japanese term for SII, "*nichibei kōzō kyōgi*."

60. Data reported in Stanley Budner and Ellis Krauss, *Communicating Across the Pacific* (Missoula, Montana: Mansfield Center for Pacific Affairs, forthcoming). The Mansfield Center conducted an extensive survey of media coverage in Japan and the U.S. of three bilateral disputes, one of which was SII. The numbers given are for stories published between April 1989 and August 11, 1990 by *Asahi shimbun*, *Nikkei shimbun*, and *Yomiuri shimbun*. The data on the balance of stories are based on content analysis conducted by the center. Of the 22.5 percent of articles that presented only one side of the dispute, 80 percent presented only the "pro-SII" side, defined as "a favorable attitude toward negotiations."

61. Note that this widely cited *Nikkei shimbun* poll showed only that more than 80 percent of Japanese supported *some* demands. The poll does not show, as USTR's Williams claimed at one point, that "80 percent of the Japanese public favored our objectives and proposals in the SII." To get to the 80 percent figure, one has to include fully 32 percent of the public who "agreed with some points, even though there are more points which are off-base (*okashii*)"—not exactly a ringing endorsement. The *Nikkei* asked 10,000 respondents by phone the following question: "America is insisting that Japan, in order to improve the trade balance, reform its domestic economic arrangements and open its markets. What do you think about this?" Of the respondents, 9 percent agreed wholly; 38.4 percent "basically agreed, even though there are a few points which are off-base (*okashii*)"; 32.9 percent gave the lukewarm response quoted above; and only 6.1 percent completely disagreed. Asked how Japan should respond to the Americans' demands, 86 percent felt the government should respond "enthusiastically" or in a "generally positive way." Only 5 percent felt there was "no need at all to respond positively."—see *Nikkei shimbun*, March 27, 1990, p. 3.

62. Sasaki Takeshi emphasizes this interpretation of the *Nikkei* poll results. See his *Seiji wa doko e mukaunoka* (Where is Politics Headed) (Tokyo: Chūkō Shinsho, 1992), pp. 50–51.

63. Interview with Japanese delegate, February 8, 1994.

64. *Japan Economic Journal*, April 21, 1990, p. 5.

65. *Japan Economic Journal*, April 21, 1990, p. 5.

66. *Yomiuri shimbun*, April 2, 1990, p. 3.

67. Interview with Williams, June 22, 1993.

68. Shigeko Fukai, "The Role of *Gaiatsu* in Japan's Land Policymaking," paper presented at the annual meeting of the American Political Science Association, Chicago, Ill., September 3–6, 1992.

69. Close readers will note that the discussion in this chapter does not analyze *all* of the tactics identified in chapter 2. For example, there is no mention here of what I called mutually advantageous issue linkage. Such linkage, readers will recall, involves facilitating agreement by linking an issue where one side makes a concession to another where the other side makes a concession. In the case of the SII talks, however, the U.S. made no attempt to use an offer of this sort in order to convince the Japanese to give up more on their side. See note 104 for chapter 3.

70. NHK, *Nichibei no shōtotsu*, pp. 270, 290–291.

71. *Shūkan tōyō keizai*, September 30, 1989, p. 18. To keep up the pressure as the negotiations continued, Baucus actually introduced such legislation in the spring of 1990. See *Wall Street Journal*, April 3, 1990.

72. *JEI Report* 44B (November 10, 1989), p. 13.

73. NHK, *Nichibei no shōtotsu*, p. 292.

74. Former USTR official Glen Fukushima tells a story that reveals how seriously Japanese officials take these struggles to make sure their ministry doesn't sacrifice more than the others. He relates an anecdote about how officials from one ministry during one set of talks insisted on breaking down one concession it was making into three or four component parts so that rival ministries would not be able to accuse it of not conceding its fair share when they counted the number of concessions each ministry had made—*Nichibei keizai masatsu no seijigaku*, p. 194.

75. NHK, *Nichibei no shōtotsu*, p. 103.

5. The Public Investment Issue

1. C. Fred Bergsten and Marcus Noland, *Reconcilable Differences? United States-Japan Economic Conflict* (Washington, D.C.: Institute for International Economics, 1993), p. 36. While I refer to *trade* surpluses and deficits here, the more precise relations are between net savings and *current account* balances. The economics behind this mechanism is explained in summary fashion as follows. Most of a nation's GNP is typically produced and consumed domestically, but two components involve international flows: the savings-investment balance (where the surplus of savings or investment leads to international capital flows) and the current account balance (where a surplus of imports or exports also leads to international monetary flows). Because money inflows must equal money outflows, in the final macroeconomic accounts, the S-I balance must equal and offset the current account balance. In practice, currency markets play the intermediary role in bringing about this equilibrium. If a nation experiences a rise in its net national savings (e.g. Japan in 1980 to 1986), its domestic interests rates tend to fall relative to those available abroad, leading capital to flow abroad. As this nation's currency is sold abroad in order to purchase foreign investments, its value drops. This makes the nation's exports cheaper and imports more expensive, helping to produce a trade surplus that equals and offsets the capital outflow. Conversely, a nation with a growing savings deficit (e.g. the U.S. in the same years) experiences rising interest rates, a stronger dollar, and a trade deficit. See Edward J. Lincoln, *Japan: Facing Economic Maturity* (Washington, D.C.: Brookings, 1988), pp. 70–71, 214-215.

2. Warwick McKibbin, Nouriel Roubini and Jeffrey D. Sachs, "Correcting Global Imbalances: A Simulation Approach," in Robert M. Stern, ed., *Trade and Investment Relations Among the United States, Canada, and Japan* (Chicago: University of Chicago Press, 1989). The study found that U.S. fiscal policy over the same period added 1.4 percentage points to the Japanese trade surplus and 1 point to the U.S. trade deficit.

3. *Japan Times Weekly International Edition*, Dec. 7–13, 1992, p. 7. The MOE survey noted that the physical strength of the older men was higher in areas with higher population densities and that the strength index had risen since the previous survey.

4. In 1980, the average new dwelling had 94.3 square meters of floor space. By 1989, the average had fallen to 80.9—See figure 7.2.

5. Newly constructed dwellings built with the help of public funds rose in size from 97.7 square meters in 1980 to 110.7 square meters in 1989—MOF data supplied to journalists as *Setsumei shiryō (zaisei tōyūshi)*, August 1991, p. 8. That the average size of new dwellings still shrank to 80.9 square meters over this period means that housing constructed privately became much smaller. These units, typically tiny rental apartments, are the "rabbit hutches" critics refer to when faulting the Japanese for their failure to invest in social infrastructure.

6. The figures cited here are for "public investment" (*kōkyō tōshi* in Japanese) the broadest category of such spending calculated by the Japanese government. It includes not just central and local public works spending but also fixed investments by other public-sector organizations and the cost of land acquisition. It is used here because the final SII deal on public investment included a commitment to add 430 trillion yen in this category of investment. Note that there are other measures of public investment (with lower numbers) that are much more frequently cited: "public-sector fixed investment" (*seifu kotei shihon keisei*) does not include the cost of land acquisition; "general government fixed investment" (*ippan seifu no kotei shihon keisei*) does not include investments by other public-sector organizations.

7. Kensetsu Daijin Kambō Seisakuka, *Nichibei kōzō mondai kyōgi to kensetsu gyōsei* (The U.S.-Japan Structural Problem Talks and Construction Administration) (Tokyo: Taisei Shuppansha, 1990), p. 36.

8. The 1990 budget, which was being drawn up as SII was being negotiated, featured a 5.2% cut in public works spending. *JEI Report*, No. 16A (April 24, 1992), p. 3.

9. America pressured Japan to adopt a growth target of 7 percent for 1978, a figure that would force the government to adopt a major deficit-funded stimulus package. Japan relented in January 1978, agreeing to the 7 percent figure. At the same time, it announced a 1978 budget which was slated to rely on borrowing for 37 percent of its funds and increased public works spending by 30 percent. At the Bonn Summit later that year, Japan again agreed to act as a locomotive along with Germany. For an interesting discussion of this previous round of macroeconomic gaiatsu, with obvious parallels to the SII negotiations on this issue, see I.M. Destler and Hisao Mitsuyu, "Locomotives on Different Tracks: Macroeconomic Diplomacy, 1977–1979," in Destler and Hideo Sato, eds., *Coping with U.S. Japan Economic Conflicts* (Lexington, MA: D.C. Heath, 1982), pp. 243–269.

10. Ōtake Hideo, *Jiyū shugiteki kaikaku no jidai: 1980 nendai zenki no nihon seiji* (An Era of Liberal Reform: Japanese Politics in the First Half of the 1980s) (Tokyo: Chūō Kōron, 1994).

11. On MOF's experience during the locomotive episode, see Destler and Mitsuyu, "Locomotives on Different Tracks," p. 254. On the after-effects, see Yoichi

Funabashi, *Managing the Dollar: From Plaza to the Louvre*, 2nd ed. (Washington, D.C.: Institute for International Economics, 1989), p. 94.

12. Funabashi was quoting MOF official Yamaguchi Mitsuhide, *Managing the Dollar*, p. 40.

13. Text of the Maekawa Report, April 7, 1986, reprinted in Ministry of Foreign Affairs, *Documents on Japan's Economic Structural Adjustment*, June 1987, pp. 19–30.

14. Quoted in Syed Javed Maswood, *Japan and Protection: The Growth of Protectionist Sentiment and the Japanese Response* (London: Routledge, 1989), p. 161.

15. Lincoln, *Japan: Facing Economic Maturity*, chapter 3; Maswood, *Japan and Protection*, pp. 152–158.

16. Funabashi, *Managing the Dollar*, p. 193.

17. Funabashi, *Managing the Dollar*, pp. 193–194; and Lincoln, *Japan: Facing Economic Maturity*, chapter 3. Note that the period in which Japan conceded to pressure for fiscal stimulus was also one in which U.S.-Japan friction came to a head over the Toshiba incident and Semiconductor Accords. The level of pressure facing Japan as it made these decision, therefore, was quite great.

18. *Japan Economic Journal*, April 23, 1988, p. 3. This plan was the one where the government was supposed to flesh out the Maekawa Commission's proposals for restructuring the Japanese economy to emphasize domestic demand-led growth. Like the Maekawa Report, however, it included no specific deficit reduction goal, and its economic growth target (3.75%) was judged by some members on the committee that drew up the plan as inadequate to achieve the restructuring needed to make a dent in current account imbalances.

19. EPA official Unno Tsuneo described the norm this way: "[those who pushed for fiscal stimulus] faced a situation in which the idea that the nation's finances shouldn't be pushed into the red had become part of the social fabric (*shakaiteki sen'i*). Everyone agreed that to push finances into the red would cause problems, that to do so would leave future generations with a big mess."—interview, May 25, 1992. Note that there is a lively academic debate about the "strength" of the MOF. On the one hand, Eamonn Fingleton portrays the ministry as dominant across the full range of policies under its jurisdiction—*Blindside: Why Japan is Still on Track to Overtake the U.S. by the Year 2000* (Boston: Houghton Mifflin Co., 1995). On the other, Matthew D. McCubbins and Greg W. Noble argue exactly the opposite, that the MOF has consistently done only what LDP politicians have wanted it to do—"Perceptions and Realities of Japanese Budgeting," in Peter F. Cowhey and Matthew McCubbins, eds., *Structure and Policy in Japan and the United States* (Cambridge: Cambridge University Press, 1995), pp. 81–115. A more balanced and nuanced argument is made by Junko Kato in *The Problem of Bureaucratic Rationality: Tax Politics in Japan* (Princeton: Princeton University Press, 1994). In my discussion of MOF here, I focus only on MOF's role in setting *fiscal policy* (overall levels of spending and taxes), and in this area I find it to be quite powerful. I am not arguing, as Fingleton does, that the ministry is similarly powerful in all areas of its jurisdiction and would happily conceed that the LDP has had a great deal of influence on how the budget was allocated.

20. Interview with Unno, May 25, 1992.

21. *Japan Economic Journal*, March 7, 1987, p. 1.

22. For the argument linking the bubble economy to Japanese fiscal and monetary policy in the late 1980s, see Yukio Noguchi, "The 'Bubble' Economy and Its Aftermath," in Foreign Press Center, ed., *The Japanese Economy in the 1990s: Problems and Prognoses* (Tokyo: Foreign Press Center, 1993), pp. 31–53.

23. The discount rate was not actually raised until May 1989, just before the sii talks got underway, but Bank of Japan administrative guidance in place since the second half of 1988 had by that time already slowed the rate of increase in bank lending.

24. NHK, *Nichibei no shōtotsu*, p. 73; Utsumi Makoto confirmed that there was such a deal in an interview, June 10, 1992. As he put it: "From the beginning, there was an agreement between the U.S. and Japan that, because macroeconomic policy is something which we deal with through the G-7, we would not deal with it in the sii talks." He called it the "Golden Rule." That there was such a deal was also confirmed by American delegation members. One U.S. official explained that the deal was a private one between Dallara and Utsumi and that other American delegation members did not learn of it until the two sides started negotiating.

25. NHK, *Nichibei no shōtotsu*, p. 254.

26. Interviews with members of American and Japanese delegations. Behind the scenes, Baker—long an advocate of a macro approach to the U.S.-Japan trade imbalance problem—was also pressing for an aggressive position on this issue. As we will see below, he was personally involved in pressing Japanese politicians on this issue in the latter stages of the talks.

27. Fauver was described as "beating up on Treasury papers" in internal meetings, pressing them to be more specific and aggressive—interview with U.S. official, August 3, 1992.

28. At the February negotiating session, the leader of the State Department delegation, Richard McCormack, described the public investment issue as "the most important of the sii issues"—NHK, *Nichibei no shōtotsu*, p. 103. Newspapers also began reporting that this was the key US demand—see *Nikkei shimbun*, February 24, 1990, p. 3.

29. NHK, *Nichibei no shōtotsu*, p. 145.

30. Interview with U.S. official.

31. One mof official called the Americans "a bunch of block heads (*tama ishi konko*)—*Asahi shimbun*, February 23, 1990, p. 5.

32. Unno called the Americans an "ally on the side of justice"—interview, May 25, 1992.

33. NHK, *Nichibei no shōtotsu*, pp. 73–74.

34. NHK, *Nichibei no shōtotsu*, p. 254. Japan's rate of general government expenditure on fixed capital formation as a share of gnp in 1989 was 5 percent, compared to 1.6 percent in the U.S., 2.3 percent in West Germany, 1.8 percent in Britain, and 3.2 percent in France—OECD, *National Accounts, Detailed Tables, Volume II, 1977–1989* (Paris: OECD, 1991). Note that the statistic for Japan is different here from the figure for 1989 "public investment" cited earlier in this chapter because the figures here

do not include investments by public corporations or land acquisition costs. See end-note 6.

35. NHK, *Nichibei no shōtotsu*, p. 274.

36. *Nikkei shimbun*, February 22, 1990.

37. NHK, *Nichibei no shōtotsu*, pp. 295–296.

38. *Nikkei shimbun*, February 23, 1990.

39. *Asahi shimbun*, March 17, 1990, p. 1.

40. *Nikkei shimbun*, March 18, 1990, p. 1.

41. Interview with Japanese official, February 8, 1994.

42. *Nikkei shimbun*, March 29, 1990, p. 2.

43. *Nikkei shimbun*, March 30, 1990, p. 3.

44. *Nikkei shimbun*, March 26, 1990, p. 1

45. *Asahi shimbun*, July 3, 1990, p. 2.

46. This position was not an entirely new one for Miyazawa who had long called for more public investment and fiscal stimulus. It is significant, however, that it was the primary issue he emphasized in his campaign to become prime minister.

47. The estimates here and in figure 5.5 are from Kensetsu Daijin Kambō Seisakuka, *Nichibei kōzō mondai kyōgi to kensetsu gyōsei*, pp. 62–63.

48. *Asahi shimbun*, July 26, 1990. John Taylor, the sɪɪ delegate for the Council of Economic Advisors, predicted that Japan's nominal growth over the decade might be as high as 6.5 percent instead of 4.75 percent as predicted by the government and assumed in the above projections. If so, he noted, 430 trillion yen would actually produce a decline in the share of GNP devoted to public investment.

49. *Japan Times Weekly International Edition*, January 7–13, 1991, pp. 1 and 5.

50. Governments of Japan and the United States, *Second Annual Report of SII Follow-up*, July 30, 1992, (version supplied by the Japanese government), p. II-2.

51. *JEI Report*, No. 39B (October 14, 1994), p. 2.

52. *Nikkei shimbun*, March 4, 1990, p. 12.

53. *Japan Economic Journal*, July 7, 1990, p. 3.

54. *JEI Report*, No. 26A (July 8, 1994), p. 3.

6. THE DISTRIBUTION ISSUE

1. The full translation of the Japanese name for the law, the *Daikibo kouritenpo ni okeru kourigyō no jigyō katsudō no chōsei ni kansuru hōritsu (Daitenhō)*, would be The Law Concerning the Adjustment of Retail Business Operations in Large-Scale Retail Stores, but an abbreviated version is used in this book.

2. According to one study, over ten percent of the goods sold by large stores are imports—OECD, *1988/89 OECD Economic Surveys: Japan* (Paris: OECD, 1989), p. 63.

3. Robert Z. Lawrence, "How Open is Japan?" in Paul Krugman, ed., *Trade With Japan: Has the Door Opened Wider?* (Chicago: University of Chicago Press, 1991), p. 30. Lawrence notes that Japanese distributors have an especially strong influence on the

market share of U.S. firms in Japan because few of these firms sell goods through majority-owned affiliates—p. 23. Refer back to discussion of foreign investment and price difference issues in chapter 3.

4. Frank Upham, "Privatizing Regulation: The Implementation of the Large-Scale Retail Stores Law," in Gary Allinson and Yasunori Sone, eds., *Political Dynamics in Contemporary Japan* (Ithaca: Cornell University Press, 1993), pp. 268–269; Hosono Sukehiro, *Posuto daitenhō* (Post-LSL) (Tokyo: Nihon Jitsugyō Shuppansha, 1991), pp. 28–33.

5. Upham, "Privatizing Regulation," pp. 269–270; Hosono, *Posuto Daitenhō*, pp. 34–36.

6. Sakata Kazukō, "Daitenhō to ōgataten mondai," (The LSL and the Large Store Problem) *Reference* (June 1991), p. 50.

7. Kent Calder, *Crisis and Compensation: Public Policy and Political Stability in Japan, 1949–1986* (Princeton: Princeton University Press, 1988), pp. 335–348.

8. Sakata, "Daitenhō to ōgataten mondai," p. 50.

9. For the argument in general, see Frances Rosenbluth, *Financial Politics in Contemporary Japan* (Ithaca: Cornell University Press, 1989).

10. Hosono, *Posuto daitenhō*, pp. 38–40; Upham, "Privatizing Regulation," p. 270; Sakata, "Daitenhō to ōgataten mondai," p. 50; and Nihon Keizai Shimbunsha, *Daitenhō ga kieru hi* (The Day the LSL is Extinguished) (Tokyo: Nihon Keizai Shimbunsha, 1990), pp. 84–88.

11. This is the main argument of Upham in "Privatizing Regulation."

12. Upham, "Privatizing Regulation," p. 271; Sakata, "Daitenhō to ōgataten mondai," p. 51.

13. The reference is to an actual case which eventually resulted in court litigation. See William L. Brooks, "MITI's Distribution Policy and U.S.-Japan Structural Talks," in Michael R. Czinkota and Masaaki Kotabe, eds., *The Japanese Distribution System* (Chicago: Probus Publishing Company, 1993), pp. 240–241.

14. Sakata, "Daitenhō to ōgataten mondai," pp. 51–53. The CAAB's were not mentioned by name in the LSL and the "coordination" work they were *required* to perform under MITI's administrative guidance was described as being optional (*if* the Large Store Council felt it was necessary) in the text of the law.

15. Hosono, *Posuto daitenhō*, pp. 54–55; Sakata, "Daitenhō to ōgataten mondai," p. 53.

16. Upham, "Privatizing Regulation," p. 272; Nihon Keizai Shimbunsha, *Daitenhō ga kieru hi*, pp. 95–98.

17. Tsuruta Toshimasa, "Kokusaika jidai no daitenhō wa dōarubekika," (What to Do with the LSL in an Era of Internationalization) *Ekonomisuto*, December 13, 1988, p. 48.

18. Sakata, "Daitenhō to ōgataten mondai," pp. 56–58.

19. Tsuruta, "Kokusaika jidai no daitenhō," p. 49.

20. Brooks, "MITI's Distribution Policy," p. 241.

21. The process took four to five years in the late 1970s, already much longer than the one-year timeframe anticipated when the LSL was passed, but delays grew

to average seven to eight years by the end of the 1980s and in some instances took 15 years—*JEI Report* 43A (November 10, 1989), p. 8.

22. MITI, *90-nendai no ryūtsū bijon*, 1989.

23. Personal interviews with MITI officials. Also, *Japan Economic Journal*, March 12, 1988, p. 4.

24. Text of the Maekawa Report, April 7, 1986, reprinted in the Ministry of Foreign Affairs, *Documents on Japan's Economic Structural Adjustment*, June 1987, p. 26.

25. Rinji Gyōsei Kaikaku Suishin Shingikai, "Kōteki kisei no kanwara ni kansuru tōshin," (Report Concerning Such Matters as the Relaxation of Public Regulations), December 1, 1988, reprinted in Rinji Gyōsei Kaikaku Suishin Shingikai Jimushitsu, ed., *Gyōkakushin: Zenshigoto* (The Administration Reform Promotion Council: Complete Works) (Tokyo: Gyōsei, 1991), pp. 110.

26. Kusano Atsushi, *Daitenhō: keizai kisei no kōzō* (The LSL: The Structure of Economic Regulation) (Tokyo: Nihon keizai shimbunsha, 1992), p. 165.

27. MITI, *90-nendai no ryūtsū bijon*, pp. 170–182.

28. *Japan Economic Journal*, July 22, 1989.

29. *Japan Economic Journal*, May 7, 1988, p. 28.

30. *Japan Economic Journal*, October 21, 1989, p. 5.

31. Kusano, *Daitenhō*, p. 170; Nihon Keizai Shimbunsha, *Daitenhō ga kieru hi*, p. 10; personal interviews with EPA and MITI officials, June 3 and May 25, 1992.

32. *Japan Economic Journal*, February 10, 1990, p. 6.

33. As an example of the kinds of deals worked out under the Large Store Law, see Higuchi Kenji, " 'Shizuoka itōyōkadō sensō' tenmatsuki," (The Details of the "Shizuoka Itōyōkadō War") *Ekonomisuto*, December 13, 1988, pp. 53–55.

34. The only way this would not be true is if economic conditions changed so much that a significant portion of the "vested interests" came to favor liberalization. That this sometimes happens, even in Japan, is evidenced, for example, by the case of the "naptha war" discussed by Frank Upham in *Law and Social Change in Postwar Japan* (Cambridge: Harvard University Press, 1987), pp. 192–196. In this case, he points out, the emergence of a huge gap between domestic and international prices for naptha, the primary feedstock for Japanese petrochemical firms, after the second oil shock led them to seek a liberalization of regulations in this area so that they could import more of the product. Similar cases in the energy industry are discussed by Richard Samuels in *The Business of the Japanese State: Energy Markets in Comparative and Historical Perspective* (Ithaca: Cornell University Press, 1987). Such rapid changes in economic conditions are less likely in sectors like the retail industry, however, which are essentially "non-traded."

35. Personal interview with MITI official, June 3, 1992.

36. Brooks, "MITI's Distribution Policy," p. 244.

37. Interview with embassy official.

38. *Japan Economic Journal*, March 12, 1988.

39. *JEI Report* 11A (March 17, 1989).

40. Interview with U.S. official, September 8, 1993.

41. Personal interview with MITI officials. Their impressions are also supported

by the way the U.S. treated the Large Store Law as just one of a large number of distribution barriers at the first negotiating session in September. See NHK, ed., *Nichibei no shōtotsu* (The U.S.-Japan Collision) (Tokyo: NHK, 1990), pp. 259–260.

42. NHK, *Nichibei no shōtotsu*, pp. 152–159; Nihon keizai shimbunsha, *Daitenhō ga kieru hi*, pp. 30–31.

43. Significant attention was given to exclusionary practices as they relate to the distribution sector, but these demands will be discussed in chapter 8.

44. Testimony of Williams, U.S. Congress, Senate Committee on Finance, *United States-Japan Structural Impediments Initiative (SII): Hearings before the Subcommittee on International Trade*, 101st Congress, 2nd sess., March 5, 1990, p. 113.

45. *Japan Economic Journal*, June 10, 1989, p. 1.

46. *Japan Economic Journal*, February 10, 1990, p. 1.

47. NHK, *Nichibei no shōtotsu*, pp. 159–160; *JEI Report* 8B (February 23, 1990), p. 5.

48. *Japan Economic Journal*, February 10, 1990, p. 6.

49. NHK, *Nichibei no shōtotsu*, p. 163; Nihon keizai shimbunsha, ed., *Daitenhō ga kieru hi*, pp. 34–42.

50. Nihon keizai shimbunsha, *Daitenhō ga kieru hi*, p. 14.

51. Nihon keizai shimbunsha, *Daitenhō ga kieru hi*, p. 17–20.

52. Text of the SII agreement reprinted in U.S. Congress, Senate Finance Committee, *United States - Japan Structural Impediments Initiative (SII): Hearings Before the Subcommittee on International Trade*, 101st Congress, 2nd sess., March 5, 1990, pp. 93–95.

53. *Asahi shimbun*, February 23, 1990, p. 1; NHK, *Nichibei no shōtotsu*, pp. 297–298.

54. Kusano, *Daitenhō*, p. 179.

55. Ibid., p. 185.

56. *Nihon keizai shimbun*, March 6, 1990, p. 1.

57. *Nihon keizai shimbun*, March 16, 1990, p. 5.

58. Personal interviews with two MITI officials, June 3, 1992.

59. Amelia Porges, "U.S.-Japan Trade Negotiations: Paradigms Lost," in Paul Krugman, ed., *Trade With Japan: Has the Door Opened Wide?* (Chicago: University of Chicago Press, 1991), p. 311.

60. Junko Kato discusses the mixed motives facing zoku veterans who aspire to be LDP leaders. See *The Problem of Bureaucratic Rationality: Tax Politics in Japan* (Princeton: Princeton University Press, 1994), pp. 100–101.

61. Kaifu's preference for abolition was reported initially on March 24 and he apparently restated this position repeatedly through March 30—Kusano, *Daitenhō*, pp. 188–190; senior LDP officials quoted Kaifu emphasizing that the U.S. would agree to nothing less than abolition in the final intra-party debate over what the Japanese position should be—*Nikkei shimbun*, April 3, 1990, p. 2.

62. Personal interview, June 3, 1992.

63. Kusano, *Daitenhō*, p. 190.

64. Nihon keizai shimbunsha, *Daitenhō ga kieru hi*, p. 13–14.

65. Interview with MITI official, June 3, 1992.

66. Nihon keizai shimbunsha, *Daitenhō ga kieru hi*, p. 84–85; Kusano, *Daitenhō*, p. 162.

67. *Asahi shimbun*, March 16, 1990, p. 5; *Nikkei shimbun*, March 5, 1990, p. 2.

68. The survey was conducted for the *Nikkei ryūtsū shimbun*, Nikkei's trade paper for the distribution and retailing sector. It polled by phone a total of 1,091 individuals aged 20–59 in Yokohama, Saitama, Niigata, Kyoto, and Kobe, all urban areas where the LSL had received extra coverage because of local disputes. Note that the results may therefore exaggerate public awareness of the law. Finding reported in Nihon keizai shimbunsha, *Daitenhō ga kieru hi*, pp. 161–164.

69. Nihon keizai shimbunsha, *Daitenhō ga kieru hi*, p. 163.

70. A leader of *Nihon Shōhisha Renmei* quoted in Nihon keizai shimbunsha, *Daitenhō ga kieru hi*, p. 164.

71. Interview with Ōta Yoshiyasu, leader of *Shōdanren*, an umbrella group representing all of the major consumer organizations, May 27, 1992.

72. A leader of *Shufuren*, the housewives association, quoted in *Asahi shimbun*, September 6, 1989, p. 9.

73. On consumer interests in Japan, see Patricia L. Maclachlan, *The Politics of Consumer Protection in Japan: The Role of Consumer Organizations in Policymaking* (dissertation, Columbia University, 1996).

74. *Nikkei shimbun*, April 3, 1990, p. 2. Those skeptical of the ability of public opinion to influence politicians often point to the limited ability of the unorganized public to *punish* politicians who fail to address their broad concerns. The public has a short attention span and often don't care enough to switch their votes based on a policy issue of this sort. But note that Kaifu's behavior here is not being attributed to a feared punishment at the polls. Instead, it is being attributed to his interest in improving his *immediate public approval rating* by taking a position known to be favored by a majority of the public.

75. Nihon keizai shimbunsha, *Daitenhō ga kieru hi*, p. 15.

76. Ibid., p. 19–20.

77. Interview with MITI official, June 3, 1992.

78. Interview with MITI official, June 4, 1992. For a discussion of how bureaucrats and politicians in Japan operate according to an "ideal" of consensus, see John Campbell, "Policy Conflict and its Resolution Within the Governnmental System," in Ellis Krauss, Thomas Rohlen, and Patricia Steinhoff, eds., *Conflict in Japan* (Honolulu: University of Hawaii Press, 1984), pp. 294–334; and Leonard Schoppa, *Education Reform in Japan: A Case of Immobilist Politics* (London: Routledge, 1991).

79. *Nikkei shimbun*, March 24, 1990, p. 3.

80. Again, those skeptical of public opinion influence will likely question why bureaucrats would really care about diffuse public interests. After all, the public (even through politicians) was not in a position to get bureaucrats fired if they didn't repond. Note, however, that I am not suggesting here that public opinion forced bureaucrats to change or act against their preferences. Many MITI officials wanted to liberalize the LSL. They had been constrained, however, by the resistance

of organized interests with a stake in the existing regulatory regime. I am arguing here that public support for liberalization brought to bear on the policy process by U.S. pressure softened up the opposition and gave bureaucrats the cover they needed to do what they wanted to do.

81. Interview with MITI official, June 4, 1992. Note that MOF was not too unhappy with this arrangement since it was able to count the funds it used to compensate small stores for their loss of LSL protection toward its own SII commitment to increase spending on social infrastructure. In this case, therefore, gaiatsu helped facilitate a deal not just through participation expansion but also by linking two previously unrelated issue areas (the LSL and public investment) in one set of international negotiations.

82. The actual program provides subsidies up to 25 percent of a projects value and up to a total per-project limit of 150 million yen ($1.5 million) for parking structures, construction of a new arcade roof, beautification of pavements, and multipurpose halls. In addition, the Ministry of Construction started a new program providing a total of 15 billion yen ($150 million) for roads and parks to serve as part of joint large and small store shopping center projects—*Nikkei shimbun*, December 29, 1990, p. 3.

83. Nihon keizai shimbunsha, *Daitenhō ga kieru hi*, pp. 18–23.

84. *Asahi shimbun*, April 18, 1990.

85. Kusano, *Daitenhō*, p. 254; *Nikkei shimbun*, July 6, 1990, p. 3. In Kyoto, four department stores announced plans to add a total of 200,000 square meters of retail space to the railway station area.

86. Interview with MITI official, June 4, 1992; *Mainichi shimbun*, December 22, 1990.

87. Note that the data comes from the Japanese retail industry rather than from MITI (the source of the data in Figure 6.2). MITI publishes its figures on large store openings only once every 10 years and so strictly comparable figures are not available. The industry's numbers, however, are not significantly different from MITI's for 1985–1987, and they show a clear increase based on the industry's own consistent classification system.

88. Emily Thornton, "Retailing Revolution in Japan," *Fortune* February 7, 1994, p. 56. Toys 'R' Us's lack of problems with the revised LSL is also reflected in the report by one U.S. Embassy official in Tokyo that the firm has not contacted them with any complaints—personal interview, May 27, 1992.

89. Thornton, "Retailing Revolution in Japan," pp. 52–56; Yumiko Ono, "Bargain Hunting Catches on in Japan," *Wall Street Journal*, May 19, 1992, B1; "Japan Shops the Wal-Mart Way," *Economist*, February 6, 1993, pp. 67–68.

90. *Nikkei shimbun*, November 22, 1994, p. 15.

91. When the CAABs were abolished, MITI beefed up its Large Store Councils by organizing nine regional boards with a total staff of 412 quasi-public servants, but these numbers were still way below the number (around 2,500) who had served on the CAABs, leading critics to suggest that MITI would end up rubber stamping local chamber recommendations—*Nikkei shimbun*, December 22, 1990, p. 3.

92. *Daily Yomiuri*, January 3, 1994, p. 5.

93. *Nikkei shimbun*, November 22, 1994.

94. *Nikkei shimbun*, November 22, 1994, p. 15.

95. *Yomiuri shimbun*, May 25, 1990, p. 1.

96. *Nikkei shimbun*, November 23, 1994, p. 10.

7. The Land Policy Issue

1. National Land Agency, *Tochi hakusho: heisei 5-nendo* (Land White Paper: 1994), 1994, p. 104.

2. Noguchi Yukio, "The 'Bubble' and Economic Policies in the 1980s," *Journal of Japanese Studies* 20:2 (Summer 1994), pp. 291–333.

3. MOFA official quoted in NHK, *Nichibei no shōtotsu* (The U.S.-Japan Collision) (Tokyo: NHK, 1990), p. 257.

4. Noguchi Yukio, "Land Problems and Policies in Japan: Structural Aspects," in John O. Haley and Kozo Yamamura, eds., *Land Issues In Japan: A Policy Failure?* (Seattle: Society for Japanese Studies, 1992), especially pp. 14–17; Noguchi, "Japan's Land Problem," *Japanese Economic Studies* 20:3 (Spring 1992), especially pp. 52–54.

5. Harada Yutaka, "Tada ichigyō no hōkaisei ga 'jūtaku' wo kaiketsu suru," (Revising Just One Line of a Law Will Fix the Housing Problem) *Ekonomisuto*, September 19, 1989, p. 12.

6. Ministry of Construction estimate cited in *JEI Report* 28A (July 20, 1990), p. 4. By building higher, central New York City, for example, accommodates six times more people per unit of land than does central Tokyo—OECD, *OECD Economic Survey 1993/94: Japan* (Paris: OECD, 1994), p. 94.

7. Noguchi, "Japan's Land Problem," p. 55. Nominal property tax rates in Japan are actually not that different from those common in other nations: 1.4 to 2.1 percent. The problem is that this rate is assessed only after the tax base is reduced through a series of steps. The tax is applied to the assessed value of the property, but this figure (in 1989) was typically only 30 percent of National Land Agency benchmark prices which were in turn only 70 percent of actual land prices, so that assessments typically came to only 20 percent of the real market value of land. Small landholders got a further advantage since their tax basis was reduced to 25 percent of the assessed value through a special break introduced in 1974 in order to help average homeowners avoid having to pay suddenly increased taxes after the land price spiral of that period. A final complicated break gave many landowners another 15 percent discount. Multiplying all of this meant that many people ended up paying tax on only 4.5 percent of the real market value of their land and that effective tax rates ended up at less than 0.1%. This number compares with effective tax rates of 1.42 percent in New York, 1.99 percent in Chicago, and 0.66 percent in Los Angeles in 1984. See *JEI Report* 28A (July 20, 1990), pp. 7–8.

8. Because taxation on urban farmland prior to SII was based on the land's agricultural productivity and had nothing to do with market values of surrounding land,

the rate relative to market value varied markedly by area. The 0.0002 figure was calculated based on actual data for Setagaya Ward of Tokyo, a residential area with some of the most expensive land in Japan, and so represents the most extreme case. See Hasegawa Tokunosuke, "Hiking the Taxes on Farmland in the Cities," *Economic Eye*, Winter 1990, pp. 17–18. Another economist, Iwata Kikuo, estimates that a more typical rate was 0.0045 percent, still a small fraction of the rate of surrounding residential land. See *JEI Report* 28A (July 20, 1990), p. 10.

9. Hasegawa, "Hiking the Taxes on Farmland in Cities," p. 18. Of course, farmland owners were not so miserly as to hold onto *all* of their land. Most could live well, however, by developing or selling just a small portion of their land each generation.

10. Noguchi, "Japan's Land Problem," p. 55. As with the property tax, a policy of underassessment and exemptions for land assets made it possible for individuals to pass on property worth as much as $1.3 million with virtually no tax liability. See *JEI Report* 28A (July 20, 1990), pp. 9–10.

11. *JEI Report* 28A (July 20, 1990), p. 5.

12. They could for "just cause," but the courts interpreted just cause so narrowly that in practice landlords have no way of forcing tenants out. See excellent discussion by John Haley, "Japan's New Land and House Lease Law," in Haley and Yamamura, *Land Issues in Japan: A Policy Failure?*, pp. 149–173.

13. The market has actually generated a substantial number of small rental apartment units (since developers know that the tenants of these tiny units will leave voluntarily once they marry and/or have children), but it has totally failed to supply decent family-sized rental accommodations since developers know that families, once settled in these, will stay throughout their lives—during which time the landowner would have lost control of the property! See Haley, "Japan's New Land and House Lease Law," p. 168; and Harada, "Tada ichigyō no hōkaisei," p. 15.

14. OECD, *OECD Economic Survey 1993–1994: Japan*, p. 98.

15. Shigeko Fukai, "Japan Land Policy and Its Global Impact," *U.S.-Japan Program Occasional Paper 90–01*, 1990, pp. 17–18; Kent Calder, *Crisis and Compensation: Public Policy and Political Stability in Japan, 1949–1986* (Princeton: Princeton University Press, 1988), pp. 390–393.

16. Fukai, "Japan's Land Policy and its Global Impact," p. 23. Ironically, as I read this account, I was doing research in Tokyo and living in a neighborhood which fit Fukai's description to the letter. My family was renting a small house in a pocket of about ten similar dwellings, surrounded on two sides by factories and on the other by a multi-story apartment building. The entire district was in fact a hodge-podge of small factories, single-family homes, and condominium and apartment complexes.

17. Fukai, "Japan's Land Policy," p. 14.

18. Noguchi, "The 'Bubble' and Economic Policies of the 1980s," pp. 296–300.

19. Calder, *Crisis and Compensation*, pp. 399–401; Fukai, "Japan's Land Policy," pp. 19–23; Yukio Noguchi, "Land Problem as an Unintended Industrial Policy: Its Mechanism and Limit," *Hitotsubashi Journal of Economics* 30 (1990), pp. 93–96.

20. Hasegawa, "Hiking the Taxes on Farmland in Cities," p. 18; NHK, ed., *Nichibei no shōtotsu*, p. 147.

21. The behavior of one urban LDP Dietman, Itō Kōsuke, perfectly illustrates the bias of the old LDP electoral system. Initially a proponent of "suburban salaried interests," Itō switched sides after he lost the election in 1986 and began campaigning for the next one by conducting an "LDP style campaign" aimed at appealing to the fewer but more organized farmers and small businessmen. After he won, he promptly found himself posted to the National Land Agency where he was placed in a position of catering to the narrow interests of these groups—Brian Woodall, "The Politics of Land in Japan's Dual Political Economy," in Haley and Yamamura, eds., *Land Issues in Japan*, pp. 138–139; Nihon Keizai Shimbunsha, ed., *Tochi wo kangaeru* (Thinking About Land) (Tokyo: Nihon keizai shimbunsha, 1990), pp. 148–150.

22. Hasegawa, "Hiking the Taxes on Farmland in the Cities," pp. 18–19; Marie Anchordoguy, "Land Policy: A Public Policy Failure," in Haley and Yamamura, eds., *Land Issues in Japan*, p. 102–103.

23. MOC data cited in NHK, *Nichibei no shōtotsu*, p. 147.

24. Fukai, "Japan's Land Policy," p. 25. Kozo Yamamura, "LDP Dominance and High Land Prices in Japan: A Study in Positive Political Economy," in Haley and Yamamura, eds., *Land Issues in Japan*, p. 68–71. The complex change introduced in 1969 reduced the tax on long-term capital gains from land sales from half of the income tax rate paid by an individual to 10 percent in 1970–1971, 15 percent in 1972–1973, and 20 percent in 1973–1974. The last rate was still well below half the income tax rate for most individuals selling large land holdings.

25. It was raised from 20 percent to 75% of the income tax rate for long-term gains over 20 million yen—Yamamura, "LDP Dominance," p. 69. Yamamura offers an interesting argument linking a long string of changes in the tax treatment of capital gains on land sales to the LDP's political calculus geared to balancing its desire to cater to its strong supporters (demanding particularistic benefits) with its desire to avoid antagonizing its weak supporters (whose interests require it to rein in particularistic benefits).

26. OECD, *OECD Economic Survey 1993–94: Japan*, pp. 100–101.

27. Local governments jealously guard their authority over the property tax especially since MOF controls almost all other sources of revenue.

28. Interview with MOF official, January 25, 1994.

29. Calder, *Crisis and Compensation*, pp. 386–390.

30. Anchordoguy, "Land Policy: A Public Policy Failure," p. 81.

31. Calder, *Crisis and Compensation*, p. 405.

32. Anchordoguy, "Land Policy: A Public Policy Failure," p. 81.

33. Fukai, "Japan's Land Policy and Its Global Impact," p. 27.

34. Anchordoguy, "Land Policy: A Public Policy Failure," pp. 81–84.

35. The most notorious case in which NLA policy was biased toward maximizing revenue was the agency's apparently deliberate decision to overestimate the expected growth in demand for Tokyo office space in 1985, just prior to a series of public land sales. This report sparked a sudden jump in land prices, which did help

the government garner additional revenue but also helped set off the land price explosion that left the price of housing beyond the reach of many urban salaried workers—Fukai, "Japan's Land Policy and Its Global Impact," pp. 5–6. These subsequent sales also are an example of the continuing ability of the LDP to use land sales to reward clients. Prime Minister Nakasone used the sales to reward real estate interests who were major contributors to his faction—Anchordoguy, "Land Policy: A Public Policy Failure," pp. 87–88.

36. *Japan Economic Journal*, April 30, 1988, p. 32.

37. The account of Tochi Rinchō's deliberations draws from Fukai, "Japan's Land Policy and Its Global Impact," pp. 28–30; Anchordoguy, "Land Policy: A Public Policy Failure," pp. 85–86; Hideo Otake, "The Rise and Retreat of a Neoliberal Reform: Controversies Over Land Use Policy," in Gary D. Allinson and Yasunori Sone, eds., *Political Dynamics in Contemporary Japan* (Ithaca: Cornell University Press, 1993), pp. 253–263; and Honma Yoshito, "Tochi rinchō no 300-nichi," (300 Days of the Advisory Council on Land Policy) *Ekonomisuto*, June 21, 1988, pp. 70–75.

38. In the end, it could do no better than a proposal to "examine the idea of reconsidering" such a step.

39. Noguchi, "Land Problems and Policies in Japan: Structural Aspects," pp. 28–29. The results of this policy initiative are discussed more fully in the final section of this chapter.

40. Fukai, "Land Policy and Its Global Impact," p. 33.

41. NHK, *Nichibei no shōtotsu*, pp. 147–148; Anchordoguy, "Land Policy: A Public Policy Failure," pp. 104–105.

42. Hasegawa Tokunosuke, "Nichibei kōzō kyōgi ni okeru tochi mondai," (The Land Problem in the SII Talks) in Abe Tetsuo, et al, eds., *Nichibei kankei no kōzu* (The Composition of U.S.-Japan Relations) (Kyoto: Minerva, 1992), p. 241. Interview with MOF official, January 25, 1994.

43. Anchordoguy, "Land Policy: A Public Policy Failure," p. 89.

44. Treasury was the driving force behind the U.S. demands in this area, and Taylor was much more skeptical in interagency meetings—personal interview with U.S. official.

45. The text of negotiating sessions in NHK, *Nichibei no shōtotsu*, pp. 256–257, 279; and *Nikkei shimbun*, November 8, 1989, p. 3. See also testimony of Charles Dallara, U.S. Congress, Senate Committee on Finance, *United States-Japan Structural Impediments Initiative (SII): Hearings before the Subcommittee on International Trade*, 101st Congress, 2nd sess., March 5, 1990, p. 45.

46. *Wall Street Journal*, March 23, 1990.

47. Because of the way that different nations measure space, comparisons of house sizes are notoriously difficult to make. See discussion of Susan B. Hanley, "Traditional Housing and Unique Lifestyles: The Unintended Outcomes of Japan's Land Policy," in Haley and Yamamura, eds., *Land Issues in Japan*, pp. 218–221.

48. Ministry of Construction, *Kensetsu hakusho: heisei 5-nendo* (Construction White Paper: 1993), 1993, p. 254. During the same period, the share of new rental housing rose from 29 percent to 49 percent. Nevertheless, the homeownership rate

for Japan remains higher than that of any European country and on a par with the rate in the U.S..

49. Jeffrey Sachs and Peter Boone, "Japanese Structural Adjustment and the Balance of Payments," *National Bureau of Economic Research Working Paper* No. 2614 (June 1988). Noguchi Yukio also cited empirical studies by Japanese economists which have shown, by comparing savings rates in high-land-price urban areas of Japan with those in low-land-price rural areas, that savings rates are not significantly affected by land prices—personal interview, March 10, 1994.

50. The CEA had trouble with this argument too. They pointed out that land prices by definition equal the expected return on land discounted for the time value of money, meaning that if land prices are high, they are high because they produce returns. Land prices cannot, therefore, be described as "expensive" to foreign firms because these firms could invest in the land and get the same type of returns Japanese firms were getting.

51. *Nikkei shimbun*, February 22, 1990, p. 1.

52. At the September session, the U.S. was so animated about land policy that the negotiators ran out of time on the first day of talks and had to come back to the issue on the second day. In contrast, they spent very little time on the issue at the February negotiating session—text of negotiations, NHK, *Nichibei no shōtotsu*, pp. 256–259, 267–269, 297. See also comments in the book on how land was deemphasized later in the year, p. 146. Interviews with a number of U.S. and Japanese officials involved in the negotiations confirm this characterization. One additional reason for the deemphasis cited by a U.S. official was the division of responsibility within the U.S. delegation for this issue. It had been Treasury's issue at the beginning, but Treasury was short-staffed and wanted State to take over more of the responsibility. In the end, no agency took full charge of the negotiations on this complex issue—interview, January 11, 1994.

53. Figure cited by US negotiator at November negotiating session, NHK, *Nichibei no shōtotsu*, p. 281.

54. For a similar evaluation, see Shigeko Fukai, "The Role of *Gaiatsu* in Japan's Land Policymaking," paper presented at the annual meeting of the American Political Science Association in Chicago, September 1992, p. 2. Fukai does, however, credit the U.S. with forcing the Japanese to pay *more* attention to public concerns.

55. Anchordoguy, "Land Policy: A Public Policy Failure," pp. 93–94.

56. EPA official Harada Yutaka, cited in NHK, *Nichibei no shōtotsu*, p. 143.

57. Noguchi, "Land Problems and Policies in Japan," p. 30–31.

58. Interestingly, the U.S. negotiators seemed to appreciate the fact that land politics were somehow more intense than the politics of other SII issue areas. As the USTR's Williams put it, "For Japanese consumers, the problem of land use was easy to see, basic, and directly impacting on their lives. And yet, this was an extremely complicated problem. Of all the issues we raised during SII, the land issue clearly had the most complicated politics. It required us to get involved in considering the interests of farmers and suburban residents, those who owned houses and those who didn't, and even the interests of varying generations. Therefore we approached this

issue extremely cautiously."—"Kagami no naka no nichibei kōzō kyōgi: #6,"
(Looking in the Mirror at the SII Talks: Part 6) *Shūkan daiyamondo*, April 18, 1992, p.
106.

59. Interviews with Hasegawa and Noguchi and with U.S. embassy officials. The
extensive contacts between U.S. officials and the reform economists is also noted by
Fukai, "The Role of *Gaiatsu* in Japan's Land Policymaking," p. 11.

60. Fukai, "The Role of *Gaiatsu* in Japan's Land Policymaking," p. 11.

61. Noguchi specifically credits the Americans with helping to get the MOF off
the ball on land tax policy—interview, March 10, 1994.

62. Interview with Noguchi, March 10, 1994; interview with Hasegawa, June 5,
1992.

63. John Kingdon, *Agendas, Alternatives, and Public Policies* (Glenview, IL: Scott,
Foresman and Company, 1984). For a similar approach applied to Japan, see John C.
Campbell, *How Policies Change: The Japanese Government and the Aging Society*
(Princeton: Princeton University Press, 1992).

64. The capital gains tax on land held over five years had ranged from 20 to 25
percent depending on the value of the gain, but was increased to 30 percent (regardless of value)—Hasegawa, "Nichibei kōzō kyōgi ni okeru tochi mondai," p. 259;
Anchordoguy, "Land Policy: A Public Policy Failure," pp. 106–107. On the history
of capital gains taxation on land, up to and including the latest changes, see Ishi
Hiromitsu, *Tochi zeisei kaikaku* (Land Tax Reform) (Tokyo: Tōyō Keizai Shimpōsha,
1991), pp. 144–171.

65. Interview with MOF official, May 22, 1992.

66. Keizai Kaikaku Kenkyūkai, *Keizai kaikaku ni tsuite* (Regarding Economic
Reform), December 16, 1993.

67. The discussion in this section is based largely on interviews with MOC officials, January 26, 1994.

68. Also, at death, heirs can avoid residential-rate inheritance taxation only if they
agree to farm land for life—Hasegawa, "Nichibei kōzō kyōgi ni okeru tochi mondai,"
p. 257.

69. Figures in National Land Agency, *Tochi hakusho: heisei 5-nendo*, pp. 162–163.

70. Noguchi points out that with an effective residential-rate property tax of
0.06 percent, a farmland owner could sell just one-eightieth of his land, deposit the
proceeds in the bank at five percent interest, and pay the tax on the remaining estate
with the proceeds—"Japan's Land Problem," p. 63. Landowners could do the same
by converting just part of their land into a parking lot and using the proceeds (often
$300 a parking space in the Tokyo area) to pay the tax.

71. NLA, *Tochi hakusho: heisei 5-nendo*, p. 162.

72. Hasegawa emphasizes this point—"Nichibei kōzō kyōgi ni okeru tochi
mondai," pp. 256–257.

73. In the Tokyo municipal district, 57 percent of urban farmland was declared
"green" while the figures for more suburban Chiba and Ibaraki were 19 and 9 percent, respectively—NLA, *Tochi hakusho: heisei 5-nendo*, p. 163.

74. Interview with MOC officials, January 26, 1994. One of the officials, who had

been posted to at a field office when landowners were making their decisions, showed me a map of his district, showing how individual decisions to divide their land had produced (literally) a checkerboard pattern.

75. Both distortions reflect the rational calculations of landowners. Landowners closest to Tokyo are the wealthiest and are therefore most worried about the impact of inheritance taxes. They realized that they could pass on land to their heirs only if they availed themselves of the "green" option. Those further out were more willing to pay higher taxes in exchange for state expenditures on infrastructure which will make their land more valuable. The patchwork pattern reflected the interest of landowners in making money off of *some* of their property for themselves even as they protected another part from taxation so that they could pass it on to their heirs.

76. Interview with M O F official, January 25, 1994.

77. The discussion in this section is based on Anchordoguy, "Land Policy: A Public Policy Failure," pp. 89–101, Fukai, "The Role of *Gaiatsu* in Japan's Land Policymaking," pp. 3–7; Noguchi, "The Loopholes in the Planned Landholding Tax," *Economic Eye*, Spring 1991, pp. 22–23; Noguchi, "The 'Bubble' and Economic Policies in the 1980s," pp. 307–308; and Ishi, *Tochi zeisei kaikaku*, especially pp. 195–231.

78. Noguchi, "The 'Bubble' and Economic Policies in the 1980s," pp. 307–308. He calculated that as a result of all the deductions, a firm with property valued at 5 billion yen ($40 million) at market rates would face an additional tax burden of only 1.5 million yen ($12,000) a year as a result of the new tax—an effective rate of just 0.03 percent.

79. Noguchi, "The Loopholes in the Planned Landholding Tax," p. 23. A similar point is made by Anchordoguy, "Land Policy: A Public Policy Failure," pp. 99–100.

80. He had calculated that the one percent tax with 500 million yen exemption would have reduced prices by 9 to 18 percent in Tokyo and Osaka and possibly cut prices in half by undercutting the myth of ever-rising prices which fed the speculative bubble—"The Loopholes in the Planned Landholding Tax," pp. 22–23.

81. Anchordoguy, "Land Policy: A Public Policy Failure," p. 95.

82. Personal interview with Noguchi, March 10, 1994. Others are more impressed with the MHA's plan. See Hasegawa, "Nichibei kōzō kyōgi to tochi mondai," p. 255.

83. Fukai makes this argument, "The Role of *Gaiatsu* in Japan's Land Policymaking," p. 10.

84. See Haley, "Japan's New Land and House Lease Law."

8. COMPETITION POLICY ISSUES

1. Eleanor M. Hadley, *Antitrust in Japan* (Princeton: Princeton University Press, 1970), pp. 121–124; Harry First, "Japan's Antitrust Policy: Impact on Import Competition," in Thomas A. Pugel and Robert G. Hawkins, eds., *Fragile Interdependence: Economic Issues in U.S.-Japanese Trade and Investment* (Lexington, MA: D.C. Heath, 1986), pp. 63–64. Note that the emphasis in this chapter is on those

aspects of competition policy which were at issue during the s11 talks. Thus, for example, I spend much less time discussing Japanese policy toward mergers (where the Bush team actually wanted Japan to relax its competition policy!) than I do on policy toward cartels and keiretsu (where the U.S. called for tougher restrictions).

2. Hadley, *Antitrust in Japan*, p. 109–110.

3. Mark Tilton, *Restrained Trade: Cartels in Japan's Basic Materials Industries* (Ithaca: Cornell University Press, 1996), pp. 27–29.

4. Hadley, *Antitrust in Japan*, p. 199; First, "Japan's Antitrust Policy," p. 64.

5. NHK, ed., *Nichibei no shōtotsu* (The U.S.-Japan Collision) (Tokyo: NHK, 1990), p. 195.

6. MITI, *Sangyō gōrika hakusho* (Industrial Rationalization White Paper), 1957, pp. 42–43—quote in Iyori Hiroshi, "Antitrust and Industrial Policy in Japan: Competition and Cooperation," in Gary Saxonhouse and Kozo Yamamura, eds., *Law and Trade Issues of the Japanese Economy* (Seattle: University of Washington Press, 1986), p. 57.

7. Interview, May 29, 1992.

8. NHK, *Nichibei no shōtotsu*, p. 196.

9. Michael Gerlach, "*Keiretsu* Organization in the Japanese Economy: Analysis and Trade Implications," in Chalmers Johnson, Laura D'Andrea Tyson, and John Zysman, eds., *Politics and Productivity: How Japan's Development Strategy Works* (New York: Harper Business, 1989), p. 158.

10. Chalmers Johnson, *MITI and the Japanese Miracle: The Growth of Industrial Policy, 1925–1975* (Stanford: Stanford University Press, 1982), pp. 282–283.

11. The FTC brought criminal charges in three cases in 1949 during the occupation but then did not attempt to use this authority again until 1969, when it filed charges in a case involving unfair advertising. Its use of criminal sanctions against the oil cartels was by far its boldest use of this authority in the agency's history—Harry First, "Antitrust Enforcement in Japan," *Antitrust Law Journal* 64:1 (Fall 1995), p. 167.

12. An average of 103 cases a year between 1987 and 1992—Department of Justice and Federal Trade Commission data cited in Ibid., p. 160.

13. André Sapir, Pierre Buigues, and Alexis Jacquemin, "European Competition Policy in Manufacturing and Services: A Two-Speed Approach?" *Oxford Review of Economic Policy* 9:2 (Summer 1993), p. 121.

14. John McMillan, "*Dangō*: Japan's Price-Fixing Conspiracies," *Economics and Politics* 3:3 (November 1991), p. 203.

15. The FTC has no discretion in determining the level of fines. For cartels involving manufacturing firms, it was legally obliged to impose fines at a rate of two percent; for retailers at a rate of one percent; for wholesalers at a rate of 0.5 percent; and others at a rate of 1.5 percent. See Iyori, "Antitrust and Industrial Policy in Japan," p. 81.

16. Ibid., p. 82. The 1981 case involved six firms operating a cartel in Kraft liner wrapping paper.

17. All of these barriers to JFTC investigations were pointed out by retired JFTC

official Iyori—interview, January 12, 1994. Note that the JFTC can use the strategy of indefinitely detaining suspects if it pursues *criminal charges* in cooperation with the Justice Ministry and the Public Prosecutors Office, but as noted above, the commission has generally preferred to pursue administrative sanctions.

18. Minoru Matsushita, *Introduction to Japanese Antimonopoly Law* (Tokyo: Yūhikaku, 1990), pp. 82–83. On the FTC's tendency to take informal actions as a way of avoiding scrutiny by the courts, see First, "Antitrust Enforcement in Japan," pp. 176–179.

19. Interview with Kikuchi Gen'ichi, June 16, 1992.

20. *JEI Report* 20A (May 19, 1989), p. 11.

21. Ibid.. In 1988, 53 cartels were export cartels, mostly set up to help administer the voluntary export quotas insisted upon by the U.S.. Another 53 were authorized under the Environment Sanitation Act, helping to prevent cutthroat competition from forcing barbers and beauticians to cut corners on sanitation. Only two were of the most problematic types: depression cartels (2) and rationalization cartels (0). See also discussion in Iyori, "Antitrust and Industrial Policy in Japan," pp. 79–81.

22. Ronald Dore, *Flexible Rigidities: Industrial Policy and Structural Adjustment in the Japanese Economy, 1970–1980* (Stanford: Stanford University Press, 1986), pp. 140–147; Robert M. Uriu, *Troubled Industries: Confronting Economic Change in Japan* (Ithaca: Cornell University Press, 1996); and Tilton, *Restrained Trade.*

23. Tilton, *Restrained Trade.*

24. Kikuchi Gen'ichi, "Ima motomerareru 'tsuyoi' kōtorii," (A "Strong" FTC Which We Can Now Demand) *Ekonomisuto,* January 23, 1990, p. 53. Interviews with Kikuchi (June 17, 1992) and Iyori (December 15, 1993).

25. McMillan, "*Dangō,*" pp. 203–207; and Brian Woodall, *Japan Under Construction: Corruption, Politics and Public Works* (Berkeley: University of California Press, 1996), pp. 36–50.

26. Masu Uekusa, "Government Regulations in Japan: Toward Their International Harmonization and Integration," in Kozo Yamamura, ed., *Japan's Economic Structure: Should it Change?* (Seattle: Society for Japanese Studies, 1990), pp. 237–269.

27. Woodall, *Japan Under Construction,* p. 48.

28. Construction investment in 1992 amounted to 18.2 percent of Japan's GNP with public sector projects accounting for roughly a third of this total—Ibid., p. 29, citing data from the Japanese construction industry newsletter, *Kensetsu gyōkai gurafu.* Tilton makes the point about how collusion in the construction industry makes possible collusion in cement and steel—Tilton, *Restrained Trade,* pp. 13–14.

29. The JFTC's policy has been that vertical restraints such as exclusive dealing contracts are illegal only when the firm enforcing such contracts has an exceptionally dominant position in a market—such as the 70 percent market share of one firm cited by the JFTC under this provision. The courts have interpreted the AML's prohibitions on vertical restraints even more narrowly, ruling in one case that a vertical restraint was not a violation of the AML's rules against cartels because there was no "*mutual*" restriction in their business activities—see discussion in Matsushita, *Introduction to Japanese Antimonopoly Law,* pp. 38–41, 60–61.

30. See F. M. Scherer, *Competition Policies for an Integrated World Economy* (Washington, D.C.: Brookings Institution, 1994), pp. 74–76.

31. Note that the term "horizontal keiretsu" refers to groups which are each made up of firms in a wide variety of *different* industries, in banking, insurance, steel, chemicals, etc. These groups should not be confused with the horizontal *cartels* discussed earlier.

32. The figure is for the three horizontal groups that started out as *zaibatsu* before World War II. The average figure for the three other bank-centered keiretsu (the Fuyo, Sanwa, and Daiichi Kangyo groups) was significantly lower, standing at 17 percent in 1985—JFTC, *The Outline of the Report on the Actual Conditions of the Six Major Corporate Groups*, February 1992, p. 21.

33. Yūsaku Futatsugi, *Gendai nihon no kigyō shūkan* (Enterprise Groups in Contemporary Japan) (Tokyo: Tōyō Shinpōsha, 1976)—cited in Michael Gerlach, "*Keiretsu* Organization in the Japanese Economy," p. 159.

34. The AML does place some absolute limits on cross-shareholding, restricting banks and other financial institutions to holdings of no more than 5 percent of a firm's outstanding shares and other large enterprises to holdings in any given firm that exceed its net worth or capital value. That the latter restriction was added in the 1977 amendments and that the limit for financial firms was lowered from 10 to 5 percent at the same time could be taken as a sign of JFTC activism on this issue— Iyori, "Antitrust and Industrial Policy in Japan," p. 69. Also, the Commercial Code contains provisions discouraging cross-shareholding above a certain level by making cross-held shares above certain levels nonvoting. While limiting the thickness of single cross-shareholding links, however, these restrictions do nothing to prevent very high levels of cross-shareholding among keiretsu groups where dozens of firms each hold small volumes of shares that nevertheless leave a significant proportion of group firm shares in the hands of other group firms.

35. John Haley, "The Myth of the Reluctant Litigant," *Journal of Japanese Studies* 4:2 (Summer 1978), pp. 359–390; J. Mark Ramseyer, "The Costs of the Consensual Myth: Antitrust Enforcement and Institutional Barriers to Litigation in Japan," *Yale Law Journal* 94: 604 (1985), pp. 604–645; and Frank Upham, *Law and Social Change in Postwar Japan* (Cambridge: Harvard University Press, 1987).

36. While those suffering from antitrust abuses have to wait for a formal JFTC ruling against a firm or a cartel before taking action *under the AML*, injured parties do have the option of filing for damages even if the JFTC does not take action under the general tort provisions of Japan's Civil Code (Article 709). In such cases, however, the plaintiffs must prove intent to cause damage and/or negligence—a burden they do not face under the AML. See Matsushita, *Introduction to Japanese Antimonopoly Law*, p. 86.

37. Ramseyer, "The Costs of the Consensual Myth," p. 617.

38. In contrast, in the U.S., plaintiffs have the advantage of less restrictive discovery rules and lighter rules of evidence on the issue of damages. Ramseyer, "The Costs of the Consensual Myth"; and personal interview with Iyori Hiroshi, January 12, 1994.

39. One case in the years between Ramseyer's analysis and the sII talks did involve a larger sum of money. In fact, in this case involving a group of Japanese construction firms who conspired to rig bids on a series of contracts with the U.S. navy at Yokosuka Naval base, the defendants ended up settling out of court for $32.6 million! The multi-million dollar resolution of this case should not be taken as a sign of a more permissive Japanese private damage system, however, for it was conducted under the shadow of *U.S.* antitrust law (given the Navy's threat to bring action in U.S. courts). In fact, the contrast between this case and the failure of a group of Japanese consumers from Tsuruoka, suing without the benefit of the threat to bring action in the U.S., to win anything in a case decided by the Japanese Supreme Court at about the same time (December 1989) serves to further document the importance of legal rules in curtailing private antitrust action in Japan. On the Yokosuka case, see Woodall, *Japan Under Construction*, pp. 125–126; on the Tsuruoka case, involving a kerosene cartel at the time of the 1973–1974 oil crisis, see *Asahi shimbun*, December 8, 1989.

40. On the last proposals, see endnote 34 above.

41. Matsushita, *Introduction to Japanese Antimonopoly Law*, p. 5.

42. Iyori, "Antitrust and Industrial Policy in Japan," p. 67.

43. Matsushita, *Introduction to Japanese Antimonopoly Law*, pp. 4–5, 30–33; NHK, *Nichibei no shōtotsu*, pp. 211–212.

44. See Daniel Okimoto, *Between MITI and the Market* (Stanford: Stanford University Press, 1989), pp. 38–39.

45. The JFTC was constrained by the constitutional prohibition on administrative "punishment" and so could set the level of fines no higher than necessary to recoup ill-gotten gains. Still, it could have used a wide variety of figures for the average level of ill-gotten gains, basing these on a range of percentages of sales or, alternatively, profits. The JFTC chose to base its fine rates on figures for average ordinary profit ratios (*keijō riekiritsu*) over a ten-year period in wholesale, retail, and manufacturing sectors. Rather than set the fine rate at the average profit rate (assuming cartels on average double their profits), however, the JFTC cut these percentages in *half* (assuming Japanese cartels only manage to increase their profits by 50 percent). According to JFTC officials, this decision to cut the figures in half was forced on them by MITI, MOF, and (because it didn't like the idea of someone other than its courts meting out punishment) the MOJ—personal interviews, December 15, 1993 and June 17, 1992.

46. Iyori, "Antitrust and Industrial Policy in Japan," p. 58. He and others made similar points in interviews.

47. Interview, June 4, 1992.

48. McMillan, "*Dangō*," p. 213.

49. Woodall, *Japan Under Construction*, pp. 47–48, 92–94.

50. Interviews with JFTC officials who pointed to LDP as well as bureaucratic opposition as the reason for why surcharge levels were set at low levels—June 17, 1992 and December 15, 1993. For the legislative history of the AML revisions, see Johnson, *MITI and the Japanese Miracle*, pp. 300–301; NHK, *Nichibei no shōtotsu*, pp. 200–213.

51. Iyori notes, for example, that the JFTC decided not to use their new power to break up firms in concentrated industries—interview, May 29, 1992.

52. The JFTC knew its action would provoke a backlash, officials told me, but felt they had to take action when the Shizuoka dangō's particularly blatant collusion (firms put down on paper who would go after whom on construction contracts) became known. Interview with Iyori, December 15, 1993.

53. Interview with Kikuchi, June 17, 1992.

54. Umezawa Setsuo, "Dokusen kinshi hō wa kaisei shinai," (We will not revise the AML) Ekonomisuto, January 23, 1990, p. 48.

55. NHK, Nichibei no shōtotsu, pp. 202–203; Nihon kōgyō shimbun, May 27, 1992. During the SII talks, interestingly, one slot went to an official from the Ministry of Foreign Affairs.

56. The account here is drawn from First, "Japan's Antitrust Policy," pp. 67–69; and the statement of John M. Andrews, President of the American Natural Soda Ash Corp (ANSAC)—U.S. Congress, Senate Committee on Finance, United States-Japan Structural Impediments Initiative (SII): Hearings before the Subcommittee on International Trade, 101st Congress, 1st sess., November 6–7, 1989, p. 88.

57. First criticizes the JFTC for failing to impose a surcharge in this case—Ibid., p. 69. JFTC officials explain that they could not issue a surcharge in this case since they had not gone after the Japanese firms for a price-raising cartel. They had merely found that the Japanese firms conspired to limit the quantity of ash they imported (raising the price of their input). Naturally, Japanese firms would not have done this to themselves unless they could collude to make sure all of them passed along this higher cost, but the JFTC did not find enough evidence to make this case. The agency felt it could shut down the cartel by eliminating its means of regulating imports—Interview with Iyori, December 15, 1993.

58. Interview with Bill Wheeler, head of FMC Asia, February 8, 1994.

59. Pickens eventually gave in. See "Koito Exec Rests Easy After Pickens Gives In," Japan Times Weekly International Edition, May 27-June 2, 1991, p. 1,7.

60. Ronald P. Dore, " 'Liberalization' Not Necessarily 'Americanization,' " Japan Economic Journal, November 4, 1989, p. 9.

61. Interview with U.S. delegate, September 8, 1993.

62. Umezawa, "Dokusen kinshi hō wa kaisei shinai," p. 49.

63. Representative of the "Japanese view" is the work of Ken'ichi Imai. See his "Japanese Business Groups and the Structural Impediments Initiative," in Kozo Yamamura, ed., Japan's Economic Structure: Should It Change?, pp. 167–202. Even the JFTC representative at the SII negotiations argued that there was no need to tighten limits on cross-shareholding—NHK, Nichibei no shōtotsu, pp. 301–2.

64. Interview with Iyori, December 15, 1993.

65. Text of the SII agreement reprinted in U.S. Congress, Senate Finance Committee, United States - Japan Structural Impediments Initiative (SII): Hearings before the Subcommittee on International Trade, 101st Congress, 2nd sess., March 5, 1990 (Hereafter cited as Final SII Report), pp. 101–102.

66. Kozo Yamamura, "Will Japan's Economic Structure Change? Confessions of a

Former Optimist," in Yamamura, ed., *Japan's Economic Structure: Should it Change?* (Seattle: Society for Japanese Studies, 1990), p. 55.

67. Iyori, "Antitrust and Industrial Policy in Japan," p. 62.

68. *Final SII Report*, p. 99–100.

69. Noda Minoru, *Ryūtsū keiretsuka to dokusen kinshihō* (The *Keiretsu*-ization of Distribution and the AML) (Tokyo: Chikuma Shobō, 1982).

70. Interview, January 12, 1994, referring to the Supreme Court case Continental TV, Inc. v. GTE-Sylvania, Inc., 433 U.S. 36 (1977).

71. *Final SII Report*, p. 96.

72. Interviews with JFTC officials.

73. Yamagata Yūichirō, "Nichibei kōzō kyōgi ga nihon wo kaeru," (The SII Talks Will Change Japan) *Shūkan tōyō keizai*, September 30, 1989, p. 16.

74. Interview with Iyori, December 15, 1993.

75. *Final SII Report*, pp. 98–100.

76. Interviews with MITI officials, June 2 and June 4, 1992. MITI officials have actually come to recognize that AML enforcement aimed at "bad" cartels serves an important role in assuring that MITI-directed industry cooperation serves state goals rather than private ones. See also Tilton, *Restrained Trade*.

77. Interview with JFTC officials.

78. Tilton makes a similar observation, though his interpretation is probably more critical of the JFTC than mine. See his *Restrained Trade*.

79. John O. Haley, "Weak Law, Strong Competition, and Trade Barriers: Competitiveness as a Disincentive to Foreign Entry into Japanese Markets," in Yamamura, ed., *Japan's Economic Structure*, p. 227.

80. Interview with Iyori, December 15, 1993.

81. S. Linn Williams, "Kagami no naka no nichibei kōzō kyōgi: #8," (Looking in the Mirror at the SII Talks: Part 8) *Shūkan daiyamondo*, April 25, 1992, p. 96.

82. Interview, June 22, 1993.

83. Patricia L. Maclachlan, *The Politics of Consumer Protection in Japan: The Role of Consumer Organizations in Policymaking* (dissertation, Columbia University, 1996).

84. *Final SII Report*, pp. 103–104.

85. Interview, September 8, 1993.

86. Interview with Iyori, May 29, 1992.

87. *Sankei shimbun*, May 16, 1992, p. 29.

88. Imokawa Tokutarō, "Rikiryō tamesareru "shin dokusen gyōsei," (Testing Out the Capabilities of the "New Anti-Monopoly Administration") *Shūkan tōyō keizai*, June 12, 1993, p. 53.

89. *Nihon keizai shimbun*, May 16, 1992, p. 35.

90. See *Sankei shimbun*, May 16, 1992, p. 29; *Nihon kōgyō shimbun*, June 2, 1992, p. 2.

91. *Japan Times*, July 29, 1994. See also First, "Antitrust Enforcement in Japan," pp. 59–61.

92. Personal interviews, 1992 and 1993.

93. Note 45 above explains how the JFTC had based its original surcharge rates

on average ordinary profit ratios (*keijō riekiritsu*), taking these figures and dividing them in half on the assumption that cartels in general increased their profits by 50 percent. Faced with the need to justify a higher penalty level after the SII talks, the JFTC based its new numbers on average operating profit ratios (*eigyō riekiritsu*) which are generally higher. The agency also decided that this time it was unnecessary to divide the numbers in half. Interview with Iyori, December 15, 1993. The defense of the numbers, in other words, was quite removed from the question of how much excess profits cartels actually earned, suggesting that it was designed mostly to provide a rationale for a particular number.

94. *Nikkei shimbun*, March 13, 1992, p. 5. Note that the law changed the criminal fine for corporations only. The maximum fine for individuals remained at the old level of 5 million yen ($40,000).

95. The four firms, including the giant Dai Nippon Ink, were part of a 15-firm cartel subjected to almost 900 million yen ($7 million) in fines in 1992 but in 1993 were accused of rigging bids on a contract for adhesive seals for use by the Social Insurance Agency—*JEI Report*, No. 9B, March 12, 1993, pp. 3–4.

96. Harry First, "Selling Anti-Trust in Japan," *Anti-Trust* 7:2 (Spring 1993), pp. 34–37; and Tilton, *Restrained Trade*, pp. 115–116. Note that this fine was calculated using the old two percent rate. If the new rate had been in effect, the fine would have come to 36 billion yen ($288 million).

97. Tilton, *Restrained Trade*, p 81.

98. See the report on the flat glass sector in the American Chamber of Commerce in Japan's *United States-Japan White Paper*, 1993, p. 50. Also, interviews with officials in the U.S. embassy in Tokyo.

99. Harry First, while quite positive in his evaluation of the JFTC's enforcement actions vis-à-vis price cartels since SII, agrees that the agency has done virtually nothing to address import access—"Antitrust Enforcement in Japan," pp. 172–173.

100. JFTC, *Survey of Transactions Between Firms in the Distribution of Flat Glass*, June 29, 1993.

101. See also First, "Antitrust Enforcement in Japan," pp. 169–173.

102. Governments of Japan and the United States, *Second Annual Report of the SII Follow-up* (version supplied by the Japanese government), July 30, 1992, p. II-38. Former JFTC official Kikuchi Gen'ichi noted in an interview, however, that many of the new staff were surplus personnel from such places as the agency that manages national forests that have now been reassigned to the JFTC—not exactly the crack investigators the commission needs. Personal interview, June 17, 1992.

103. JFTC-supplied data.

104. There have been two cases filed in recent years, one by a group of Saitama citizens claiming that they lost tax dollars due to the Saitama *dango*'s anticompetitive activities and the other by the Social Insurance Agency aimed at claiming the damages it lost due to bid-rigging by the four printing firms subject to criminal sanctions by the FTC. The first is given little chance of success. See Egawa, "Rikiryō tamesareru "shin dokusen gyōsei," pp. 54–56. The continued weakness of the private damage remedy is critical because it makes the JFTC's own enforcement efforts more diffi-

cult. One reason the JFTC has failed to act against group boycotts like the one organized by the cement cartel discussed above is because it has had difficulty finding
firms that are willing to testify against their long-term suppliers. In the absence of a
functioning private damage remedy system, potential witnesses have no incentive to
risk the retaliation of their suppliers. In the U.S., the prospect of winning a civil suit
and collecting treble damages induces victims of anti-competitive practices to cooperate with authorities.

105. On the recent spate in shareholder suits, see Fusahiro Tanaka, "Whose
Company is it Anyway? The Corporate Governance Controversy," *Tokyo Business
Today*, August 1993, pp. 14–16.

106. See the "Comments of the U.S. Delegation" appended to Governments of
Japan and the United States, *First Annual Report of the SII Follow-up*, May 5, 1991 (version supplied by the Japanese government).

107. *Washington Post*, April 21, 1992, p. C1.

9. THE CLINTON FRAMEWORK TALKS

1. *Washington Post*, June 29, 1995, p. A32.

2. Edward Lincoln traces the changes in many of these indices in *Japan's New
Global Role* (Washington, D.C.: Brooking Institution, 1993). He notes that the ratio
of manufactured imports to GDP grew from 2.6 percent in 1985 to 3.8 percent in
1990 but that this rate remained less than half the level of the United States—p. 85.
He also notes that the intra-industry trade index grew 12 percent between 1988 and
1992, describing this change as only "modest"—p. 88. In contrast, the asymmetry in
cumulative foreign investment levels became even more pronounced over the same
period—pp. 70–77.

3. *Washington Post*, April 24, 1993.

4. For an excellent account of the bargaining leading to this deal on the format
for the Framework Talks, see Peter Ennis, "U.S. and Japan Reverse Roles in
Economic Framework Negotiations," *Tokyo Business Today* (October 1993), pp.
56–57.

5. "Text of Clinton's Statement," reprinted in full in *The Daily Yomiuri*, February
13, 1994, p. 3.

6. This seems to be the most popular interpretation given in media reports about
U.S. trade policy. See, for example, *Daily Yomiuri*, February 13, 1994, p. 1.

7. See discussion of Nye Report below.

8. This line of argument drew heavily on Judith Goldstein, *Ideas, Interests and
American Trade Policy* (Ithaca: Cornell University Press, 1993).

9. Goldstein, *Ideas, Interests, and American Trade Policy*, p. 13.

10. *JEI Report*, No. 39A, October 14, 1994, pp. 2–3.

11. Peter Ennis, "Inside Clinton's Japan Team," *Tokyo Business Today*, July 1993, pp.
6–11.

12. Clinton had backed NAFTA during the campaign but insisted on side agreements on worker standards and environmental regulation, and continued to hedge

on the issue well into 1993, letting Ross Perot and NAFTA opponents within his party have the field—I. M. Destler, *American Trade Politics*, 3rd ed. (Washington, D.C.: Institute for International Economics, 1995), pp. 218–228. It was exactly during this time, when the administration was being blasted by labor unions, that the Clinton administration was formulating its trade policy toward Japan.

13. *JEI Report*, No. 39A, October 14, 1994, p. 8.

14. *JEI Report*, No. 22B, June 18, 1993, p. 8.

15. *Washington Post*, July 11, 1993, p. A18.

16. Ennis, "U.S. and Japan Reverse Roles in Economic Framework Negotiations," pp. 56–57.

17. *JEI Report*, No. 40B, October 29, 1993, pp. 9–10.

18. This specific proposal was contained in draft agreements in the government procurement areas submitted in November—*JEI Report*, No. 43B, November 19, 1993, p. 10; Kawashima Mutsuho, " 'Kyakkan kijun' de oshimakuru beikoku," (America is Pushing Hard for "Objective Criteria") *Shūkan tōyō keizai*, November 6, 1993, p. 44.

19. *JEI Report*, 40B, October 29, 1993, p. 10.

20. *JEI Report*, 43B, November 19, 1993, pp. 10–11.

21. On the May deal, see *Wall Street Journal*, May 25, 1994. Note that neither side was actually conceding much. The Americans had been saying all along that they were not asking for "numerical targets," and the Japanese had agreed to "quantitative criteria" back in July 1993.

22. At the time negotiations were restarted in May, the two sides aimed to come to an agreement on the three priority issues by the time of the Naples G-7 Summit in early July, but that proved impossible. The U.S. then announced that its July 31 deadline for resolution of the government procurement issues, set under U.S. trade law but already postponed twice, would not be postponed again—but this date too passed without a deal, leading the U.S. to initiate sanctions proceedings on this issue. According to press accounts, the major stumbling block preventing agreement in each case was the issue of "objective criteria." See *Daily Yomiuri*, August 1, 1994, p. 1.

23. The critical phrase was cited in the previous paragraph, but is reproduced here with emphasis on words requiring an element of interpretation. Japan agreed that follow-up assessments of the agreement would be based on an "annual *evaluation of* progress in the value and share of procurement of foreign [medical technology/ telecommunications] products and services *to achieve*, over the *medium term*, a *significant* increase in *access* and sales of *competitive* foreign [medical technology/telecommunications] products and services."

24. This was, however, a purely "defensive" victory for the Americans, who avoided losses in market share as a result of discriminatory implementation of deregulation, but failed to win concessions that promised to bring U.S. firms a significant increase in market share. See *JEI Report*, No. 38B, October 7, 1994, pp. 8–9.

25. Text of statement issued by Mickey Kantor and USTR Press Release, May 10, 1995.

26. "Unilateral estimation" was the term used by MITI official Hisashi Hosokawa to describe the numbers in the deal—*Washington Post*, June 30, 1995, p. F1.

27. Quoted in *New York Times*, June 29, 1995, p. D6.

28. Toyota, "Press Information: Toyota Announces New Global Business Plan," released June 28, 1995.

29. The Government of Japan also promised to reiterate that it would be considered a violation of the Anti-Monopoly Law for the automakers to pressure their dealers not to offer foreign cars.

30. Toyota, "Press Information," pp. 6–7.

31. *JEI Report*, No. 15A (April 23, 1993), p. 9.

32. Toyota, "Press Information," p. 8.

33. *New York Times*, June 29, 1995, p. D6.

34. *Washington Post*, June 22, 1995, p. D1.

35. *JEI Report*, No. 15A, April 23, 1993, p. 13.

36. MITI vice-minister for international affairs Hatakeyama Noboru, quoted in the *Washington Post*, April 25, 1993, p. A28.

37. The views of former EPA Vice-minister Miyazaki Isamu, discussed in Hiroshi Fukunaga, "Arguments over Numerical Goals," *Tokyo Business Today* (May 1994), p. 39.

38. *Asahi shimbun*, February 9, 1994.

39. *Asahi shimbun*, February 13, 1994.

40. Results of poll on popular support for leading contenders in the race to succeed Murayama as prime minister, cited in *Washington Post*, June 27, 1995, p. D4.

41. Keidanren, for example, called for changes not too different from those ultimately adopted after American pressure, including a "review of the contents of the periodic motor vehicle inspections (frequency of inspections, the number of inspection items) to reflect the development of automobile-related technology," in its *Toward an Open, Transparent and Fair Market Economy: Proposals for Deregulation*, July 7, 1992, p. 6.

42. For the U.S. position, see USTR, *1994 National Trade Estimate Report on Foreign Trade Barriers*, pp. 177–178. Also, USTR, "Written Statement by USTR Mickey Kantor and USTR Press Release," May 10, 1995.

43. *Nikkei Weekly*, June 26, 1995, p. 1.

44. Motorola had been completely closed out of the corridor until 1989 when American pressure had succeeded in convincing the Japanese government to set up the marriage with IDO and authorize that firm to start building a system that would run Motorola phones. For background, see Laura D'Andrea Tyson, *Who's Bashing Whom?* (Washington, D.C.: Institute for International Economics, 1992), pp. 66–71. Motorola was especially eager to get IDO moving because it knew the cellular phone market would explode as soon as consumers were allowed to buy (rather than lease) phones, a change slated to take effect in April 1994.

45. Robert Orr, "The *Gaiatsu* Game Between the U.S. and Japan," *Tokyo Report* 19:6 (June 1994)—produced by Hotel Okura and published as special section of *Nikkei Weekly*, May 30, 1994. Also, personal interview with Orr, the Director of Government Relations-Japan for Motorola's Tokyo office, May 24, 1994.

46. Personal communication with Robert Orr, August 7, 1995.

47. Raymond J. Ahearn identifies a "gaiatsu is dead" perspective in his recent work "Japan's Response to U.S. Trade Pressures: End of an Era?" *Congressional Research Service Report for Congress*, June 12, 1995.

48. On bargaining leading up to the 1992 auto accords, see *JEI Report*, No. 2B, January 17, 1992, pp. 15–18; and *JEI Report*, No. 15A, April 23, 1993; On the semi-conductor accords, see Ellis Krauss, "U.S.-Japan Negotiations On Construction and Semiconductors, 1985–1988: Building Friction and Relation-Chips," in Peter B. Evans, Harold K. Jacobson, and Robert D. Putnam, eds., *Double-Edged Diplomacy: International Bargaining and Domestic Politics* (Berkeley: University of California Press, 1993), pp. 266–277.

49. *The Daily Yomiuri*, March 5, 1994. For background on the Clinton adminis-tration and Super 301, see Thomas O. Bayard and Kimberly Ann Elliott, *Reciprocity and Retaliation in U.S. Trade Policy* (Washington, D.C.: Institute for International Economics, 1994), pp. 44–49.

50. The 200,000 total exports at stake broke down as follows: Toyota, 86,578; Nissan, 33,743; Honda, 35,631; Mitsubishi, 10,671; Mazda, 37,700—*Nikkei Weekly*, May 22, 1995, p. 1.

51. *Daily Yomiuri*, November 12, 1993.

52. Testimony of Summers in U.S. Congress, House Committee on Government Operations, *United States-Japan Framework Talks on Trade: Hearings before the House Subcommittee on Commerce, Consumer, and Monetary Affairs*, 103rd Congress, 2nd sess., February 24 and March 23, 1994, pp. 108–109.

53. On the cabinet plan, see *Japan Economic Survey* 18:10 (October 1994), pp. 1–2. I have emphasized here the tax cut component of stimulative fiscal policy, but there was also a public works aspect. Here, the American concern was that MOF—having spent much of the 430 trillion yen in public investment it had promised for the decade in an effort to combat the recession—would slow down public works spending in the latter half of the decade. Unless there was another 10-year plan with significantly higher numbers, a slowdown was inevitable. Politicians and govern-ment officials began discussing such a plan during the summer of 1994 and eventu-ally adopted a plan to spend 630 trillion yen over the years 1995–2005. This too was delayed by MOF's insistence that the new cabinet commit to a consumption tax first, and analysts estimated that the new plan would boost public works spending by only 3 percent a year in nominal terms—See *JEI Report*, 39B, October 14, 1994, pp. 1–3.

54. *Daily Yomiuri*, November 12, 1993; and Bruce Stokes, "Immovable Mandarins," *National Journal*, April 30, 1994, p. 1008.

55. "Text of Hosokawa's Statement," reprinted in full in *The Daily Yomiuri*, February 13, 1994, p. 3.

56. Export market dependence, of course, is just one dimension of the bilateral economic relationship where asymmetries may have shifted. One might suggest, for example, that the emergence during the last decade of Japan's power as a source of capital (and America's corresponding shift to debtor status) might explain why Japan is now able to say "no" to the U.S. While such shifts probably do have something to

do with greater Japanese assertiveness, they cannot explain why the U.S. was more successful in using gaiatsu under Bush than under Clinton since U.S. dependence on Japanese capital was greatest in the late 1980s and has declined somewhat in the 1990s.

57. The U.S.-Japan Security Treaty has long served to reassure Japan's neighbors who might otherwise be worried that Japan would rearm and threaten them again militarily as it did during World War II. Japan recognizes that the treaty serves this stabilizing function and remains hesitant to risk upsetting the alliance, especially when China and other nations in the region are already in the midst of a moderate arms race. See Aaron L. Friedberg, "Ripe for Rivalry: Prospects for Peace in a Multipolar Asia," and Desmond Ball, "Arms and Affluence: Military Acquisitions in the Asia-Pacific Region," both in *International Security* 18:3 (Winter 1993–94), pp. 5–33 and 78–112; Michael T. Klare, "The Next Great Arms Race," *Foreign Affairs* 72:3 (Summer 1993), pp. 136–152.

58. For a realist account emphasizing Japan's continuing "dependence and vulnerability" relative to the U.S. on the military side, see Kenneth N. Waltz, "The Emerging Structure of International Politics," *International Security* 18:2 (Fall 1993), p. 65.

59. See section on threats in chapter 2.

60. The U.S. was particularly dependent on Japanese cooperation in this case because one of North Korea's most valuable sources of hard currency was the flow of funds sent to the country by North Koreans living in Japan. Unless the Japanese agreed to cut off these flows, a politically sensitive step, an embargo aimed at forcing North Korea to submit to nuclear inspections was unlikely to be effective.

61. A U.S. businessman who has been following the talks closely quotes U.S. Commerce Undersecretary Jeffrey Garten reporting that in interagency meetings, State and Defense Department officials made comments such as this—personal interview, June 15, 1994.

62. *Nikkei shimbun*, May 25, 1994, p. 1.

63. *Washington Post*, February 19, 1995, p. A48; *JEI Report*, April 21, 1995.

64. Department of Defense, *United States Security Strategy for the East Asia-Pacific Region*. See also Joseph S. Nye, Jr., "The Case for Deep Engagement," *Foreign Affairs* 74:4 (July/August 1995), pp. 91–102.

65. Chalmers Johnson and E. B. Keehn, "The Pentagon's Ossified Strategy," *Foreign Affairs* 74:4 (July/August 1995), p. 105. In the endgame leading up to the 1995 auto accords, a comment by the White House press secretary expressing concern about the impact of trade tensions on U.S.-Japan security relations was briefly interpreted in Japan as a signal that, the Nye Report not withstanding, the U.S. *did* intend to use its leverage on the security side. This impression was quickly corrected, however, by Mondale, Clinton, and other administration officials who reassured Japan that it should have no worries about the American security guarantee.

66. Ozawa Ichirō, *Blueprint for a New Japan* (Tokyo: Kōdansha, 1994), p. 94.

67. *Washington Post*, May 20, 1995, p. D1.

68. Ennis, "U.S. and Japan Reverse Roles," p. 56–57.

69. Joseph M. Grieco, *Cooperation Among Nations: Europe, America, and Non-Tariff Barriers to Trade* (Ithaca: Cornell University Press, 1990).

70. Robert O. Keohane, *After Hegemony: Cooperation and Discord in the World Political Economy* (Princeton: Princeton University Press, 1984).

71. On the new dispute settlement procedure and how it differs from the old, see Jeffrey J. Schott, *The Uruguay Round: An Assessment* (Washington, D.C.: Institute for International Economics, 1994), pp. 125–132.

72. Ibid.

73. Most trade experts predicted that Japan would win a WTO case against unilateral American sanctions—*Washington Post*, May 11, 1995, A18.

74. Nezu Risaburō, quoted in *Nikkei Weekly*, December 20, 1993, p. 1.

75. *Daily Yomiuri*, March 5, 1994, p. 21.

76. Trade minister Hashimoto also met with the new WTO head, Renato Ruggiero, in Tokyo—*Nikkei Weekly*, May 1, 1995, p. 1.

77. Letter from Kantor to Ruggiero, dated May 10, 1995, released by the USTR.

78. Greg Mastel of the Economic Strategy Institute was quoted repeatedly predicting the U.S. could win a WTO case against Japan—*Washington Post*, May 6, 1995, p. D1.

79. This was a real risk. To get the WTO through Congress, Clinton had been forced to agree to set up a committee of federal judges to review WTO rulings to see if they were fair. A pair of big rulings against the U.S., judged unfair by such a panel, would have probably led the U.S. government to, in effect, walk out of the WTO. For background see *Financial Times*, May 12, 1995.

80. That Japan was conscious of such worries was suggested by the comments of trade minister Hashimoto a few days before the settlement when he said, "The U.S. and Japan went through a lot of trouble to make the WTO. We cannot destroy the system with our own hands," quoted by Reuter, reporting from Geneva, June 26, 1995.

81. See *Washington Post*, May 25, 1995.

82. *New York Times*, June 14, 1995, D1, 5.

83. For these worries, see Iwao Nakatani, "WTO Victory Would be Pyrrhic," *The Japan Times Weekly International Edition*, June 26–July 2, 1995, p. 9.

84. The clearest evidence of this is in the reports I received from Dietmen and Japanese journalists in 1993–1994 about trends in political party contributions by businesses and interest groups which indicate that LDP fund-raising suffered greatly and that interest groups are starting to shop around (or cover their bets) with their campaign giving.

85. This logic is summarized in Peter F. Cowhey and Matthew D. McCubbins, "Conclusion," in Cowhey and McCubbins, eds., *Structure and Policy in Japan and the United States* (Cambridge: Cambridge University Press, 1995), pp. 256–259.

86. Peter Ennis, "Inside the Clinton-Hosokawa Summit," *Tokyo Business Today* (May 1994), p. 37.

87. Ozawa, *Blueprint for a New Japan*. See also Sasaki Takeshi, *Seiji wa doko e mukaunoka* (Where Is Politics Headed?) (Tokyo: Chūō Kōronsha, 1992).

88. Interview with senior MOFA official, March 22, 1994.

10. Conclusions

1. My purpose is not too different from that which motivated Alexander George and Richard Smoke to evaluate the utility of deterrence theory in their seminal work, *Deterrence in American Foreign Policy: Theory and Practice* (New York: Columbia University Press, 1974).

2. Thomas O. Bayard and Kimberly Ann Elliott, *Reciprocity and Retaliation in U.S. Trade Policy* (Washington, D.C.: Institute for International Economics, 1994), p. 86.

3. The authors do not present their findings in this format. I have derived these tables from the authors' "Summary Table of All Section 301 Cases," pp. 355–368. The authors calculated the "degree to which American negotiating objective was achieved" by asking not just whether an agreement was reached but also whether the American goal (improved market access, reduced export subsidies, improved intellectual property protection, etc.) was in fact achieved when the agreement was implemented. See their pp. 59–64. I have reported outcomes of all 301 cases that were not dropped by the American side for a lack of evidence involving the nation with the most 301 cases. Where the authors used a few idiosyncratic terms to describe outcomes (e.g. "no" instead of "not at all"; and "yes" instead of "largely successful"), I have employed one of the standard four terms that the authors used.

4. These cases provide a wide variety of opportunities to show through comparative analysis how factors other than raw power affect negotiating outcomes. Bayard and Elliott, for example, do detailed case studies of the Super 301 cases where the U.S. tagged Japan, Brazil, and India as "unfair traders" and sought, during the period of 1989–90, to use this ultimate weapon of U.S. trade law to achieve market-opening objectives. While India completely refused to accept American demands, Japan agreed to most American demands—an outcome that does not correspond to the relative power positions of India and Japan—see their pp. 101–170. Odell, in a separate study, contrasts America's difficulty in imposing its demands on Brazil in the informatics case with its greater success in winning concessions from Europe on feedgrains although on all counts Europe should have had the greater power to resist American demands—John Odell, "International Threats and Internal Politics: Brazil, the European Community, and the United States, 1985–1987," in Peter Evans, Harold Jacobson, and Robert Putnam, eds., *Double-Edged Diplomacy: International Bargaining and Domestic Politics* (Berkeley: University of California Press, 1993), pp. 233–264.

5. While I use Bayard and Elliott's data here, I should note that the authors themselves do not break down the results of 301 cases by country and attempt to analyze why some countries are overall more responsive than others. They do make note of Japan's unusual responsiveness, however, noting that just three Japan cases (beef, tobacco, and semiconductors) account for $3 billion of the $4 billion total increase in U.S. exports that can be attributed to 301 cases—*Reciprocity and Retaliation*, p. 334.

6. Bayard and Elliott, *Reciprocity and Retaliation*, p. 94.

7. The authors seem to draw the term "participation expansion" from my earlier

published work, adding the term "positive" to distinguish it from the threat-derived variety. They are not able to test the impact of this factor (whether the U.S. has allies in the target country that support change for their own reasons) in their quantitative regression, but they do look for it and find it in their detailed case studies— Ibid., p. 85.

8. Ibid., pp. 85–89, 332–333.

9. Bayard and Elliott do include a few other attributes of nations in their regression analysis which, they could claim, explains the variation across nations. They factor in, for example, whether or not a nation had counter-retaliated against the U.S. in the past: Canada had retaliated in the past, so U.S. pressure was less effective; Japan had never retaliated, so U.S. pressure was more effective. This exercise offers little more than circular reasoning, however, for it doesn't explain why these nations were bold enough to counter-retaliate in the first place.

10. Though their recommendations are not focused specifically on Japan, Bayard and Elliott make a similar recommendation based on their reading of how new WTO rules will impact U.S. bargaining leverage—*Reciprocity and Retaliation*, pp. 329–351.

11. Bayard and Elliott, *Reciprocity and Retaliation*, p. 345; Jeffrey J. Schott, *The Uruguay Round: An Assessment* (Washington, D.C.: Institute for International Economics, 1994), pp. 14–15.

12. Some would probably emphasize this advantage of a multilateral approach over and above the "legitimacy" advantage. While it too is clearly important, I emphasize the latter factor since Japan (in contrast to the EC) never took advantage of legal opportunities that *were* available even under GATT to challenge unilateral U.S. threats. It did not do so, I propose, not so much because the GATT process was weaker (it was also weaker for the EC, remember) but because U.S. pressure enjoyed greater legitimacy in those days.

13. Amelia Porges, "Japan: Beef and Citrus," in Bayard and Elliott, *Reciprocity and Retaliation*, p. 263.

14. Keidanren, *Toward an Open, Transparent and Fair Market Economy: Proposals for Deregulation*, July 7, 1992; and Keidanren, "Kisei kanwa no dankō wo motomeru," (Calling for Decisive Deregulatory Action) *Keidanren shiyrō* 5 (May 1994).

15. For a summary of Japanese demands, see William H. Cooper, "Japan-U.S. Trade: The Structural Impediments Initiative," *Current Politics and Economics of Japan* 1:1 (1991), pp. 79–81.

16. The case of U.S.-Japan talks aimed at harmonizing their intellectual property regimes illustrates the potentials of two-way bargaining: Japan agreed to speed up the processing of patent applications in return for a U.S. concession where it promised to eliminate the nuisance of "submarine patents" by publishing all applications within 18 months of filing. Though this 1990 deal grew out of the SII talks, it was not discussed in detail in this book because the negotiating *was* unusually two-way. See William E. Thomson, Jr. and Sean A. Luner, "Sweet Patent Pacts," *Managing Intellectual Property*, November 1994.

17. See C. Fred Bergsten and Marcus Noland, *Reconcilable Differences? United*

States-Japan Economic Conflict (Washington: Institute for International Economics, 1993), pp. 210–219.

18. A variety of economists and political scientists—many of them cited in chapter 3—have provided evidence that Japan does maintain barriers and that at least some of these are "strategic" in that they help Japanese firms gain competitive advantages when they sell abroad. Even if one does not accept these arguments, however, there is another important reason why it is in the U.S. interest to tackle these barriers: failure to deal with what are *perceived* to be unfair trade practices in Japan will reduce support for the liberal trading system in the U.S. and abroad.

19. OECD, *OECD Economic Surveys 1993/94: Japan* (Paris: OECD, 1994), p. 92.

20. "Repairing the U.S.-Japan Relationship," *ACCJ Journal*, June 1994, pp. 8–15. When this article was circulated to President Clinton in January 1993, he reportedly scribbled "agree with this" next to this passage. Good advice, too late.

BIBLIOGRAPHY

Advisory Committee on Trade Policy and Negotiations. *Analysis of the U.S.-Japan Trade Problem*. February 1989.

Ahearn, Raymond J. "Japan's Response to U.S. Trade Pressures: End of an Era?" *Congressional Research Service Report for Congress*. June 12, 1995.

Allison, Graham T. *Essence of Decision: Explaining the Cuban Missile Crisis*. Boston: Little, Brown and Company, 1971.

American Chamber of Commerce in Japan. *United States-Japan White Paper*. 1993.

Anchordoguy, Marie. "Land Policy: A Public Policy Failure." In John O. Haley and Kozo Yamamura, eds., *Land Issues In Japan: A Policy Failure?* Seattle: Society for Japanese Studies, 1992, pp. 77–111.

Armacost, Michael H. *Friends or Rivals: The Insider Account of U.S-Japan Relations*. New York: Columbia University Press, 1996.

Axelrod, Robert. *The Evolution of Cooperation*. New York: Basic Books, 1984.

Baldwin, David. "Interdependence and Power: A Conceptual Analysis." *International Organization* 34:4 (Autumn 1980): 471–506.

Baldwin, Robert E. *The Political Economy of U.S. Import Policy*. Cambridge: MIT Press, 1985.

Ball, Desmond. "Arms and Affluence: Military Acquisitions in the Asia-Pacific Region." *International Security* 18:3 (Winter 1993–94): 78–112.

Bayard, Thomas O. and Kimberly Ann Elliott. *Reciprocity and Retaliation in U.S. Trade Policy*. Washington, D.C.: Institute for International Economics, 1994.

Bello, Judith Hippler, and Alan F. Holmer. "The Heart of the 1988 Trade Act: A Legislative History of the Amendments to Section 301." In Jagdish Bhagwati and Hugh T. Patrick, eds., *Aggressive Unilateralism: America's 301 Trade Policy and the World Trading System*. Ann Arbor: University of Michigan Press, 1990, pp. 49–89.

Bergsten, C. Fred, and Marcus Noland. *Reconcilable Differences?: United States-Japan Economic Conflict*. Washington, D.C.: Institute for International Economics, 1993.

Bergsten, C. Fred, and William R. Cline, *The United States-Japan Economic Problem*. Washington, D.C.: Institute for International Economics, 1987.

Brooks, William L. "MITI's Distribution Policy and U.S.-Japan Structural Talks." In Michael R. Czinkota and Masaaki Kotabe, eds., *The Japanese Distribution System*. Chicago: Probus Publishing Company, 1993, pp. 231–248.

Budner, Stanley, and Ellis Krauss. *Communicating Across the Pacific*. Missoula, Montana: Mansfield Center for Pacific Affairs, forthcoming.

Burton, John. *World Society*. Cambridge: Cambridge University Press, 1972.

Calder, Kent E. *Crisis and Compensation: Public Policy and Political Stability in Japan, 1949–1986*. Princeton: Princeton University Press, 1988.

Calder, Kent E. "Japanese Foreign Economic Policy: Explaining the Reactive State." *World Politics* 40:4 (July 1988): 518–541.

Caldwell, Dan. *The Dynamics of Domestic Politics and Arms Control*. Columbia, SC: University of South Carolina, 1991.

Campbell, John C. *How Policies Change: The Japanese Government and the Aging Society*. Princeton: Princeton University Press, 1992.

Campbell, John C. "Policy Conflict and its Resolution within the Governmental System." In Ellis Krauss, Thomas Rohlen and Patricia Steinhoff, eds., *Conflict in Japan*. Honolulu: University of Hawaii Press, 1984, pp. 294–334.

Chinworth, Michael W., and Dean Cheng. "The United States and Asia in the Post-Cold War World." *SAIS Review* 11:1 (Winter-Spring 1991): 73–91.

Choate, Pat. *Agents of Influence*. New York: Alfred A. Knopf, 1990.

Coase, R. H. "The Problem of Social Cost." *Journal of Law and Economics* 3 (1960): 1–44.

Cohen, Stephen S., and John Zysman. *Manufacturing Matters: The Myth of the Post-Industrial Economy*. New York: Basic Books, 1987.

Cooper, William H. "Japan-U.S. Trade: The Structural Impediments Initiative." *Current Politics and Economics of Japan* 1:1 (1991): 73–81.

Cowhey, Peter F. "Domestic Institutions and the Credibility of International Commitments: Japan and the United States." *International Organization* 47:2 (Spring 1993): 299–326.

Cowhey, Peter F., and Matthew D. McCubbins, eds. *Structure and Policy in Japan and the United States*. Cambridge: Cambridge University Press, 1995.

Curtis, Gerald. *The Japanese Way of Politics*. New York: Columbia University Press, 1988.

Deardorff, Alan V., and Robert M. Stern. "American Labor's Stake in International Trade." In Adam S. Walter, ed., *Tariffs, Quotas and Trade: The Politics of Protectionism*. San Francisco: Institute for Contemporary Studies, 1979.

Destler, I. M. *American Trade Politics: System Under Stress*, 1st, 2nd, and 3rd eds. Washington, D.C.: Institute for International Economics, 1986, 1992, and 1995.

Destler, I. M., and Hideo Sato, eds. *Coping with U.S.-Japanese Economic Conflicts*. Lexington, MA: D.C. Heath and Co., 1982.

Destler, I. M., and Hisao Mitsuyu. "Locomotives on Different Tracks: Macroeconomic Diplomacy, 1977–1979." In Destler and Hideo Sato, eds.,

Coping with U.S. Japan Economic Conflicts. Lexington, MA: D.C. Heath and Company, 1982, pp. 243–269.

Destler, I. M., and John S. Odell, *Anti-Protection: Changing Forces in United States Trade Politics.* Washington, D.C.: Institute for International Economics, 1987.

Destler, I. M., Hideo Sato, Priscilla Clapp, and Haruhiro Fukui. *Managing an Alliance: The Politics of U.S.-Japan Relations.* Washington, D.C.: Brookings, 1976.

Dore, Ronald. *Flexible Rigidities: Industrial Policy and Structural Adjustment in the Japanese Economy, 1970–1980.* Stanford: Stanford University Press, 1986.

Dornbusch, Rudiger. "Policy Options for Freer Trade: The Case for Bilateralism." In Robert Z. Lawrence and Charles L. Schultze, eds., *An American Trade Strategy: Options for the 1990s.* Washington, D.C.: Brookings, 1990.

Drucker, Peter. "Japan's Choices." *Foreign Affairs* 65:5 (Summer 1987): 923–941.

Economic Planning Agency. *Bukka Repooto.* (Price Report). Annual.

Economic Planning Agency. *Nenji keizai hōkoku.* (Annual Economic Report). Annual.

Eckstein, Harry. "Case Study and Theory in Political Science." In Fred Greenstein and Nelson Polsby, eds., *Handbook of Political Science, vol. 7.* Reading, MA: Addison-Wesley, 1975, pp. 79–138.

Encarnation, Dennis J. *Rivals Beyond Trade: America Versus Japan in Global Competition.* Ithaca: Cornell University Press, 1992.

Ennis, Peter. "Inside Clinton's Japan Team." *Tokyo Business Today* (July 1993): 6–11.

Ennis, Peter. "Inside the Clinton-Hosokawa Summit." *Tokyo Business Today* (May 1994): 34–38.

Ennis, Peter. "U.S. and Japan Reverse Roles in Economic Framework Negotiations." *Tokyo Business Today* (October 1993): 56–57.

Evans, Peter. "Building an Integrative Approach to International and Domestic Politics: Reflections and Projections." In Peter Evans, Harold K. Jacobson, and Robert Putnam, eds. *Double Edged Diplomacy.* Berkeley: University of California Press, 1993, pp. 397–430.

Evans, Peter, Harold K. Jacobson, and Robert Putnam, eds. *Double Edged Diplomacy: International Bargaining and Domestic Politics.* Berkeley: University of California Press, 1993.

Fallows, James. "Containing Japan." *Atlantic* (May 1989): 40–54.

Ferguson, Charles. "America's High Tech Decline." *Foreign Policy* 74 (1989): 123–144.

Ferguson, Thomas. *Golden Rule: The Investment Theory of Party Competition and the Logic of Money-Driven Political Systems.* Chicago: University of Chicago Press, 1995.

Fingleton, Eamonn. *Blindside: Why Japan is Still on Track to Overtake the U.S. by the Year 2000.* Boston: Houghton Mifflin, 1995.

First, Harry. "Antitrust Enforcement in Japan." *Antitrust Law Journal* 64:1 (Fall 1995): 137–182.

First, Harry. "Japan's Antitrust Policy: Impact on Import Competition." In Thomas A. Pugel and Robert G. Hawkins, eds., *Fragile Interdependence: Economic Issues in U.S.-Japanese Trade and Investment.* Lexington, MA: D. C. Heath, 1986, pp. 63–76.

First, Harry. "Selling Anti-Trust in Japan." *Anti-Trust* 7:2 (Spring 1993): 34–37.

Friedberg, Aaron L. "Ripe for Rivalry: Prospects for Peace in a Multipolar Asia." *International Security* 18:3 (Winter 1993–94): 5–33.

Friman, H. Richard. "Side-Payments Versus Security Cards: Domestic Bargaining Tactics in International Economic Negotiations." *International Organization* 47:3 (Summer 1993): 387–410.

Fukai, Shigeko. "Japan Land Policy and Its Global Impact." *U.S.-Japan Program Occasional Paper* 90–01 (1990).

Fukai, Shigeko. "The Role of *Gaiatsu* in Japan's Land Policymaking." Paper presented at the APSA annual meeting in Chicago, September 3–6, 1992.

Fukunaga, Hiroshi. "Arguments over Numerical Goals." *Tokyo Business Today* (May 1994): 39.

Fukushima, Glen. "The Nature of United States-Japan Government Negotiations." In Valerie Kusuda-Smick, ed., *United States / Japan Commercial Law and Trade*. Transnational Juris Publications, 1990, pp. 660–667.

Fukushima, Glen. *Nichibei keizai masatsu no seijigaku*. (The Political Science of U.S.-Japan Economic Disputes). Tokyo: Asahi Shimbunsha, 1992.

Fukushima, Glen. "Repairing the U.S.-Japan Relationship." *American Chamber of Commerce in Japan Journal* (June 1994): 8–15.

Funabashi, Yoichi. *Managing the Dollar: From the Plaza to the Louvre*, 2nd Ed. Washington, D.C.: Institute for International Economics, 1989.

Futatsugi, Yūsaku. *Gendai nihon no kigyō shūdan*. (Enterprise Groups in Contemporary Japan) Tokyo: Tōyō Shinpōsha, 1976.

Galtung, Johan. "On the Effects of International Economic Sanctions, With Examples from the Case of Rhodesia." *World Politics* 19 (April 1967): 378–416.

George, Alexander, and Richard Smoke. *Deterrence in American Foreign Policy: Theory and Practice*. New York: Columbia University Press, 1974.

George, Aurelia. "Japan's America Problem: The Japanese Response to U.S. Pressure." *The Washington Quarterly* 14:3 (Summer 1991): 5–19.

Gerlach, Michael. "*Keiretsu* Organization in the Japanese Economy: Analysis and Trade Implications." In Chalmers Johnson, Laura D'Andrea Tyson, and John Zysman, eds., *Politics and Productivity: How Japan's Development Strategy Works*. New York: Harper Business, 1989, pp. 140–174.

Gilpin, Robert. *U.S. Power and the Multinational Corporation*. New York: Basic Books, 1975.

Governments of Japan and the United States. *First Annual Report of the SII Follow-up*. May 5, 1991. (version supplied by the Japanese government).

Governments of Japan and the United States. *Second Annual Report of the SII Follow-up*. July 30, 1992. (version supplied by the Japanese government).

Gowa, Joanne. *Allies, Adversaries and International Trade*. Princeton: Princeton University Press, 1994.

Goldstein, Judith. *Ideas, Interests, and American Trade Policy*. Ithaca: Cornell University Press, 1993.

Grieco, Joseph M. *Cooperation Among Nations: Europe, America, and Non-Tariff Barriers to Trade*. Ithaca: Cornell University Press, 1990.

Haas, Peter, ed. Special Issue on Epistemic Communities. *International Organization* 46:1 (Winter 1992).

Hadley, Eleanor M. *Antitrust in Japan.* Princeton: Princeton University Press, 1970.

Haley, John. "Japan's New Land and House Lease Law." In John O. Haley and Kozo Yamamura, eds., *Land Issues In Japan: A Policy Failure?* Seattle: Society for Japanese Studies, 1992, pp. 149–173.

Haley, John. "The Myth of the Reluctant Litigant." *Journal of Japanese Studies* 4:2 (Summer 1978): 359–390.

Haley, John O. "Weak Law, Strong Competition, and Trade Barriers: Competitiveness as a Disincentive to Foreign Entry into Japanese Markets." In Kozo Yamamura, ed., *Japan's Economic Structure: Should It Change?* Seattle: Society for Japanese Studies, 1990, pp. 203–235.

Hall, Peter. *Governing the Economy: Politics of State Intervention in Britain and France.* New York: Oxford University Press, 1986.

Hanley, Susan B. "Traditional Housing and Unique Lifestyles: The Unintended Outcomes of Japan's Land Policy." In John O. Haley and Kozo Yamamura, eds., *Land Issues In Japan: A Policy Failure?* Seattle: Society for Japanese Studies, 1992, pp. 195–222.

Harada, Yutaka. "Tada ichigyō no hōkaisei ga 'jūtaku' wo kaiketsu suru." (Revising Just One Line of a Law Will Fix the "Housing" Problem) *Ekonomisuto* (September 19, 1989): 10–15.

Hardin, Russell. *Collective Action.* Baltimore: Johns Hopkins University Press and Resources for the Future, 1982.

Hasegawa, Tokunosuke. "Hiking the Taxes on Farmland in the Cities." *Economic Eye* (Winter 1990): 17–19.

Hasegawa, Tokunosuke. "Nichibei kōzō kyōgi ni okeru tochi mondai." (The Land Problem in the SII Talks) In Abe Tetsuo, et al, eds., *Nichibei kankei no kōzu.* (The Composition of U.S.-Japan Relations) Kyoto: Minerva, 1992, pp. 239–266.

Higuchi, Kenji. " 'Shizuoka itōyōkadō sensō' tenmatsuki." (The Details of the "Shizuoka Itōyōkadō War") *Ekonomisuto* (December 13, 1988): 52–55.

Hirschman, Albert O. *National Power and the Structure of Foreign Trade.* Berkeley: University of California Press, 1945.

Honma, Yoshito. "Tochi rinchō no 300-nichi." (300 Days of the Advisory Council on Land Policy) *Ekonomisuto* (June 21, 1988): 70–75.

Hosono, Sukehiro. *Posuto daitenhō.* (Post-LSL) Tokyo: Nihon Jitsugyō Shuppansha, 1991.

Iida, Keisuke. "When and How Do Domestic Constraints Matter?: Two-Level Games With Uncertainty." *Journal of Conflict Resolution* 37:3 (September 1993): 403–426.

Ikenberry, G. John, David A. Lake, and Michael Mastanduno, eds. *The State and American Foreign Economic Policy.* Ithaca: Cornell University Press, 1988.

Imai, Ken'ichi. "Japanese Business Groups and the Structural Impediments Initiative." In Kozo Yamamura, ed., *Japan's Economic Structure: Should It Change?* Seattle: Society for Japanese Studies, 1990, pp. 167–202.

Imai, Ken'ichi. "The Legitimacy of Japan's Corporate Groups." *Japan Echo* 17 (Autumn 1990): 23–28.

Imokawa, Takutarō. "Rikiryō tamesareru "shin dokusen gyōsei." (Testing Out the Capabilities of the "New Anti-Monopoly Administration"). *Shūkan tōyō keizai* (June 12, 1993): 52–58.

Inoguchi, Takashi. "Japan's Images and Options: Not a Challenger, but a Supporter." *Journal of Japanese Studies* 12:1 (Winter 1986): 95–119.

Inoguchi, Takashi, and Iwai Tomoaki. *'Zoku giin' no kenkyū*. (Research on Policy Tribes) Tokyo: Nihon Keizai Shimbunsha, 1987.

Ishi, Hiromitsu. *Tochi zeisei kaikaku*. (Land Tax Reform) Tokyo: Tōyō Keizai Shimpōsha, 1991.

Iyori, Hiroshi. "Antitrust and Industrial Policy in Japan: Competition and Cooperation." In Gary Saxonhouse and Kozo Yamamura, eds., *Law and Trade Issues of the Japanese Economy*. Seattle: University of Washington Press, 1986, pp. 56–82.

Janow, Merit E. "Trading With an Ally: Progress and Discontent in U.S.-Japan Trade Relations." In Gerald L. Curtis, ed., *The United States, Japan, and Asia: Challenges for U.S. Policy*. New York: W. W. Norton, 1994, pp. 53–95.

Japanese Fair Trade Commission. *Kōsei torihiki iinkai nenji hōkoku—dokusen kinshi hakusho*. (Fair Trade Commission Annual Report—The Anti-Monopoly White Paper). Annual.

Japanese Fair Trade Commission. *The Outline of the Report on the Actual Conditions of the Six Major Corporate Groups*. February 1992.

Japanese Fair Trade Commission. *Survey of Transactions Between Firms in the Distribution of Flat Glass*. June 29, 1993.

Jensen, Lloyd. *Bargaining for National Security*. Columbia, SC: University of South Carolina, 1988.

Johnson, Chalmers. "How to Think About Economic Competition From Japan." In Kenneth Pyle, ed., *The Trade Crisis: How Will Japan Respond?* Seattle: Society for Japanese Studies, 1987, pp. 71–83.

Johnson, Chalmers. *MITI and the Japanese Miracle: The Growth of Industrial Policy, 1925–1975*. Stanford: Stanford University Press, 1982.

Johnson, Chalmers. "MITI, MPT, and the Telecom Wars: How Japan Makes Policy for High Technology." In Chalmers Johnson, Laura D'Andrea Tyson, and John Zysman, eds., *Politics and Productivity: How Japan's Development Strategy Works*. New York: Harper Business, 1989, pp. 177–240.

Johnson, Chalmers. "Trade, Revisionism, and the Future of Japanese-American Relations." In Kozo Yamamura, ed., *Japan's Economic Structure: Should it Change?* Seattle: Society for Japanese Studies, 1990, pp. 105–136.

Johnson, Chalmers, and E. B. Keehn. "The Pentagon's Ossified Strategy." *Foreign Affairs* 74:4 (July/August 1995): 103–114.

Kato, Junko. *The Problem of Bureaucratic Rationality: Tax Politics in Japan*. Princeton: Princeton University Press, 1994.

Kawashima, Mutsuho. "'Kyakkan kijun' de oshimakuru beikoku." (America is Pushing Hard for "Objective Criteria") *Shūkan tōyō keizai* (November 6, 1993): 44–47.

Keidanren. "Kisei kanwa no dankō wo motomeru." (Calling for Decisive Deregulatory Action) *Keidanren shiryō* 5 (May 1994).

Keidanren. *Toward an Open, Transparent and Fair Market Economy: Proposals for Deregulation.* July 7, 1992.

Keizai Kaikaku Kenkyūkai. *Keizai kaikaku ni tsuite.* (Regarding Economic Reform). December 16, 1993.

Kensetsu Daijin Kambō Seisakuka. *Nichibei kōzō mondai kyōgi to kensetsu gyōsei.* (The U.S.-Japan SII Talks and Construction Administration). Tokyo: Taisei Shuppansha, 1990.

Kensetsu Keizai Kenkyūjo. *Nihon keizai to kōkyō tōshi.* (The Japanese Economy and Public Investment). Various issues.

Keohane, Robert O. *After Hegemony: Cooperation and Discord in the World Political Economy.* Princeton: Princeton University Press, 1984.

Keohane, Robert O., and Joseph S. Nye. *Power and Interdependence,* 2nd Ed. Glenville, IL: Scott, Foresman, 1989.

Kiewiet, D. Roderick, and Matthew D. McCubbins. *The Logic of Delegation: Congressional Parties and the Appropriations Process.* Chicago: University of Chicago Press, 1991.

Kikuchi, Gen'ichi. "Ima motomerareru 'tsuyoi' kōtorii." (A "Strong" FTC Which We Can Now Demand) *Ekonomisuto* (January 23, 1990): 50–55.

Kindleberger, Charles. *The World in Depression.* Berkeley: University of California Press, 1973.

King, Gary, Robert O. Keohane, and Sidney Verba. *Designing Social Inquiry: Scientific Inference in Qualitative Research.* Princeton: Princeton University Press, 1994.

Kingdon, John W. *Agendas, Alternatives, and Public Policies.* Glenview, IL: Scott, Foresman and Company, 1984.

Klare, Michael T. "The Next Great Arms Race." *Foreign Affairs* 72:3 (Summer 1993): 136–152.

Knopf, Jeffrey W. "Beyond Two-Level Games: Domestic-International Interaction in the Intermediate-Range Nuclear Forces Negotiations." *International Organization* 47:4 (Autumn 1993): 599–628.

Knorr, Klauss. *The Power of Nations.* New York: Basic Books, 1975.

Krasner, Stephen D. "Global Communications and National Power: Life on the Pareto Frontier." *World Politics* 43:3 (April 1991): 336–366.

Krasner, Stephen D. "Japan and the United States: Prospects for Stability." In Takashi Inoguchi and Daniel Okimoto, eds., *The Political Economy of Japan, vol. 2: The Changing International Context.* Stanford: Stanford University Press, 1988: 381–413.

Krasner, Stephen D. "State Power and the Structure of International Trade." *World Politics* 28 (April 1976): 317–347.

Krasner, Stephen D. "Trade Conflicts and the Common Defense: the United States and Japan." *Political Science Quarterly* 101:5 (1986): 787–805.

Krauss, Ellis S. "U.S.-Japan Negotiations on Construction and Semiconductors, 1985–88: Building Friction and Relation-chips." In Peter B. Evans, Harold K.

Jacobson and Robert D. Putnam, eds., *Double-Edged Diplomacy*. Berkeley: University of California Press, 1993, pp. 265–299.

Krauss, Ellis S., and Elizabeth Coles. "Built-in Impediments: The Political Economy of the U.S.-Japan Construction Dispute." In Kozo Yamamura, ed., *Japan's Economic Structure: Should It Change?* Seattle: Society for Japanese Studies, 1990, pp. 333–358.

Krauss, Ellis S., and Simon Reich. "Ideology, Interests, and the American Executive: Toward a Theory of Foreign Competition and Manufacturing Trade Policy." *International Organization* 46:4 (Autumn 1992): 857–897.

Kusano, Atsushi. *Amerika gikai to nichibei kankei.* (The U.S. Congress and U.S.-Japan Relations) Tokyo: Chūkō Sōsho, 1991.

Kusano, Atsushi. *Daitenhō: keizai kisei no kōzō.* (The LSL: The Structure of Economic Regulation) Tokyo: Nihon keizai shimbunsha, 1992.

Lake, David. "Beneath the Commerce of Nations: A Theory of International Economic Structures." *International Studies Quarterly* 28 (1984): 143–170.

Lawrence, Robert Z. "Efficient or Exclusionist? The Import Behavior of Japanese Corporate Groups." *Brookings Papers on Economic Activity* 1 (1991): 311–330.

Lawrence, Robert Z. "How Open is Japan?" In Paul Krugman, ed., *Trade With Japan: Has the Door Opened Wider?* Chicago: University of Chicago Press, 1991, pp. 9–37.

Lawrence, Robert Z. "Imports in Japan: Closed Markets or Closed Minds?" *Brookings Papers on Economic Activity* 2 (1987): 517–548.

Lax, David, and James K. Sebenius. *Manager as Negotiator: Bargaining for Cooperation and Competitive Gain.* New York: The Free Press, 1986.

Lehman, Howard P., and Jennifer L. McCoy. "The Dynamics of the Two-Level Bargaining Game: The 1988 Debt Negotiations." *World Politics* 44:4 (July 1992): 600–644.

Lincoln, Edward J. *Japan: Facing Economic Maturity.* Washington, D.C.: Brookings, 1988.

Lincoln, Edward J. *Japan's New Global Role.* Washington, D.C.: Brookings, 1993.

Lincoln, Edward J. *Japan's Unequal Trade.* Washington, D.C.: Brookings, 1990.

Maclachlan, Patricia L. *The Politics of Consumer Protection in Japan: The Role of Consumer Organizations in Policymaking.* Dissertation, Columbia University, 1996.

Magee, Stephen P., and Leslie Young. "Endogenous Protection in the United States, 1900–1984." In Robert M. Stern, ed., *U.S. Trade Policies in a Changing World Economy.* Cambridge: MIT Press, 1987, pp. 145–195.

Mansfield, Edward. "Alliances, Preferential Trading Arrangements and Sanctions." *Journal of International Affairs* 48:1 (Summer 1994): 119–139.

Mastanduno, Michael. "Do Relative Gains Matter? America's Response to Japanese Industrial Policy." *International Security* 16:1 (Summer 1991): 73–113.

Mastanduno, Michael. "Framing the Japan Problem: the Bush Administration and the Structural Impediments Initiative." *International Journal* 47:2 (Spring 1992): 235–264.

Mastanduno, Michael. "Setting Market Access Priorities: The Use of Super 301 in US Trade with Japan." *World Economy* 15:6 (November 1992): 729–753.

Maswood, Syed Javed. *Japan and Protection: The Growth of Protectionist Sentiment and the Japanese Response*. London: Routledge, 1989.

Matsushita, Minoru. *Introduction to Japanese Antimonopoly Law*. Tokyo: Yūhikaku, 1990.

Mayer, Frederick W. "Managing Domestic Differences in International Negotiations: The Strategic Use of Internal Side-Payments." *International Organization* 46:4 (Autumn 1992): 793–818.

McCubbins, Matthew D., and Greg W. Noble. "Perceptions and Realities of Japanese Budgeting." In Peter F. Cowhey and McCubbins, eds., *Structure and Policy in Japan and the United States*. Cambridge: Cambridge University Press, 1995, pp. 81–115.

McKean, Margaret. "State Strength and the Public Interest." In Gary D. Allinson and Yasunori Sone, eds., *Political Dynamics in Contemporary Japan*. Ithaca: Cornell University Press, 1993, pp. 72–104.

McKibbin, Warwick, Nouriel Roubini, and Jeffrey D. Sachs, "Correcting Global Imbalances: A Simulation Approach." In Robert M. Stern, ed., *Trade and Investment Relations Among the United States, Canada, and Japan*. Chicago: University of Chicago Press, 1989, pp. 379–424.

McMillan, John. "*Dangō*: Japan's Price-Fixing Conspiracies." *Economics and Politics* 3:3 (November 1991): 201–218.

Milner, Helen V. "The Political Economy of U.S. Trade Policy: A Study of the Super 301 Provision." In Jagdish Bhagwati and Hugh T. Patrick, eds., *Aggressive Unilateralism: America's 301 Trade Policy and the World Trading System*. Ann Arbor: University of Michigan Press, 1990, pp. 163–180.

Milner, Helen V. *Resisting Protectionism: Global Industries and the Politics of International Trade*. Princeton: Princeton University Press, 1988.

Milner, Helen V., and David B. Yoffie. "Between Free Trade and Protectionism: Strategic Trade Policy and a Theory of Corporate Trade Demands." *International Organization* 43:2 (Spring 1989): 239–272.

Ministry of Construction. *Kensetsu hakusho*. (Construction White Paper) Annual.

Ministry of Foreign Affairs. *Documents on Japan's Economic Structural Adjustment*. June 1987.

Ministry of International Trade and Industry. *90-nendai no ryūtsū bijon*. (Vision for the Distribution Industry in the 1990s) 1989.

Ministry of International Trade and Industry. *Sangyō gōrika hakusho*. (Industrial Rationalization White Paper) 1957.

Moravcsik, Andrew. "Introduction: Integrating International and Domestic Theories of International Bargaining." In Peter B. Evans, Harold K. Jacobson and Robert D. Putnam, eds., *Double-Edged Diplomacy*. Berkeley: University of California Press, 1993, pp. 3–42.

Muramatsu, Michio. "Patterned Pluralism Under Challenge: The Policies of the 1980s." In Gary D. Allinson and Yasunori Sone, eds., *Political Dynamics in Contemporary Japan*. Ithaca: Cornell University Press, 1993, pp. 50–71.

Muramatsu, Michio, and Ellis Krauss. "The Conservative Policy Line and the Development of Patterned Pluralism." In Kozo Yamamura and Yasukichi Yasuba, eds., *The Political Economy of Japan, vol. 1: The Domestic Transformation.* Stanford: Stanford University Press, 1987, pp. 517–554.

NHK, ed. *Nichibei no shōtotsu.* (The U.S.-Japan Collision) Tokyo: NHK, 1990.

Naka, Norio. *Predicting Outcomes in United States-Japan Trade Negotiations: The Political Process of the Structural Impediments Initiative.* Westport, CT: Quorum Books, 1996.

National Land Agency. *Tochi hakusho.* (Land White Paper) Annual.

Nihon Keizai Shimbunsha, ed. *Daitenhō ga kieru hi.* (The Day the LSL is Extinguished) Tokyo: Nihon Keizai Shimbunsha, 1990.

Nihon Keizai Shimbunsha, ed. *Tochi wo kangaeru.* (Thinking About Land) Tokyo: Nihon Keizai Shimbunsha, 1990.

Noda, Minoru. *Ryūtsū keiretsuka to dokusen kinshihō.* (The *Keiretsu*-ization of Distribution and the AML) Tokyo: Chikuma Shobō, 1982.

Noguchi, Yukio. "The 'Bubble' and Economic Policies in the 1980s." *Journal of Japanese Studies* 20:2 (Summer 1994): 291–330.

Noguchi, Yukio. "The 'Bubble' Economy and Its Aftermath." In Foreign Press Center, ed., *The Japanese Economy in the 1990s: Problems and Prognoses.* Tokyo: Foreign Press Center, 1993, pp. 31–53.

Noguchi, Yukio. "Japan's Land Problem." *Japanese Economic Studies* 20:3 (Spring 1992): 51–77.

Noguchi, Yukio. "Land Problem as an Unintended Industrial Policy: Its Mechanism and Limit." *Hitotsubashi Journal of Economics* 30 (1990): 87–99.

Noguchi, Yukio. "Land Problems and Policies in Japan: Structural Aspects." In John O. Haley and Kozo Yamamura, eds., *Land Issues In Japan: A Policy Failure?* Seattle: Society for Japanese Studies, 1992, pp. 11–31.

Noguchi, Yukio. "The Loopholes in the Planned Landholding Tax." *Economic Eye* (Spring 1991): 22–23.

North, Douglass C. *Institutions, Institutional Change and Economic Performance.* New York: Cambridge University Press, 1990.

Nye, Joseph S., Jr. "The Case for Deep Engagement." *Foreign Affairs* 74:4 (July/August 1995): 91–102.

Nye, Joseph S., Jr. "Coping with Japan." *Foreign Policy* 89 (Winter 92/93): 96–115.

Odell, John. "International Threats and Internal Politics: Brazil, the European Community, and the United States, 1985–1987." In Peter B. Evans, Harold K. Jacobson and Robert D. Putnam, eds., *Double-Edged Diplomacy.* Berkeley: University of California Press, 1993, pp. 233–264.

OECD. *National Accounts, Detailed Tables, volume II, 1977–1989.* Paris: OECD, 1991.

OECD. *OECD Economic Surveys 1986/87: Japan.* Paris: OECD, 1986.

OECD. *OECD Economic Surveys 1988/89: Japan.* Paris: OECD, 1989.

OECD. *OECD Economic Surveys 1993/94: Japan.* Paris: OECD, 1994.

Okimoto, Daniel. *Between MITI and the Market.* Stanford: Stanford University Press, 1989.

Olson, Mancur. *The Logic of Collective Action.* Cambridge: Harvard University Press, 1965.

Olson, R. S. "Economic Coercion in World Politics: With A Focus on North-South Relations." *World Politics* 31:4 (July 1979): 471–494.

Orr, Robert M., Jr. *The Emergence of Japan's Foreign Aid Power*. New York: Columbia University Press, 1990.

Orr, Robert M., Jr. "The *Gaiatsu* Game Between the U.S. and Japan." *Tokyo Report* 19:6 (June 1994)—produced by Hotel Okura and published as special section of *Nikkei Weekly*, May 30, 1994.

Ōtake, Hideo. *Jiyū shugiteki kaikaku no jidai: 1980 nendai zenki no nihon seiji* (An Era of Liberal Reform: Japanese Politics in the First Half of the 1980s) Tokyo: Chūō Kōron, 1994.

Ōtake, Hideo. "The Rise and Retreat of a Neoliberal Reform: Controversies Over Land Use Policy." In Gary D. Allinson and Yasunori Sone, eds., *Political Dynamics in Contemporary Japan*. Ithaca: Cornell University Press, 1993, pp. 242–263.

Oye, Kenneth. *Economic Discrimination and Political Exchange: World Political Economy in the 1930s and 1980s*. Princeton: Princeton University Press, 1992.

Ozawa, Ichirō. *Blueprint for a New Japan*. Tokyo: Kōdansha International, 1994.

Pastor, Robert A. *Congress and the Politics of Foreign Economic Policy*. Berkeley: University of California Press, 1980.

Pempel, T. J. "The Unbundling of 'Japan, Inc.': The Changing Dynamics of Japanese Policy Formation." *Journal of Japanese Studies* 13:2 (1987): 271–306.

Porges, Amelia. "Japan: Beef and Citrus." In Thomas O. Bayard and Kimberly Ann Elliott. *Reciprocity and Retaliation in U.S. Trade Policy*. Washington, D.C.: Institute for International Economics, 1994, pp. 233–266.

Porges, Amelia. "U.S.-Japan Trade Negotiations: Paradigms Lost." In Paul Krugman, ed., *Trade With Japan: Has the Door Opened Wider?* Chicago: University of Chicago Press, 1991, pp. 305–327.

Prestowitz, Clyde V. *Trading Places: How We Are Giving Our Future to Japan and How to Reclaim It*. New York: Basic Books, 1988.

Putnam, Robert. "Diplomacy and Domestic Politics: The Logic of Two-Level Games." *International Organization* 42 (Summer 1988): 427–460.

Pyle, Kenneth. *The Japanese Question*. Washington, D.C.: AEI Press, 1992.

Raiffa, Howard. *The Art and Science of Negotiation*. Cambridge: Harvard University Press, 1984.

Ramseyer, J. Mark. "The Costs of the Consensual Myth: Antitrust Enforcement and Institutional Barriers to Litigation in Japan." *Yale Law Journal* 94: 604 (1985): 604–645.

Ramseyer, J. Mark, and Frances M. Rosenbluth. *Japan's Political Marketplace*. Cambridge: Harvard University Press, 1993.

Rinji Gyōsei Kaikaku Suishin Shingikai Jimushitsu, ed. *Gyōkakushin: Zenshigoto*. (The Administration Reform Promotion Council: Complete Works) Tokyo: Gyōsei, 1991.

Ripley, Randall B., and Grace A. Franklin. *Congress, the Bureaucracy, and Public Policy*. Homewood, Ill.: The Dorsey Press, 1976.

Rosenbluth, Frances M. *Financial Politics in Contemporary Japan*. Ithaca: Cornell University Press, 1989.

Sachs, Jeffrey, and Peter Boone. "Japanese Structural Adjustment and the Balance of Payments." *National Bureau of Economic Research Working Paper* No. 2614 (June 1988).

Sakata, Kazukō. "Daitenhō to ōgataten mondai." (The LSL and the Large Store Problem) *Reference* (June 1991): 48–87.

Samuels, Richard. *The Business of the Japanese State: Energy Markets in Comparative and Historical Perspective*. Ithaca: Cornell University Press, 1987.

Samuels, Richard. *"Rich Nation Strong Army": National Security and the Technological Transformation of Japan*. Ithaca: Cornell University Press, 1994.

Sapire, André, Pierre Buigues, and Alexis Jacquemin. "European Competition Policy in Manufacturing and Services: A Two-Speed Approach?" *Oxford Review of Economic Policy* 9:2 (Summer 1993): 113–132.

Sasaki, Takeshi. "Nichibei kōzō kyōgi: 'motareai' no kiken." (The SII Talks: The Danger of "Reliance"). *Ekonomisuto* (November 7, 1989): 104–107.

Sasaki, Takeshi. *Seiji wa doko e mukaunoka*. (Where is Politics Headed?) Tokyo: Chūkō Shinsho, 1992.

Satō, Seizaburō, and Matsuzaki Tetsuhisa. *Jimintō seiken*. (LDP Rule) Tokyo: Chūō Kōronsha, 1986.

Saxonhouse, Gary R. "Comparative Advantage, Structural Adaptation, and Japanese Performance." In Takashi Inoguchi and Daniel I. Okimoto, eds., *The Political Economy of Japan, vol. 2: The Changing International Context*. Stanford: Stanford University Press, 1988, pp. 225–248.

Schattschneider, E. E. *Politics, Pressures, and the Tariff*. New York: Prentice-Hall, 1935.

Schattschneider, E. E. *The Semisovereign People: A Realist View of Democracy in America*. New York: Holt, Reinhart and Winston, 1960.

Schelling, Thomas. *The Strategy of Conflict*. Cambridge: Harvard University Press, 1960.

Scherer, F. M. *Competition Policies for an Integrated World Economy*. Washington, D.C.: Brookings Institution, 1994.

Schoppa, Leonard J. *Education Reform in Japan*. London: Routledge, 1991.

Schoppa, Leonard J. "Two-Level Games and Bargaining Outcomes: Why *Gaiatsu* Succeeds in Japan in Some Cases But Not Others." *International Organization* 47:3 (Summer 1993): 353–386.

Schoppa, Leonard J. "*Zoku* power and LDP power: A Case Study of the *Zoku* Role in Education Policy." *Journal of Japanese Studies* 17:1 (Winter 1991): 79–106.

Schott, Jeffrey J. *The Uruguay Round: An Assessment*. Washington, D.C.: Institute for International Economics, 1994.

Sebenius, James K. "Challenging Conventional Explanations of International Cooperation: Negotiation Analysis and the Case of Epistemic Communities." *International Organization* 46:1 (Winter 1992): 323–365.

Sebenius, James K. "Negotiation Arithmetic: Adding and Subtracting Issues and Parties." *International Organization* 37:2 (Spring 1983): 282–316.

Sebenius, James K. *Negotiating the Law of the Sea: Lessons in the Art and Science of Reaching Agreement*. Cambridge: Harvard University Press, 1984.

Skidmore, David. "The Politics of National Security Policy: Interest Groups, Coalitions, and the SALT II Debate." In David Skidmore and Valerie M. Hudson, eds., *The Limits of State Autonomy*. Boulder: Westview Press, 1993, pp. 205–233.

Snidal, Duncan. "The Limits of Hegemonic Stability Theory." *International Organization* 39:4 (Autumn 1985): 579–614.

Stokes, Bruce. "Immovable Mandarins." *National Journal* (April 30, 1994): 1005–1008.

Takagi, Shintarō. "Nihon no chika, jūtaku kakaku wa takasugiru?" (Are Japanese Land and Housing Prices Too High?) *Nihon keizai kenkyū* 20 (May 1990): 108–122.

Takeuchi, Yasuo. "Tackling the Impediments to Trade." *Japan Echo* 17:3 (Autumn 1990): 6–7.

Talbott, Strobe. *Endgame: The Inside Story of SALT II*. New York: Harper & Row, 1979.

Tanaka, Fusahiro. "Whose Company is it Anyway? The Corporate Governance Controversy." *Tokyo Business Today* (August 1993): 14–16.

Thayer, Nathaniel B. "Competition and Conformity: An Inquiry into the Structure of Japanese Newspapers." In Ezra F. Vogel, ed., *Modern Japanese Organization and Decision-Making*. Berkeley: University of California Press, 1975, pp. 284–303.

Thornton, Emily. "Retailing Revolution in Japan." *Fortune* (February 7, 1994): 52–56.

Tilton, Mark. *Restrained Trade: Cartels in Japan's Basic Materials Industries*. Ithaca: Cornell University Press, 1996.

Tollison, Robert D., and Thomas D. Willett. "An Economic Theory of Mutually Advantageous Issue Linkages in International Negotiations." *International Organization* 33:4 (Autumn 1979): 425–449.

Tsebelis, George. *Nested Games: Rational Choice in Comparative Politics*. Berkeley: University of California Press, 1990.

Tsuruta, Toshimasa. "Kokusaika jidai no daitenhō wa dōarubekika." (What to Do with the LSL in an Era of Internationalization) *Ekonomisuto* (December 13, 1988): 44–51.

Tyson, Laura D'Andrea. *Who's Bashing Whom? Trade Conflict in High-Technology Industries*. Washington, D.C.: Institute for International Economics, 1992.

Tyson, Laura D'Andrea, and John Zysman. "Developmental Strategy and Production Innovation in Japan." In Chalmers Johnson, Tyson and Zysman, eds., *Politics and Productivity*. New York: HarperBusiness, 1989, pp. 59–140.

U.S. Congress. House Committee on Government Operations. *United States-Japan Framework Talks on Trade: Hearings Before the House Subcommittee on Commerce, Consumer, and Monetary Affairs*. 103rd Congress, 2nd sess., February 24 and March 23, 1994.

U.S. Congress. Senate Committee on Finance. *Super 301: Effectiveness in Opening Foreign Markets: Hearings Before the Subcommittee on International Trade*. 101st Congress, 2d sess., April 27, 1990.

U.S. Congress. Senate Committee on Finance. *United States - Japan Structural*

Impediments Initiative (SII): Hearings before the Subcommittee on International Trade. 101st Congress, 1st sess., July 20, 1989.

U.S. Congress. Senate Committee on Finance. *United States-Japan Structural Impediments Initiative (SII): Hearings before the Subcommittee on International Trade.* 101st Congress, 1st sess., November 6–7, 1989

U.S. Congress. Senate Committee on Finance. *United States - Japan Structural Impediments Initaitive (SII): Hearings before the Subcommittee on International Trade.* 101st Congress, 2nd sess., March 5, 1990.

U.S. Department of Defense. *United States Security Strategy for the East Asia-Pacific Region.* 1995.

U.S. Trade Representative. *1994 National Trade Estimate Report on Foreign Trade Barriers.* 1994.

Uekusa, Masu. "Government Regulations in Japan: Toward Their International Harmonization and Integration." In Kozo Yamamura, ed., *Japan's Economic Structure: Should it Change?* Seattle: Society for Japanese Studies, 1990, pp. 237–269.

Upham, Frank. "Privatizing Regulation: The Implementation of the Large-Scale Retail Stores Law." In Gary Allinson and Yasunori Sone, eds., *Political Dynamics in Contemporary Japan.* Ithaca: Cornell University Press, 1993, pp. 264–294.

Upham, Frank. *Law and Social Change in Postwar Japan.* Cambridge: Harvard University Press, 1987.

Umezawa, Setsuo. "Dokusen kinshi hō wa kaisei shinai." (We will not revise the AML) *Ekonomisuto* (January 23, 1990): 46–49.

Uriu, Robert M. *Troubled Industries: Confronting Economic Change in Japan.* Ithaca: Cornell University Press, 1996.

van Wolferen, Karel. *The Enigma of Japanese Power: People and Politics in a Stateless Nation.* New York: Knopf, 1989.

van Wolferen, Karel. "The Japan Problem." *Foreign Affairs* 65:2 (Winter 1986/87): 288–303.

Wagner, R. Harrison. "Economic Interdependence, Bargaining Power, and Political Influence." *International Organization* 42:3 (Summer 1988): 461–483

Walton, Richard, and Robert McKersie. *A Behavioral Theory of Labor Negotiations.* New York: McGraw-Hill, 1965.

Waltz, Kenneth N. *Theory of International Politics.* Reading, MA: Addison-Wesley, 1979.

Waltz, Kenneth N. "The Emerging Structure of International Politics." *International Security* 18:2 (Fall 1993): 44–79.

Williams, S. Linn. "Kagami no naka no nichibei kōzō kyōgi: 1–9." (Looking in the Mirror at the SII Talks: Parts 1–9). *Shūkan daiyamondo* (March 14–May 16, 1992).

Winham, Gilbert R. *International Trade and the Tokyo Round Negotiations.* Princeton: Princeton University Press, 1986.

Woodall, Brian. *Japan Under Construction: Corruption, Politics, and Public Works.* Berkeley: University of California Press, 1996.

Woodall, Brian. "The Politics of Land in Japan's Dual Political Economy." In John O.

Haley and Kozo Yamamura, eds., *Land Issues In Japan: A Policy Failure?* Seattle: Society for Japanese Studies, 1992, pp. 113–148.

Yamagata, Yūichirō. "Nichibei kōzō kyōgi ga nihon wo kaeru." (The SII Talks Will Change Japan) *Shūkan tōyō keizai* (September 30, 1989): 10–18.

Yamamura, Kozo. "LDP Dominance and High Land Prices in Japan: A Study in Positive Political Economy." In John O. Haley and Kozo Yamamura, eds., *Land Issues In Japan: A Policy Failure?* Seattle: Society for Japanese Studies, 1992, pp. 33–75.

Yamamura, Kozo. "Will Japan's Economic Structure Change? Confessions of a Former Optimist." In Kozo Yamamura, ed., *Japan's Economic Structure: Should It Change?* Seattle: Society for Japanese Studies, 1990, pp. 13–64.

Yamamoto, Taketoshi. "The Press Clubs of Japan." *Journal of Japanese Studies* 15:2 (Summer 1989): 371–388.

Zaller, John R. *The Nature and Origins of Mass Opinion.* Cambridge: Cambridge University Press, 1992.

INDEX

Boone, Peter, 198
Boskin, Michael, 72
Brady, Nicholas, 74, 106
Brazil, U.S. pressure on, 23
Brittan, Leon, 288
Brown, Ron, 258, 262
Bubble economy, and land prices, 187;
    MOF policy leading to, 129
Bureaucracy (in Japan), power relative
    to politicians, 325n27; segmentation
    and rivalry in, 97, 190–92, 346n74;
    see also specific Japanese ministries
    (e.g. Ministry of Finance)
Bush Administration, and initiation of
    SII talks, 10; interest in LSL leading
    up to SII, 161; political calculus
    behind SII launch, 78; trade policy
    of, 69–76; see also Structural
    Impediments Initiative talks
Bush-Kaifu Palm Springs summit, 105,
    166
Bush-Uno communique, 85
Business Roundtable, 70, 78

Calder, Kent, 191, 342n27
Cartels, continuing de facto exemp-
    tions for, 222; in cement, 249;
    Japanese attitudes toward, 228, 246;
    large number exempted under the
    Anti-Monopoly Law, 218, 222; MITI
    retains faith in, 228
Carter, Jimmy, 28
Council of Economic Advisors, origins
    of SII involvement, 79; Tyson named
    head of, 260; views on Super 301,
    72; see also John Taylor
Cellular phones issue, 274–75
Cheney, Richard, 114
China, and failure of linkage, 37; mod-
    ernization of military forces, 259
Choate, Pat, 333n30
Clinton administration, announcement
    touting Framework deal, 254; auto
    talks endgame, 268–69; demands for

Japanese fiscal stimulus, 277; effort
    to influence Chinese human rights
    policy, 36; embrace of revisionism,
    260; political logic behind getting
    tough with Japan, 262; reform of
    trade policy institutions, 260; sanc-
    tions threat on luxury autos, 15, 268
Clinton-Hosokawa summit, 14, 258
Cold War, effect of its end on U.S.-
    Japan trade relations, 9, 57, 259–60,
    281–85; and Japan's "1955 System,"
    102–3; Japanese response to its end,
    284–85; persistent effect on institu-
    tions, 284; role in legitimizing U.S.
    pressure on Japan, 102; shock of its
    end opens door to new ideas, 260;
    slow end in Asia, 60; and U.S. trade
    institutions, 64; and U.S. trade poli-
    cy, 51, 59
Collective action theory, 30
Commerce department, addition to SII
    process, 80; and FSX talks, 71,
    334n42; push for semiconductor
    accords, 68; support for results-
    oriented trade policy, 77; views on
    trade policy toward Japan, 71, 75
Commercial Activities Adjustment
    Boards, 152, 157, 175
Competition policy, difficulty of
    appealing to public, 242; a dysfunc-
    tional private damage remedy sys-
    tem, 225–26; exemption for con-
    struction industry, 223; importance
    of functioning private damage reme-
    dy, 369n104; lack of native tradition
    in, 217; lax sanctions under, 221;
    most important practices affecting
    imports, 241; reform initiative in
    1970s, 227–28; resale price mainte-
    nance issue, 241; soda ash case,
    231–32; tendency toward informal
    enforcement, 219–21; weak distrib-
    ution guidelines, 250
— and SII, summary of SII demands

ties, 240, 247; preference for case-
by-case land policy, 191; pressures
JFTC over Saitama dangō, 245; prolonged rule of, 96; reliance on gaiatsu, 100–101; and segmentation of
policy process, 97–98, 99, 158; and
small shopkeepers, 150, 158, 164;
tendency toward particularism, 159,
188; ties to contruction industry,
229–30; see also zoku
Legitimacy, role in favoring reverberation, 33; and threats, 36
Lincoln, Edward, 87, 370n2
Linkage, 24; conditions generating synergy, 36–37, 38, 40; mutually advantageous, 37–38; power politics variety, 36; Robert Putnam on, 36,
38–39; target-nation variety, 38–40

Macroeconomic policy coordination,
history of U.S.-Japan bargaining on,
118, 123, 124–27; under Clinton,
264; see also public investment, fiscal
policy (in Japan)
Maekawa Haruo, 125
Maekawa Report, background on,
338n96; recommendations for distribution system, 156; as source of
SII demands, 81, 105; statement on
fiscal policy, 125
Managed trade, see results-oriented
trade policy
Market-Oriented Sector-Specific talks,
65, 216
Mass media (in Japan), coverage of LSL
during SII, 169; opposition to U.S.
Framework demands, 272; role in
facilitating effects of U.S. pressure,
100–101; as U.S. ally during SII,
107–8
Mastanduno, Michael, 323n14,
332n24, 336n70, 336n73, 337n91,
339n104
Matsushita, 274

McCormack, Richard, 80, 105,
338n92, 349n28
McCubbins, Matthew, 348n19, 375n85
McKean, Margaret, 99
Miki Takeo, 229
Ministry of Commerce and Industry,
149
Ministry of Construction, implentation
of urban farmland tax reform, 208;
involvement in dangō process, 223;
and land policy, 183, 188
Ministry of Finance, autonomy relative
to LDP politicians, 127, 348n19;
Budget Bureau of, 127; complex
views on land policy, 203; control
over only some land taxes, 190;
deficit reduction goals, 123, 127;
and "locomotive" experience, 124;
and Maekawa report, 126; objects to
macro targets, 264; oppostion to no-
offset tax cut, 278–79; policy contributing to "bubble economy," 129;
preference for G-7 as forum for discussing fiscal policy, 129; pursuit of
fiscal autonomy, 124, 126; push for
new land tax, 206; refusal to compromise on public investment, 134;
struggle to contain LDP demands
for spending, 343n36; tries to maintain fiscal course despite SII pledge,
142; views on capital gains tax, 206;
see also public investment
Ministry of Foreign Affairs, urges moderation in July 1993, 285
Ministry of Home Affairs, acquiescence
to LSL reform after SII, 168; belated
campaign to raise land tax assessments, 212; control over property
taxes, 190; opposition to LSL
reform in 1989, 157; opposition to
new land tax, 203, 211
Ministry of International Trade and
Industry, changing attitudes of
younger officials, 284; effect of pub-